THE
BEGINNINGS
OF
NEW FRANCE

MARCEL TRUDEL

THE BEGINNINGS OF NEW FRANCE

1524-1663

Translated by Patricia Claxton

The Canadian Centenary Series

McClelland and Stewart Limited

0-7710-8610-5

The Canadian Publishers
McClelland and Stewart Limited
25 Hollinger Road, Toronto 374

à ma femme, Micheline

For material in the illustration sections of this
book, acknowledgement is made to the
following sources:

PUBLIC ARCHIVES OF CANADA for Part of the "Harleian" Map
of the World; New France in 1550; New France in 1569; the
Habitation of Chauvin at Tadoussac; Jacques Cartier's *La
Grande Hermine*; the Habitation of Ste Croix; the Habitation
of Port Royal; the Habitation of Quebec; Portrait of Champlain; Face from Champlain's 1632 map of New France.

THE AUTHOR for Remains of some of those who spent the
winter of 1604-1605 at Ste Croix.

ARCHIVES NATIONALES DU QUEBEC for The Côte de Beaupré
and the Isle of Orleans; Monseigneur de Laval; Marie de
l'Incarnation.

MCGILL UNIVERSITY LIBRARY for Montreal, 1642.

ARCHIVES OF THE QUEBEC SEMINARY for Quebec in 1660.

WATSON'S STUDIO, Midland, for Modern reconstruction of
Fort Ste Marie.

METROPOLITAN TORONTO LIBRARY BOARD for The taking of
Quebec by the English, 1629; Plan of the fort at Quebec; Plan
of the Habitation of Quebec; The first entries in the registry
book of Notre Dame Church, in Montreal.

CENTRE MARGUERITE BOURGEOYS, Montreal, for Marguerite
Bourgeoys.

Printed and bound in Canada by
THE HUNTER ROSE COMPANY

THE
CANADIAN
CENTENARY
SERIES

A History of Canada

W. L. Morton, EXECUTIVE EDITOR
D. G. Creighton, ADVISORY EDITOR

VOLUMES STARRED ARE PUBLISHED

†ALSO AVAILABLE IN PAPERBACK

CONTENTS

The Beginnings of New France

ILLUSTRATIONS

Facing page 116

Part of the "Harleian" Map of the World – New France in 1550 – New France in 1569 – The Habitation of Chauvin at Tadoussac – Replica of *La Grande Hermine* – The Habitation of Ste Croix – Remains of some of those who spent the winter of 1604-1605 at Ste Croix – The Habitation of Port Royal – The Habitation of Quebec – Portrait of Champlain

Facing page 180

Face from Champlain's 1632 map of New France – The Côte de Beaupré and the Isle of Orleans, in 1641 – Quebec, 1660 – Montreal, 1642 – Modern reconstruction of Fort Ste Marie – The taking of Quebec by the English, 1629 – Plan of the fort at Quebec – Plan of the Habitation of Quebec – Notre Dame Church registry book – Monseigneur de Laval – Marie de l'Incarnation – Marguerite Bourgeoys

The Canadian Centenary Series

Half a century has elapsed since *Canada and Its Provinces*, the first large-scale co-operative history of Canada, was published. During that time, new historical materials have been made available in archives and libraries; new research has been carried out, and its results published; new interpretations have been advanced and tested. In these same years Canada itself has greatly grown and changed. These facts, together with the centenary of Confederation, justify the publication of a new co-operative history of Canada.

The form chosen for this enterprise was that of a series of volumes. The series was planned by the editors, but each volume will be designed and executed by a single author. The general theme of the work is the development of those regional communities which have for the past century made up the Canadian nation; and the series will be composed of a number of volumes sufficiently large to permit adequate treatment of all the phases of the theme in the light of modern knowledge.

The Centenary History, then, was planned as a series to have a certain common character and to follow a common method but to be written by individual authors, specialists in their fields. As a whole, it will be a work of specialized knowledge, the great advantage of scholarly co-operation, and at the same time each volume will have the unity and distinctive character of individual authorship. It was agreed that a general narrative treatment was necessary and that each author should deal in a balanced way with economic, political, and social history. The result, it is hoped, will be an interpretative, varied, and comprehensive account, at once useful to the student and interesting to the general reader.

The difficulties of organizing and executing such a series are apparent: the overlapping of separate narratives, the risk of omissions, the imposition of divisions which are relevant to some themes but not to others. Not so apparent, but quite as troublesome, are the problems of scale, perspective, and scope, problems which perplex the writer of a one-volume history and are magnified in a series. It is by deliberate choice that certain parts of the history are told twice, in different volumes from different points of view, in the belief that the benefits gained outweigh the unavoidable disadvantages.

The Centenary Series is fortunate to add to its volumes, and the Editors welcome a contribution made by the best French scholarship. Professor Marcel Trudel brings to the history of the founding of New France, a story often told and at least once in classic form, new information, novel emphases, fresh nuances of interpretation and a firmness of outline and a clarity of insight not before attained. In especial, his unrivalled carto-graphic learning, the scope of his demographic analysis and his sympathetic knowledge of the Indian and Indian culture give the volume an authority and a distinction all its own. Such a contribution, moreover, greatly aids the growing integration of the Series: *enfin les fleurs-de-lys!*

W. L. MORTON,
Executive Editor,
D. G. CREIGHTON,
Advisory Editor.

The Beginnings of New France

This book is a condensation of my three volumes devoted to the early years of New France: *Les vaines tentatives, 1524-1603; Le comptoir, 1604-1627; La seigneurie des Cent-Associés, 1627-1663;* and Chapter 18 is based on two other volumes of mine, recently completed: *Le terrier du Saint-Laurent en 1663* and *La population du Canada en 1663.* The establishing of the French colony in North America extends over the whole of this long period of 1524-1663. Its history begins with the year 1524, the year of Verrazano's discovery of the Atlantic coast between Florida and Newfoundland, a region to which he gave the name *Nova Gallia* or New France. From that time until 1603, as the French sought vainly for a foothold in the new world, history records only a succession of fruitless efforts. Not until 1604 did they finally narrow their sights to the northeastern corner of the American continent. Even then there was hesitation over the exact location of their foothold, for they were in search of an ideal site for colonization, but from that date onward their occupation of that part of America was continuous, sometimes in Acadia, sometimes in the St Lawrence, and sometimes in both regions at once. As yet, however, New France existed for no other purpose than the barter of furs; it could not even be considered a commercial colony, for it consisted only of one or more trading posts. It was in 1627 that French authorities launched an ambitious commercial organization, the Company of the Hundred Associates, with the intention of establishing an integrated colony for the exploitation and development of the natural resources of America; New France, theoretically extending from Florida to the north pole, then became a seigneury. This third period in many ways still resembled the second; for example, in economic life, in social insecurity, and in the numerical weakness of the population. But there were important new developments. This period saw the introduction of a system of land distribution and the appearance of social structures transplanted from France. However, the Hundred Associates, sorely beset from the very beginning, were unable to establish the powerful colony that had been hoped for. Their intermediary, the Communauté des Habitants, also failed to do so, and in 1663 New France was brought under the direct control of the King. The colony underwent a far-reaching reorganization, and the former seigneury of a commercial company became, in effect, an overseas French province. The early years of New France, this long period of repeated disappointments, thus came to a close.

I cannot terminate this preface without expressing gratitude to those who have lent their support and encouragement throughout my years of research. I wish most particularly to thank the Canada Council, whose grants have been invaluable.

MARCEL TRUDEL

CHAPTER 1

Fleurs-de-lis in the New World at Last

1524

A great deal of mystery shrouds the first years of the history of North America, the years from 1497 to 1521. Twentieth-century historians are still posing the same questions that faced their predecessors of the nineteenth century, and are just as baffled. Where exactly did John Cabot, the Corte-Reals and Fagundes put to shore? How much of the coastline did they visit? Did any of these mariners sight or even explore that "great bay" which is now the Gulf of St Lawrence? Did any of them penetrate into it as far as the river? All these questions, and others too, remain without satisfactory answers. With admirable skill and learning, historians have developed intriguing theories, but evidence to support them is still lacking.

In 1524, thanks to an Italian explorer sailing in the service of France, the veil is lifted, at least for a time.

Following a voyage accomplished in that year, a map appeared which bore the legend *Nova Gallia* along the coast of the North American continent. Thus, New France enters history for the first time; throughout more than two centuries, under this same name, it was to occupy a more or less extensive portion of the continent. New France was born in 1524. If the British Empire in America owed its origin to an Italian, Giovanni Caboto, the French Empire originated with another Italian, Giovanni da Verrazano.

France was the last of the Atlantic nations to join the race to Asia. True, since 1504, Breton fishermen had made frequent use of the route to Newfoundland, but fishing voyages undertaken regardless of science or politics earned no credit for France as a contributor to contemporary knowledge of the world, nor any rights to the possession of land.

France was well acquainted with the Newfoundland route, and she was not without material resources, navigators, or vitality. How was it, then, that the most populous of the Atlantic countries was the last to engage

1

in the westward search for Asia? Why was it that France only came on the scene thirty years after the discovery of America?

The answer lies in the foreign policy of the kings of France. That policy was entirely focused upon the Mediterranean, which explains why France had made no attempt to embark on Atlantic enterprises since the reign of Louis XII. She finally made her bid in 1523, although she was still at war with Charles V of Spain, and it was the return of the Magellan expedition of 1519-22, bringing a wealth of spices, that pressed her into action at this time.

The great Spanish circumnavigation of the world became known to Europe through the publication of the narratives of Pigafetta and of his companion Transylvanus in 1522 and January of 1523. In France, Louise of Savoy, the mother of Francis I, at once had Pigafetta's journal translated into French. Beyond a doubt, there was a cause-and-effect relationship between Magellan's expedition and Verrazano's, which was organized in 1523.

The Italians of the sixteenth century might be compared with the English of the nineteenth century. They were business men with international interests and leaders in large-scale undertakings, to the extent that Italian had become the international language of commerce. It happened that a number of Italian bankers, having been driven from their homeland by the turbulence of the times, had established themselves in Lyons for strategic reasons: "For the kingdom of France, Lyons was the main gateway to Italy and the Orient, and the continental market-place closest to Upper Germany, a rendezvous for merchants operating between that area and Mediterranean Spain." At this international commercial crossroads, the Italians played a crucial role.[1]

And so these Italian bankers of Lyons laid plans for the discovery of a commercial route that would be shorter than Magellan's and would thus assure France of a monopoly in Asian products.

Unfortunately, we know almost nothing of Verrazano prior to his arrival on the scene. He was a citizen of Florence, and had undoubtedly gone to sea at an early age. He must have distinguished himself in seafaring if business men, who were not in the habit of taking senseless risks, saw fit to put him in charge of the enterprise. In any case, from his letter to Francis I recounting his voyage, Verrazano appears to have been both an expert cosmographer and a well-read, discriminating Renaissance figure. His letter does credit to Florence, a Mecca of humanism, and to Italy, then the world's centre of learning in cosmography.

But though it was backed by the Italian bankers of Lyons, this was not a private undertaking. It is true that there is no known official document attesting to Francis I's intention of sending Verrazano on a voyage bound for Asia. Nevertheless, aside from the fact that it was quite usual for the

King to entrust his ventures to private interests, there are a number of indications to justify the view that the Verrazano expedition was an official one. The map prepared in 1529 by the navigator's brother bears the inscription: "perordine et Comandamto del Christianissime Re di Francia" ("by order and command of His Most Christian Majesty of France"). Furthermore, the letter sent to Francis I by Verrazano on his return makes reference to the vessels sent by the King. "I wish," writes Verrazano, "to relate to Your Majesty the order of our navigation with respect to its cosmographic aspects," and he adds, "I hope to be able to present in person to Your Majesty a more complete exposition of these theoretical data."[2] We have here the clear impression of a navigator back from a mission and duly reporting to the competent authority.

What was it that Verrazano proposed to do? We should keep in mind his own statement: "It was my intention, in the course of this voyage, to reach Cathay and the eastern extremity of Asia." His entire account demonstrates that his aim was to find a passage somewhere between Spanish Florida and Newfoundland that would put France directly into contact with Asia. But how much was known about North America when Verrazano set out on his journey? The answer is important in evaluating the Florentine's role and assessing the extent of his contribution to contemporary knowledge of the New World.

The Caribbean Sea was blocked to the south and west, and also to the north: in 1519, the Spaniard Pineda had searched in vain in that direction for a passage to the Asian Sea, but he did discover an important river which was to bear the name Spiritu Santo before it came to be called the Mississippi. To the east, this coastline ended in a peninsula discovered in 1513 by Ponce de Leon on Palm Sunday or *Pascua florida*, hence the name Florida. To what was this peninsula attached? The map of the world attributed to Leonardo da Vinci, which is thought to have been drawn about 1514, represents it as an island in an ocean touching on Japan. In 1521 the Spaniards, sent by Lucas Vasquez de Ayllon, returned to Florida and pushed a little further northward, probably as far as South Carolina. They took possession of the territory without being able to solve the geographical problem.

Next to become known in America were Nova Scotia, Cape Breton, the southern and eastern coasts of Newfoundland, and Labrador, all of which were visited by the English and Portuguese; their cartography was becoming more and more precisely defined, but the speculation was still that these regions were an extension of Asia. There remained a major enigma; what lay between Florida and the "land of the baccalaos"? Did the continental barrier stretching from the Tierra del Fuego to Florida extend as far as Cape Breton? Or was there a sea where the waters of the Atlantic mingled with those of the Asian Sea? No navigator had as yet supplied an answer, and this void in what was known of America remained to be filled. In the unknown expanse between Florida and Cape Breton, then, lay a last chance for France to make up her twenty-five-year lag in exploration.

In 1523, the Italian bankers of Lyons launched their enterprise with a fleet of four ships under Verrazano's command. They chose Dieppe as the point of departure, no doubt because the Italian bankers of Rouen were associated with those of Lyons and also because Dieppe was the home port of Jean Ango, a powerful shipowner always interested in long-range expeditions. The vessels put to sea, but a storm "suffered in the northern regions" forced Verrazano to take refuge in Brittany with two of his ships, the *Dauphine* and the *Normande*. He effected repairs to both and, judging perhaps that it was too late to resume the westward voyage, he had them outfitted as warships and went off to do some privateering along the coast of Spain. Finally, he decided to "follow the previously-planned route with the *Dauphine* alone."[3]

And so, on January 17, 1524, the *Dauphine* set sail on her long voyage of exploration from an island near Madeira, with a complement of fifty men and "enough provisions for eight months, arms and other engines of war and seafaring." There were two known routes which could lead Verrazano to America, the North Atlantic route which was followed by European fishermen, and the route which involved a detour via the West Indies. The latter was to be used several times by the English on voyages to Virginia. On leaving the Madeira archipelago, Verrazano took neither of these two courses, but struck out on a new and direct route, an initiative which bore witness to his daring.[4] In twenty-five days, with a "pleasingly gentle" following wind, the *Dauphine* logged 800 leagues before encountering a storm. Pushing westward and "bearing slightly north" for a further twenty-five days, she covered another 400 leagues; and then, wrote Verrazano, "there appeared a new land which no one had ever seen before, either in earlier times or in our own." To establish the position of this territory in relation to Florida, Verrazano sailed south for a distance of some fifty leagues, and then, noting that the shoreline continued unbroken and fearing to "fall foul of the Spaniards," he turned about, sailed northward to the "point previously sighted," and went ashore.[5] This was at the 34th parallel in the neighbourhood of Cape Fear in what is now North Carolina. The date being March 25, he named his point of arrival Annunciation, after the festival celebrated on that day.[6]

Following the coast northeastward, they found a land that was inhabited, fertile and very pleasant, but an obstacle nevertheless, since their purpose was to reach the Asian Sea. Then, suddenly, the goal seemed to be within sight, on the far side of "an isthmus a mile wide and 200 miles long," to which Verrazano gave his name. His description has a touching air of desperation about it: "From the ship, we caught sight of the eastern sea toward the northwest. That sea is doubtless the one that washes the shores of India, China and Cathay. We sailed the entire length of this island, in the unyielding hope of finding some strait, or, better still, a promontory terminating this land toward the north, so that we might penetrate to the blessed shores of Cathay."[7] If only that "unyielding hope" had been rewarded, da Gama's and Magellan's routes would have been superseded and the day won for France! But the sea remained inaccessible, and, on their return, all Verrazano and his companions could do was show on the maps how close the waters of Asia had come, at that point on the coast-line, to mingling with the waters of the Atlantic.[8] And it was no more than an illusion, for what they had taken to be the Asian Sea was Pamlico Sound, closed by a sandy isthmus.

There was no choice but to continue along the coast. The *Dauphine* had brought them fifty leagues northeast from Annunciation when they came to a country which, "by reason of the beauty of its trees," Verrazano called Arcadia.[9] With due allowance made for sixteenth-century distances and maps, this was probably the Accomack Peninsula at the entrance to Chesapeake Bay, in Virginia. After three days of reconnoitring there, Verrazano moved along the coast, investing geographical features with French names.

The *Dauphine* also dropped anchor at a place of great renown in our day, which Verrazano was the first European to visit and describe, namely New York. Here, since he was in search of a passage to Asia, he travelled up the river "to a point half a league inland," encountering natives all the way. However, on account of a "contrary wind that blew from the sea," he was unable to prolong his exploration and was obliged to return "re-gretfully" to the *Dauphine*.[10]

Next, he stopped for two weeks to take on supplies in a "very beautiful harbour" which has been identified as Newport (Narragansett Bay, Rhode Island). Because of its favourable features, this harbour was given the name Refuge. As well as the convenience of the location, the friendliness of the natives proved to be a most valuable asset. They were, in fact, "the most handsome and best disciplined" of all the peoples that Verrazano had encountered during his voyage.

On May 6, the expedition resumed its journey "without ever losing sight of land," and soon came to a very different region, which was dubbed "the land of evil men." "The natives," wrote Verrazano, "bore no resem-blance to those we had seen previously. These were as cruel and vicious as the others were courteous. They were so barbarous that, for all our friendly signals, we were never able to communicate with them; [. . .] the advances we made had no effect on them, and when there was nothing left to barter" (for there was barter, but only "by means of a rope"), "as we were pulling away, the men began demonstrations of scorn and obscenity of every kind conceivable by the vilest of creatures." Penetration inland was possible only by force of arms. No trace of cultivation was to be seen, and Verrazano assumed that "the soil, by reason of its sterility, was capable of producing neither fruit nor grain."[11]

This was the future New England, perhaps the Boston region, or more probably that of Casco Bay in Maine. The barbaric and intractable natives are strangely reminiscent of the Skraelings who had been so troublesome to the Vikings of Vinland. When Champlain was to come to this region in 1606, he, too, would have to contend with extremely ill-disposed natives.

Still following the shoreline in a northeasterly direction, Verrazano sailed the whole length of a coast "more accessible and devoid of forests," dominated "by high mountains sloping down towards the shore," and fringed with many small islands.[12] This was the first description of Maine, written in 1524.

Ultimately, Verrazano reached "that land discovered long ago by the Bretons and which is at 50 degrees"; he pushed further north again, as far as 54 degrees, it would seem, but the continental barrier still loomed relentlessly. Verrazano noted, moreover, that the Portuguese had followed this coastline "still further north as far as the arctic circle, but without glimpsing an end to it."[13] Both the English and the Portuguese had already explored the "land of the Bretons" and the "new-found land" at length, which was doubtless why Verrazano, once he had left the coast of Maine behind, no longer took the trouble to note what he saw, if indeed he saw anything at all; not a word about the great inlet of the Bay of Fundy; no suggestion of it on either Maggiolo's or Verrazano's map; complete silence on the strait separating Cape Breton from Newfoundland, through which Verrazano might have discovered the St Lawrence Gulf and River if he had pushed on in that direction. But he did not consider it necessary to repeat the explorations of the Portuguese, and the *Dauphine*, after taking on supplies, headed back to France.[14]

Somewhere in the fifteen hundred miles between Florida and Cape Breton, Verrazano had hoped to find the breach leading from the Atlantic to Asia, but everywhere his way had been blocked by the continental barrier. And yet his voyage was still a spectacular success. Until 1524, nothing whatever was known of what lay between Florida and Cape Breton; Verrazano established the existence of a single, continuous coastline from one to the other, thereby removing this expanse from the realm of conjecture. The Atlantic seaboard of the North American continent was now charted in its entirety for the first time in history.

But for all that, the "blessed shores of Cathay," whose spices were to bring riches to France, had not been reached. Did this intervening con-

tinent offer sufficient compensation? For the most part it was a beautiful
country, and its climate healthy. Almost every time he went ashore,
Verrazano returned to his ship filled with enthusiasm. But what about
spices, and gold? The financiers of Lyons and Rouen would certainly
expect something that would bring in a good profit. As to this, Verrazano
was not able to offer any certainty. Some of the mountains appeared to
him to be "rich in mineral matter"; in "the land of evil men," there might
be metals hidden beneath the hills, for he had seen the natives wearing
pendant earrings of copper.[15] He is said to have brought back "a selection
of gold, potions and other aromatic liquors from his voyage so that, after
an audience with His Majesty, he might confer with numerous merchants
[in Lyons]."[16] But it was a far more precious cargo that Magellan's
Vittoria had brought home to Spain in 1522!

Verrazano also brought back a map; he had compiled a portolano chart
of his voyage and sketched the land that he had seen, and "in a little
book geometrically determined the interval between one meridian and
another, adding observations on the height of the tides in each climate,
in every kind of weather and at each hour of the day, which may well
be useful to navigators."[17] This "little book," which would have furnished
us with some of the scientific findings of the expedition, has never been
found, nor has the portolano chart which Verrazano was to present to the
King. We do, however, have two maps drawn on the basis of information
supplied by Verrazano himself, one, dated 1527, by Vesconte de Maiollo
or Maggiolo,[18] and the other, dated 1529, by Girolamo da Verrazano, the
navigator's brother.[19] On these maps, for the first time in the history of
cartography, the coastline extending from Florida to Cape Breton bears
European place-names, largely French in origin if not in form, and on
Maggiolo's the royal fleurs-de-lis of France make their first appearance on
a map of the New World.

The *Dauphine* arrived in France during the summer of 1524.[20] It was
an unfortunate time for Verrazano's return. Francis I was on his way
down the Rhône and would not soon be back; he was to devote himself
entirely to war, not only in defence of his possessions but also with the
intention of re-entering the Italian scene. But, on February 26, 1525, came
the Italian debacle; at Pavia, Francis I suffered defeat and capture. From
Italy he was taken to Madrid, where he remained for a year as the prisoner
of his elated rival, Charles V. This was enough to postpone Verrazano's
next voyage indefinitely.

While the Florentine cooled his heels, the Spaniards undertook to turn
New France into a New Spain. No sooner had Verrazano returned to
Dieppe than a Spanish ship set out for Newfoundland. Her captain was
Estevan Gomez, a Portuguese who, like Magellan, with whom he had
sailed for some time, had entered the service of Spain. Putting to sea in

August 1524, Gomez steered straight for Newfoundland and, reversing Verrazano's course, made this his starting point for a voyage down the coast, taking soundings of all the bays and river mouths as he went. He concluded his exploration after rounding Cape Cod, sailed on to Cuba and from there back to Spain, where he arrived in June 1525, bringing with him a number of natives whom he had captured on the coast of Maine. Changes on the map were in store. The entire area explored by Gomez was named Estevan Gomez Land and an abundance of Spanish place-names replaced the French names introduced in 1524. These were to remain current until the seventeenth century.

Immediately another explorer, Lucas Vasquez de Ayllon, came along to add to the claims of Spain. It will be recalled that in 1521 some Spaniards under his command had returned to Florida and had sailed up the Atlantic coast as far as South Carolina. He resumed his exploration in June 1526, this time with three ships and accompanied by Dominican friars. His primary object was to find a strait that would open the way to Asia. Returning to South Carolina, a little beyond the point reached five years earlier, the Spaniards sailed north and anchored in Chesapeake Bay, the entrance to which had raised hopes of the discovery of a strait. There a small colony was established, called San Miguel. But shortly this new enterprise was menaced by sickness. Ayllon succumbed among his colonists in October and was buried in San Miguel. Dissension then forced the survivors to withdraw to the West Indies. The first Spanish effort at colonization north of Florida had failed and no passage to Asia had been found. But progress had been made in the establishment of Spanish place-names on the map of North America; the territory between Florida and Gomez Land became known as Ayllon Land, and here, too, a whole list of Spanish names supplanted Verrazano's place-names.

While the New France of 1524 was in the process of becoming a Spanish continent divided into Gomez Land in the north, Florida to the south and Ayllon Land in between, Verrazano was preparing a new expedition for the spring of 1526. Everything was in readiness, but 1526 wore on and no start was made; 1527 passed and still the expedition to North America did not materialize.

On June 10 of that same year, two ships dispatched by Henry VIII left England for Newfoundland; they were the *Mary Guildford*, under the command of John Rut, who was accompanied by Canon Albert de Prato, and the *Sampson*. The two vessels first explored the coast north of Newfoundland, but the precise nature of the tasks performed by this official mission is not known. In August, the *Mary Guildford* stopped at the port of St John's, from where Rut and Canon de Prato wrote to England. Then the two ships (not distinguished one from the other by name) turned south to pursue their investigations. One of them visited Cape Breton and the coast of "Arembec" (Verrazano's *Oranbega* or *Norembègue*, corresponding to New England), and then returned to England in October of the same year; the other sailed all the way down the coast of Gomez and Ayllon Lands, and turned up in the West Indies in November.[21] This expedition, faring no better than its predecessors, found no route to Asia. However, it did enable England to assert her rights on the Atlantic seaboard along with France and Spain, and moreover it was she, the latecomer, who was to gain possession of this long coastline in the end.

Verrazano's expedition finally got under way in the spring of 1528. Was he still seeking a passage through the continental barrier which he had probed four years earlier and which had effectively stopped Gomez, Ayllon and the 1527 English expedition after him? Was he hoping to find the hypothetical strait thought by Maggiolo to be situated in the isthmus of Panama? Or had he really set out to explore the coast of Brazil, as the Portuguese ambassador believed in 1527?[22]

Verrazano set sail, but, as in the case of the celebrated Corte-Real brothers, no one knows for certain what became of him. Some authors have taken the view that, under the name of Jean Florin (for John the Florentine), he fell into Spanish hands and was summarily hanged as a pirate. In response to this theory, it has been asserted that the Jean Florin in question was one Jean Fleury, a notorious corsair from Honfleur who had no connection with Jean (Giovanni) de Verrazano. Other writers have claimed that, in disappointment with France, Verrazano returned to Italy to die. Today, more credence is generally given to the tragic story told by the navigator's brother to the poet Paul Jove. According to this story, Verrazano was seized by West Indian natives and, before the very eyes of his companions, who had stayed aboard their ship, was cut to pieces and devoured.[23] Be that as it may, in 1528 the curtain fell on the career of the first great navigator sent by France to North America.

From Cape Breton to Florida, along a coast whose features were still unidentified and unnamed, Verrazano had spread a French map in 1524. What became of it subsequently?

The names Angoulesme and Refuge made their last appearance on a map in 1561.[24] *Francesca*, the name Verrazano gave in honour of Francis I to the land he had discovered, was not employed more than a dozen times by cartographers and was no longer in use after 1562. The Asian Sea, which the navigator thought he had sighted on the far side of an isthmus and to which he had given his name, disappeared from the maps after 1583, and with it the name of Verrazano. American geography very quickly forgot Francis I and his Florentine navigator; Verrazano's contribution to cartography perished with his own century. Except, that is, for three names: *Norembègue*, *Nouvelle-France*, and *Arcadie*.

The name Norembègue first appeared in mapmaking after Verrazano's voyage: his brother Girolamo inscribed *Oranbega* on his map, probably to designate the Rhode Island region. Later, *Norombega*, *Norumbega*, and then *Norembègue* were applied to the Penobscot region of Maine and invested with legendary wonders that had their origin "in the enthusiastic description of Refuge by Verrazano." Norembègue continued to be talked of in the seventeenth century; Champlain and Lescarbot were to try to establish its location, and it was still shown on a map as late as 1677, but the origin of the name has remained in the realm of conjecture.

Nouvelle-France, a name which appeared in 1529 in its Latin form of *Nova Gallia*, lent itself quite naturally to the designation of land discovered by France. It was applied to various regions of America and was to retain a place there for more than two centuries before finally disappearing with the English conquest of 1760.

The idyllic name, Arcadie, is still in use in the form *Acadie* or *Acadia*. Verrazano, the Renaissance humanist, had plucked it from his knowledge of literature as an appropriate name for Virginia, a land of strikingly beautiful trees. Then, without deliberate intent, sixteenth-century cartographers shifted it little by little toward the northeast; in 1566, we find it located between Norembègue and Newfoundland, covering the present territory of Nova Scotia and New Brunswick.[25] The name was still in use in the form *Arcadie* on a map of 1572 and in a printed work dated 1575.[26] Then, at the end of the sixteenth century, under the influence of a purely coincidental resemblance to native place-names,[27] there was a period of several years of hesitation between *Arcadie* and *Acadie*. Considering the maps which first showed the form *Arcadie* and then gradually transferred the name to the area that is historically Acadie, the period of hesitation between the two forms on the part of writers, and particularly the exclusive use of the form *Arcadie* by Champlain in 1603, we may safely assert that it was Verrazano's name *Arcadia* that ultimately produced *Acadie* and *Acadia*. Today, that name is the sole remaining relic of the illustrious voyage of 1524.

CHAPTER 2

The Discovery of a Great Highway into the Continent

1535

Though France was the last Atlantic power to enter the scene in the New World, a continental coastline had been discovered for her by Verrazano in which there might well lie a direct route to Asia. Even failing such a route, there was a land here that could still become the seat of a great empire. Francis I was not a man to neglect such a stroke of good fortune.

Brazil at that time was more attractive than North America to Ango and other shipowners, but in 1532 an influential figure came forward to refocus France's attention on the route initiated in 1524. This was Jean Le Veneur, Bishop and Count of Lisieux, Abbé of Mont St Michel and Grand Almoner of France. In 1532, Francis I made a pilgrimage to Mont St Michel. The Bishop, who received him there, brought before him a pilot, Jacques Cartier, a relative of the bursar of the abbey. He assured the King that Cartier, "by virtue of his voyages to Brazil and the New Land," was well able "to lead ships in the discovery of new territories in the New World." Le Veneur even pledged himself, "if the King would consent to entrust this mission to Jacques Cartier, to provide chaplains and contribute to the cost of these voyages of discovery from his own resources."[1]

Francis I, who had sponsored the voyage of the *Dauphine*, could hardly remain unresponsive to his offer, but the question of the freedom of the seas posed a problem. The bulls of Rome had reserved new territories to Portugal and Spain. True, the bulls were not universally recognized as having such far-reaching force. Nevertheless, it was not expedient for Francis I to offend Pope Clement VII, who had become his political ally against Charles V. A marriage between the son of Francis I and the Pope's niece provided the occasion for a discussion of the bulls. The Pope, who was more interested in Italian politics than in unknown lands, raised no difficulties. He is reported to have stated "that the papal bull dividing up the new continents between the crowns of Spain and Portugal concerned only already-known continents and not lands subsequently discovered by the other crowns."[2] Thus, Francis I was now able to pursue his policy of exploration as he saw fit without coming into conflict with his ally the Pope, and Bishop Le Veneur was at liberty to give rein to his dreams of "the blessed shores of Cathay."

And so the King called upon Jacques Cartier to continue Verrazano's work. Cartier was a pilot from St Malo, born in 1491; in 1520, he had married Catherine Des Granches, who came of a more prominent family than his own; in documents we find him present at baptisms, either as a godfather or simply as a witness.[3] This, from purely documentary sources, is all we know of him for certain before Le Veneur's recommendation to the King. That there had been no mention of Cartier in connection with long-range expeditions before 1532 is no proof that he was new to the game, and as far as Newfoundland is concerned it would be very surprising if a St Malo pilot over forty years of age had never been there. Nothing, after all, is known of Verrazano's seagoing experience before 1523, yet from that date onward he showed himself to be an outstanding navigator. Costly enterprises were not entrusted to men of unproven competence, and the one thing certain is that Cartier's previous experience was sufficient to earn him the support of Bishop Le Veneur, the Admiral of France and the King himself.

What was Cartier's objective in 1534? The commission authorizing his departure has never been found, but a royal order for payment of the cost of equipment gives us part of the answer: Jacques Cartier was "to voyage to that realm of the *Terres Neufves* to discover certain isles and countries where it is said there must be great quantities of gold and other riches."[4] The rest of the answer may be deduced from the account of the voyage: Cartier's insistence on discovering a passage that would lead him further still, the care he took to make soundings of bays and rivers, and his disappointment when he found himself at a dead end, all show clearly that he was following Verrazano's lead in seeking the fissure that would open up the continental barrier.

Cartier left St Malo on April 20, 1534, with two ships and sixty-one men;[5] "with good sailing weather" he reached *Bonne Viste* on May 10.[6] There are no other details: a routine crossing, evidently, and made in the record time of twenty days. Ice forced him to take refuge further south, in a harbour that already bore the name Ste Catherine, but ten days later he sailed north to the *isle des Ouaiseaulx*, obtained a plentiful supply of meat there, and on May 27 entered the *baye des Chasteaux*. This "bay" between Newfoundland and Labrador, which we know as the Strait of Belle Isle, had already been named and had appeared on maps; Cartier had been instructed to make it his first objective.[7]

Immobilized by wind and ice until June 9, Cartier then made an examination of the harbours and islands, described the hazards to be avoided, and recorded distances. At this time he conferred his first place-name, giving to an island the name of Ste Catherine, doubtless in honour of his wife. But he was not yet in unknown territory. In the harbour of Les Islettes, a league to the west of Blanc Sablon, he noted that "much fishing" was carried on. Ten leagues beyond this place there was a harbour which already bore the name of Brest;[8] Cartier put to shore there to take on water and wood. On the 12th, as he continued his examination of harbours, he conferred names on places that so far had none: Toutes Isles for a group of islands, St Antoine for one harbour and St Servan for another, where he raised his first cross, and St Jacques for a river. He had penetrated as deep as a hundred miles into the continental barrier, yet there he met a ship from La Rochelle that had intended to fish in the harbour at Brest but had passed by it during the night. Cartier went aboard and guided the ship into a harbour situated further west, "one of the good harbours of the world," which he named Jacques Cartier.[9]

This vessel from La Rochelle, encountered more than a hundred miles from the Atlantic, was Cartier's last contact with European civilization. The same day, June 12 or 13, he came upon his first natives, whom he qualified as "sturdy enough," but "frightful and savage." For the land he had seen so far, Cartier had nothing but profound contempt: "It should not be called new land, but [a name suiting its] frightful and ill-shapen stones and rocks; for I saw not one cartload of land in all that northern coast." He believed, he added, "that this was the land God gave Cain." After this less than encouraging sight, he returned to the harbour of Brest. On the 15th, he weighed anchor and steered "for the south."[10] From that moment, Cartier was entering the unknown; the voyage of discovery had begun.

It is perfectly legitimate to suspect that Cartier was not the first European to visit the Gulf of St Lawrence. And yet not one of the known maps long studied by specialists depicts the Gulf; the most authoritative maps show no more than an indentation between Labrador and Newfoundland which was called the Baie des Châteaux, and the fact that it was called a bay is proof enough that the contours of the Strait of Belle Isle were unknown. If any Europeans had recognized the Gulf of St Lawrence for what it was, there is no sign of it in cartography. Until 1534, the hinterland of Newfoundland and Cape Breton was deeply veiled in mystery; Cartier, in discovering the Gulf, was the first to tear through the veil.

Steering a southerly course, then, Cartier sailed down the west coast of Newfoundland, leaving French names strung like the beads of a chaplet all along that yet unmapped coast.[11]

Had he kept on this southward course in 1534, he would have established then that Newfoundland was an island and demonstrated the existence of a passage between it and Cape Breton. But he did not pursue his investigations any further in that direction, contenting himself with

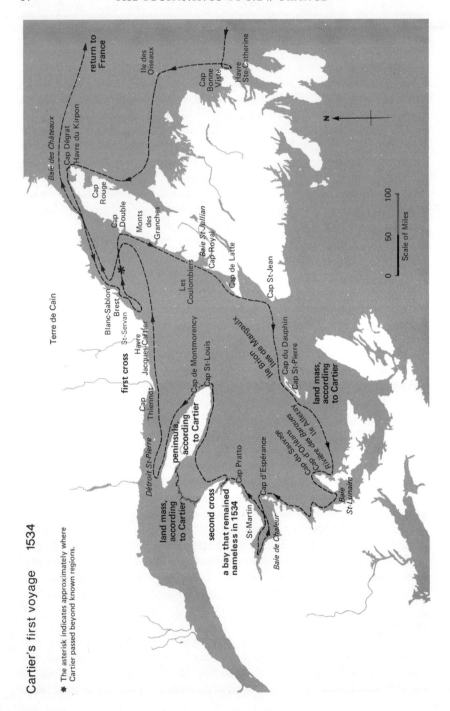

Cartier's first voyage   1534

* The asterisk indicates approximately where
  Cartier passed beyond known regions.

assuming, on account of the heavy tides, that there was "a passage between the *Terre Neuffve* and the land of the Bretons," and cherishing the hope that, if this were the case, it "would mean a great reduction in both time and distance."[12] More eager to find the route to Asia, he left the coast of Newfoundland at Cape Anguille and veered away to the west.

He soon came upon three islands "as full of birds as a meadow [is] of grass," and a goodly provision was laid in. These islands received the name Margaulx. At last, on June 25, he discovered something he had not seen since his arrival: some good land, "the best land we have seen, for an acre of this ground is worth more than the whole of the *Terre Neufve*." It was an island rich in trees, wild wheat, peas and fragrant herbs. To this lush island, the description of which reminds us of Verrazano's Arcadia, Cartier gave the name Brion,[13] in honour of the Admiral of France. On June 26, some other islands hove into view, the Magdalen Islands, but Cartier took these to be the beginning of the mainland.

On June 29 he was still running westward, but "without having any cognizance of land," except that in the evening, as the sun set, he sighted what looked like two islands. Next day, a prolonged examination showed that the land was much more extensive than he had first believed. He went ashore at several points on both the east and the west coasts, and had nothing but praise for what he saw. He took this to be the mainland, though in fact he was on Prince Edward Island. Finally, as he sailed around this "mainland," he sighted an expanse of water which he took to be a bay, and he named it St Lunaire. It was a strait, but one which could only have taken him back to where he had come from.

When he had set his course southward along the Newfoundland coast, Cartier's intention had been simply to reconnoitre the country, but on turning westward he had reverted to his prime preoccupation, the passage to Asia. From that moment onward, he examined every opening that came into view. Continuing toward the north, he sighted on July 3 "a large bay and opening"; the Baie de Chaleur, with its deep waters, a width of about fifteen miles at its entrance and a penetration of about a hundred miles inland, seemed to justify every hope. "And because of the depth and tide marks and changing nature of the land, we had hopes of finding the passage there, in like manner to the passage of the Chasteaulx." Cartier gave the name Cap d'Espérance to the southern point of the entrance. He brought his ships into the shelter of a small harbour, the "conche sainct Martin," on the north shore of the bay, and from July 4 to July 12 he pursued a systematic investigation.[14]

On the 6th, while exploring a newly-discovered cape "to see how the land fell away behind," he encountered a large number of Micmacs who joyfully held out their furs on sticks from a distance, but the French, seeing themselves outnumbered, tried to slip away. The Micmacs caught up with them; Cartier made signs to them to go away, but in vain. With natives all around, Cartier ordered his men to fire over their heads. There was a general stampede, then the Indians came back; in the end, Cartier was unable to shake them off until he let fly "two fire-lances which passed among them." The next day they were back at St Martin's Cove to offer their furs again. This time the two parties achieved a better understanding and some bartering took place, the French receiving furs in exchange for trivial objects. That date, July 7, 1534, marked an important occasion, the first duly recorded ceremony of commercial exchange between Europeans and the natives of the Gulf. Not that it was the first time that trading had taken place, by any means. The eagerness of the Micmacs to receive the strangers and their insistence on offering their goods were ample proof that these natives were in the habit of trading with Europeans; explorers and fishermen before Cartier are known to have returned home with furs, but this is the first time that we are given a description of the actual trading ceremony.

The exploration progressed. On July 8, Cartier sailed twenty-five leagues into what he took to be a strait. Next morning there was great disappointment in store for him; "we became aware of the end of the bay, which saddened and afflicted us;" above the land that closed the bay, the party could make out "very high mountainous land." No road to Asia that way! To this bay Cartier gave the name Baie de Chaleur; not that it was particularly warm there but perhaps because it was a pleasant place to be. It might better have been called Disappointment Bay.

Cartier left the Baie de Chaleur on July 12 and continued his search northward. On the 14th he finally reached and entered what he called a river, but it was in fact a bay, which would soon bear the name Gaspé. Very strong winds, so strong that one ship lost an anchor, compelled him to push on another seven or eight leagues, where he found a good harbour. On account of the bad weather, he remained there from July 16 to 25.[15]

This prolonged stay enabled Cartier to establish historic relations with a new nation of natives. These were not the Micmacs with whom he had just been trading in the Baie de Chaleur, nor were they the "frightful" people he had seen in June; these natives were different enough to warrant a pause in Cartier's account so that they might be described in meticulous detail.

These were the Iroquois. They had invaded the St Lawrence Valley around the year 1200, introduced the cultivation of corn, beans, pumpkins and tobacco, and finally imposed their domination along the whole length of the river.[16] In that month of July 1534, Cartier established the first European relations with a nation that was to play a leading role in the lands of the St Lawrence until almost the end of the eighteenth century. This historic event took place in an atmosphere of gaiety and merriment. Cartier distributed "knives, glass beads, combs, and other articles of small value"; to the women, he gave small tin bells. The Indians sang and danced.

July 24 saw another historic moment. On Pointe Penouille, at the entry to the harbour, Cartier raised a thirty-foot cross with an escutcheon embossed with three fleurs-de-lis and a wooden plaque carved in large letters with the legend, Vive le roi de France. The navigator nowhere declares that he formally took possession of the country, and no contemporary text claims any such formal act; nevertheless, the raising of that cross with its inscription in honour of the King of France was clearly tantamount to a solemn assertion of the rights of France over that land.

At this, Donnacona, chief of the Iroquois, felt himself to have been deeply wronged. When the French had re-embarked, he got into a canoe with three of his sons and his brother, approached the ship and began a harangue, "pointing to the cross and making the sign of the cross with two fingers; then he pointed to the land all around us, as if to say that all the land was his, and that we should not have planted the cross without his leave." He had cause to regret it. On the pretext of pacifying him, Cartier made as if to give him an axe in exchange for his fur; the moment Donnacona moved to touch his acquisition, the canoe was made fast, some of the French jumped into it and the natives were hustled aboard the ship, "at which they were greatly astonished."

Cartier, however, sought to reassure his guests, feasting them and explaining to Donnacona that the cross was only there to serve as a sea-mark. The French, he said, intended to return, and wished to take with them two of Donnacona's sons, whom they would bring back. Despite misgivings, Donnacona agreed. He and his braves said their farewells to the departing sons, and the French and Indians parted on the best of terms.

It was customary for explorers to carry off natives and take them home from their voyages as evidence or as an additional memento, but Cartier fully intended to return to North America. These natives came from inland, and were in a position to hand him the key to the continent. When the French returned they would need guides who had learned to speak their language during a stay in France, for up to then the visitors had understood little of what was said. Cartier had brought off a masterly coup by means of a very simple trick, arousing Donnacona's greed with the offer of an axe. With skill and cunning, he had carried off two of Chief Donnacona's sons, and yet had succeeded in preserving friendship between the French and the Iroquois.

Convinced by sign language that the cross would be respected, Cartier left the Bay of Gaspé on July 25. He should then have veered westward and entered a great river, but a mirage effect caused him to believe that his path was blocked; thus it was that in 1534 he failed to discover the river that would have launched him at once into the interior of the continent.

And so he headed east and, until July 29, sailed along and around the end of what he took to be a peninsula but which was really Anticosti Island. Would he, once off its northern coast, at least detect the 25-mile strait that separated the supposed peninsula from the north shore? From August 1 to 5, in the teeth of high winds, "we sailed close inshore on a northwesterly course, first on one side and then on the other, to see whether this was a bay or a passage." The adventurers reached the narrowest part of the strait, but the sea was still very rough and they returned to the Anticosti side and went ashore. There, from a cape, they observed the land begin "to fall away to the southwest."

Here again, Cartier had been within an ace of discovering the river. Once again he had failed to do so, not because he thought the way was blocked, for he had seen an opening (which he named St Peter's Strait), but because the weather was against him. All the members of the expedition assembled to consider what should be done; they elected to withdraw.

With a following sou'wester, Cartier headed straight for Newfoundland, then turned north. By August 9, he was back at Blanc Sablon. On the 15th, "after hearing mass," he set sail for the Atlantic crossing. Except for three days in a heavy storm, the weather was favourable and the expedition ultimately found itself back in St Malo on September 5, 1534, after an absence of four and a half months.[17]

Cartier was returning to France, then, to announce that he had not reached the objective he had been set, those "isles and countries where it is said there must be great quantities of gold and other riches." Beyond the Atlantic facade of Newfoundland, he had seen a rather disappointing country; on the northern coast, ill-formed rockland, without a cartload of earth, ground that God had reserved for Cain; to the south, however, fertile islands, alive with game; on the west, mainland with a climate, soil and trees that called forth Cartier's unreserved enthusiasm. But one cannot help wondering whether the praise was not due to the striking contrast between the last-named areas and the "land of Cain." At all events, there was no gold, nor other metals; the natives Cartier had encountered were poor and wore on their persons no trinkets of the slightest worth.

But even without gold or other metals, the country nevertheless was worth something. There was a great, even teeming abundance of cod, such as Cartier had noted off the west coast of Newfoundland. Furs were another potential source of profit. Cartier could not have foreseen the brilliant future in store for furs; his account twice observes that the skins worn by the natives were "a thing of little value." However, in July 1534, the Micmacs were probably not expecting customers; as for the Iroquois, they had come down to the coast for no other purpose than to lay in a provision of fish.

The voyage of 1534 ended in failure, as that of 1524 had done; the passage to the Asian Sea had not been found. No such passage existed, as we well know today, but Cartier, in the course of two months of exploration behind Newfoundland, should at least have discovered the great watercourse that could have taken him deep into the interior of the continent. Nevertheless, he had worked well, taking soundings of all the bays, particularly the Baie de Chaleur; between the Gaspé Peninsula and Anticosti, he believed he had seen nothing but land. In the strait north of Anticosti, winds had robbed him of an opportunity to continue his soundings; there remained therefore the assumption that a passage existed here which might lead further. This assumption was in itself an advance, another step westward and, perhaps, toward Asia.

Moreover, that first voyage provided a valuable addition to contemporary knowledge of America in establishing the existence of a sea beyond Newfoundland. Cartier may not have been the first to enter it, but he was the first to map it. His map contained serious errors; he did not see the strait separating Newfoundland from Cape Breton; he took the Magdalen Islands to be the beginning of the mainland; he described the strait between Prince Edward Island and New Brunswick as a bay; and he showed Anticosti Island as a peninsula. Taken as a whole, the Gulf of St Lawrence, as seen by Cartier, was one large lake with only one fully charted exit, namely the Strait of Belle Isle, and another north of Anticosti which he did not have time to examine.

The discovery of an inland sea, a visit to a new country, an alliance with natives from the west, a hypothetical passage that might open the way to further exploration, the possibility of commercial gain; all this was enough to justify a second attempt, the more so since Cartier had brought home two natives who, with their initiation in the French language, were to stimulate interest in this new venture. Domagaya and Taignoagny spoke of a great river which flowed from their territory, and of a kingdom called Saguenay from which copper came. The tales they told, whether true or false, could not fail to have a decisive effect.

Cartier had arrived home in St Malo on September 5, 1534. By October 30, he had received a commission from Admiral Chabot to undertake a second voyage. Like the first, it was to be carried out "at the desire and command of the King," and Francis I put 3,000 livres into the enterprise. This was a more ambitious venture than the first. In 1534, Cartier had sailed with only two ships, carrying a complement of sixty-one men. This time there were to be three ships: the *Grande Hermine*, with Cartier on board as commander and pilot, the *Petite Hermine*, and the *Emerillon*. The ships were equipped and victualled for a voyage of a year and a half, and they carried about 110 men.[18] The two Indians embarked with Cartier.

His official objective in 1535 was the continuation of the first voyage.

The commission signed by Admiral Chabot was explicit: "completion of the navigation in the lands beyond the *Terres Neufves* whose discovery you have already begun"; and when the King signed an order for payment in favour of Cartier, it was to be used "to pursue the discovery of certain distant lands."[19]

On May 16, 1535, which was Whit Sunday, the ships' companies went to confession, took communion and received the episcopal blessing. On the 19th, the expedition set sail. This time, the east-to-west crossing was not such an easy one; on the 26th "the weather turned to fury and tempest, which lasted for us, with contrary and raging winds, as long as any that ever were had by vessels crossing this sea, without abatement." Cartier arrived at last at the Ile des Oiseaux on July 7, after a crossing that took fifty days, whereas the previous crossing had taken no more than twenty. Entering the Baie des Châteaux, he sailed across it and dropped anchor at Blanc Sablon. The second voyage of exploration was at last beginning, more than two months after his departure from St Malo.

Cartier had only one immediate preoccupation, and that was to take up his investigations where he had left them the previous year, in St Peter's Strait. He steered west along the north shore on the Gulf, adding to the existing place-names as he went. Next he sailed toward Anticosti, searching in vain for a harbour, then turned again to the north shore. There, the account notes, "we found a large and very beautiful bay, full of islands and good entrances," which he named St Laurent. This was the name which, some thirty years later, came to be used to designate first the entire gulf and then the river.

At length, on August 13, Cartier made the most important breakthrough of all his explorations. Turning southwest again, he sailed toward the westernmost point of what, in 1534, he had taken to be a peninsula, and it was then that he grasped the broad geographic scheme of the area. Having reached this region, Domagaya and Taignoagny were rediscovering places that were familiar to them because they had come there from the interior to fish, and since they now spoke French they were able to communicate their knowledge. The place they were approaching, they told Cartier, was not a peninsula but an island; on the far side of this, it was possible to travel to Honguedo, where they had boarded ship with him; on the northern side, two days' journey from the island, the Kingdom of Saguenay began, and still beyond was Canada. A little more of the unknown west was revealed, and that day, August 13, 1535, the word Canada took its place in history.[20]

Cartier landed on the island on August 15 and gave it the name Assumption; from it, on the far side of the strait, he saw the high mountains of the south shore. But the two Indians insisted that the north shore "was the beginning of Saguenay and inhabited country and that from there came the red copper." Did Cartier still hesitate? The Indians assured him that this river was the road to Canada and to Hochelaga, that it ran "ever narrowing as far as Canada; that then there is fresh water in the said river, which goes so far that no man has ever been to the end." A river that became narrower as one went upstream, water that turned from salt to fresh and that came flowing from such a distance that no man in memory had reached its source; if the Indians were not lying, this meant that the all-important water route had been found, that the passage across the continent sought by the French must lie in that direction.

And so Cartier took "the road to Canada," but, in order not to miss any possible opening, he zigzagged from shore to shore as he went. On September 1, he set sail upriver, "bound for Canada." En route, he encountered a river on his right that was "very deep and swift," a river flowing "between high mountains of bare rock, with but little soil, yet notwithstanding, quantities of trees grow there." The guides told him that this was the "way to the kingdom and land of Saguenay," but he barely penetrated into its mouth. There they met a fishing party come from Canada, and Domagaya and Taignoagny renewed acquaintance with their compatriots. Then the expedition continued along the "road toward Canada." At last, on September 7, they reached a group of fourteen islands (one of them the Ile d'Orléans) that marked the "beginning of the land and province of Canada."

For what it may be worth, then, it can be said that Cartier arrived in Canada on September 7, 1535.

He dropped anchor between the north shore of the river and the Ile d'Orléans and went to meet the island natives. The Indians at first fled, but after Domagaya and Taignoagny, no doubt in European dress, had revealed their identity, they brought eels, coarse millet (corn), some large melons (probably pumpkins), and a feast was held; Domagaya and Taignoagny must have longed for corn while they were away. The next morning appeared the Iroquois chief whom Cartier had met at Honguedo in 1534: Donnacona, lord of Canada. He was reunited with his two sons and had them tell him about their journey to France. More feasting followed. When the palavers were over, Cartier ordered out the long-boats and went off in search of a harbour. Hugging the shore for about ten leagues, he found a "very beautiful and pleasant fork in the waters, at a place where there is a small river and harbour with a bar." It was September 14 when he put in there, and he named the place Ste Croix, after the festival celebrated on that day.

Cartier was in the St Charles River and the harbour he had chosen was a little way upstream, at the confluence of its waters with the stream called the Lairet. Nearby, on a "double ridge of land, at a good height and cultivated all about," stood Stadacona, the "demeurance" or dwelling-place of the lord Donnacona. It consisted of a cluster of huts which, contrary to Iroquois custom and no doubt owing to Montagnais influence, was not, it seems, protected by an enclosure. Stadacona was surely established on Cape Diamond, but the precise location has never to this day been found.

Before they returned to their ships, the French made a tour of the large island near which they were anchored, a place "most beautiful to behold, and level," rich in fine trees and with no "tillage," where the natives engaged in fishing. They were astonished by the profusion of vines, the first they had seen, and Cartier named this island the Ile de Bacchus, which he changed in the course of this same voyage to Ile d'Orléans. Afterwards, he guided his ships into harbour at Ste Croix.

Cartier was in haste to reach the Hochelaga that his Indian guides had talked of and where they had promised to take him. But no sooner had he established his base at Ste Croix than Domagaya and Taignoagny began to show signs of dissatisfaction. On September 15, while he was setting up river markers, Cartier observed the leading personalities of Stadacona talking together on a point of land and staying clear of the French. When Cartier went to join them, Taignoagny told him that Donnacona was angry because the French were carrying "so many war sticks," but Cartier, observing that Donnacona did not look angry, realized that the two guides were stirring up trouble. He quickly found out that what was upsetting the Indians of Stadacona was the forthcoming journey to Hochelaga.[21]

The Iroquois of the St Lawrence, who had come from the southwest three centuries earlier, should not be regarded as forming a single political and cultural entity. They are thought to have been made up of two quite distinct groups; one, which had settled at Hochelaga, is believed to have been Onondaga in origin; the other, concentrated about Stadacona, was more probably a family of Mohawks who had long lived under the influence of the Montagnais. The Onondagas and the Mohawks did, however, have sufficient ethnic elements in common to give them the appearance of belonging to one and the same nation.[22] It was Hochelaga that had supremacy among the occupants of the St Lawrence Valley, holding Stadacona and eight or nine other nations living on the banks of the river in a state of dependence. Whether he had learned from the European experience of his sons or was naturally endowed with a measure of political acuity, the Stadacona chief was anxious to keep for his own village the benefits of the promising trade about to take shape with the French. It was he who had first met the French and it was through his sons that they had found their way to Stadacona; he firmly intended to act henceforth as intermediary between the whites and his own race, seeing this as a potent means of extricating himself from domination by Hochelaga. If, on the other hand, the French were to establish relations of their own with Hochelaga further up the river, Stadacona would lose its acquired advantage and would continue to live in subjection. Donnacona was therefore bent on doing everything possible to isolate Hochelaga.

On September 16, as Cartier was busy securing the two *Hermines* and manoeuvring the *Emerillon* into the roadstead for the journey to Hochelaga, the people of Stadacona appeared with Donnacona. After an exchange of courtesies, Taignoagny spoke for his people: "Donnacona is angry with your plan," he told Cartier, "and is against my going to Hochelaga as I promised to do." What was the supposedly serious reason offered by Taignoagny? The river, he said, was of no worth! (A century later, Quebeckers were to tell Maisonneuve not to go to Montreal because the island was overrun with Iroquois.) "I shall go nevertheless," replied Cartier, "because I am commanded by the King to go as far as it may be possible; if you come, Taignoagny, we shall make you a present and feast you; in any case, all we wish to do is to see Hochelaga and come back." Taignoagny still refused, and the two sides parted.

Donnacona returned the following morning and, after a long harangue, offered Cartier a little girl and two boys on condition that the voyage to Hochelaga should not take place; so, at least, said Taignoagny as interpreter. Cartier stood firm. Domagaya then intervened to say that Donnacona was making these presents "out of sincere affection and as a mark of confidence," and he declared himself willing to go to Hochelaga. A lively discussion ensued between the two interpreters, "from which we perceived that Taignoagny was a worthless fellow and that his intent was naught but treachery and malice, not only from this but also other evil tricks we had seen him play." Cartier, in any case, accepted the three children and presented Donnacona with two swords and a brass bowl. Volleys were fired to crown the celebration, but the Iroquois thought that the heavens were falling upon them and set up "such a howling and yelling that it seemed that hell itself had been loosed." Taignoagny spread the rumour that some natives had been killed during the celebration, and the Iroquois fled in disorder.

The plot was thickening. While Taignoagny had refused to go to Hochelaga, Domagaya assured the French that he would go with Donnacona's consent. Would Taignoagny be alone in his treachery? Judging from what was to follow, we have the impression that Domagaya's intent was only to recoup Taignoagny's failure by pretending to side with Cartier. In fact, all three Indians, Donnacona and the two interpreters, were playing out a farce; a display of witchcraft staged for Cartier's benefit on September 18 gave proof of it.

Doggedly, Donnacona made one last attempt, saying that he would allow the interpreters to go to Hochelaga if Cartier would leave a hostage to stay with him. Cartier would tolerate no compromise; he preferred to go without interpreters. In any case, Domagaya and Taignoagny were no longer to be trusted. On September 19, the *Emerillon* moved out of the roadstead and sailed up-river.

On September 28, Cartier entered a large lake, only two fathoms deep, which was to bear the name Angoulême on maps until Champlain renamed it Lac St Pierre. At its head this lake appeared to be "entirely closed, without any river." Cartier dropped anchor and scouted by boat for a passage; he saw then that the main river entered by way of four or five branches. Being unable to take the *Emerillon* through, he left the ship where the river discharged into the lake and continued the journey in boats with some thirty men. The party reached Hochelaga on the evening of October 2.[23]

A thousand people "showing wondrous joy" were there to receive them, bringing great quantities of fish and of their corn bread, which they showered into the boats; after distributing small gifts, Cartier and his men retired to their boats for the night while the natives continued to dance joyously around their fires until morning came.

Cartier then set out with about twenty of his men and three Iroquois to "go to see the town and dwelling-place of these people." In the meadows below a mountain which Cartier named *mont Royal*, he found Hochelaga. The town was "completely round and palisaded with timber in three tiers," and provided with a single "gate and entrance secured with bars, having above it, and in several places on the palisade, galleries of a kind, and ladders leading up to them, which are stocked with stones and rocks for guarding and defending the place"; exactly the type of fortified town that Champlain was to encounter in Iroquois country in 1615. It contained fifty wooden houses covered with bark, each fifty paces long and twelve to fifteen wide; each house was subdivided into chambers with a larger room in the centre where a fire burned and where the people lived in community; in the loft was stored the corn from which they made a dough that they baked on hot stones. They also made soups of corn and other vegetables and ate a great deal of dried fish which they preserved in "large vessels, like earthenware casks." Salt was unknown to them. They made themselves garments of furs, but the majority went about "almost completely naked." They lived in the main by "tillage and fishery." They were a sedentary people; the account notes that they did not stir from their land "and were not *embulataires*, like those of Canada and the Saguenay," and that nevertheless other tribes along the river were subject to them.

Their most precious possession, which for them took the place of gold and silver, was *esnoguy*, a small snow-white shell from which they made "a manner of rosary." This was Cartier's first sight of wampum, the strings and belts which would be so frequently mentioned in the history of Franco-Indian relations; he was perhaps the first European to see it.

Inside the town, the very cordial reception turned into a sort of religious ceremony, in the course of which the Indians demonstrated a belief that they would receive a cure for all their ills from these strangers. The king of Hochelaga, a man of only about fifty, was already completely crippled; he ordered himself to be carried before Cartier and showed him his limbs, as if asking for "healing and health." Cartier did the best he could for him by massaging his arms and legs. Then the people rushed toward the healer. Moved by their trust, Cartier recited the Gospel of St John, made the sign of the cross over the sick, and prayed to God to vouchsafe them the grace of "Christianity and baptism." Then he read them the Passion of Christ, "word for word," amid the most profound silence. The ceremony ended with a distribution of gifts; axes, knives, rosaries and *Agnus Dei* medals of pewter.

Leaving Hochelaga, Cartier climbed Mount Royal and from there beheld the region spread out before him: far away to the north as to the south, a chain of mountains, then smooth, flat country, the river, and "the most impetuous cataract that it would be possible to see" (which today we call the Lachine Rapids). Even though there were no interpreters, he tried to have the Indians describe to him what lay beyond these rapids; he gathered that there were three similar cataracts higher up, and that above them the river could be navigated for more than three moons; he further understood that, on the north, a large tributary (here we recognize the Ottawa) flowed from the west, as did the great river itself. Cartier con-cluded at once that this tributary was the same river that passed through the Kingdom of Saguenay. It was explained to him, still in sign language, that it was from this river that gold and silver came, while copper was obtained from Saguenay. Along this river, he was told, lived the *agojuda*, that is to say, enemies "armed to the fingertips" who made constant war. Because of the language barrier, it was difficult to learn more. At last the French returned to their boats, and when they departed the Indians followed them a long way down the river.

Cartier's visit to Hochelaga had lasted only a day. Having arrived there on the evening of October 2, he set off down the river again in the course of the next day. The *Emerillon* was safe and sound where he had left it, and on the 5th he set sail "to return to the province of Canada." On October 7, he halted in the mouth of a river coming from the north, where there were four large islands. He named it *rivière de Fouez*, and thereupon the St Maurice River took its place in history.[24]

On his return to the harbour at Ste Croix on October 11 after a journey of three weeks, he found some new developments. Near the vessels lying at anchor, his men had constructed a fort to guard against any possible attack, "completely enclosed by heavy timbers planted upright and joined one to another, and armed with artillery all around." This unfortunately is all the description the account has left us of the first structure built by Europeans in the St Lawrence Valley.[25]

Donnacona and the interpreters came to greet Cartier, feigning great joy, and Cartier went to Stadacona to follow up the exchange of courtesies. But there the friendliness disappeared. The reason was, of course, the journey to Hochelaga that Cartier had made despite Donnacona's opposition. The interpreters, moreover, were losing no opportunity to plot and scheme. It would seem that, having been introduced to commerce in France, they had been reproaching their Indian brothers for accepting trifling gifts of no value in return for the provisions they supplied. The Iroquois, already turning into hardened traders, were beginning to demand more. Furthermore, they wished to recover the three children whom Donnacona had entrusted to Cartier, and they did, in fact, secure the escape of one girl. Relations were broken off.

Fearing an attack, Cartier had wide ditches dug around the fort, reinforced the palisade and instituted a night watch. After some time had passed, the Iroquois began to regret having incurred Cartier's "ill grace" and made a fresh approach. Cartier let them beg and beseech for a time, and then agreed to resume relations. A feast was held, and the two sides began to pay each other visits again "with as much affection as earlier."[26]

At the witchcraft display that they had staged in September, the Iroquois had claimed that their god had spoken at Hochelaga, predicting so much snow and ice that all would perish. Cartier had retorted that their god was nothing but a fool. Poor man, he had known only Brittany winters of light snowfalls and twig-fed fires, and he had no idea of what lay in store! The Indian interpreters, who were in a position to compare the European and Laurentian winters, were well aware how little he knew.

The god Cudouagny turned out to be no fool. From mid-November to mid-April, the ships were locked in ice two fathoms thick; the snow lay four feet deep and more, rising above the level of the ships' sides. The "beverages" froze in their casks with the cold, and a coat of ice four fingers thick formed inside the ships. The entire river froze as far up as Hochelaga.[27] The Europeans were having their first taste of Canadian winter.

More terrible even than the winter was the scurvy. The term "scurvy," a word of Norwegian origin, was first applied "to the disease that afflicted fishing crews who lived almost entirely on sour milk." A distinction was made between two types of scurvy; land scurvy, which ravaged those countries of the north where the population was "deprived for part of the year of fruits and green vegetables" (this sickness disappeared with the introduction of the potato), and sea scurvy, which afflicted mariners, and for which the cure, from the seventeenth century on, was eating oranges and lemons. Potatoes, oranges, lemons and wine or medicinal herbs later provided the vitamin C that gave protection against scurvy for both the people of northern countries and those spending long periods at sea.

In 1535, neither Cartier nor anyone in Europe for that matter knew of any defence against the malady.[28] It broke out in December among the Indians of Stadacona; then, in spite of the sanitary cordon that the French tried to set up against infection, it attacked them too. By mid-February, of the 110 men of the expedition no more than ten were still in good health; the sick were barely able to help one another any longer, which was "a pitiful sight to see, considering where we were." By then eight had died, and all their comrades could do was bury them beneath the snow, because of the frost in the ground.

In these dire straits, Cartier turned to prayer. He had an image of the Virgin set up against a tree outside the fort, and one Sunday the party made its way there in procession, and mass was recited and sung before the image. Cartier vowed to make a pilgrimage to Roc-Amadour if God should "grant him grace to return to France." The sickness continued to rage; a total of twenty-five men died, and hope was abandoned for some forty others; barely three or four were left unscathed, Cartier among them.

This was most fortunate, because it enabled him to ensure the safety of this tiny group of Frenchmen in their distress. Fearing greatly that the natives of the country might become aware of "our pitiable condition," the French were obliged to play a game of bluff. Whenever any Indians came near the fort, Cartier would go out, to be followed after a while by one or two others; he would then put on a show of anger against these men who could think of nothing better to do than saunter about, and would order them back into the fort, shouting abuse after them; then he would explain to the Indians that everybody inside the fort was hard at work, and the sick men would meanwhile do their utmost to make as much noise as possible. This was their last resort, in their extreme hardship; had the natives known the real situation, they would undoubtedly have taken advantage of it to rid themselves of these strangers who had become a thorn in their side.

The sufferers had almost given up hope of ever seeing France again when they discovered "a remedy against all our sickness, the most excellent that was ever seen or found on earth." This time, the interpreter Domagaya unknowingly served them most usefully. Cartier had seen him affected by scurvy, with one of his legs badly swollen, his teeth "lost and decayed, and his gums rotted and stinking." Ten days later, Cartier saw him again, "healthy and resolute." There was a remedy, then, and one that acted rapidly; but how could they discover what it was without letting it be known that the French were in the most serious distress?

Once again, Cartier took to artifice. "How did you cure yourself?" the captain asked Domagaya. "With the juice from the leaves of a tree," replied the Indian. "Are there any such trees hereabouts?" Cartier inquired again, "and could you show me some? For I have a servant who came back infected from our visit to the lord Donnacona." Domagaya sent two women with Cartier to find some, and they showed him how to crush the bark and leaves of the *annedda*. "Put the whole to boil in water, then drink the water every other day, and put the pulp on the swollen and diseased legs," they told him. Cartier had some of the concoction prepared. At first the sick men refused even to taste it, but the few who ventured to do so felt better at once, by a "true and manifest miracle," even to the extent that one of them found himself "clearly cured" of the pox. The men now rushed to drink the brew.[29] The source of this marvellous remedy was the *thuya occidentalis* or white cedar, whose leaves have a high content of ascorbic acid (vitamin C); it came to be called the *arbor vitae*, the tree of life.[30]

As Champlain was to do at a later date when he wintered among the Hurons, Cartier occupied his spare time enriching his knowledge. Since his return from Hochelaga, he had made it a habit to converse and come and go "with the peoples living nearest by." He would observe and question them, and return home with a profusion of details which would find their way into the account of the voyage, or which he would impart to inquiring minds like that of the Franciscan friar Thevet; details which, when assembled, yield a most valuable body of fact.

Cartier was the first European to provide precise information about the customs of the natives of the St Lawrence Valley. They lived "almost in community of property." They were sedentary, and if Cartier, in comparing those of Canada with their brother Indians at Hochelaga, described them as *embulataires*, this was most likely because they travelled every year to Honguedo to fish. As well as fishing, they practised agriculture, harvesting grain "as big as peas" (corn), melons (probably pumpkins), and peas and beans. Cartier noted that the women worked, both at fishing and at farming, "incomparably more than the men." In winter time, hunting provided them with an ample supply of food. Both meat and fish were dried and eaten raw, without salt.

Their clothes were made of skins, but these Iroquois were "more hardened to the cold than beasts"; in the "most severe cold that we have seen, which was harsh and a thing to marvel at," they came to the ships every day across the ice and snow, most of them almost naked, "something which is unbelievable for those who have not seen it."

One custom made a vivid impression on Cartier, as it did on the Spaniards of the same period, and that was the taking of tobacco. The tobacco plant, which Cartier did not name, was gathered in great quantities by the Iroquois during the summer. Cartier gives the following description of the way they made use of it: "They dry it in the sun, and wear it around their necks in a little animal's skin forming a bag, with a small horn of stone or wood. Then, at any time, they crumble the herb and put it into one of the two ends of the horn; next they put a burning ember to this and suck at the other end until they fill their bodies with smoke and it comes out through the mouth and nostrils as if it were pouring from a chimney." Cartier tried out the "horn" and it seemed to him "to have ground pepper in it."[31]

In that spring of 1536, having been to Hochelaga and having talked at length with the Iroquois, Cartier was able to assess the progress he had made since 1534. He now possessed a quite extensive view of the country's geography.

A mighty river emptied its waters at Assumption Island (Anticosti) and Honguedo (Gaspé), where the Iroquois came to fish every year. On his way up this river, Cartier had seen a number of other rivers, their mouths swarming with whales and "sea-horses" (walruses, to us); the most important of these was the one that led toward the Kingdom of Saguenay. Above the Ile aux Coudres, beginning at the archipelago that included the Ile de Bacchus or Ile d'Orléans, one entered the Kingdom of Canada, "where there are several populations in unenclosed villages." On a cape stood the capital, Stadacona. Upstream, on a mountain, was the village of Tequenonday and, in the plain, Achelacy. Continuing upstream, one came to the Rivière de Fouez, a tributary flowing from the north, and then the river broadened into a large lake (perhaps already named Angoulême). Of the watercourses that flowed into this lake, the following were noted as the most important: the Chateaubriand River (probably the present Nicolet River), the Montmorency River, which probably corresponds to the St Francis, and another which came from the southwest (the future Richelieu River) and remained nameless. Cartier gathered from the Indians that this last river originated in a region where there was neither ice nor snow and where oranges grew, and concluded that this region must lie toward Florida. Beyond Lac d'Angoulême, one entered another Iroquois kingdom, Hochelaga, whose capital was situated near Mount Royal. At Hochelaga, navigation was interrupted by rapids, but travel by the water route could be resumed higher up, and after negotiating three more rapids it was possible to travel westward by water for three months. Above Hochelaga, a sizable river flowing from the west emptied into the main river, and this tributary led to two or three big lakes and a "freshwater sea of which no man is known to have seen the end." The continental barrier was thus much wider than anyone had believed.

Cartier was intrigued by the mysterious Kingdom of Saguenay. Donnacona, who claimed to have been there, described it with enthusiasm as a land "where there are infinite quantities of gold, rubies and other riches and where there are white men, as in France, dressed in woollen cloth." How far away was this wondrous kingdom? Today one thinks of the region of Lac St Jean and the Saguenay River, but a close examination of the account reveals that it is impossible to place Cartier's Saguenay geographically. Was it just a fairy-tale kingdom—a product, pure and simple, of the Indian imagination? Or was it not, rather, a synthesis of traditional folklore retold by Donnacona for his own purposes, as happens among primitive peoples? Attempts have been made to link this Saguenay myth with the Norwegian expedition of 1362: a treasure-hunt by white men dressed indeed in cloth. But if, travelling west of Hochelaga, Donnacona and his compatriots really had seen white men dressed in cloth, and an abundance of precious metals, then it must be supposed that they had ascended the Ottawa River (the "straight and good road" to Saguenay), navigated the Great Lakes, entered the Mississippi river system and reached the Spanish possessions. Viewed in this way, the Kingdom of Saguenay did actually exist, but another century and a half would pass before Frenchmen retraced that route.

For the French, the ethnic, linguistic and political unity of the St Lawrence Valley was a great advantage. Certainly, the Iroquois had enemies: south of the river, the Toudamans, who were probably Micmacs or Etchemins, blocked their route to the Honguedo fishing grounds from time to time; Donnacona had some Toudaman scalps in his house. And to the northwest of Hochelaga, on the great tributary that came from the west, were the Agojudas, who made constant war on the Iroquois. But for all that, the Iroquois seemed to Cartier to be firmly entrenched in positions of strength. What, then, could be more favourable to a French penetration inland than to have found not only a great river but a unified nation that was in control of the whole valley?

Cartier's friendship with the Laurentian Iroquois lacked stability, however, thanks to the intrigues of Domagaya and Taignoagny. Through the winter, visits were exchanged with a fair measure of cordiality, it is true, and it was Domagaya who, unaware of the plight of the French, introduced them to the wonder-working infusion. But with the coming of spring, the mutual distrust revived.

On April 21, Donnacona returned to Stadacona after a lengthy absence, with "a number of people who were handsome and powerful and whom we were not accustomed to see." Domagaya came to the harbour of Ste Croix to announce Donnacona's return, but would not cross the river. This degree of distrust was unusual and aroused in Cartier "a suspicion of treachery." On the pretext of paying a courtesy call, Cartier sent two of his men to Stadacona to see what was going on, but Donnacona feigned sickness and would not receive them. The emissaries then went to see

Taignoagny and found large numbers of people in all the huts, but Taignoagny would allow no visits and carefully escorted the ambassadors back
to the harbour. On the way, they learned at last what was happening.
An internal dispute had broken out among the Indians of Stadacona; one
clan, led by an Iroquois named Agona, had risen against Donnacona. In
apprising his visitors of the situation, Taignoagny expressed the desire that
Cartier should rid the country of Agona by carrying him off to France.
He undertook, in return, to do anything that Cartier should ask. As the
situation was urgent, Taignoagny requested a reply the following day.

Donnacona's supporters were thus counting on Cartier to eliminate
Agona, but Cartier was wilier than they, and "resolved to trick them."
Donnacona and his sons had become a danger to the French alliance, he
reasoned, and since there was a crisis inside Stadacona and a choice must
be made between two clans, the essential move would be to spirit away
Donnacona, Domagaya, Taignoagny and other dangerous individuals. The
way would then be cleared for a new ruling faction and, as an added
benefit, Donnacona would himself come to Europe to relate to Francis I
"what he had seen of the wonders of the world in the lands of the west."
All that was needed now was to bell the cat.

Cartier first sent an answer to the effect that he wished to see Taignoagny, but two days passed and no visitor appeared. The Indians were
avoiding the French "as though we would have sought to kill them. Now
we perceived their wickedness." Finally, on the third day, Donnacona and
his interpreters appeared at the harbour. Only the interpreters were
prepared to cross the river, however. They proposed to Cartier that he
should seize Agona and take him away to France. In order to reassure
Donnacona, whom he was anxious to get his hands on, Cartier replied that
the King had forbidden him to bring "either a man or woman back to
France, but would allow me to bring two or three little boys, to learn the
language"; nevertheless, he said, he would be glad to carry Agona off as far
as Newfoundland and leave him on some island. The interpreters were
satisfied; Agona would be eliminated and, as they understood it, they themselves could breathe easy; no attempt would be made to take them back to
France. They promised to return the next day with Donnacona and all
the people of Stadacona for the festival of the Holy Cross.

Cartier's trick was working. To carry out his scheme he had chosen
May 3, the festival commemorating the discovery of the Holy Cross. Intending, perhaps, to make this a solemn occasion on which he would
take possession of the country for France (though the account does not
say this in so many words), the French leader restaged the scene enacted
at Honguedo by putting up a cross thirty-five feet high. Toward noon, the
Iroquois of Stadacona thronged to the site for the ceremony, and Cartier
learned that Donnacona, the interpreters and others of their party were

on the way. He was overjoyed at the news, "hoping to seize them." At about two o'clock, Donnacona appeared near the ships and Cartier went to greet him; Donnacona returned his courtesies, "one eye on the woods, and wondrous fearful." On the advice of Taignoagny, Donnacona refused to enter the fort; the women moved off and only the men remained. Everyone was on the alert.

Meanwhile, Cartier secretly gave orders to his men to seize Donnacona, Taignoagny, Domagaya and two other important personages upon his signal. Now he again invited the Iroquois into the fort. They entered, but suddenly Taignoagny warned Donnacona to get out. At this, Cartier shouted an order and the French threw themselves on those marked for capture, the other Indians taking to their heels in confusion "like sheep before a wolf, some across the river, the others into the woods, each to save his own skin." The prisoners were placed "under safe guard."

Cartier was elated; the old chief of Stadacona, the two interpreters and two others had been removed from power, and Agona was free to take over.

"Wailing and howling all night, like wolves," the Iroquois demanded their chief. At noon the next day they were still there shouting, "in as great numbers as we have seen during the voyage." In the end, Cartier had Donnacona appear before them.

Cartier had told Donnacona that in ten or twelve months' time, when he had seen the King of France and described Saguenay to him, he would return home with a splendid gift from the King. Full of confidence in spite of what had just taken place and very pleased with Cartier's promise, Donnacona told his people about it and they all rejoiced at the turn of events. The Iroquois presented Cartier with twenty-four strings of *esnoguy*, "which is the greatest wealth they have in this world." There was further parleying, but Donnacona was obliged to resign himself to his fate, and he ordered provisions (corn, meat and fish) to be brought to him "to eat at sea." To the women who brought them, for the men would no longer come near, Cartier renewed his assurance that Donnacona would be back in twelve moons, but the author of the account immediately adds: "and this he said to pacify them."[32]

On May 6, Cartier left the harbour of Ste Croix with the *Grande Hermine* and the *Emerillon*, leaving the bodies of twenty-five of his companions at rest in Canadian soil and, for want of sufficient crewmen, the hulk of the *Petite Hermine*. He took with him ten captive Iroquois: the old chief Donnacona, his sons Domagaya and Taignoagny, the girl of twelve and two little boys who had been given to him by Donnacona in September 1535, a girl of eight or nine whom he had received in the same period from the chief of Achelacy, and three Indians (two of them personages of importance) who are not further identified. In his cargo he carried a small amount of gold, real gold, a dozen nuggets from Saguenay carved in the shape of small goose-feathers; there is no information as to when and through whom the gold had come into Cartier's hands.

The return journey was almost without incident. This time, Cartier passed between Honguedo and Anticosti, "which passage had not hitherto been discovered" because nothing but land had been seen there. He steered straight for the Ile de Brion to shorten his route, because he wanted to emerge from the Gulf not by way of the Strait of Belle Isle but through the channel whose existence between Cape Breton and Newfoundland he had hopefully assumed in 1534. He established the fact that Les Araines (later called the Iles de la Madeleine) were not the beginning of the mainland, as he had believed in 1534, but islands. On June 1 or 2, he reached the northwest coast of Cape Breton, sailed down it for a time and then, no doubt because he found no way through, sailed back to the northern tip and set his course eastward. On June 3 he was at Newfoundland, in a harbour which he named St Esprit; two days later he arrived at the islands of St Pierre and Miquelon, where he stayed until the 16th. Then, favoured by good weather, he crossed the ocean in thirty days. On July 16 he entered the port of St Malo after an absence of fourteen months.[33] The ten Iroquois set foot on a continent which they were never to leave.

This voyage of 1535-36 had been far more fruitful than its predecessor. From a geographical point of view, the progress Cartier had made was enormous. He had inaugurated a new way of access to the Gulf through the strait separating Cape Breton from Newfoundland, and in so doing had proved that Newfoundland was an island. His mapping of the Gulf was more accurate, now showing the Magdalens as an archipelago and not part of the mainland, and Anticosti as an island and not a peninsula.

What was much more important, and this was Cartier's crowning accomplishment, he had discovered a great river which was to become the essential axis of French penetration into North America. He had travelled up that river, discovering tributaries which would remain strategic routes: the Saguenay, the St Maurice and the Richelieu. He had journeyed as far as Hochelaga, where his way was barred by rapids, but he had learned that beyond those rapids it was possible to go great distances toward the west, and to reach a freshwater sea.

Cartier's achievement in 1535-36 marked the peak of French exploration in America in the sixteenth century. All St Lawrence cartography of that century drew its inspiration from Cartier; no further light would be shed on the American interior at those latitudes until seventy-five years later, with the discoveries of Champlain.

CHAPTER 3

The First French Colony in America

1541–1543

Like Verrazano in 1524, Cartier returned to France at an unfortunate moment. When he moored in St Malo on July 16, 1536, Francis I had just dismissed the Spanish ambassador. War broke out in the Pyrenees and in the Alps, and in the King's preoccupations Savoy took precedence over America.

Cartier seems to have been reduced to inactivity. His name does not appear in any official document until May 10, 1537, when the King made him a gift of the *Grande Hermine* in repayment of costs incurred during his voyage of 1535. The decision to do so resulted, no doubt, from the audience accorded to the St Malo navigator by Francis I at about this time. Cartier had presented a report, "as well by writing as by word of mouth," of his voyage of discovery. Map in hand, he talked to the King about the river that was eight hundred leagues long and might well lead to Asia. He brought a dozen pieces of genuine gold, and furs that could be sold at a handsome price, and spoke of wondrous things. Donnacona, who came with him, was questioned by the King and confirmed what Cartier said.[1]

The war between Francis I and Charles V was short-lived, coming to an end with the Truce of Nice on June 18, 1538. And so from the end of summer, America once again became the order of the day. Outstanding debts of the last expedition were settled: payment was made to Cartier, by order of the King, of some 3,500 livres still due on his voyages, plus about 100 livres owed him on account of his own remuneration as well as the feeding and upkeep of "a number of savage persons" over a period of two years.[2]

For reasons which are difficult to fathom, the new project was not able to take shape until the latter half of the year 1540. Then the King's first move was a gesture that was sure to alarm his rivals, Spain and Portugal; in August, 1540, he accorded universal permission to all his subjects to go to the "new lands," including the Portuguese territories. On the following October 17, he gave Cartier a commission to leave on a third expedition.

34

Cartier was named "captain general and master pilot of all ships and other seagoing vessels" to take part in this new expedition. He was to go to the lands of "Canada and Ochelaga and as far as the land of Saguenay, if he can reach it." With him would go a good number of the King's subjects "of willing disposition and of all professions, arts and industries." The commission does not specify the number of ships, stating only that Cartier might take the *Emerillon*, "now old and decaying," and transfer its fittings to the other vessels. (In the event, however, the *Emerillon* was not demolished but repaired.) Nor does it fix the expedition's strength in manpower, although it authorizes Cartier to choose fifty men from among prison inmates, excepting counterfeiters and those judged guilty of heresy or lese-majesty against God or man. Already the instructions were fuller than in 1534 and 1535; the expedition was to "enter deeper into these lands, to converse with the peoples found there and to live among them, if need be."[3] The immediate objective in the autumn of 1540 was not therefore the foundation of a French colony in America; Cartier was to continue his exploration, broaden his relations with the natives, and only live among them "if need be." Up to this point the aim was simply to resume the undertaking of 1535.

Having received this commission, Cartier set to work immediately. In January 1541, however, there came a complete change of plans; the enterprise passed from the hands of the St Malo captain into those of a gentleman of the Court, and the voyage of exploration turned into a substantial effort at colonization. On January 15, Francis I directed a commission to Roberval, a Protestant, who thereby took charge of the new enterprise, with the most comprehensive powers.

Although he signed his name "La Rocque" and was known by this name in his own time, Jean-François de La Rocque is remembered in Canadian history by the name of Roberval, after one his estates, perhaps to avoid confusion with Mesgouez de La Roche, who founded a short-lived colony toward the end of the century. Roberval was descended from high-ranking nobility, of Languedoc on his father's side and of Picardy, where his estates were situated, on the side of his mother, Isabeau de Poitiers. He had fought in the Italian wars as an officer attached to the Duc de Bouillon, and with his estates of Roberval, Bacouel, Noé-Saint-Rémy, Poix and others, had all the attributes of a great nobleman. He attended the Court assiduously, figuring in the immediate entourage of Francis I; an important personage indeed, as attested by the dedication of two poems to him by Clément Marot in 1525. Although it is not known precisely why, he was nicknamed *le petit roi de Vimeu*. As a Protestant, he was obliged to take flight in 1535, as did the poet Marot. He soon returned, however, under the protection of Francis I and the King's sister, Marguerite of Navarre.[4] His military career, his skill at fortification, his experience in land development, his enterprising nature, his financial resources, the prominence of his family and his success as a courtier may all go to explain why a Protestant would be entrusted with the command of the first French colony in America.

To these lands "of Canada and Ochelaga and others around and about them," wrote the King, and even in "all lands beyond and bordering the seas uninhabited or not possessed and dominated by any Christian prince," he had decided to send a goodly number of gentlemen and others, "both men-at-arms and of the populace, of each sex and every liberal and mechanic art," to go far into these lands "and to the very land of Saguenay." As provided in Cartier's instructions, they were to "converse with these foreign peoples" and live among them if necessary, but Roberval's commission provided much more: the building and establishment of "towns and forts, temples and churches for the communication of our Holy Catholic faith and Christian doctrine"; the institution of laws and law officers, that these peoples might live "with reason and order in the fear and love of God." To give, continued the King, "greater order and dispatch to the accomplishment of this enterprise," there must be named "some excellent personage of great loyalty and integrity toward us" to be its "head and leader"; he had therefore chosen Jean-François de La Rocque, Seigneur de Roberval.

To Roberval would belong the choice of captains, ships' masters, pilots and other men-at-arms and mariners, command in all things, including the imposition of corporal, civil and monetary penalties at sea and on land, the authority to come and go "in these foreign lands" and to bring them "into our hands by friendly means or by force of arms," the right to build strongholds, to appoint and to dismiss, to make laws and issue political ordinances, and to punish by the death penalty. All those who were to go on this expedition, finally, were to "swear upon oath to serve us well and loyally and with obedience to the orders of our said Lieutenant-General."[5]

A breath-taking recitation of absolute powers! It was reported to Charles V that Roberval had been appointed King of Canada,[6] and with reason. As Lieutenant-General endowed with near-regal powers, he might indeed behave like a king. Only a man of gentle birth, "some excellent personage," could be invested with such authority in distant lands. For all his merits in seafaring, Cartier could never hope to have as much.

To this great enterprise, Francis I assigned the noblest goal toward which human travail could be directed; the propagation of the Christian faith. Anyone observing France from the time she first turned her attention to the "new lands" might well find this religious proselytism somewhat startling. In 1524 Verrazano had given not a thought to the religious question. Nor at any time did Cartier behave as though he had been charged by his king with the propagation of the Christian faith.

It was only about 1540 that Francis I began to put a religious stamp on his American enterprises, and that the colonial project of 1538 was graced, after the fact, with a religious preamble.[7] This preamble would have us believe that Francis I, being assured that there was neither gold nor silver to be had in Canada, sent Cartier there solely for the purpose of conquering "an infinity of souls for God." This ridiculous pretence is belied beyond ·question by Cartier's accounts, by the content of Francis I's conversations with the Portuguese informer, Lagarto, and by the total absence of any evangelical activity in Canada up until then; it was an attempt at all costs to give these past enterprises a religious character which they never had. In this period we are supposed to see the awakening of motives nobler than purely secular ones, at least as far as America was concerned, motives which would henceforth clothe the extra-territorial activities of the kings of France in apostolic respectability.

Indeed, the foreign policy of the kings of France was from then on to be labelled RELIGION. In the commission he delivered to Cartier on October 17, 1540, Francis I stated that in sending out earlier expeditions of discovery, his purpose had been to have knowledge of lands peopled by "savages living in ignorance of God and without reason"; those who had been brought back to France " we have long kept in our kingdom, having them instructed in the love and fear of God and of His holy law and Christian doctrine, intending that they should be taken back to these lands in company of a goodly number of our willing subjects, so that the other peoples of these lands might be more easily led to embrace our holy faith." In the light of this recital in contradiction of the facts, to what end were the French to attempt to live among the natives? "The better to realize our said intention and to do that which is the will of God our creator and redeemer and shall glorify His holy and sacred name and our Mother, the holy Catholic Church, of which we are the declared and appointed first son."[8]

In later official texts, no opportunity was to be missed for declaring, with the same luxuriance, that France was toiling first and foremost for the glorification of God's name. The commission delivered to the Protestant Roberval in January 1541 repeats word for word the religious declaration of Cartier's commission. When the King gave Roberval authority to recruit prisoners the following February, he wrote that this measure was undertaken "in honour of God our Creator." In giving Roberval priority in his choice of ships, the King recalled that the expedition was effected "for the glorification and enhancement of our holy Christian faith and Holy Mother the Catholic Church."[9]

Why this sudden ostentatious show of missionary zeal? Only political considerations could explain such posturing on Francis I's part. Since the Pope had divided all new territories between Spain and Portugal in 1493, there was only one way that France could enter the scene without offending the Holy See, and that was to take up a missionary role.

Whether motivated by missionary zeal or by a thirst for riches, France in this enterprise stood to run foul of the Spanish empire and its ally, Portugal. Charles V, the sworn enemy of Francis I since 1521, reacted immediately. Upon learning that, in August, 1540, the King of France had authorized his subjects to go to the "new lands," he declared flatly that Francis I was violating the Treaty of Nice; if the King of France refused to renounce his decision and if the French fleets put to sea, grave consequences could ensue; Spain and Portugal must prepare themselves to defend their interests.[10]

And yet the French king had been at pains to reassure his rivals. In his commission to Cartier, had he not represented Canada as "forming a tip of Asia"? A feeble precaution, it is true, since, from the time of Verrazano's voyage, Francis I was convinced that Canada was not part of Asia, and England, Spain and Portugal were even more convinced of it in 1540. A much safer precaution was the restriction he imposed upon Roberval (which he had not imposed upon Cartier), to the effect that he must absolutely not go into lands "occupied, possessed and dominated" by the princes, his allies, nor "likewise by our very dear and beloved brothers the Emperor and the King of Portugal." When the Spanish ambassador continued to protest, Francis I replied that he could not refuse to allow his subjects to go wherever they desired, but that they would keep away from territory under Spanish authority, going only to lands discovered by his predecessors and which had belonged to his crown thirty years before Spanish and Portuguese ships even set sail for the Indies. The Spanish ambassador could extract no more than a promise that the French would not set foot on Spanish territory. He was not greatly reassured, since it indeed appeared that Francis I meant only territories settled and defended by Spain; "to pass by and discover by eye," said His Majesty in the course of the conversation, "is no title of possession."[11]

Besides claiming for France the discovery of "new lands" thirty years previous to 1492 (a claim made very late in the game and never substantiated), Francis I was proposing a principle which promised to be a real thorn in the side for Spain and Portugal: effective occupation, and not simple discovery, should constitute the right to possession. This was a complete novelty which, even though it deprived France of the discoveries of 1524, endangered the magnificent partition that Spain and Portugal had secured for themselves in 1493. In any case, they had good reason to expect the French to set foot in territories that they had never really occupied; the King of France himself had said they would do so.

In answer to this new principle, the ambassador put forward an argument which he considered a weighty one: the Holy See had reserved the "new lands" to Spain and Portugal. Francis I replied that if the popes had spiritual jurisdiction, they did not have jurisdiction in the apportionment of land among kings, and besides, neither the kings of France nor the other Christian kings had been invited to share in the partition. When another Spanish dignitary, the Comendador Mayor of Alcantara, also invoked this celebrated partition, Francis I replied banteringly that the sun gave warmth to him as well as to others and that he would very much like to see Adam's last will and testament to learn how he had divided up the world.[12]

In the meantime, the Marquis de Aguilar, Charles V's ambassador to Rome, was lodging a complaint with the Pope about the fleet that the French were preparing to send to the Indies, invoking the Treaty of Nice and the bulls of Alexander VI. Pope Paul III was quick to reaffirm the treaty and the bulls, but to gain time he asked to see the bulls, of which there ought to be a copy somewhere. The ambassador wrote to Spain for copies of the documents,[13] but there was no more talk of papal intervention. If in 1493 the Spanish pope Alexander VI had been only too glad to favour his compatriots, the Italian Paul III had no such reason. After all, Francis I was proclaiming, with much fanfare, that his primary concern was to carry out an apostolic mission. How could he be refused the right to bring the Indians into the bosom of the Church? And there was another motive; the King of France could yet provide powerful support for the papacy against the formidable power of Spain, as indeed he had already done in the Cognac League in 1526. It was essential, then, to avoid rendering a judgement which could mean trouble for the papacy and which would probably not be listened to anyway.

Portugal, which was just as much involved as Spain, did nothing. To Charles V's urgent requests, John III replied consistently with excuses. All the same, when it was learned in the autumn of 1541 that Cartier had landed in Canada (or, as it was said, in the New Land of the King of Portugal), John III felt he must make a gesture. His ambassador lodged a complaint with Francis I, but the latter replied that conquests and voyages were his right as well as that of other princes of Christendom. John III did not pursue the matter further; as the Infante of Portugal admitted, the King's needs were so urgent everywhere that it was better not to see certain things.[14]

While the Spaniards spied diligently, Roberval and Cartier worked to get their expedition under way. A sum of 46,350 livres was collected, of which 45,000 came from the King and the rest was borrowed by Roberval; of this sum, Cartier was entrusted with 31,350 livres for the repair and outfitting of the five chosen ships. Since this was not enough, Cartier was obliged to put up money of his own; the repair of the *Emerillon*, which belonged to the King, cost him 1,000 livres, and altogether he spent 8,600 livres from his own pocket. Enough food was bought to last two years. Besides agricultural tools and ready-made carts, a number of domestic animals were put on board to work on the land and "to multiply there": 20 cows, 4 bulls, 100 sheep, 100 goats, 10 hogs and 20 horses and mares.[15] These were to be the first European livestock in the St Lawrence Valley, if not in all of North America north of Florida.

For the execution of this ambitious colonial plan, a considerable number of people would have to be recruited. In order to attract gentlemen and others "of excellent virtue or industry" to the enterprise, the King created two institutions for America which were to be long-lived; the seigneurial régime and commercial monopoly.

Roberval was in effect authorized to distribute land in perpetual fief and seigneury. The seigneurs receiving these lands would, however, be responsible for the defence and upkeep of the country. At the same time, the King stipulated that only Roberval's associates, to the exclusion of all others, might enter the "passages and straits leading to the said countries of Canada, Ochelaga, Saguenay and others circumjacent." Profits were to be divided three ways: a third for the King, a third to remain with Roberval, so that he might carry on the voyage "in the space of the next five years" and in payment for his services, and the remaining third to be divided among the associates.[16] In 1541 the pattern for the Company of the Hundred Associates was thus already set; the participants in the enterprise, landholders and merchants of the commercial monopoly, were to accept the colony as their responsibility.

Nobles looking for seigneuries or commercial profits would no doubt come forward in great numbers, but how were the much-needed common folk to be recruited, the men-at-arms, artisans and labourers? Such folk might well hesitate to embark, wrote the King, "because of the far distance of these lands and the dread of shipwrecks and maritime and other hazards, [and] being loth to leave their possessions, relatives and friends, fearing to make this voyage"; or else, once arrived, they might not want to stay.

To overcome the lack of volunteers, the King resorted to the conscription of criminals, outlaws and fugitives. In commuting sentences of death "to an honest and beneficial voyage," he thought to perform a "merciful and meritorious" act toward the wrongdoers, so that they might do homage to the Creator and change their lives. The criminals to be chosen would have their confiscated possessions restored, but they would have to contribute to the cost of their transport across the ocean and to their upkeep during the first two years. If they returned without the King's permission, they would be condemned without hope of mercy. Where the return was authorized, the King would be ready to pardon them if they had done their duty. Certain categories of criminals were excluded from this conscription, however; those guilty of lese-majesty against God and man, heresy, counterfeiting "and other too-grievous cases and crimes." Also excluded were those whose trials had not been completed and who had not yet received their "sentences of death."[17]

On February 7, 1541, Roberval was accordingly authorized to seek recruits in prisons under the jurisdiction of the *Parlements* of Rouen, Paris, Dijon, Bordeaux and Toulouse. His aides were soon sent on the hunt.

As to the result of this vast conscription, we do not have all the names nor even the total number of criminals who were to comprise the majority of the first colonists of New France. The available information is fragmentary to say the least. A complete list of these conscripts would have been of great interest, and would have allowed us a better appreciation of the atmosphere of the first French colony in America.

The departure of Roberval's expedition had been set for the spring of 1541. The prisoners were to come to St Malo by April 10, and it was hoped that the voyage would begin shortly after. Cartier was ready; in May, his five ships were "furnished and set in good order" and Roberval could see "the ships fallen downe to the roade, with their yards acrosse full ready to depart and set saile." Roberval had not yet received "his artillery, powder and munitions and other things necessary [. . .] which he had provided for the voyage, in the Countreys of Champaigne and Normandie." He could not leave without these things. But the King insisted that Cartier should leave immediately, and Roberval therefore gave Cartier "full authoritie to depart and goe before, and to governe all things as if he had been there in person." On May 23, 1541, Cartier put to sea with five ships, having made his will, in which he bears the title "captain and master pilot to the King for the *Terres Neuffves*." The ships were the *Grande Hermine*, which was his personal possession, the *Emerillon*, the *Saint-Brieux*, the *Georges* and another unidentified ship.[18]

The crew list has never been found, and we do not even know the total emigrant population. The Spanish spy Santiago was to write later that Cartier left with 1,500 men, which is not unlikely.[19] Of Cartier's companions, the most important should be noted: two brothers-in-law of Cartier, Gyon Des Granches, Vicomte de Beaupré, and the pilot Macé Jalobert; a nephew, Etienne Noël; Olivier du Breil, who was charged with "the conduct of the King's ships" and who was to die during the voyage; and the ship's master Thomas Fromont dit La Bouille. In a letter written from France to Henry VIII, an Englishman reported that the poet Clément Marot, being obliged to fly on account of heresy, had embarked with Cartier as an infantry captain. Either this was a mistake or Captain Marot changed his mind, for the celebrated poet never came to Canada to wield either the sword or the pen.[20]

Not a single Iroquois was on the voyage. Following his coup of May 1536, Cartier had told the Indians of Stadacona that Donnacona would return in ten or twelve moons, but only to pacify them. The old Indian chief had seen Francis I and had told him of the wonders of Saguenay, and the moons had passed. In spite of anything affirmed in the commission of October 1540, Cartier had no intention of taking Donnacona back to Stadacona. He had removed him to make way for a chief whom he considered more reliable. Even less was there any question of taking back the two interpreters, Domagaya and Taignoagny, who had caused so much trouble. The ten Indians brought to France in 1536 (six adults, two boys, and two girls) had since been living at the King's expense. Three were baptized in March 1539, but the register does not identify them and we know only that they were male. Could it be that these were baptisms *in articulo mortis?* It was about this time, in any case, that the aged Donnacona disappeared from view. According to Thevet, who must have questioned him at length, Donnacona spoke French and died a good Christian. The other Indians died about the same time; in the spring of 1541, only one little girl was left. She was not taken back to the land of her birth and it is not known what became of her.

It took "three full months" to reach Stadacona. At sea there were constant "contrary winds and continuall torments"; the fleet did not have "in all that time 30. houres of good wind to serve us to keepe our right course"; the ships were scattered and only reunited at Newfoundland at the end of June. On the way they were short of water and the "cattell, as well Goates, Hogges, as other beastes which we carried for breede in the Countrey" had to be given cider to drink. Cartier was obliged to make a long stop at Newfoundland to take on water and wait, in vain, for Roberval. Finally, without having done any exploration, it would seem, and having lost two precious months, Cartier appeared at Stadacona before the harbour of Ste Croix on August 23, 1541.[21] He had not been there for five years.

The Iroquois were still living at Stadacona. Led by Agona, Donnacona's successor, they came to meet Cartier with great demonstrations of joy. Cartier was at once asked for news of Donnacona. "He died in France," replied Cartier. In view of Donnacona's advanced age, his death seemed only natural. But what had become of the nine others? To reply that eight of them had died would have given a bad impression; once again, Cartier squeezed by with a lie. The others, he said, had retired in France, where they were living like *grands seigneurs;* they had married and did not wish to return to their own country. Agona took it all in good humour, "because he remained Lord and Governor of the countrey." The Indians then presented the French with wampum: Agona removed from his own head and placed upon Cartier's what served him for a crown, "a piece of tanned leather of a yellow skin edged about with *Esnoguy* (which is their riches and the thing which they esteeme most precious, as wee esteeme gold)."

He also placed his bracelets of *esnoguy* on Cartier's arms, "colling [hugging] him about the necke and shewing unto him great signes of ioy." Cartier returned the crown to Agona's head and distributed small gifts.[22]

However, Cartier did not establish his colony in the harbour of Ste Croix. Whether he took the trouble to see what was left of the fort of 1535 and the cross, the account does not say. Nor does it give us the underlying reasons for making a move. Was it only for material reasons that Cartier did not reoccupy the same site? It seems more likely that he had learned to distrust the Iroquois. He was by now accustomed to their joyous manifestations, recognized them to be only an outward show to mask hostility, and knew what else to expect. He fully intended to go up-river to Hochelaga, which Stadacona had not pardoned him for doing in 1535 and which he would be no more readily pardoned for doing in 1541. He had removed Donnacona and other important figures to make way for Agona, but he had promised to bring them back; he had not done so, and Agona, although not anxious for the return of his adversaries, knew that he himself could suffer the same fate. Finally, with the coming of five ships and a considerable population, the Iroquois began to have apprehensions for their continued possession of the country. Between the French and the Iroquois there lay a deeper gulf than five years' absence.

The harbour of Ste Croix was too close to Stadacona, but if there was to be a move it would have to be to some strategic point. Cartier went up-river in a long-boat and chose such a point at the western end of Cape

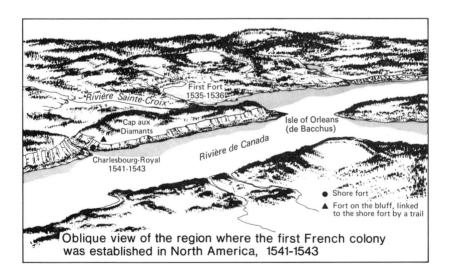

Oblique view of the region where the first French colony was established in North America, 1541-1543

Diamond, where the Cap Rouge River emptied into the St Lawrence. This river seemed to him "better and more commoditous to ride in and lay his ships, than the former." From this position on the cape, he could much more easily control the river route and at the same time have direct access to the valley of the St Charles. Having decided upon this place, which he named Charlesbourg Royal, he brought his five ships to anchor there.

There was reason to be pleased with the spot: "very good and faire grounds, full of as faire and mightie trees as any be in the world"; oaks, "the most excellent that ever I saw in my life," laden with acorns; beautiful maples, and above all the *annedda*, the white cedar, "which hath the most excellent vertue of all the trees of the world." There was also hemp, "which groweth of its selfe, which is as good as possibly may be seene, and as strong," and there were vines laden with grapes "as blacke as Mulberies, but they be not so kind as those of France because the Vines bee not tilled." In short, it was "as good a Countrey to plow and mannure as a man should find or desire."

But what was all that, compared with the marvels they were discovering as though in a new Peru? Besides "a goodly Myne of the best yron in the world," there was observed at the foot of the mountain a "kind of slate stone blacke and thicke, wherein are veines of mynerall matter, which shewe like gold and silver"; on the river-bank, "certaine leaves of fine gold as thicke as a mans nayle"; on the height of the cape, "good store of stones, which we esteemed to be Diamants," and here and there, "we have found stones like Diamants, the most faire, pollished and excellently cut that it is possible for a man to see. When the Sunne shineth upon them, they glister as it were sparkles of fire." The riches of Cipango within reach!

Cartier put his men to work. On the shore at the foot of the promontory, he set them to building a fort; up the steep cliff he "made a way in maner of a payre of staires," and at the summit he established a second fort to assure the protection of the first and the control of the river. There, very close to the fort, was a beautiful spring. While some worked at building, the others worked on the land; in one day, twenty men ploughed an acre and a half and sowed seeds of "Cabbages, Naveaus or small Turneps, Lettises and others, which grew and sprong up out of the ground in eight dayes."

On September 2, as the King had commanded him to do, Cartier sent two ships back to France, the *Saint-Brieux* and the *Georges*. Macé Jalobert and Etienne Noël, both "skilfull and excellent pilots," carried letters to the King, "to advertise him what had bene done and found." They were also to announce the death of the ship's master, Thomas Fromont dit La Bouille. They arrived at St Malo on October 3, 1541.[23] Francis I's reaction that autumn is not known. If those letters from Charlesbourg Royal, the first mail sent from the St Lawrence Valley, spoke of silver, gold, and diamonds glittering with "sparkles of fire," he must have believed himself at last to be as rich as Charles V!

The prime objective assigned to Cartier and Roberval had been Saguenay, the storied kingdom so highly praised by Donnacona. Of the two routes which led there, Cartier had opted for the one through Hochelaga in 1535, but his way had been barred by rapids. In 1541, he renewed his attempt.

He gathered some gentlemen, masters, and pilots together, and it was decided to leave immediately for Hochelaga. For the moment, there was only one object, "to view and understand the fashion of the *Saults* of water, which are to be passed to goe to Saguenay." Then, in the course of the winter, they would prepare themselves to "be the readier in the spring to pass farther." They were thus launching upon an extensive plan of penetration into the interior of the continent. On September 7, having provided for the safety of Charlesbourg Royal, which he left under the command of his brother-in-law, the Vicomte de Beaupré, Cartier set forth with a number of gentlemen and sailors in two boats. This time the sorcerers of Cudouagny made no attempt to bar the route; besides, the Indians of Stadacona were no longer supposed to know much about what the French were doing. Cartier stopped at Achelacy to pay a call on the chief, who had shown him friendship in 1535, giving him a little girl and warning him of the treachery of the interpreters. He entrusted two boys to this chief, so that they might learn the Iroquois language, and was generous with his gifts, "a cloake of Paris red, which cloake was set with yealow and white buttons of Tinne, and small belles," two brass bowls, hatchets and knives. Since his experience with native interpreters had not been a happy one, he was changing his method. These two boys left by Cartier at Achelacy in 1541 were inaugurating the system that was to be used in the seventeenth century, that of training French interpreters by having them live with a tribe of Indians.

At last, on September 11, Cartier found himself once more at the Island of Montreal, but, as in 1535, rapids barred his way. He took his place in one of the boats, which was "double manned" in an attempt to overcome the current, but there were "great rockes, and so great a current, that we could not possibly passe any further." So they landed and found "hard by the water side a way and beaten path" leading upstream. The path led to a village. The natives (still Iroquois) showed themselves to be friendly. As best he could, for he had no interpreters, Cartier explained that they were on their way to the rapids and were in search of Saguenay. Four guides put themselves at his disposal and led him to another village beside some other rapids (the Lachine rapids). After a presentation of "Pottage and Fish," Cartier inquired "as well by signes as wordes, how many more *Saults*" there were on the way to Saguenay and what was the distance there. The Indians replied "with certaine little stickes, which they layd upon the ground in a certain distance, and afterwarde layde other small branches betweene both, representing the *Saults*." Cartier understood from this that there was only one rapid still to be passed, but that the river was not navigable as far as Saguenay. Since this Saguenay was just a vague realm somewhere to the west or the southwest, Cartier's interpretation is puzzling; either he misunderstood the reply of the Iroquois, or else the Iroquois had misunderstood his question.

Since he had come only to see the "fashion of the *Saults* of water," Cartier did not press further and returned to his boats. Four hundred Indians had gathered there, and they seemed to rejoice in the coming of the French. Cartier distributed hatchets and hooks to their chiefs, and to the others trinkets, "as combs, brooches of tynne and copper, and other smal toyes." There was no reception at Hochelaga, the capital of the Iroquois country, nor reading from *In principio*, nor laying of hands on the sick; the account does not even mention the town of Hochelaga. Could the capital have declined as much as all that in only six years? Or should Hochelaga be identified with the "Towne of Tutonaguy" which was two leagues distant from the first rapids? Did the capital have two names, or had the Iroquois moved it in order to be closer to Lake St Louis? The account of the voyage says not a word about the magnificent reception given the French there in 1535, and this suggests strongly that its author had not been on the previous voyage.

The return of the French from Hochelaga was marked by a renewal of hostility on the part of the natives, just as in 1535. When Cartier stopped at Achelacy, where he had left the two French boys, the chief was not there. According to his son, he had gone to Maisouna two days earlier; in fact, he had gone to Stadacona "to conclude with Agona, what they should doe against us." Franco-Iroquois relations had deteriorated to the point where even the most faithful ally had begun to plot and scheme. On his arrival at Charlesbourg Royal, Cartier learned that the Iroquois were no longer coming to the fort as they had before; "they were in a wonderful doubt and feare of us." At Stadacona, there were "a wonderfull number of the Countrey people assembled together." Cartier looked to the state of the fort's defences. And there the story abruptly ends.[24]

What went on in the course of that winter? It would seem that there was another epidemic of scurvy, but that it was easily overcome, thanks to the white cedar infusion.[25] Did the voyage beyond Hochelaga that was planned for the spring ever take place? We may suppose so, from the account's evaluation of the hospitality shown by the Iroquois of Hochelaga: "if they had thought they had bene too strong for us, then would they have done their best to have killed us, as we understood afterward."[26] Judging from the last part of this sentence, Cartier did carry out his plan of exploration, but we do not know how far he went.

One thing seems certain; the Iroquois had declared war on the French. Cartier was to tell Roberval in June of 1542 that "hee could not with his small company withstand the Savages, which went about dayly to annoy him." According to French fishermen from Newfoundland, the Indians had killed carpenters at work in Canada and generally shown their savagery. Indians who had come to *la Grande-Baie* (the Gulf) and gone aboard a Spanish ship bragged of having killed more than thirty-five of Cartier's men.[27] The long Franco-Iroquois conflict certainly began that winter of 1541-42.

In June, 1542, Cartier broke camp. A Frenchman from Bayonne reported that he left two ships and three hundred men at Charlesbourg Royal. According to another witness, he left only his dead;[28] it would seem that this second report was the more accurate. Whatever the case, Cartier was pleased to have left, as he thought, with a most precious cargo; diamonds and gold. One report speaks of eleven barrels of gold and about a bushel of precious stones; another enumerates ten barrels of gold ore, seven of silver, and seven quintals of pearls and precious stones.[29] With this cargo, Cartier met Roberval at Newfoundland in mid-June.

Roberval was a year late with his project. Not having all his artillery and other essential equipment in May of 1541, he had let Cartier go ahead with the five ships and had gone to Honfleur to complete his own preparations. There he bought the ship *Marie* and signed a contract for the use of the *Sainte-Anne* and the *Valentine*. Since he was short of money, he sold his seigneury of Bacouel in June 1541 for 2,000 livres and a mill for 1,200 livres, thus committing his personal wealth to the enterprise, as had Cartier. He kept hoping to leave shortly, but in July he was still in France, which the King found strange, and the Spanish ambassador began to believe that the whole enterprise would "go up in smoke."[30]

With what was Roberval busying himself, now that his fleet would be unable to leave before the following year? Nothing is said of him until the autumn of 1541, and he was then at sea, engaged in privateering. This Verrazano had also done after his false start in 1523; it was a means of enriching the coffers to help meet the costs of the expedition.

Roberval at last set sail from La Rochelle on April 16, 1542. Aboard the three large ships were "200. persons, aswel men as women," gentlemen as well as "souldiers, mariners, and common people."[31] Neither the account of the voyage nor any document of 1542 mentions anything about churchmen. And yet the official purpose of this expedition was one of evangelism, although it is hard to believe that the Protestant Roberval was setting forth to devote himself to the establishment of Catholicism in America. Documents of 1542 (the few that have been found) reveal no concern whatever for evangelism.

Did Roberval have on board any of the prisoners conscripted the previous year? The account gives no information on this point; those to whom Roberval was later to mete out punishment were not necessarily prisoners. It may be supposed, since Cartier left with five ships and Roberval had only three, that the conscripts, or most of them, had embarked in 1541. Besides the crew and passengers, it would seem that the ships carried cows, bulls, sheep and horses, as well as many items of feminine appeal, no doubt destined for barter with the Indians.[32]

Shortly after the departure, the fleet encountered a "quite contrary" wind and was obliged to take refuge at Belle-Isle-en-Mer in sight of Brittany and to stay there for some time. Roberval set out again, with the return of good weather, and the crossing was thenceforth uneventful. He dropped anchor on June 7 at the port of St Jean on the east coast of Newfoundland.[33]

It was here that Roberval saw Cartier arrive from Stadacona with his entire company. Cartier came to do "his duetie" to his superior, announce to him that he was bringing back gold ore and diamonds, and explain his abandonment of Charlesbourg Royal by his inability to withstand the Indians. Since Roberval had brought forces of ample strength, he commanded Cartier to return with him to Canada, but Cartier, who wanted to "have all the glory of the discoverie of those partes," according to the author of the account, waited until the following night and then slipped away unseen to return to France.[34] He reached St Malo early in September, 1542.[35]

Apparently he was determined to be the first to present the King of France with diamonds and gold. But his fleet carried a cargo of illusions; it is true that a preliminary appraisal at Newfoundland had confirmed that his gold ore was of good quality, but another more serious appraisal in France reduced it to worthless iron pyrites! As for the diamonds, alas, they were only quartz! Of Cartier's precious cargo, nothing remained but a proverb: "false as Canadian diamonds."[36] A beautiful dream evaporated and Cartier's flight turned into a ridiculous act of insubordination.

Roberval was delayed for a considerable time in Newfoundland, taking on provisions and "composing and taking up of a quarell" between the French and the Portuguese. He did not put to sea again until June 30, 1542. He entered the Grande Baie through the Strait of Belle Isle and sailed along Anticosti Island, Cartier's *Assomption*, which is called *Ascension* in the account and also in the *Cosmographie* of Roberval's pilot, Jean Fonteneau dit Alfonse. This change was perhaps unintentional. Another, important though short-lived, should be noted: the St Lawrence, or Rivière de Canada as it was until then, since that was where it led, was named *France-Prime* or *François-Premier* by Roberval.[37]

As the fleet sailed up the river, careful observations were made of the north shore, and it would seem that it was on this occasion that an exploration up the Saguenay was carried out. In 1535 Cartier had done no more than enter its mouth; in 1542 Roberval, or perhaps only his pilot, went at least two or three leagues up the river, far enough to observe that it was wider upstream; Alfonse concluded that this must be an arm of the sea, through which one could reach "the Pacific sea or indeed the sea of Cathay." Then the fleet continued its course toward the Isle of Orleans, making virtually no changes or additions to Cartier's place-names, to judge from the *Cosmographie*. When Alfonse describes navigational routes he is more precise than Cartier, and it is easier to know what he means; he is the first, moreover, to note the existence of Montmorency Falls.[38]

Four leagues west of the Isle of Orleans, Roberval chose "a convenient place to fortifie our selves in, fitte to commaund the mayne River, and of strong situation against all invasion of enemies." This was evidently Cap Rouge, which Cartier had just left; the site is recognizable from the description given in the account: "a fayre Fort, neere and somewhat West-ward above Canada, which is very beautifull to beholde, and of great force, situated upon an high mountaine"; and, at the foot of the mountain, near the little river, "another lodging."

But the account tells us that Roberval had this double fort "built." Had Cartier destroyed his settlement before leaving? Or had the Iroquois strip-ped the place to prevent its reoccupation? If these were not Cartier's build-ings refurbished, Roberval had rebuilt along the same lines. The account gives a number of details about Roberval's establishment that are lacking for Cartier's. In the fort on the cliff, "there were two courtes of buyldings, a great Towre, and another of fortie or fiftie foote long: wherein there were divers Chambers, an Hall, a Kitchine, houses of office, Sellers high and lowe, and neere unto it were an Oven and Milles, and a stoove to warme men in." The fort on the shore consisted of "another lodging, part whereof was a great Towre of two stories high, [with] Two courtes of good buylding." Perhaps it was Cartier's. One thing certain is that, on arriving at this spot, Roberval and his men found wheat that Cartier had sown before his departure; on a single ear, Alfonse counted 120 grains.

The colony spent the month of August and part of the following month settling in. The place was no longer called Charlesbourg Royal but *France-Roy*; according to other documents, it was variously called *fort Henri-Charles* or again *France-neufve*. On September 14, Roberval sent two of his three ships back to France under the command of Admiral Sauveterre and Captain Guinecourt to report to the King and to "bring newes out of France how the King accepted certaine Diamants which were sent him." Sauveterre and Guinecourt had orders to return the following year "with victuals and other things." Now it happened that Sauveterre had killed a sailor by the name of Laurent Barbot on Christmas day of 1541, and was threatened with prosecution for the deed. Roberval exercised his judicial right and drew up letters of acquittal in Sauveterre's favour, invoking legitimate self-defence. This document, of September 9, 1542, dated at France Roy on the France Prime, is the oldest known official text in the history of French administration in Canada.[39]

With the two ships gone and everyone housed, attention turned to preparations for the winter. The first necessary decision was not an encouraging one; the colony would already have to be put on short rations of bacon, beef and beans, with cod on Wednesdays, Fridays and Saturdays. We are not told whether the French took to hunting in this country so rich in game and fish. Shad could in any case be had from the Indians in exchange for knives and trinkets.

The colony was hard-hit by sickness; "many of our people fell sicke of a certaine disease in their legges, reynes [loins], and stomacke, so that they seemed to be deprived of all their lymmes." Some fifty colonists perished.[40] This scourge was scurvy once again, and there is nothing in the account to suggest that Roberval was aware of the wonder-working infusion of the white cedar. Cartier's absence was having disastrous consequences.

The Canadian winter seemed long for these people who were tasting it for the first time. The author of the account carefully notes that the ice did not begin to melt until April. These difficulties were compounded by unruly behaviour on the part of some of the colonists. Michel Gaillon was hanged for theft (this was the first hanging in Canada), Jean de Nantes was thrown into irons along with a number of others, and several colonists were given the whip, "as well men as women." Some historians have used this evidence to accuse Roberval of undue harshness. It is unfair to call him a buccaneer, as some have done, and the colony's leader can hardly be reproached for applying the disciplinary measures of his time. Theft, for example, led straight to the gallows, and so it still was in the nineteenth century. Being a career soldier and having, perhaps, some former convicts among his charges, he was bound to impose strong discipline. Moreover, the author of the account observes that Roberval "used very good justice" and that, in this way, the colonists "lived in quiet.[41] What more could be asked of a leader?

All we know of the behaviour of the Indians toward the French is that they came to barter shad. Since Roberval had military strength at his disposal, they seem to have been less aggressive than in Cartier's time, and the account (incomplete, it is true) makes no allusion to any attack. The pilot Alfonse saw these Indians as "good and gentle folk, so that they do no harm to anyone who does none to them." What had become of Agona, whom Cartier had put into power and who turned against his ally? What had become of the chief of Achelacy, the long-time faithful friend who had gone over to the other side in the end? No more is said of them. Neither this account of Roberval's voyage nor Alfonse's *Cosmographie* add much to what Cartier's accounts had already revealed about the Indians, apart from one important detail: "they are very white [. . .] but they paynt themselves for feare of heat and sunne burning." In the following century, there would be talk of *Peaux-Rouges* as opposed to *Visages-Pâles*, but the author of this account makes no mistake; the Iroquois were not a red-skinned race! And he adds what time has subsequently proved: "if they were apparelled as the French are, they would bee as white and as fayre."[42]

The winter had been disastrous. In the spring of 1543, a decision was made; the colony would return to France in the course of the summer. But there still remained the final objective assigned to Roberval: Saguenay, that mysterious country where gold and silver and precious metals abounded. Reading the account, one gets the impression that Roberval was in no great hurry to go in search of it. Though he arrived at France Roy in August of 1542, it was only in June of 1543 that he set out for the "province of Saguenay."[43]

Nothing in the account indicates that Roberval went by way of Hochelaga in search of Saguenay, but the planisphere of 1550 by Desceliers dispels any doubt that this was the case, with an inscription entered just west of Hochelaga: "as far as here came mons^r de roberval."[44] Did he intend to found a colony on the Island of Montreal, as has been suggested? Nothing in the account, nor on maps of the period, nor in the writings of Alfonse, gives grounds for this hypothesis. The decision to return to France clearly contradicts it, moreover. The account, the only text to tell the story of this voyage, says clearly that an expedition went in search of Saguenay; Roberval, like Cartier, intended to get there by way of Hochelaga.

He designated sixty-nine men to accompany him, of whom eight are known by name. The rest of the colony, that is to say some thirty people, were to stay at France Roy under the command of Royèze. Since this Saguenay was thought to be fairly close to Hochelaga, Roberval expected to return at the beginning of July, or in a month's time. Following that, the colony would take ship for France.

On June 5, "after supper," the party embarked in eight boats equipped with sails, and the next day the flotilla began the ascent of the river toward Hochelaga. Since the author of the account was not on the voyage, and since the account is incomplete in any event, we know practically nothing of what happened during this expedition. A week after Roberval's departure. one group returned to France Roy; they announced that one of the boats had been lost and that eight men had been drowned. On June 19, five voyagers returned, bringing 120 pounds of grain and word that the departure for France was postponed until July 22.[45] There, the account ends abruptly.

What had happened? Where had the grain come from? Where had the

boat been lost? On the way up the river, in an attempt to negotiate the
Lachine Rapids, or on the way back to France Roy? The account is exas-
peratingly uninformative on all these questions. As to how far Roberval
had got in his voyage of exploration, only one document gives an answer,
and that is Desceliers's map of 1550; the inscription already mentioned
would seem to indicate that Roberval had entered the Ottawa River, but
we cannot be quite sure of this because cartographers so often wrote their
inscriptions and place-names in whatever spaces were available rather than
at the exact spot they wished to indicate. There is no document that con-
firms that Roberval had passed the Lachine Rapids. Alfonse's *Cosmographie*
reveals nothing new about the region of Hochelaga, and there is no map
that shows anything more than what Cartier had already made known.
The interruption of the narrative and the absence of official records leaves
many question-marks.

It is not until the following September that there is further word of
Roberval.[46] By that time he was in France and the French colony had been
repatriated.

Why this withdrawal to Europe? Although we do not know the precise
reasons, the return had been decided upon early in June at the latest,
before the Saguenay expedition, and the abandonment of the Laurentian
colony therefore did not arise from the failure of that expedition. There
were other causes, revealed by only one document of the period, the
Desceliers map, on which there is an inscription stating that the impos-
sibility of trade with the Indians "by Reason of Their austerity," the
climate of the country and "small profit" had driven the French home,
although they hoped to return to Canada when it should please the King.

It will be remembered that Roberval had sent Paul d'Aussillon de Sauveterre to France with two ships in September 1542 to report to Francis I
on what had happened and to bring back supplies the following year. On
January 26, 1543, d'Aussillon was authorized to return to Canada with
two ships loaded with "food and other things of which [Roberval] has
great need and necessity." In France, then, there was no question of
repatriating the Canadian colony. All that was known there was that
Roberval needed food, and he was being sent it. One of these ships left
France between March 13 and May 29, 1543, but it could not have arrived
at France Roy until after June 19.[47]

At all events, everyone was back in France by September 11 and the
adventure was at an end.[48] Those who had prophesied calamity for France
were proven right: the building of a New France in the new lands of the
north had foundered. The *Castilliens* and the *Portugallois* could now relax.

And the failure was a resounding one. Relations with the Indians, on
which the success of any European establishment depended above all, had
worsened disastrously. The Iroquois, masters of the valley, had been friends

at first, then distrustful allies; once they had turned into bloodthirsty enemies, how could a settlement be maintained there? Colonization in general
acquired a bad name. The enormous waste of money was long to be
remembered by kings and subjects alike, and in the seventeenth century
tireless efforts would be necessary to make colonization in the St Lawrence
Valley look attractive again.

For the exploration of the continent by way of the St Lawrence, the
failure was no less resounding. Cartier's third voyage added nothing to his
prestige as a navigator, and Roberval's and Alfonse's navigational achieve-
ments consisted in supplying further details of the gulf and river. The
great unanswered questions raised by the voyage of 1535 remained unanswered still.

It was a Spaniard, De Soto, who was responsible for the progress made
during this period in the exploration of the North American continent.
Between 1539 and 1542, De Soto explored South Carolina, Georgia and
Alabama and crossed the Mississippi 450 miles from its mouth to reach
into Oklahoma; a spectacular feat that clearly showed up Cartier's and
Roberval's timidity.

On the great highway of the St Lawrence, where everything had pointed
to a rapid French advance toward the West, progress ground to a halt
after 1535. If there had been at least a permanent settlement by the time
of this halt, the French foothold would have been effectively established.
It was established, in fact, only in the cartography of the day; all sixteenth-
century maps that appeared after the voyage of Cartier and Roberval, of
French or other origin, showed the St Lawrence River and Gulf dotted with
French place-names. A precarious foothold, to be sure; it will be recalled
that in 1524 Verrazano had left a string of French names all along the
coast from Florida to Cape Breton, and that the following year they were
supplanted by a Spanish nomenclature that was respected even by French
cartographers. But history's wheel of fortune decreed that the names
created by Cartier and Roberval should survive the temporary abandonment of the St Lawrence; while European geographers all represented the
Atlantic coastline as Spanish, they continued to show on their maps of the
St Lawrence Valley the details and names that they had learned from
Cartier and Roberval. This was how France kept her foothold after 1543,
when the veil of mystery fell once more about the great river of Canada,
not to be raised again for a half a century.

CHAPTER 4

Commerce Brings France Back
to North America
1577–1602

The first major French colonial program was undertaken in the time of Admiral Coligny. This was a time of bitter religious strife, and Coligny devised a plan to found a colony overseas which might serve as a refuge for the Huguenots. The first attempt was made in 1555, when Villegaignon founded a colony in Brazil, but the Portuguese destroyed it in 1560. Two more Huguenot settlements were established by Ribault and Laudonnière in Florida in 1562 and 1564, but by 1565 both had been destroyed by the Spaniards. For the foundation and support of these colonies, French authorities had launched a systematic effort which would not be equalled until the seventeenth century. By comparison, Roberval's enterprise was only, as one might say, an accident of French policy.

On August 24, 1572, the Feast of St Bartholomew, there was a whole-sale massacre of the Huguenots in Paris and throughout France, and Coligny was its first victim. From then on, France was rocked by turmoil for many years. In the western provinces, whence expeditions to far-flung places must necessarily set forth, chaos reigned. La Rochelle became the centre of resistance for the Protestants, and from England an army of Huguenots invaded Normandy. By the Edict of Beaulieu of May 1576 and the Peace of Bergerac of September 1577, the Huguenots obtained the disavowal of the massacre of St Bartholomew, partial freedom of worship, and designated places of refuge. But this religious tolerance proved to be fragile, for the Holy League (La Sainte Ligue) had been formed in 1576. Its declared and uncompromising aim of "One faith, one law, one king" demanded the exercise of a single, Catholic faith. Under the leadership of the family of Guise and backed by Philip II, King of Spain, it was to stop at nothing.

In 1577, however, there was a truce, or, more properly speaking, a lull in the fighting, and the colonial policy that had been set aside ten years earlier could once more come to the fore. But who was there to carry it out? Throughout this dramatic period of French history, from 1576 to 1589, a period that has been called "the history of the decomposition of a great State," a dynamic colonial policy could no longer be looked for from either the king or the admiral. It was private citizens, already commercially active in the region, who provided the initiative and were to take hold of the northeastern corner of America.

Neither the Brazilian nor the Florida adventure had in any way affected the fisheries of Newfoundland. The shipowners of Normandy, Brittany and elsewhere continued to send out their fishing expeditions as they always had; they were there before Cartier, they were still there in the time of Charlesbourg Royal and France Roy, and they continued to return each year, hoping to corner the inexhaustible supply of cod at the expense of their Basque, Spanish and Portuguese competitors.

It would be easy to show that the economy of western France depended in great measure upon the Gulf of St Lawrence during the years 1560 to 1570. That it continued to do so is indicated by the fact that the voyages to Newfoundland continued in the following years. For proof of the constant exploitation of the Gulf of St Lawrence we need only look to the ordinance of March, 1584, which fixed norms of equipment for ships sailing to Newfoundland.[1]

Throughout the second half of the sixteenth century, then, the French went to Newfoundland every year. They were in contact with the Indians and, like Cartier, brought a few of them back to France from time to time. There was, for instance, a Newfoundland Indian who was baptized at St Malo in 1553, and two others who were mentioned in 1584 and 1585. With these annual fishing voyages to Newfoundland and these contacts with the Indians, France had been constantly present in the northern regions of America, in spite of Roberval's retreat in 1543 and in spite of later official preoccupation with Brazil and Florida. If France was still to make a place for herself across the Atlantic, it was natural to expect that she might do so in this part of the New World.

But if such a thing were to come about, it was essential that there be both a policy favourable to colonization and bold and adventurous leaders. All those who had already been to America (Cartier, Roberval, Villegaignon, Ribault and Laudonnière) were dead. A new man was to come forward: Mesgouez, Seigneur de La Roche.

In 1577 this Breton marquis, former page and favourite of the Queen Mother, Catherine de Médicis, obtained authorization from Henry III to found a New France. In somewhat obscure circumstances, he persuaded Henry III that, without offending the neighbouring princes, the King possessed "the means of conquering and taking possession of some newly discovered lands and countries occupied by barbarous peoples, from which he may and hopes to bring much benefit to this our Kingdom, both for traffic and commerce and for other excellent purposes." The declared motives were the same as those brought into fashion in Roberval's time: "in the zeal and fervent devotion he bears for God's service as a Christian and for our own Majesty and that of our successors as well as in singular affection for the prestige of the name of France, and for the furtherance, assurance and benefit of the commerce and traffic, well-being, profit and utility of the entire public of this Kingdom."

Under the terms of his commission of 1577, La Roche would be permitted to go to the New Lands and others adjacent, to make those he occupied his own, to build fortresses and possess the country in his own and his successors' right, "perpetually and for always as their own domain and rightful acquest." In January, 1578, the King went further still and named La Roche "Governor and our Lieutenant-General and Viceroy of the said *Terres neuves* and countries which he shall conquer and take from these barbarians."[2]

Here indeed was a project of sweeping proportions, and an entrepreneur who found himself hoisted to a pinnacle. La Roche was to become viceroy of the lands he might occupy, besides acquiring them as his personal property! La Rocque de Roberval enjoyed very extensive powers in 1541, but he never bore the heady title of Viceroy; he could grant seigneuries, but the country was never his personal property. Neither Roberval nor Villegaignon nor Ribault had had such privileges as were now given to La Roche.

Another significant fact was that Henry III was no longer considering carving out a New France from the Portuguese empire, as had his father Henry II, nor on the borders of the Spanish empire, as had his brother Charles IX. He was reverting instead to the policy of his grandfather, Francis I, envisaging a New France in the northern regions of America. Thus he brought thirty-four years of official abstention to an end.

It is possible that the project was not immediately put into execution. According to La Roncière, whose information is not always reliable, La Roche organized the departure of two vessels, the larger of which was seized by the English.[3] If, however, two vessels did in fact set sail under the command of the first viceroy of the New Lands, the documents of the day reveal neither their destination nor the strength of their complements. In any event, the two royal commissions of 1577 and 1578 confirmed the renewal of interest in the northern regions of America on the part of French officialdom.

The most important economic fact of North American history in the sixteenth century was the initiation of the fur trade. Since very early times, Basques, Bretons and Normans had come yearly to North America in quest of cod for the market places of Europe, but as the early explorers became more familiar with the American coast, they found a new and unexpected commercial commodity in the furs to be had there. One after the other, Cartier, Roberval and Jean Alfonse had noted that the Indians were in the habit of storing up quantities of magnificent furs with a view to barter among themselves. The Europeans soon learned to participate.

Trade was slow in getting under way. Not all cod fishermen came into contact with the Indians; "green cod" fishermen stopped above the continental shelf, well off-shore, salted their fish on board their ships and, having completed their catch, returned direct to Europe. It was the "dry cod" fishermen who settled ashore for the season. From their base port, they would go out to fish and then return with their catch to lay it out for the long drying process. They found it necessary, besides, to venture quite far inland in search of wood and game. The dry cod fishermen thus became old hands in the country. Among them was a Captain Champagne who was reported to have been in the Bay of Fundy about 1568 on board the *Gargarine*, and particularly a Basque fisherman by the name of Savalette who was encountered in Acadia in 1607 and who, it would seem, was then on his forty-second voyage, which would mean that he had first visited the region about 1565.[4] These fishermen were under contract to cod merchants, and when they brought furs back to Europe at the end of the fishing season it was as curiosities mainly, or for their own pleasure. But interest increased as the furs became more luxurious and plentiful. Fishing vessels added more and more of them to their cargoes, as did a vessel in 1569 which returned to France with a cargo of furs of excellent quality. Beginning in 1581, the merchants of St Malo, Rouen and Dieppe organized voyages specifically for trading in furs up the St Lawrence; Hakluyt reports having seen a consignment of a variety of furs in Paris in 1583 which was valued at the staggering sum of 20,000 crowns.[5] By this time cod fishermen were no longer content to await chance encounters with the Indians; they went out in search of furs, and more and more often their voyages were organized for this purpose. The Indian civilization of Northeastern America was to undergo profound changes as a result. Whereas these native peoples had been oriented until then toward the sea because it provided them with food, little by little they were to turn away from it in order to store up furs for barter, and their way of life was to undergo a transformation in consequence. The sixteenth-century fishing fleets were thus to bring about a major revolution for the Indians.

During this initial period in the history of the fur trade, an important expedition was undertaken by a merchant of Rouen, Etienne Bellenger. According to his English friend, Hakluyt, who met him in France, Bellenger went to Cape Breton at the expense of Charles de Bourbon and, from there, sailed down the coast for a distance of two hundred leagues. A hundred leagues from Cape Breton, he came upon a sizable village where the houses were covered with bark. He bartered at ten or twelve places and brought home some ore said to contain silver, as well as several varieties of fur (beaver, otter, marten and others), all dressed and painted on the inside. These furs sold at Rouen for some four hundred crowns, while the trinkets that Bellenger had given the Indians in exchange had cost him only forty.[6]

This voyage was of considerable geographic interest as well, for, according to Hakluyt, Bellenger brought back a meticulous description of the coast. It seems likely, according to Ganong, that it was from Bellenger that Hakluyt obtained certain precise details, in particular of the bay called *Menim* or *Menan*, which opened into the Atlantic west of Cape Breton and which was undoubtedly the Bay of Fundy.

This fruitful voyage of Bellenger's in 1583 no doubt explains in part why La Roche reappears in 1584, the same La Roche of whom nothing had been heard for six years. He had obtained his viceroyalty of the New Lands at an unpropitious time, for France was still embroiled in war and would remain so until the death of the Duke of Anjou in June 1584. Even then, internal peace was not assured, since the first in line as heir to the throne was a Protestant, Henry of Navarre, cousin of Henry III. However, there was at least a pause in military operations in 1584, and it was in that year that the question of La Roche's expedition was revived. Financed by Cardinal de Bourbon, Archbishop of Rouen, and by Admiral de Joyeuse, La Roche embarked three hundred colonists to people the new country, but his principal vessel of 300 tons broke up near Brouage, which put an end to the enterprise.[7]

In this same year of 1584, merchants of St Malo organized a commercial expedition and ascended the St Lawrence. Their five ships returned so heavily laden with furs that they prepared a fleet of ten ships for the following year, to the great despair of the observer Hakluyt, who feared that the English were about to be shouldered aside as the French carried off all the riches for themselves under their very noses.[8] And so European merchants invaded the St Lawrence in force. In 1587, a fight broke out there between rival traders, probably all of them French. Jacques Noël and his company had three small vessels burned and another captured by their adversaries.[9] For the shipowners of Brittany and Normandy, cod maintained its place because it was essential as a food, but it was decidedly furs that took the limelight in commercial circles in the last quarter of the sixteenth century, and with them, the St Lawrence River.

For the merchants of St Malo who had initiated the trade in Canadian furs, the most dangerous threat did not come in the form of foreigners or religious wars, but from fellow citizens of St Malo wanting it all to themselves. On January 12, 1588, a twelve-year monopoly for Canada and adjacent countries was obtained from Henry III by Jacques Noël and Etienne Chaton de La Jannaye.

This La Jannaye's religious persuasion is unknown, but he was an enemy of the Holy League, although he had fought against the Huguenots. He had never been to Canada.[10] Jacques Noël, a nephew of Cartier and half-brother of the Etienne Noël who had sailed with Cartier in 1541, had already been in Canada, perhaps as a pilot. In the course of one of these voyages he actually retraced his uncle's footsteps, seeing with his own eyes what remained of by-gone forts (Ste Croix, whose vestiges Champlain was also to see, and Charlesbourg Royal) which, he wrote, had fallen into ruins from neglect. He travelled up the river as far as the rapids of Hochelaga and climbed Mount Royal. Cartier's nephew did not advance his uncle's work, although he possessed something that would have permitted him to take up the task, for he had found a work by Cartier, "a book made in manner of a sea chart." He prepared a book himself in the same form, following the lines of Cartier's. June of 1587 found him once more in St Malo, from where he wrote to correct the position that a map, dedicated to Hakluyt, had given to the *Grand Lac* above the *Saults*. In that same year 1587, his two sons, Michel and Jean, were in Canada with their father's "sea chart" in hand. They lost four small ships there, and so that year the "traffic" was worth nothing to them.[11]

Immediately following the return of this disastrous expedition of 1587, Jacques Noël set about making his own preparations. In association with Chaton de La Jannaye, he presented a petition to the King, basing his request for a commercial concession on the losses suffered long before by his uncle.

Their wish, said Noël and La Jannaye, was "to carry on the memory" of Cartier. They cited the trade in furs, the relations established with the Indians, the copper which had been discovered, and the old forts which were lying there in ruins and were a waste, in view of all that the country had to offer. Invoking the 8,630 livres which remained owing to Cartier since Francis I's time and the "work and services" accomplished by the St Malo navigator, as well as emoluments owed by the King to La Jannaye for the last twelve years, the two associates requested a subsidy ("a few deniers") so that they might return to Canada and build "some fortresses for the assurance and retreat of their persons and vessels" against incursions "which might be made against them by our subjects and other nations." In addition to this financial aid, they begged the King to accord them an exclusive monopoly for mines and fur pelts for a period of twelve years.

Since he was unable to repay what remained due to Cartier's heirs and what La Jannaye was claiming as emoluments, Henry III readily consented to the grant of a commercial concession. In doing so he granted the same powers that Francis I had accorded Cartier on October 17, 1540. This was therefore a revival of a commission that was a half century old. Noël and La Jannaye were to enjoy the right to all the trade and commerce of

Canada both in mining and furs. As in Cartier's commission, sixty prisoners, both men and women, would be sent to the concessionaires each year "to populate the country," to work in the mines and, along with the soldiers and mariners, "to live as subjects and in the fear of God in the Apostolic and Roman Catholic Religion," to trade with the savages "in every peaceful fashion, to attract and attempt to instruct and lead them to acquaintance with God and His Christian faith."[12]

The exclusivity of the Catholic religion in 1588 has interesting sidelights. For the first time since the essentially Protestant ventures in Brazil and Florida, Protestantism was being excluded by a plan of colonization. Henry III was here breaking with the policy followed by Henry II and Charles IX. Did he do so out of personal conviction? In the policy of kings, personal conviction has always been outweighed by the *raison d'Etat*. It was essential to rule out the possibility of Spanish intervention across the Atlantic on the pretence of saving Catholicism; Philip II could not be allowed the opportunity of repeating the same politico-religious manoeuvres in the St Lawrence that he had executed in Florida. The circumtances of 1588 demanded that New France should be exclusively Catholic.

The monopoly of January 12, 1588, threatened to drive out those merchants who had been carrying on a profitable business in the St Lawrence. The merchants of St Malo determined to appeal to the *Parlement* of Rennes. The monopoly, they declared, had been obtained on false pretences. On the other hand they hesitated to request this monopoly for themselves, because it would obligate them to build and maintain fortifications.

The *Etats* of Brittany then joined the outcry against the monopoly and called for freedom of "traffic and commerce." Henry III decided that the call was justified; on May 5 he proclaimed freedom for all in fishing and trade, except in lands that La Jannaye and Noël might discover. On July 9, in his letters of revocation, the King restricted the proposed monopoly further; La Jannaye and Noël were to have no exclusive rights except over "minerals that they had searched out and discovered."[13] Thus they could no longer count on the immense profit that would derive from the commerce that was already established, but must await the development of mines as yet unproven. Under these conditions the plan of colonization would no longer be profitable, and they withdrew. Jacques Cartier's family took no further part in the development of the St Lawrence.

This was above all a victory for free trade. For the first time in the history of New France, the problem of conflict between merchants and colonizers had been clearly demonstrated, the merchants wanting simply to barter in the St Lawrence and the colonizers hoping to be assured of commercial revenues and intending to apply them in part to the foundation of a new country. In this first round, the partisans of pure and simple trade had carried the day. The merchants of St Malo stubbornly refused to believe in the fertility of the country and maintained that it was good for nothing but as a source of pelts. What they wanted, of course, was commercial gains without the burden of colonization, whereas the foundation and maintenance of a colony would be impossible without the support of an exclusive monopoly. There was therefore a complete cleavage of interest between commerce and colonization.

Either freedom of commerce for all and no colony, or exclusive monopoly and colonization; the year 1588 posed the dilemma for the first time, and freedom of commerce emerged the victor. Many other such victories were to follow, to the detriment of the cause of New France. This same dilemma was to provide drama throughout the career of Champlain.

But the merchants' victory was not a conclusive one. There was still Viceroy La Roche to be reckoned with, for sooner or later he might attempt to exercise his prerogatives. However, the events of the day were against him. La Roche was an adversary of the Holy League, and in 1589 he fell into the hands of the Duc de Mercœur, who, although he was brother to the Queen, was the leader of the League in Brittany; Mercœur imprisoned La Roche in the Château de Nantes and did not release him until 1596.

A monopoly was too attractive a prize to be left lying untouched. In 1591 a man by the name of La Cour Pré-Ravillon is said to have succeeded to the concession held by Noël and La Jannaye, but no document has yet been found to substantiate this speculation. Pré-Ravillon perhaps only laid claim to a concession restricted to the development of mines. It is known, in any case, that Pré-Ravillon did attempt to establish a foothold in the Magdalen Islands.

It was becoming more and more urgent toward the end of the sixteenth century for the French to establish a solid base in North America if they were not to lose the resources of the Gulf and the commercial highway of the St Lawrence. Circumstances were now in fact beginning to take a favourable turn. Henry IV, having become a Catholic, was gradually winning back military and political control of his kingdom. The last to yield was the Duc de Mercœur's Brittany, which made its peace early in 1598, and the following May the Treaty of Vervins confirmed the ultimate failure of the aggressive tactics of Philip II. Henry IV had just issued the Edict of Nantes, moreover, and the end of the long series of religious wars at last ushered in an era of peace.

La Roche, having been released by Mercœur in 1596, was already taking advantage of the imminent peace to organize a new voyage to America. In November 1596, he was in Honfleur attempting to obtain repayment of some 5,000 crowns owed to him. On February 16, 1597, he obtained "power" from the King and the Admiral of France. On March 4, he concluded an agreement for the transport of his colony to Sable Island. On April 17, he made a request to the *Parlement* of Rouen that all convicts condemned to the galleys be turned over to him, but it is not certain that he obtained them.[14] After so many abortive attempts, was a New France at last to come into being?

Sable Island, ninety miles off Cape Canso, is the sole point rising above sea level from the sub-oceanic plateau long known to navigators as *les Bancs* or the Banks; with its area of 16,000 acres, it is twenty-five miles long, shaped like "a bow whose string is stretched from east to west"; it is entirely surrounded by a broad beach, and here and there are hillocks of sand; a part of its area is taken up by a lagoon or *barachois*, which once was joined to the sea by an inlet. The island has excellent pasturage and plenty of fresh water. There are no trees, only shrubs, wild roses, cranberries, blueberries and strawberries. Its fauna includes walruses, seals, sea-lions, a great many foxes, and horses which were left there at some time by Europeans and have reproduced and become wild. Its climate is the same as New England's.[15]

This is probably the island which, having been visited early in the sixteenth century by the Portuguese, bears the name *S. Cruz* on the Reinel map of 1505. Toward the middle of the century, it reappeared on various maps as *Isolla del Arena* or *Ile de Sable*. Either a certain Baron de Léry, whose story remains very obscure, or some Portuguese are thought to have abandoned some equipment there intended for an agricultural settlement. In 1583, Humphrey Gilbert ran aground there and lost a ship.

La Roche did not sail with the voyage he organized in 1597. On March 4, he chartered the *Catherine*, a ship of about 160 tons which belonged to the Norman sea captain Thomas Chefdhostel. The ship was provisioned with food by La Roche and was to carry thirty-three sailors and men-at-arms under the command of Captain Kerdement, Lieutenant Kéroual and Ensign Mondreville. It was to leave at the first appropriate moment, take on salt at Brouage, and then go to fish at Sable Island.[16] To all appearances this was a fishing voyage, but it was also a voyage of reconnaissance, as subsequent events would show; and no doubt it was profitable, since La Roche set to work immediately to prepare for his own and his colony's transport to Sable Island in 1598.

First of all he had his letters patent renewed by Henry IV. These new letters, obtained on January 12, 1598, envisaged a project similar to the projects of 1541, 1555, 1562 and 1578. Recalling that Henry III had already elected La Roche for such a mission, Henry IV declared that he wished to continue the work begun by Francis I who, "moved by zeal and concern for the exaltation of the Christian name," had entrusted Roberval with a mission of conquest. "For this holy work and advancement of the Catholic Faith," therefore, La Roche was named the King's

Lieutenant-General for the countries of *"Canada, Hochelaga, Terres-neuves, Labrador, rivière de la grand Baye, de Norembergue"* and adjacent lands which were not inhabited "by subjects of any Christian Prince." He could construct fortresses, make laws, grant lands in *"Fiefs, Seigneuries, Chastelenies, Comtez, Vicomtez, Baronnies,"* whose beneficiaries in return would assure the defence of the country. No one would be permitted to trade without authorization from La Roche. Finally, profits were to be divided into three parts: one would remain with La Roche, the second would be divided amongst those who made the voyage, and the last would serve for the maintenance of the colony.[17]

With his official objective ("the advancement of the Catholic Faith"), Henry IV was carrying on the policy of Henry III and of his distant great-uncle Francis I. It was no particular indication that the Holy League had imposed its will on foreign policy, or that the neophyte Henry IV was conducting himself unswervingly as a "Very Christian King"; as in Henry III's case, it demonstrated above all that France was hoping not to unduly alarm an intolerant Philip II, with whom a difficult peace was in the making. Henry IV was echoing Francis I with the powers that he was giving La Roche, too. Roberval had been named Lieutenant-General, could construct fortresses, make laws and grant lands in fief and seigneury, and held a commercial monopoly. The terms were to be exactly the same for La Roche. It will be observed, however, that while La Roche had received the titles of Viceroy and Proprietor of the New Lands in 1578, he no longer had these titles in 1598. This was apparently a deliberate omission. Henry IV had already had more than enough trouble recovering his kingdom from those powerful nobles who, during the wars of religion, had carried France back to the state of fragmentation prevailing before the reign of Louis XI.

La Roche set out to recruit colonists from among beggars and vagabonds, and rounded up two hundred men and fifty women. In mid-March, Chefdhostel and Jean Girot placed the *Catherine* of about 160 tons and the *Françoise* of 90 tons at his disposal for the transport of the colony. They agreed to take La Roche and his colonists to Sable Island, then they would stop on their return from fishing to bring him back, by which time he would have been able to establish his settlers.[18]

La Roche embarked toward the middle of April and was set ashore on Sable Island, the site which had been examined on his behalf the previous year. He settled his colonists on the northern shore of this island, to which he gave the name Bourbon, close by the inlet which ran from the salt lake to the sea and which was named Rivière Boncœur; there he had a storehouse and dwellings built. When Chefdhostel and Girot had finished their fishing they came to collect La Roche, and the colonists stayed behind under the command of Querbonyer, with Captain Coussez in charge of the storehouse. In October, 1598, La Roche was once more in France busily recruiting colonists; Henry IV, well satisfied with this beginning, gave him 12,000 crowns.[19]

It has taken a long time to unearth the truth about these and subsequent events in the Sable Island adventure. For many years, on the strength of versions reported by Champlain, Lescarbot, Charlevoix, Garneau and others, historians repeatedly wrote that La Roche had stopped at the island only to await the choice of a suitable site on the mainland, and that a raging storm had driven him back to France on this and later occasions when he tried to bring help to his colonists; in the end, it was said, after five years of appalling hardship, these unfortunates were repatriated on an order from the *Parlement* of Rouen. The actual details of the story have been brought to light by documents published by the Bréard brothers in 1889, and through research by Gustave Lanctôt and Joseph Le Ber.[20]

In 1599, La Roche sent Chefdhostel to take more settlers and food supplies to Sable Island; in 1600 and in 1601, relations between La Roche and his colony were still perfectly normal. Thanks to Chefdhostel, fresh supplies arrived there and skins and oils were sent back to France. In 1602, however, there was no such voyage, and no one knows why. Contact was resumed in 1603. On February 21, Chefdhostel agreed to transport food to the island aboard the *Catherine*; a commissioner was to sail with him, because it seemed that the King wished to have precise information so that he might decide what should become of the colony and the monopoly; this commissioner would inspect the island and its fertility and the cattle and pigs there. On his return voyage, Chefdhostel might bring back Commander Querbonyer and some ten others with their baggage; the ship would be loaded with skins, oils and other merchandise as had been done on each previous voyage.

And so Chefdhostel set sail in the spring of 1603 for Sable Island. When he arrived, he discovered a dramatic situation which had perhaps existed since the preceding year; Commander Querbonyer, the storekeeper Coussez and several others had been assassinated. Why and how had it happened? It is thought that the colonists (several of whom were ex-convicts) had revolted and ransacked the storehouse when the annual supplies failed to arrive in 1602. Only eleven colonists remained, which suggests that a large number of settlers had taken flight. Chefdhostel took the survivors aboard, as well as the skins and oils that he would normally have taken, and returned to France. Henry IV called the eleven colonists before him, hoping to find out what had happened on Sable Island. The survivors told him a convincing story in their own favour; they received letters of pardon, the right to two thirds of the profits realized on the skins and oils that had been brought back, and a compensation payment of fifty crowns each.[21]

La Roche could do no more for his island. For four or five years he had had to contend with stiff competition; his 1598 enterprise, already at a disadvantage from the very fact of its isolation, was further undermined by those who were casting covetous eyes at his monopoly. In 1603 he found himself brushed aside, and it was a Protestant, Chauvin de Tonnetuit, for whose benefit the greater part of his immense domain was sliced away, on the pretext that the conditions of his monopoly had not been respected.

On November 22, 1599, Pierre Chauvin de Tonnetuit had obtained the exclusive monopoly of trade "in the country of Canada, the coast of Acadia and others of New France," along with the title of King's Lieutenant. Until then the Huguenots had been denied access to New France, and Henry IV in his letters patent to La Roche had assured the exclusivity of an established Catholic faith in the colony, but a mere ten months later a large part of La Roche's monopoly was taken from him and placed in the hands of the Protestant Chauvin. The reason for this radical change in policy was that, between the issuance of La Roche's letters patent and Chauvin's, two decisive events had taken place: the signing of the Edict of Nantes, that "attempt at co-existence" between Catholics and Protestants which allowed Huguenots to hold public office, and of the Treaty of Vervins, which restored peace between France and Spain. Now there was very little danger that the weakened Philip II might intervene against a New France in which Protestants had a part.

Chauvin, a native of Dieppe, had served Henry IV at the head of Calvinist troops against the Duc de Mercœur, and he may have taken part in the King's campaign in the region of Caux. From 1596, he was a merchant and mariner at Honfleur. He lent money to shipowners operating in the fisheries of Newfoundland, and two of his own ships, the *Espérance* and the *Bon Espoir*, came to Newfoundland in 1597. In 1598 he had part ownership, along with some St Malo merchants, in a ship that had been captured from foreigners "at the Island of Orleans, in Canada." Early in 1599, his ship the *Don-de-Dieu* undertook a cod-fishing voyage with Henri Couillart. The following November, he secured the monopoly for Canada and Acadia, undertaking to "live in the country and build a stronghold." He proposed to take five hundred men to America, and Champlain, who was severely critical of Chauvin on other occasions, although he recognized him to be "a man most expert and knowledgeable in navigation," was overjoyed at the new enterprise. "This is the beginning of a fine endeavour," he wrote, "without cost to the King, if what is in this commission shall be realized."[22]

A "beginning of a fine endeavour" indeed, but Chauvin had to reckon with stiff opposition. This opposition came first from La Roche, who saw himself dispossessed of a sizable portion of his monopoly at a time when he still had his Sable Island colony to maintain. La Roche defended his position vigorously, and Henry IV amended his decision. On January 15, 1600, he named Chauvin only "one of the lieutenants" of La Roche and limited the area of his monopoly to a hundred leagues along the St Lawrence as far as Tadoussac. Chauvin submitted to this reduction; in a contract of the following month he styled himself "Lieutenant for the King, in the country of Canada, in the absence of the Marquis de La Roche," and once Tadoussac was established La Roche added it to the territories under his jurisdiction.[23] Chauvin's enterprise was therefore subordinated to La Roche's and Tadoussac belonged to Sable Island. But this was only in principle, because in fact La Roche and Chauvin seemed to have nothing to do with each other and the history of Tadoussac remained completely independent of that of Sable Island.

There was also opposition from the merchants. The *Communauté* or merchants' guild of St Malo delegated Jean Gouverneur to represent to the King, if Chauvin's monopoly should become operative, the "prejudice that would ensue from it for the inhabitants of Brittany," who had been carrying on trade there since time immemorial, not counting the fact that their vessels were already outfitted and about to put to sea. In 1588 it had suited the merchants of St Malo to belittle Cartier's voyages in an attempt to frustrate his nephew, Jacques Noël, but in 1600 they made these very voyages one of their principal arguments; it was, they said, a citizen of St Malo, Jacques Cartier, who had discovered Canada.

The St Malo merchants had won in 1588, but in 1600 they fared less well; this time colonization won the round against trade and, since La Roche seemed to be making no headway, it looked as though Chauvin would indeed and at last become the founder of New France.

With his monopoly upheld, Chauvin organized his first voyage in the spring of 1600. With his own four ships,[24] he mobilized the biggest fleet to set sail for Canada under a single command since 1542. Nothing as ambitious as this had been attempted in the St Lawrence for sixty years.

As Chauvin's assistant, there sailed a man who was to play an important role in Canada over a number of years: François Gravé, called in historical texts variously *Dupont-Gravé*, *Dupont*, *Le Pont* or *Pont-Gravé*. Born about 1554 in St Malo and a Catholic, Gravé had, like Chauvin, been a career soldier before becoming a merchant. Described as "most knowledgeable about voyages at sea, from having made a number of them," he had already come to the St Lawrence to trade with the Indians. He had been up the river as far as Trois Rivières before 1599, and it was perhaps thanks to him that the names Trois Rivières and Quebec made their first appearance on a map (the Levasseur map of 1601). His experience was of great value. According to Champlain, it was Gravé who had taken the necessary steps at Court for obtaining the monopoly, which would explain why La Roche accused him of betraying "all those who do commerce in St Malo and have been His Associates." In fact, Gravé left St Malo in 1600 and moved to Honfleur.[25]

There was another important passenger on the voyage, although this time it was "for his own pleasure" only: Pierre Du Gua de Monts.[26] This gentleman was of Italian origin and was born in Saintonge about 1560. Like Chauvin, he was a Huguenot and, also like him, had taken part in the religious wars in Normandy under the Protestant banner. He later became Governor of Pons in Saintonge.[27] When he sailed on board the *Don-de-Dieu* as an observer in 1600, de Monts began an American career which, though lasting only a few years, was of great importance, because it was to point the way for Champlain. Without de Monts, it can easily be imagined that there would have been no Champlain.

While La Roche continued to sustain his colony of Sable Island, Chauvin sailed direct to Tadoussac, at the entrance to the Saguenay River. This spot had already been visited by Cartier in 1535 and by Roberval in 1542, and had become a trading post for the French, though it is impossible to determine precisely when. The name Tadoussac appears as *Thadoyzeau* about 1550 in *Le grand insulaire* by Thevet. On the Hakluyt-Wright map of 1599-1600, the name is written *Tadouscu*, and it turns up again in 1601 on the Levasseur map spelled *Tadoucaq*, but here it is placed to the west of the mouth of the Saguenay. Its first official mention occurred on January 15, 1600, in the royal letters addressed to La Roche and Chauvin.

Champlain severely criticizes the place that Chauvin had chosen. It was in a region of high mountains, "where there was little soil, if not all rocks and sand [...] the most disagreeable and unfruitful place there is in this country"; the land was "very poorly disposed to allow any good cultivation," and whenever there was an ounce of cold forty leagues up-river, there was a pound of it at Tadoussac. The choice, it would seem, had been made by Chauvin despite opposition from his advisers; Gravé, who knew the river as far as Trois Rivières, would have liked to settle much further upstream, and de Monts would have liked to cast about for something new.[28] All Chauvin was interested in at first was trading, and from this point of view Tadoussac was indeed the ideal place, but in view of the conditions the destiny of New France was likely to be no more felicitous here than on Sable Island.

Chauvin did nevertheless make an attempt to establish something durable by leaving a number of men at Tadoussac to remain until the return of the ships the following year. He therefore constructed a crude building measuring about 24 feet by 18 and 8 feet high, covered with planks and surrounded by light fencing and "a little ditch dug in the sand"; a very rudimentary establishment that Champlain gleefully pokes fun at, referring to it as "a country cottage." With his trading finished, Chauvin left sixteen men there and, without having made the least attempt at exploration or discovery, went back to France.[29]

The winter of 1600-1601 at Tadoussac was disastrous. Chauvin's sixteen stalwarts found out then "what difference there was between France & Tadoussac"; they also quickly consumed the food that had been left for them, and Tadoussac soon became "la cour du Roy Petault," a Bedlam where each thought he should be master. Indolence and then sickness reduced them "to dire necessity." They were obliged to leave their habitation and take refuge with the natives. Some of them died and the others "languished" as they waited for the ships to return.[30] Though the French had spent three winters in the St Lawrence Valley a half century earlier, they had not yet learned to survive on their own; without the natives, the minute colony of Tadoussac would have flickered and died.

Happily, relief arrived in spring of 1601, as it did for Sable Island. Chauvin sent his ship Espérance to Tadoussac, commanded by Guyon-Dières of Honfleur. As for that voyage, the only comment we have is Champlain's sarcastic observation that it was "as fruitful as the first." There was no more talk of spending the winter. But the trading at least must have been profitable, since Chauvin led another voyage in April 1602, on which we once again find the Espérance commanded by Guyon-Dières and the Don-de-Dieu under the command of Henri Couillart. The expedition spent four months at Tadoussac, busying itself with trade and fishing. Chauvin had agreed to deliver 100,000 dried fish to Rouen merchants, but he was unable to complete his cargo and was obliged to pay them compensation. His fleet brought home three St Malo men whom a ship's captain had abandoned in "the isle of Canada," and it was perhaps on this occasion that two Indians from Tadoussac went to France and were presented to Henry IV, returning home in 1603 "to make report on what they had seen in France."[31]

These were meagre results. The intention had been to found a New France in the St Lawrence Valley at the expense of the monopoly accorded to La Roche, but Tadoussac remained simply a trading post where the French had even given up spending the winter. Chauvin's fortunes had been no happier than La Roche's.

Since no progress was being made, and this enterprise of "discovery and inhabitation of the lands and realms of Canada" must needs be "strengthened and pressed forward," in the autumn of 1602 Henry IV authorized the merchants of Rouen to join forces with Chauvin. New France remained Normandy's preserve, for the Communauté of St Malo was still excluded from its commerce. On December 21, 1602, the St Malo merchants resolved to protest to the Parlement of Rennes and to the King. Henry IV's reply was encouraging; it was to hasten the colonization of Canada, declared the King, that he had granted permission to the citizens of Rouen to join with Chauvin, and in so doing it had not been his intention to deny the rights of the St Malo merchants, who had long traded in Canada and who knew its "peoples, customs, shores and dwelling places"; for this reason, he continued, the first President of Normandy, Vice-Admiral de Chaste and the Sieur de La Cour would be at Rouen at the end of January to meet there with the merchants of St Malo, "so that all might confer more fully on the most prompt and suitable expedients for the accomplishment of such a useful and praiseworthy purpose, assuring therewith profit, security and contentment for all our good subjects." And so on January 3, 1603, the merchants of St Malo were invited to come to Rouen to meet Chauvin and his new associates. Since Chauvin could not alone provide for "the discovery and inhabitation of the Province of Canada," as the invitation reads, it was the King's wish that the citizens of Rouen and St Malo should join with him. Pending the conclusions to be reached at this meeting, no ship going to Canada would be allowed to go "further than Gaspay."[32]

Thus, as Henry IV was preparing to send a commissioner to Sable Island to see what had been done there and estimate the chances of success, a decision was made to promote the colonization of Canada with the formation of a company on a much larger scale, in which Chauvin and the merchants of Rouen and St Malo would be in partnership. In this we see an active policy of colonization, for whose realization the biggest problem was finding powerful financial backing.

For the merchants, of course, colonization would entail additional expenditure; Chauvin's future associates would be obliged to contribute to costs which they judged would be unproductive as far as their commerce was concerned. The Communauté of St Malo backed away in this month of January 1603, letting their claims drop and giving as their reason "the small worth of the returns from the said Canadian trade to this city in general."[33] They would deprive themselves of business rather than bear any of the costs of colonization. Henry IV was thus denied badly-needed support for his colonial program. Chauvin and his Rouen associates were left alone to carry it out, but Chauvin died soon afterwards, probably in February of 1603.[34]

Chauvin's role in America over three years may well appear to have been a complete failure. The tiny dwelling he built at Tadoussac had been insufficient to spend even one winter in; far from becoming the heart of an empire, Tadoussac remained no more than a trading post, and a mere place of seasonal barter at that. No progress had been made in discovery, either. Champlain blames the failure on Chauvin's Protestantism,[35] but religion is no explanation; there is not a single document that alludes to religious dissent within Chauvin's enterprise. The valid explanation lies in the slimness of Chauvin's means. His resources were dependent on the success of his trade and fishing. Henry IV, who had the colonization of Canada at heart, understood this very well, but his efforts to unite the Rouen and St Malo merchants in support of Chauvin's enterprise had failed, and Chauvin's death put an end to it before it could be known whether or not the support of the Rouen merchants alone would have given it greater scope. The dilemma of 1588 remained: either a colony sustained by an exclusive monopoly, or free trade and no colony.

In spite of all, Chauvin's role as an initiator was an important one. The port he chose, Tadoussac, remained the sole maritime port of the St Lawrence for the next thirty years. Above all, his efforts marked an important milestone; since Roberval's time and in the wake of the hapless Brazil, Florida and Sable Island ventures, he was the first to return to the St Lawrence with constructive intent. It was through Chauvin that the French effectively resumed their occupation of the great valley discovered by Jacques Cartier more than half a century earlier.

CHAPTER 5

A Reassessment of the St Lawrence

1603

Since 1543 there had been many changes in the great valley of the St Lawrence.

In the time of Cartier and Roberval, the valley was the domain of the Iroquois, with their settlements on the strategic island of Hochelaga and at Achelacy, Stadacona and a number of small neighbouring villages. Through their somewhat loose confederacy, the Iroquois controlled the entire river down to the Gulf, where they would go from Stadacona and perhaps other settlements to fish.

When the French returned a half century later the whole picture in the St Lawrence had changed. The river banks were deserted, or very nearly; in 1603 Champlain met a few natives near Ile aux Lièvres, and below Ile aux Coudres he noted on the north shore a little river where the Indians sometimes came and camped in huts; opposite the Isle of Orleans he observed Algonquins similarly camped, and at the mouth of the Riche- lieu River there were the huts of other Indians.[1] All were nomadic; there were no longer any fixed settlements. Champlain saw not a single in- habitant when he arrived at Quebec. He makes no reference to the old Stadacona nor to Achelacy. When he came to the St Louis Rapids, not once did he write the name Hochelaga, or Tutonaguy either. The former masters of the St Lawrence had gone. When Champlain speaks of the Iroquois, he locates them far to the southwest, near Lake Ontario and Lake Champlain.

How did all this come about? The voyagers of those times are mute on the subject, and their silence is disconcerting; from 1543 to 1603, there is not a shred of information to enlighten us on this upheaval in the ethnic and political structure of the St Lawrence. From Jacques Noël, who came to the St Lawrence in 1585, saw the ruins of forts built by his uncle, Jacques Cartier, and travelled up the river as far as Hochelaga, we have no clue whatever. He does not even reveal whether or not the natives he saw were the same ones that Cartier had known forty years earlier.

71

Perhaps the upheaval had already begun at that time, or perhaps it was already complete. It seems most likely that it occurred fairly soon after the voyages of Cartier and Roberval. Champlain is said to have reported that "old hands in the country" had never seen anything of Hochelaga, and according to Lescarbot, who published his work in 1618, the French who "today haunt" the St Lawrence "understand nothing" of the glossary prepared by Cartier on "the language of Canada." And yet between Cartier and Lescarbot only half a century had gone by! On the other hand, there may be reason to believe that the revolution was of later date, possibly about 1600; in 1608, Lescarbot used the expression "a few years ago."

Was this change due to war? That is Champlain's view. Lescarbot writes that the Iroquois were taken by surprise "in their enclosure" by an enemy force of eight thousand, who destroyed them. The author of the Jesuit *Relation* of 1644 reports that the Algonquins had defeated their Iroquois enemies everywhere and become their masters. In a memorandum of 1697, La Chesnaye recounts the tradition that the Algonquins "had driven the Iroquois from the site and vicinity of Quebec, which was once their dwelling-place; we were shown their villages and hamlets all covered with new growth." This is a likely explanation. Even in Cartier's day the Iroquois were beset by the Toudamans, who killed about two hundred of their people in 1534 on an island opposite the mouth of the Saguenay. They also were constantly at war with the Agojudas, who were "armed to the very fingers" and wore armour "of cords and wood, lashed and woven together."[2]

Or was it simply that the Iroquois had migrated, rather than being exterminated by their enemies? It was the custom of the Iroquois nations, as with others, to move their settlements at varying intervals once the soil had been exhausted. Driven by economic imperatives and perhaps by an increasing need for security, the Iroquois may have chosen to retire to the interior to be among other peoples of their language and culture.

According to a recent hypothesis, the disappearance of the Laurentian Iroquois was due to the formation to a league between the Algonquins of the Ottawa River, the Montagnais of the Saguenay and the Etchemins of the south shore, an alliance which was consolidated well before 1603. Since Cartier's day, the St Lawrence had become a magnificent fur market for the French. Their suppliers were the hunting peoples, Algonquins, Etchemins and Montagnais, for whom the water route was blocked by the sedentary nation of Laurentian Iroquois. Hochelaga presented a barrier that was reinforced by the existence of Achelacy and Stadacona. To escape the control of the Iroquois, the hunting peoples resorted to two long by-passes involving portages, the Algonquin route by way of the Gatineau, and the route up the St Maurice to the Lac St Jean basin and thence down-river to Tadoussac. Moreover, bartered European commodities

were quickly distributed among the allies and even, through the Algonquins, as far as the lands of the Hurons; among these commodities there
was iron, which was available to the nations of the league from the sixteenth century onward and was to serve them well both in defence and
attack. The league, controlling the entire hinterland of the St Lawrence
and becoming increasingly powerful through the use of European equipment, may have gained the upper hand, ultimately destroying the Iroquois
of Stadacona and Hochelaga or forcing their migration.[3]

Whatever the reason, the St Lawrence Valley had regained a certain
political unity. With the league of Montagnais, Etchemins and Algonquins, which had the armed support of the Micmacs or Souriquois of
Acadia and the Hurons of far-away Georgian Bay, there was a new
hegemony that favoured the French of the seventeenth century. Because
they were nomadic, the nations of the St Lawrence would facilitate European colonization, and because they were counting more and more heavily
on barter with the Europeans, they would be strongly motivated to defend
the valley against attack from the sedentary Iroquois living to the south
of Lake Ontario.

Colonization was on the threshold of a new era. Early in 1603, Henry
IV was striving to bring together the merchants of Rouen and St Malo in
support of Chauvin, the St Lawrence monopoly-holder. He also dispatched
a commissioner to Sable Island to make a precise evaluation of La Roche's
endeavours. From 1603 on, the kings of France were to follow a colonial
policy that became a sustained tradition, and no longer spasmodic.

Following the death of Chauvin, would the St Lawrence monopoly
revert in its entirety to La Roche? At this time, early in 1603, La Roche
was still maintaining Sable Island and was preparing yet another voyage
to carry supplies to his colony. Invoking his letters patent, he still claimed
Tadoussac as part of his domain, but Henry IV did not seem convinced
of the soundness of his work;[4] the King passed him by and chose as successor to Chauvin the man who was to have presided at the meeting of
Rouen and St Malo merchants, Commander Aymar de Chaste.

De Chaste's European career had been impressive; Knight of Malta,
Grand Prior of Auvergne, Commander of Limoges, Grand Master of the
Order of St Lazare, he had been sent to Portugal in 1582 to replace Strozzi,
who had perished in the struggle against Spain. De Chaste came back
defeated, but a hero of knightly combat. In 1586, he seized the island
of Oléron from the Huguenots. As Vice-Admiral of France and Governor
of Dieppe in 1589, he served the cause of the Protestant King Henry IV,
as did Chauvin, Gravé and de Monts. This service was not only military,
since in 1593 de Chaste was the King's creditor to the tune of 93,000
livres. With the war ended, he formed an association of merchants, of

which Gravé was a member. In 1602, he went to England as ambassador extraordinary for Henry IV.[5] An imposing personage, and a Catholic.

For all the importance of the new monopoly-holder, the merchants of St Malo still refused to enter into association with the merchants of Rouen. For them, colonization was a thankless burden. But they continued to claim freedom of trade, by virtue of the discovery of Canada which, they said, had been accomplished "with great expense by their predecessors." For the year 1603, Henry IV permitted them to outfit a vessel which would go and trade in Canada under the command of Captain Gilles Eberard du Coulombier; this ship might even sail in company with the ships of Aymar de Chaste.[6] But the monopoly remained intact.

De Chaste then assembled a company of Rouen merchants alone. As his representative in America, he appointed Gravé, a man who already had a long record of experience in the St Lawrence, and he chartered two ships, the *Bonne-Renommée* and the *Françoise*, the latter still commanded by Captain Jean Girot as in 1598. Jean Sarcel de Prevert of St Malo, an associate of Gravé's, joined the expedition, but aboard his own ship. Gravé left Honfleur on March 15, 1603, just as La Roche was dispatching his last ship to Sable Island.[7]

Aymar de Chaste was never to see his fleet again. He died two months later, even before Gravé had reached Tadoussac. His role had been brief but important. History will remember him as the organizer of the celebrated voyage of 1603, but Canadian geography has preserved his name only in that of a cape, Cap de Chaste, which, moreover, underwent a deformation and is now Cap Chat.

Among the passengers taking ship that month of March 1603 was Samuel de Champlain. He sailed not as lieutenant, as has been written, but, like de Monts in 1600, simply as an observer. According to his own statement, he had been invited by Aymar de Chaste to "see this country, & what its promoters were doing there." De Chaste obtained the necessary permission for him to sail, and Gravé was instructed to "receive him aboard his vessel" and to "show him the country & all that might be possible in these parts."[8] At some thirty years of age, Champlain was feeling out his way for the future.

What had he been doing before 1603?

It is generally calculated that he was born about 1570, or perhaps 1567. Attempts have been made to paint him either as the issue of poor fisherfolk, or as the bastard son of a great family. His marriage contract of 1610 identifies him as the son "of the late Antoine de Champlain, Naval Captain in his lifetime, and of Dame Marguerite Le Roy,"[9] which enlightens us very little; it was easy enough to insert *de* in the name and give titles to parents in a notarial act. Champlain was himself a naval captain, and so had been able to follow in his father's footsteps. We know nothing else about his parents, and the identity of the mysterious "uncle from Provence" who played an important role in Champlain's early career remains to be clarified.

We do not know whether Champlain was baptized a Catholic or a Protestant. His biblical Christian name, which was hardly ever given in Saintonge except in Protestant families, and the fact that Brouage, his birthplace, was a Huguenot city at that time, suggest that Champlain was born a Protestant. That he opposed the Catholic League means little, for opposition to the League was common to monarchists both Catholic and Protestant. Nor does his choice of a Protestant wife prove anything. But though he may have been born a Protestant, he very soon became a Catholic, like the Jesuit Paul Le Jeune, who was born a Huguenot and became a Catholic upon attaining his majority. Whatever the case, Champlain was a Catholic when he began his Canadian career in 1603, and the doctrine which he expounded to the Indians of Tadoussac was the Catholic doctrine.[10]

Was he a nobleman? Probably not by birth, but in certain legal documents, the earliest in 1615, and in the official list of the Hundred Associates of 1627, which was drawn up before the King had issued the Company twelve letters of nobility to be conferred on Associates who were commoners, Champlain was styled *écuyer*, a title borne by gentlemen of the lowest rank of nobility.[11] It could be concluded that he was elevated to the nobility before 1615, probably in 1612, when he became the lieutenant of a viceroy; it is most unlikely that a Bourbon de Condé would have considered being represented in New France by a commoner invested with extensive powers which theoretically only a noble might properly wield. This is a hypothesis which only the discovery of new documentation will substantiate.

Of his early career, we know little for certain. He may have practised the art of painting or draftsmanship, a most valuable one for a geographer. Champlain was indeed an excellent draftsman. He must have begun to go to sea at an early age, since he told the Queen in 1613 that he had been attracted to the art of navigation since his "early childhood." He stated in 1632 that he had served in Henry IV's army against the League until 1598, with the rank of *maréchal-des-logis*, or billeting officer. When the Spanish troops maintained by Philip II in Brittany set sail from Port Blavet (today Port Louis, in the department of Morbihan), Champlain went with them. From Spain, according to what he told the King in 1630 and repeated in 1632, he undertook a voyage to the West Indies which kept him away for two years and a half. His presence was noted in Cadiz in July 1601; after that he returned to France, and at Court enjoyed a pension granted to him by the King. It was then that he came tò know Commander de Chaste, and to be invited by him to sail with Gravé.[12] In 1603,

Champlain was still an enigmatic figure, and his presence on this voyage might have passed unnoticed if he had not published his account of it— the only account we have.

On the 7th of May, Aymar de Chaste's expedition, led by Gravé, was in sight of Newfoundland. On the 20th it arrived at Anticosti Island and the next day, after sighting "Gachepé," entered the St Lawrence River and sailed up it as far as Bic, from where it crossed the river to Tadoussac, finally arriving on May 26.[13]

A league from there, on Pointe St Mathieu (today Pointe aux Alouettes), some hundred Indians were holding a "tabagie" or feast presided over by Chief Anadabijou. One of the Indians brought back from France by Gravé told them of "the excellent reception that the King had accorded them & the good treatment that they had received in France," the "fine Castles, Palaces, houses & peoples that they had seen, & our way of life." The King, this Indian assured his countrymen, "wished them well, & desired to people their land, & bring peace with their enemies (who are the Irocois) or else to send forces to conquer them." Anadabijou declared that he was delighted to have the King "as his great friend" and would be very happy for him to people the country and make war on his enemies. Then there was dancing to celebrate a recent victory over the Iroquois, and afterwards all the Indians, numbering about a thousand (Algonquins, Etchemins and Montagnais), went to Tadoussac with their birchbark canoes laden with furs.[14]

During the trading, from May 26 to June 18, Champlain studied the Indians at his leisure. On June 11, he took time to go twelve or fifteen leagues up the Saguenay, visiting in particular that part which resembled more a fjord than a river. The Indians described to him a "mightily impetuous torrent of water" from which this river flowed, a torrent preceded by eighteen falls and rapids, beyond which one could reach a great lake fed by rivers. Here, already, was the entire hydrographic plan of the Kingdom of Saguenay with its principal falls (Arvida-Shipshaw) and Lac St Jean. Beyond the sources of these rivers that emptied into the lake, the Indians told him, there were other lakes. By these water routes, the nations of the north came down to trade beaver and marten skins with the Montagnais in exchange for what the Montagnais had obtained from the French. These nations of the north, according to the Indians, were "within sight of a salt-water sea." Instead of concluding immediately that this must be the Asian Sea, as other travellers might in their eagerness have done, Champlain wrote, with startling assurance, "it is some gulf of this sea [the Atlantic] whose waters enter from the North into the lands, & in truth it can be nothing else."[15]

Champlain, probably the first explorer to penetrate so far up the Saguenay, thus notes two factors of great importance for an understanding of this part of the New World: on the one hand the existence of a salt-water sea which was not the Asian Sea, and on the other hand the route followed by the nations of the north to come down to trade with the Montagnais, a commercial route which, it would seem, had been established for some considerable time.

On June 18, with the "tabagie" and trading over, Gravé set out up the river which Champlain still called Rivière de Canada, as Cartier had done. Gravé intended to go by boat as far as the St Louis Rapids. Until then he had never been beyond Trois Rivières, although he had wanted to push further upstream in 1600. Champlain went with him. On this journey up the St Lawrence in 1603, however, Champlain made no discoveries; what was new to him was not new to other Frenchmen of his time. For half a century the river as far as Hochelaga had been represented cartographically with fair accuracy.

On June 22, they dropped anchor "at Quebec which is a strait of the said *rivière de Canadas.*" Quebec was an Indian name for a narrowing, and its usage had been confirmed by the Levasseur map two years earlier. Here Champlain's observations are geographic generalities: if the land were cultivated, it would be as good as that of France; like Cartier, he saw "diamonds in the slate rocks, which are better than those of Alançon." Convinced that Cartier's establishment had been further upstream, he was not dabbling in historical reminiscence, nor was he thinking of any project for the future; the site impressed him, but that was all. Besides, the stop was brief; Gravé was on familiar ground here, and he pushed on upstream the following morning.

Champlain noted some rapids which one day would bear the name of Richelieu (between Deschambault and Lotbinière), and then Trois Rivières, "where the climate begins to moderate, the weather being somewhat different to that of Ste Croix." It is here that the future pioneer begins to reveal his exceptional qualities. An island "which faces the channel" of the river and commands the neighbouring islands draws his attention, and he writes, "This would be in my judgement a place suitable for habitation, & could be quickly fortified, for its situation is strong in itself, & close to a large lake." This is the first time since his arrival in North America that Champlain mentions habitation, but the habitation he had in mind would be related to the trade in furs. By paddling up the river that emptied here (the St Maurice today), it would be possible, with portages, to reach the lake from which the Saguenay springs (Lac St Jean), and from there to arrive at Tadoussac; a settlement at Trois Rivières would be "a boon for the freedom of several nations who dare not pass that way, for fear of the Irocois, their enemies, who hold all this River of Canada in their grasp: but [were the place] inhabited, the said Irocois & the other Savages could be brought to friendship; or at the very least, under the protection of this habitation, the said Savages would come freely without fear & danger." As it happened, Champlain was to establish his settlement first of all on the strait of Quebec; upon his order, a fort would be built at Trois Rivières by Laviolette twenty-six years later.

An expedition up the St Maurice was brought to a halt before "a very narrow fall of water," and the voyage up the St Lawrence was resumed. On June 29, the Feast of St Peter, the French entered the lake previously called Angoulême, which on Champlain's initiative was to become Lac St Pierre. Champlain noted rivers that he did not name and also thirty small islands at the head of the lake. He also entered the "Rivière des Irocois" (today the Richelieu River) which he was anxious to examine, because it was from there that the Iroquois invaded the St Lawrence. A band of Montagnais on their way to make war on the Iroquois had erected a palisade reaching from the St Lawrence to the smaller river for the protection of their canoes. Beginning in a long-boat and then changing to a skiff, Champlain went up the river, but rapids prevented him from going further than the site of the present village of St Ours. The Indians gave him a good description of the country further upstream: the Chambly Rapids, the river which led through many islands to Lake Champlain and Lake George, "at the end of which are camped the Irocois," and another river (in which we recognize the Hudson) whose mouth was "some hundred or hundred and forty leagues away" on the Atlantic coast, still called the "coast of Florida."

Finally, on July 3, 1603, "sailing before the wind," Gravé's party came in sight of the St Louis Rapids. This country was new for him as well as for Champlain. "We at once made ready our skiff, which had been specially constructed for passing these rapids." Gravé and Champlain took their places in it, a number of Indian guides took to a canoe, and thus they arrived at the foot of the rapids, but not without difficulty; "never have I seen a torrent of water rage with such violence [. . .] there is a marvellous seething from the force & tumbling of the water as it passes this cataract." The obstacle was a formidable one; "to carry the boats is a task which may not be done in such brief time." But it would be possible to go beyond with canoes and "see all that might be possible, good or bad, in a year or two."[16]

For the moment, the explorers must be content with putting questions to the Indians. Cartier had been there in 1535 and again in 1541, but without interpreters. In 1603, Indians who could be understood gave the French the first description of the *pays d'en haut* that clearly corresponded with reality.

Beyond the rapids, the Indians explained, there was a first lake, into which emptied "a river which led to the home of the Algoumequins," sixty leagues away. This was the Ottawa River, on which, 65 leagues from its mouth, was the land of the Algonquins. This first lake, into which this tributary emptied, was separated from another lake further up the main river by more rapids; here we recognize Lake St Francis. Still more rapids and then a lake 80 or 150 leagues long; this was our Lake Ontario, which is in reality about 65 leagues long. Above this last lake there was a cataract "of some height" (the first allusion in Canadian literature to Niagara Falls) and then a second large lake of about 60 leagues in length; this was Lake Erie which is in fact 83 leagues long. Above this, a strait and then another great lake whose water was "*mauvaise*"; Lake Huron. The guides had not seen the end, because they had gone no further; "so big is it, that they will not risk putting out into its midst." Champlain thought that this lake whose water was undrinkable and whose end was unknown might be the *mer du Su* or Asian Sea.

During the return journey, the expedition met with some well-travelled Algonquins who provided further details. The last great lake (Lake Huron) was to the northwest. From the north shore of the first great lake (Lake Ontario), where the water never froze over, there emptied a river by which the Algonquins came from the interior. This would be the River Trent, which, with portages, would communicate with Rice Lake, Lake Simcoe, and Georgian Bay. From south of this first great lake came a river from the land of the Iroquois (the Oswego River or Black River), by way of which the Iroquois and Algonquins made war upon each other. The country of the Iroquois was very fertile; there was "corn aplenty" and other fruits of the land which the Algonquins did not have. A nation known as the *bons Irocois* (this would be the Hurons, who were related to the Iroquois) were in the habit of coming among the Algonquins to buy French merchandise from them. According to these "good Iroquois," there was a mine of pure copper in the north country. Champlain took due note of the divergences in the information provided (water which was salt or not, distances which were longer or shorter), and he concluded that the great expanse of water whose end the Indians had not seen could only be "*la mer du Su*, the Sun setting where they say it does."[17]

Even though the French of 1603, like Cartier, were unable to overcome the obstacle of the St Louis Rapids for lack of time, their understanding of the geography of the country took an immense step forward, a step which might have been attained in 1535 if only Cartier had had his interpreters with him. The entire upper St Lawrence system was taking shape, with proportions that were remarkably close to reality. And there was the further revelation of a great trade route existing above the site of the former village of Hochelaga; French goods that the Algonquins acquired by barter in the St Lawrence were finding their way up the Ottawa River into the land of the Hurons. The sixteenth century had barely come to a close and already European articles, mostly made of metal, were reaching the natives of the interior some fifteen hundred miles from the Atlantic coast.

Immediately after their return to Tadoussac on July 11, Gravé and Champlain set out for Gaspé, where they stayed from the 15th to the 19th, no doubt to lay in a provision of fish. During these few days of respite, Champlain was able to obtain a general impression of the area: Gaspé Bay, the river emptying into it, the Baie des "Molues," Ile Perçée and the Ile de "Bonne adventure," all places where there was fishing, "both dry and green." From the Indians he obtained information on parts of the country that he was not able to see for himself: the Baie de Chaleur, haunt of a "frightful monster," the Gougou; up a river flowing into this bay, a lake where there could be found "in the earth, a foot or a foot & a half deep, a manner of metal" resembling silver; and a way from this river to another, the Matane, which emptied into the St Lawrence. The Indians spoke to Champlain about the Souriquois River (flowing into the Bay of Fundy) where the St Malo mariner Sarcel de Prevert had gone with the Indian chief Secoudon from the St John River in search of a copper mine "near the sea on the South side," probably at Cap d'Or, at the entry of the Bassin des Mines or Minas Basin. They also spoke of the Ile St Laurent (our Cape Breton), where the Souriquois or Micmacs spent the winter, of the coast of Acadia which, when followed, would lead into a bay (the Bay of Fundy), "which adjoins the said copper mine," and of the river (the St John River) which emptied into that bay and by way of which the Indians of Acadia would go to make war on the Iroquois.[18]

A land rich in promise for its minerals, this Acadia, according to Champlain. There was a high mountain jutting out over the sea, "brilliant in the light of the Sun, where there are quantities of verdigris which comes from the said copper mine" and from which fell pieces of copper; lower down toward the coast of Acadia, a "mountain of black pigment, with which the Savages paint themselves"; then an island where "a manner of metal" was to be found which was neither tin nor lead, but which resembled silver. Prevert had given the Souriquois wedges and chisels so that they might bring him pieces from the mines the following year. In the lands of the Almouchiquois (on the coast of Maine), there were other mines, but there the Souriquois would not dare to go unless accompanied by the French to drive off their enemies. Champlain makes efforts to fix, hypothetically, the positions of these places spoken of by Prevert, adding, "All this country is very beautiful, & flat, where are found all the kinds of trees that we saw on our way to the first cataract of the great River of Canada."[19]

As he considered Prevert's description of the Acadian coast, Champlain's thoughts turned to the major preoccupation of the century before, the quest for a passage to Asia. The Indian interpreters had talked to him of a great lake beyond the St Louis Rapids which might perhaps be the Asian Sea, but Champlain began to hope that it might be more easily accessible from the Atlantic coast. "It would be a great benefit to find in the coast of Florida some passage which would lead close to this great salt-water lake, both for the navigation of vessels, which would not be subject to so many perils as they are in Canada, & for the shortening of the route by more than three hundred leagues."[20]

In Acadia there was beautiful countryside, with beautiful trees. These could be found in the St Lawrence, too, but Acadia offered many mines and perhaps a faster route to the Asian sea. Acadia might be an alternative to the St Lawrence, where navigation was long and difficult and where there were so many conflicts. In 1603 it was Acadia rather than the St Lawrence that intrigued Champlain.

On July 19, Gravé and Champlain left Ile Perçée to return to Tadoussac, but because of bad weather they spent some time visiting the north shore of the Gulf from Sept Iles upstream. On August 3, there was a great feast at Tadoussac, led by Chief Begourat, to celebrate a victory won in the land of the Iroquois. Montagnais women danced naked before the French and staged a mock battle in the water, beating at each other with paddles. With this delightful scene to remember, Gravé and Champlain left Tadoussac once more on August 16 and rejoined Prevert at Ile Perçée two days later.[21] Five years would go by before Champlain again set foot in these parts.

CHAPTER 6

The Search for an Ideal Location on the Atlantic

1604–1607

At the beginning of the seventeenth century, few of the countries of Europe still had any chance of establishing themselves on the American continent north of Florida. Already eliminated were Norway, Denmark, Italy, and the countries of the Holy Roman Empire. The remaining competitors were Holland, England, France, Spain and Portgual.

In the fifteenth and sixteenth centuries, Spain and Portugal had astounded the world; they had leapt to an unforeseen and impressive lead in exploration which ensured to each of them, by the Demarcation Line of 1493, possession of half the non-Christian territories of the globe. Before the end of the sixteenth century, however, Portugal had slipped far behind in the race for occupation of North America. For want of an heir to her throne, she had been joined to Spain since 1580; her strength sapped, besides, by her prodigious efforts of earlier years, she had long since lost interest in North America. But what of Spain? To all outward appearances, she remained a major and magnificent power. Already possessed of a rich empire stretching from Central America over three quarters of South America and across the Pacific to the Philippines, she had also gained sway over the immense Portuguese dominions in Brazil, Africa and the East Indies. In Europe she possessed Sardinia, Sicily, the Kingdom of Naples and a number of Italian dukedoms. The seventeen provinces of the Netherlands were under her protectorate. But the picture from within was less rosy. Since the death of Philip II, Spain had been in decline; at home she was suffering the effects of inflation, and the revenues of her colonies no longer made up the deficits. She could no longer seek to expand in North America, and the colonial powers therefore ceased to have anything to fear from her north of Florida. In 1598, in fact, by a secret clause of the Treaty of Vervins, she had granted freedom of action to France beyond a so-called Friendship Line which passed through the westernmost of the Canary Islands.

Thus there remained in the race only three Atlantic countries: Holland, England, and France.

The northern provinces of the Netherlands had as yet neither the unity nor the independence they were to achieve in 1648. They were still under the protectorate of Spain, but, led by their *stadhouder*, Prince Maurice, they continued a struggle for liberty that had begun long before. Holland- ers and Zeelanders provided maritime transport for the Spaniards, whom they supplied with wheat, but they also, in spite of Spain, carried on a brisk trade in the Mediterranean; they sailed northern seas that had hitherto been inaccessible; they followed the Portuguese spice routes and, on March 20, 1602, they founded their East India Company. North America had as yet seen neither explorers nor merchants from the Netherlands, but both were soon to make their presence known.

As for England and France, both were now ripe for colonial endeavour. During the sixteenth century, each had carried out methodical exploration, a necessary preliminary. Both of them, and the Netherlands too, were entering the golden age of mercantilism.

Under the autocratic Queen Elizabeth, England had overcome the great political and military crises of the sixteenth century, while her mariners, already of legendary reputation, went forth in search of a passage to Asia in the icy reaches of the American continent or plundered riches in the Spanish Indies. Merchants of London and other cities joined in companies of "Merchant Adventurers" who supplied capital for voyages afar. At this point England was favoured with a most happy combination of circum- stances. James I, who as James VI of Scotland already had eighteen years' experience in ruling a kingdom, succeeded to the throne of England and took up the reins of one of the best-governed states of Europe; the Irish wars had just come to an end, and in 1604 a treaty terminated the conflict between England and Spain. For the kingdom of James I, twenty years of peace were in store. Secure at home and powerful at sea, England was manifestly ready to strike root in North America.

At the beginning of the century the situation for France, too, was excel- lent. To the threat of being overrun by Spain, France had replied with a victorious internal union of Catholics and Protestants. The Huguenot King Henry IV espoused Catholicism in 1593, proclaimed the Edict of Nantes in 1598, and won back his kingdom from Spain, the Netherlands, and those powerful families who had carved out independent domains within the kingdom during its long period of disintegration. France was once again firmly united. To the task of restoring her to full health in every sense, Henry IV, with the help of Sully, gave himself with astonish- ing energy, and by 1603 France was again becoming a major economic power. Now she was ready to reassert her historic rights in North Amer- ica. At the end of 1603, moreover, the entire continent, with the exception of Florida, was still unoccupied by European powers; the New France of 1524 was still there for the taking.

In the autumn of 1603, the Protestant Pierre Du Gua de Monts, who had come to Tadoussac in 1600, took charge of French colonization. On October 31, the Admiral of France granted him a commission as Vice-Admiral and, on November 8, Henry IV granted him, as his Lieutenant-General, authority over all the territory between the 40th parallel and the 46th (the latitude of Cape Race) and a ten-year monopoly of trade with the Indians on the Atlantic coast and on both shores of the St Lawrence.[1]

While private investors were entirely at liberty to associate themselves with this new monopoly, they hung back from committing themselves to a colonial enterprise whose costs looked as though they would run higher than the estimated profits; the King therefore reduced to sixty from the originally envisaged one hundred the number of persons to be taken to America. A number of merchants of Rouen (headquarters for the enterprise), St Malo, La Rochelle and St Jean de Luz signed up for at least the first two voyages, and from them the company obtained a capital of 90,000 livres.[2] No more ambitious project, nor one backed by greater resources, would materialize before that of the Hundred Associates in 1627.

Swayed, no doubt, by Champlain's account published in 1603, de Monts turned to Acadia in 1604 in search of a location embodying all the ideal conditions for colonization: proximity to the sea, friendly Indians, plentiful mining, fertility of soil, and a nearby waterway which might possibly lead toward Asia.

The company's fleet of three ships[3] set sail early in March, 1604.[4] With it sailed de Monts, his Catholic lieutenant François Gravé, Jean de Biencourt de Poutrincourt, a gentleman who was soon to play an important role, and Champlain, who was to act as geographer but carried no official title or instructions. The spiritual needs of the expedition were provided for; there were two Catholic priests, one, whose name is unknown, who was to spend the winter in Acadia, and the other Nicolas Aubry, who was travelling for his own pleasure; for the Protestants there was at least one minister, of unknown identity. As for the common folk aboard in 1604, we have no precise information; of the minimum of sixty persons that de Monts was pledged to take to Acadia, how many were the vagabonds whose conscription had been authorized we do not know.

After touching land at Port au Mouton, where he waited three weeks for Gravé's ship to join him,[5] de Monts sent Champlain to pick out a spot for a temporary settlement, pending the choice of a permanent site. Champlain sailed down the coast, doubled Cape Sable and found a harbour in St Mary's Bay where their largest vessel might be anchored in safety.[6] He led the expedition to this spot, but since it would have taken too long to fortify, they decided to look elsewhere. Leaving this bay on June 16 through Long Island Strait, de Monts set out in a pinnace to examine the great bay to which he gave the name Baie Française, today the Bay of Fundy. Not far up the coast, the party came upon a bay which Champlain described as "one of the most beautiful harbours that I have seen in all these coasts, where two thousand vessels could [shelter] in safety." This large bay with its magnificent valley stretching away toward the north was indeed "the most pleasant & appropriate [place] for habitation that we have set eyes upon"; Champlain named it Port Royal.[7] Poutrincourt, even more captivated than the others, asked that it be conceded to him in seigneury, which was done on August 31 of that year.[8]

Having explored this bay and fifteen leagues up the valley, however, de Monts still insisted on pursuing the search. He continued to the end of the Baie Française, hoping to find the mines of which Prevert had heard tell in 1603, and here entered Chignecto Bay.[9] Then, turning toward the south, he sailed along the coast of what is now New Brunswick, carefully noting the location of iron mines all the way. The mouth of a river, "the biggest & deepest that we have yet seen," received the name Rivière St Jean because the day was June 24, the feast of St John the Baptist; there a cross was raised.[10] Further to the south, the ship entered a large bay, later called Passamaquoddy, where there was "so great a quantity of islands, that we scarce could know the number, & of very fair appearance." Into this bay emptied a river which was half a league wide at its mouth; this river, then called Rivière des Etchemins, was later to receive the name Ste Croix, because of its form.

Making its way up this watercourse, four miles from its mouth, the expedition saw a small island in the middle of the river, about half a mile from the shore. Here, wrote Champlain, on instruction from de Monts, was "the place that we judged the best, for its situation, goodly country, & for the communication that we would have with the savages of these coasts & of the interior of these lands." The island was "of sound disposition, & the soil about very good, the climate mild.[11] This island had definite advantages; it would have any vessel sailing up the river at its mercy, and also had a small landlocked harbour. However, being still little acquainted with America, the Europeans had overlooked a number of serious shortcomings. It would be necessary, wrote Lescarbot, "at every hour of the day, morning, noon and night, to cross with great effort a large expanse of water in order to bring such things as might be needed from the mainland"; an island, he added, "is not appropriate to commencing the establishment of a colony," and besides, there was neither fresh water nor firewood there.[12] The same mistake was being made, then, that had been made by Villegaignon in the bay of Rio de Janeiro; the same mistake that had been made by La Roche with his isolated colony on Sable Island. The Europeans still had a lot to learn.

De Monts brought his principal vessel from St Mary's Bay and the moving-in was begun. Having installed a battery of cannon on the southern point, he erected on the northern part of the island a fort consisting of three buildings inside a palisade. Other living quarters were built outside the fort proper, and all these structures, fort and lodgings, were grouped about an open space. The men did not live only on the island; more fertile soil was to be found on the west bank of the river, and there they were later to build a mill and prepare charcoal. Land would be cleared even further afield for cultivation; three leagues upstream, near some rapids (today called St Stephen) on the western branch of the river, the soil would be tilled and grain would ripen.[13]

At the end of August, de Monts sent his ships back to France with Gravé and Poutrincourt, while he himself stayed behind to spend the winter with some seventy-nine others.[14]

Champlain, having searched in vain for mines around Chignecto Bay,[15] set out on September 2 for the Norembègue country. Ste Croix Island was still only a makeshift, and a site for a permanent settlement remained to be found. This voyage was to last a month.[16]

Until this time, the French in Acadia had been in communication only with the Souriquois, also called Micmacs, who lived by hunting in the Acadian peninsula and on Cape Breton and the Gaspé Peninsula. On their arrival at the Pentagouët River (today the Penobscot) they were to form an alliance with another ethnic group, the Etchemins. Called Etchemins, Pentagouëts, Penobscots (by the English) and also Malecites, these Indians of the Algonquian linguistic family lived along this coast without distinguishable boundaries between one tribe and another. In the style of their huts, their fur clothing and their nomadic life, they resembled the Souriquois. Chiefs Bessabez and Cabahis received Champlain with cordiality, and Champlain invited them to make peace with the Souriquois and the "Canadiens," adding that de Monts wished to "inhabit their land, & show them how to cultivate it, so that they might no longer lead so miserable a life as they did."[17]

On September 17, Champlain set out for a river called "Quinibequy," but his Indian guides refused to follow him. Hampered by poor weather, he was then obliged to turn back toward Ste Croix, having gone only as far as Pemaquid, in Muscongus Bay, between the Pentagouët and Kennebec rivers. He had examined 150 miles of coastline and penetrated fifty miles into the interior up the Pentagouët. He was not the first to visit this coast, but he was the first to give a sufficiently accurate description of it for us to recognize its features. He came back somewhat disappointed; altogether, he wrote, this coast offered no more than that of Ste Croix.[18]

Then winter came, six months of it, during which three or four feet of snow fell. It was the colonists' misfortune that the winter that year was very severe. Unaccustomed as they were to North American winters, no one had thought to dig cellars, chink cracks in the walls or lay in a plentiful supply of firewood; since they had neither spring nor brook, they were reduced to drinking melted snow; on their daily menu, there was only salted meat.[19]

There was scurvy, too. In the colony of Ste Croix, it was known that Cartier's men had cured themselves with "the herb called Aneda," but what was this herb? The Indians of Acadia did not know the secret, and no remedy could be found. Of the eighty members of the colony, thirty-five or thirty-six were carried off by the illness, another twenty came very close to death, and only about ten remained unaffected.[20]

With the arrival of spring, Gravé came back from France to announce the dispatch of supplies by the company. The disastrous winter had clearly shown the urgency of relocating elsewhere, and de Monts decided to look for a place "of better temperature" to the south.[21] He set out aboard a pinnace accompanied by Champlain and a number of others, including twenty sailors,[22] and reached Pemaquid on July 1, just after the Englishman George Weymouth had departed, having examined the mouth of the Kennebec.

This was the country of the Almouchiquois, of the same Algonquian linguistic family as the Etchemins and the Souriquois. De Monts travelled up the river and made alliances with the chiefs, but the river was dangerous for ships and the country looked poor. The search must be extended further south. De Monts continued his examination of the coast, making alliances with the Indians that he met and observing their customs. Thus, working from one cape to another and from one bay to another, he eventually came to a cape (called Cape Cod by Gosnold in 1602) to which he gave the name Cap Blanc; he rounded this promontory and on the other side of the isthmus he found a harbour, which received the uninspiring name of Mallebarre. On July 25, after having covered some four hundred miles but being by now short of supplies, the expedition was obliged to turn back toward Ste Croix.[23] Along this coast, where a flourishing New England was to take root twenty years later, de Monts had not found his ideal spot for colonization; where the country was attractive and the climate pleasant, he judged the coast to be of difficult access, or else it was the soil itself which was unpromising, or again the Indians did not appear sufficiently reliable.

Since the first winter on Ste Croix Island had been disastrous, de Monts decided to transport his colonists to the other side of the bay, to Port Royal, until such time as he should "make more ample discovery." Gravé and Champlain chose a spot of some elevation on the north shore of the basin, "opposite the island which is at the entrance" of the Rivière de l'Equille, later the Rivière du Dauphin. To speed the building, the houses of Ste

Croix were dismantled and reassembled at Port Royal. This time a more practical plan was adopted; instead of the buildings being scattered, there was a closed quadrangle which would be protected by a gun-platform armed with four cannon at the southwest corner. Gardens were made on the outside.[24] For the French there was the added advantage of having as neighbours a large band of Souriquois who dwelt sometimes on the nearby St Mary's Bay and sometimes on the bay of Port Royal itself. This group's loyalty to the French was to be unswerving. Their chief was Membertou, a man "of prodigious size, and taller and stronger-limbed than most, bearded like a Frenchman" while "not one of the others had hair on his chin"; according to local legend, he was more than a hundred years old, and he claimed to have seen Jacques Cartier.[25]

With the colony re-established at Port Royal (but only until a spot could be found south of Cape Cod), de Monts decided to return to France to report to the King and obtain "what would be needed for his enterprise." Gravé became commander of the colony, and some forty men were left to spend the winter with him.[26]

Not much of note came to pass, that winter of 1605-6 at Port Royal. Scurvy again took its toll, but the losses were less severe than at Ste Croix. Between six and twelve colonists perished, among whom were the Catholic priest and the Protestant minister, who were buried in the same grave, "to see whether they could rest in peace together in death, since they were unable to reach agreement in life."[27]

In the spring of 1606, Gravé was prepared to set out in search of a permanent site for the colony to the south, as he had been charged to do by de Monts. However, his departure was delayed by a navigational accident, then he suffered a heart attack, and subsequently his pinnace ran aground and broke to pieces.[28] There was nothing left to do but await the help that was coming from France. In mid-July, when still no help had come, it was decided to leave Port Royal in the care of two French settlers, and to try to return to France aboard fishing boats. On July 24, near Cape Sable, the party met the Sieur de Monts's secretary coming to tell them that supplies and a large number of additional colonists were on their way, and so Gravé and his men turned about and went back to Port Royal. The *Jonas* had just arrived, commanded by Poutrincourt, who had come to take command in Acadia in place of de Monts.[29] He had brought with him the lawyer Marc Lescarbot who, as a poet, was to delight Port Royal with the grace of his pen and who, as a historian, was to leave a most distinguished and important document on Acadia. Among this group of 1606 there came, as volunteers, an apothecary from Paris, Louis Hébert, who was a first cousin of Poutrincourt's, and two natives of Champagne who, like Poutrincourt, came from St Just and were to play an important part in the history of Acadia, namely Claude Turgis de Saint-Etienne et de La

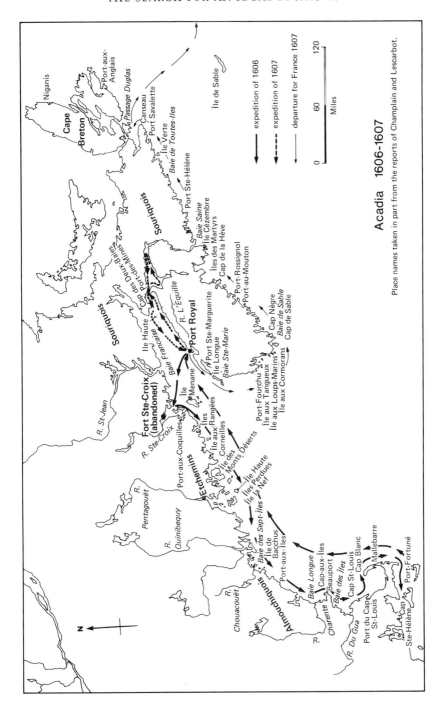

Acadia 1606-1607

Place names taken in part from the reports of Champlain and Lescarbot.

expedition of 1606
expedition of 1607
departure for France 1607

0   60   120
Miles

Tour and his young son Charles, aged about fourteen. The ship had left without a priest, and when it arrived in Acadia it was learned that the only priest that de Monts had left there had died. Presumably there was no priest present throughout the winter of 1606-7. Once again, no women were brought to Acadia.

De Monts, who was no more enthusiastic about Port Royal than about Ste Croix, had requested that the party should search south of Cape Cod for a place that would be "truly habitable." It was agreed that an exploration would be undertaken during the autumn, after the sowing of the crops.[30]

Instead of heading straight for Cape Cod, which should have been the point of departure for this new exploration, time was lost in "re-examining the discoveries" that de Monts had already made, and this is why the expedition, having left Port Royal on September 5, did not arrive at Mallebarre (Nauset Harbor), until October 2. In the month of October, 1606, very late in the season, the planned exploration was therefore only just beginning. From Mallebarre, Poutrincourt rounded the cape and dropped anchor in a harbour on the south coast which, because of the unfortunate incident that followed, was to be called Port Fortuné. This was fine country, with fertile soil, rich fishing grounds and friendliness (at least so it appeared) on the part of the Indians, but the harbour was not deep enough nor its entrance sufficiently safe; yet another place which did not measure up to all the required ideal conditions. Then came a surprise attack from the Indians, which cost the French some losses and obliged Poutrincourt to leave. The famous Refuge (the bay of Rhode Island or Narragansett Bay), where Verrazano had sojourned with such pleasure, was very close; owing to the winds, however, it was impossible even to reach Martha's Vineyard. Poutrincourt decided to return to Port Royal, but before leaving he promised that the following year the French would come to live beyond Mallebarre.[31]

This month and a half of exploration had been almost a total waste of time. Even though a temporary alliance of the Almouchiquois, Etchemins and Souriquois had been achieved, the friendship of the Indians to the south had been lost and the 1605 expedition's exploration had been advanced no more than the width of Cape Cod! This was as far south as the French were ever to go, for all Poutrincourt's promise that they would come back another year to settle further to the south. It was the last French exploration along this coast. The history of New France in these parts thereupon came to an end; the history of New England was about to begin.

Poutrincourt returned to Port Royal on November 14, 1606, heavy-hearted with disappointment, but Lescarbot had prepared a masque to lift his spirits with its merriment: the *Théâtre de Neptune*,[32] "in French rhymes penned in haste." With this play, theatre in North America was born.

That year the colony had the good fortune to enjoy a pleasant winter. There was plenty of food and plenty of wine too, and there was no shortage of fresh meat. In short, wrote Champlain, "we passed this winter most joyously, & fared lavishly." In this atmosphere of geniality, Champlain founded the "Ordre de Bon Temps." There was some scurvy, nevertheless, but its victims this time were few; seven according to Champlain, and only four according to Lescarbot.[33]

Came the spring and the idyllic contentment of the winter gave way to an anxious question: would there be help coming from France? If no ship came, there could be no hope of surviving on the resources of the country alone. The colonists would have to prepare some boats and go to join the fishing fleets. On May 24, 1607, it was not a mighty fleet with de Monts at its head that hove into view, but a small pinnace charged with bringing the news of a catastrophe.[34] The trading privilege had been revoked, mainly because of persistent opposition from Normandy and Brittany.

It had been an illusory monopoly, in any case. The immense preserve had been invaded by everyone. Among the intruders were the Dutch, who had carried off the lion's share of the furs of the St Lawrence in 1606,[35] but by far the greatest number were other Frenchmen. There were even some who were members of de Monts's company. The commercial operations of the associated merchants were supposed to be pooled, in principle, with no activity carried on privately in New France nor profits reaped outside the company. But good faith within the company was far from intact. If certain notarized instruments are to be believed, De Bellois, treasurer of the company, Lieutenant Gravé and (who would have believed it?) de Monts himself had been attempting to defraud the company![36] The methods of gathering furs, besides, were not always of a nature calculated to facilitate relations with the Indians or, consequently, the trade itself. In fact, the conditions under which trade was carried on were at times such as to render "the French name odious and deserving of contempt"; French poachers would even go as far as violating Indian burial grounds to lay their hands on "Beaver skins that these poor folk put over their dead as a last act of kindness upon burial."[37]

In any event, from the spring of 1607, de Monts knew that his monopoly, which would normally have had another seven years to run, had been cut short. An edict of July 17 confirmed the fact and put an end to any remaining hope.[38] The French left Port Royal on August 11 for Canso, leaving to Membertou and his people, along with ten barrels of flour, "possession of the *manoir*, if they wished to use it." During the voyage Champlain renewed his acquaintance with the coast and made "a map [of it] as of the rest." He noted, in particular, "a very sound bay seven or eight leagues long, where there are no islands in the channel save at the end." Here, described for the first time in 1607 and called Baye Saine, with the Rivière Platte which emptied into it, was the future harbour of Halifax.[39] This was Champlain's last look at Acadia, for he never came there again.

By an ironic twist of fate, at the very time that the French were forced to abandon the continent for lack of support, the English were coming to settle permanently in North America. In April 1606, they had founded two great trading companies, the London Company and the Plymouth Company, and had appropriated the entire Atlantic Coast of North America from Acadia (including Port Royal) down to Cape Fear. Their first party of 105 colonists left England in December of 1606, arrived in Chesapeake Bay in April of 1607, and on May 13 stopped at a point a little way up a river and founded Jamestown. A second party set out on May 31, 1607 and, while Poutrincourt and Champlain were spending their last moments at Port Royal, with the rest of the colony waiting at Canso to take ship for France, Raleigh Gilbert and George Popham were on their way to establish a settlement at the mouth of the Kennebec. The forty-five English of the Kennebec River and the 105 colonists of Virginia were the only Europeans to spend that winter of 1607-8 in America north of Florida.

But the years spent by the French in Acadia from 1604 to 1607 had not been an entirely wasted effort. Geographic understanding of the area had made spectacular progress; where the vast peninsula of Acadia had formerly been undefined and confused with the rest of the coast, it was now separated from the continent with the insertion in its proper place of the great bay known today as the Bay of Fundy; there remained only the inland regions of Acadia to be further defined. And the map of Acadia was a French one.

These three years spent by the French in Acadia had made it possible for them to establish a lasting relationship with the Indians. The existence of *sagamis*, each the domain of a *sagamore*, gave the French the advantage of dealing with well-defined groups led by recognized chiefs. The French were sure they had found a land of great promise here. Moreover, Ste Croix and Port Royal had provided them with an invaluable lesson in adaptation; they would never again abandon a colony for reasons of climate. In short, Acadia had lost nothing of its original attraction. For all the obstacles that had confounded de Monts, there was reason to believe that if ever there were to be a New France it would be here in Acadia.

CHAPTER 7

The Return to the St Lawrence

1608–1614

The St Lawrence, forsaken by French officialdom after Roberval's and Cartier's fruitless efforts, had been brought back into the public eye by Champlain in 1603 with the publication of his account of that year's expedition. It was only in 1608, however, that the French returned to the region. Du Gua de Monts had turned his attention to Acadia, hoping to discover an ideal site for colonization, but had found nothing to fulfil all his requirements. The King, moreover, had cut short his ten-year monopoly; in 1608 it had only one year to run. This time, Champlain offered arguments that caused de Monts to revert to the option of the St Lawrence: there would be better protection against European competition, and the country would be easier to defend; the league binding the natives of the valley and their alliance with other nations living on the shores of an inland sea would be advantageous to the French; the fur trade looked more promising there than in Acadia; and then, it was the St Lawrence that offered the best chance of finding a route to Asia. These were Champlain's principal reasons for advising de Monts "to go and settle on the great St Lawrence River."[1]

And so de Monts sent out three ships from Honfleur in April 1608, among them the *Don-de-Dieu*, commanded by Champlain and with a cargo "of the things necessary and appropriate for a habitation."[2] Aboard this ship, it should be noted, was a "young boy," Etienne Brûlé, who was destined for a career as an interpreter.[3] De Monts's company had sent priests on the voyage to Acadia, but there were none on this voyage, even though it was planned to spend the winter in America. Nor were there any women.

Samuel de Champlain was the leader of this entire expedition of 1608. Neither at Tadoussac in 1603 nor in Acadia between 1604 and 1607 had he occupied any superior post. With "his lieutenancy in the country of New France,"[4] de Monts therefore gave him his first position of command in his career in America.

De Monts's men were being sent to the St Lawrence in the expectation
of finding tranquillity, but a rude surprise awaited them at Tadoussac on
June 3. A party of Basques, under the command of a man named Darache,
had established themselves there by force of arms and were carrying on
trade in spite of the ban decreed by Henry IV the preceding January.
When ordered by Gravé to withdraw, they replied with cannons and mus-
kets. Gravé was wounded and was relieved of his arms and munitions. It
was agreed that the dispute should be settled in France,[5] but by then it
was abundantly clear that the truncated monopoly left to de Monts was
an illusory one; since the Basques had already seized control of Tadoussac
(the terminus of the inland fur routes), the fur trade that year could no
longer yield much of value for de Monts.

Champlain travelled up the Saguenay as far as the waterfall above the
present city of Chicoutimi, obtained from the Indians a new description
of the hydrographic system of this region, then returned to Tadoussac
and set out in a pinnace on June 30 "to go to Quebecq."[6] He arrived there
on July 3 and scouted for an appropriate location for his settlement. At the
foot of Cape Diamond where the river narrowed (as the name Quebec
signified), he chose the spot that seemed to him the most practical, where
there was a natural landing-place on the water's edge. The Habitation he
built was no copy of its Acadian predecessors. At Ste Croix the buildings
had been scattered and at Port Royal de Monts had built a quadrangle.
Here, there were three buildings joined by a second-floor gallery; this gallery and a continuous outside wall unified the three buildings into a single
block; around it was a moat which could only be crossed by a drawbridge.
Around the whole, finally, was a palisade to provide the outermost line
of defence to the entire system. Here at Quebec in 1608 was a reproduction
in miniature of a European fortress.[7]

The Quebec enterprise was barely launched when a conspiracy very
nearly ruined it. It would seem that the instigator was a locksmith, Jean
Duval, who, with his eye on a quick and handsome profit, had been
scheming ever since leaving France to deliver the fort of Quebec into the
hands of the Basques or the Spaniards; Darache's victory at Tadoussac had
fitted very nicely into his plan. As it happened, however, one of the con-
spirators went to the pilot Le Testu and confessed everything. The others
were arrested. Three were first condemned to the gallows but were finally
sent back to France for punishment. Duval was hanged, and work on the
Habitation continued with the criminal's head in full view, impaled on
the end of a pike.[8]

All who were not staying for the winter departed on September 18 with
Gravé. The only Europeans left on the continent north of Florida were the
English of Virginia and the twenty-eight French of Quebec. It was this

little band, possessed of not so much as a single rowboat, that was to brave the fifth winter spent by Europeans in the valley of the St Lawrence.

The winter does not seem to have been particularly severe. It was scurvy that turned it into a disaster. The sickness began in February 1609 and lasted into April. Cartier had cured his men with the *annedda*, but the Laurentian natives were of a different ethnic group from those of 1535 and appear to have been ignorant of it. That winter at Quebec, the French were just as defenceless against the scourge as they had been in Acadia. Besides the seven men who died of dysentery, another thirteen were carried off by the scurvy, the surgeon Bonnerme among them. In May 1609, of the twenty-eight Frenchmen left at Quebec in September 1608, there were no more than eight survivors![9]

After Gravé's arrival at the end of May, a voyage of "discovery" in the lands of the Iroquois was agreed upon, a voyage that was to turn into a military excursion. At this point there appeared a party of Algonquins, bringing with them some Indians of a nation that the French had never before encountered. This was the nation of the Ouendats, who shared the same culture and virtually the same language as the Iroquois. The French called them Hurons because of the way they wore their hair, which resembled the bristly ridge of the boar's head (*hure*).[10] These Hurons, who dominated trade between nations on the Great Lakes, had long been anxious to enter into an alliance with the French, whose merchandise they had known since the preceding century.

With an alliance concluded at Quebec, the planned expedition was taken up once more. At the mouth of the Richelieu River the French found themselves in some difficulty with their Indian allies, and only about sixty agreed to go on with Champlain. On July 14, the little band of three Frenchmen and sixty Indians entered the "very large lake" which had been mentioned in 1603 and which was at once named Lac de Champlain. When he discovered the Green Mountains to the east and the Adirondacks to the south, Champlain was indeed entering a region frequented by the Iroquois, but their home territory was further away, south of Lake Ontario. Five nations of common origin lived there in a confederation which was still more cultural than political. From east to west, they were the Mohawks, the Oneidas, the Onondagas, the Cayugas and the Senecas. It was the Mohawks, the habitual invaders of the St Lawrence, with whom the French were at odds. It should be remembered that when Champlain speaks of Iroquois (a disparaging term used by their enemies), it was the Mohawks that he meant and not the five nations as a whole.

On July 29, on Ticonderoga Point (site of the fort and battle of Carillon), not far from the falls by which the waters of Lake George spill into Lake Champlain, the French leader and his party came upon a band of Iroquois. Both sides erected barricades and throughout the night danced and hurled insults at one another. On the morning of the 30th the Iroquois began to advance, about two hundred in number, led by three chiefs easily recognizable by their tall plumes. While his two French companions concealed themselves in the woods with a number of Indians, Champlain marched toward the enemy, hidden in the ranks of his Indian allies; the allies then opened their ranks and Champlain advanced ahead of them, his arquebus charged with four bullets. He walked to within thirty paces of the enemy and then, just as the Iroquois were about to let fly their arrows, he fired, killing two of the chiefs and mortally wounding the third. Then one of the French fired a shot "from within the woods," which threw the Iroquois into a panic. A good number of them were killed (some fifty, according to Lescarbot), and a dozen more were taken prisoner. Among the allies there were only fifteen wounded, and lightly at that. There were victory dances, and then the party set out for home.[11]

Champlain's victory had been no more than a brilliant skirmish. He had been content to put the band of warriors to flight, without attempting to pursue them or invade their territory. This victory, however, contributed to a growing sense of defeat on the part of the Iroquois, who saw themselves being excluded on all sides from the great North American fur trade.

This brief military expedition also made it possible for the French to lay claim to a new territory, the Richelieu Valley and the region of Lake Champlain. The Sieur de Monts's lieutenant had been the first European in the mountains of Vermont and New York.

Some historians have blamed Champlain for the long series of Iroquois wars that the country was to endure. They have overlooked the fact that Champlain was under orders from the Sieur de Monts, and could not act on his own initiative. Besides, neither Champlain nor de Monts can be held responsible for this warfare, for it had been going on since the century before, and the military alliance by which they were bound had been concluded before either had come to the St Lawrence in any official capacity. In 1603 the French were already committed to the Indians of the St Lawrence either to persuade the Iroquois to make peace or to conquer them by force of arms. In 1609, the French had no choice but to carry out their earlier promise.

Champlain returned to France the following October at de Monts's request and reported to his superior and to the King on the state of affairs in America. De Monts did not succeed in having his monopoly renewed, however; all he received was the right to collect a sum of 6,000 livres from others trading in the St. Lawrence. This, observed Champlain, was like giving him the ocean to drink.[12]

For all that, de Monts did not give up his dream of a New France. While Poutrincourt went back to Acadia hoping to revive the colony of 1607, he prepared a new expedition, but this time Champlain was able to bring with him only goods for barter and the bare necessities for the men wintering at Quebec. When he arrived at Tadoussac on May 19, 1610, he found ships that had already been there for a week. Since trade was to be open to everyone, the early arrival of these ships did not bode well for de Monts's company.

The Indians had promised to take Champlain "to explore the three rivers, as far as a place where there is so great a sea that they can see no end to it, & return by way of the Saguenay to Tadoussac." They were proposing to travel up the St Maurice River as far as Hudson Bay and to return through Lac St Jean and down the Saguenay. Had this long journey materialized in 1610, the French would have reached Hudson Bay several weeks before the English and would have discovered Lac St Jean thirty-seven years earlier than in fact they did.[13] But the Indians were not going to take Champlain to Hudson Bay or even to Lac St Jean; they would open up the back country only at such time and to such extent as they judged would be useful to them. Each year their promise was for the following year, and solely to assure themselves of armed support from the French.

And so these grand schemes of discovery had to be shelved in order to undertake another military expedition, this time to dislodge a band of Iroquois who had established themselves behind barricades on the Richelieu a league and a half from its mouth. Before Champlain arrived on the scene, his Indian allies had launched an assault against this entrenchment and had been thrown back with heavy losses. In the end, the Iroquois resistance crumbled before the French arquebuses and a well-coordinated assault, and the enemy was exterminated. Champlain emerged from the engagement with a slight wound to his ear, with which he was marked for the rest of his days.[14] For a number of years the name Cap de Victoire commemorated this second triumph of the French over the Iroquois.

It was after this battle that a young Frenchman was entrusted to the Algonquins and Hurons; this young man was beyond a doubt Etienne Brûlé, although Champlain refers to him only as "my servant" without naming him.[15] Champlain and Gravé were eager to send him with these allies "to learn what was the nature of their country, to see the great lake, observe the rivers, what manner of peoples inhabit them; withal to discover what mines & most rare things may be found among these places & peoples." In return, the allies asked that Champlain should take a Huron called Savignon to France.[16] Brûlé was thus the first European to travel up the Ottawa River, to enter the country of the Algonquins, and to reach the Great Lakes.

Meanwhile, on August 3, the English arrived in Hudson Bay; they pressed on into James Bay, and there on its southern coast they spent the winter.

The situation was becoming very unhappy for New France in the St Lawrence. The fur trade had been a disaster for everyone in 1610. Without the revenues of the fur trade, de Monts's company could do nothing for Quebec. True enough, Poutrincourt's Acadia seemed assured of success, thanks to the capital invested in it by the Marquise de Guercheville. On the other hand, the English were gaining more and more ground in territory that the French persisted in calling New France. They had discovered and occupied Hudson Bay; John Guy, the same year, established a colony of some forty people in Newfoundland, while Quebec's population was less than twenty; Jamestown in Virginia already had five hundred inhabitants! And in France, fate had struck a cruel blow; on May 14, 1610, Henry IV was assassinated. The monarch who had backed Chauvin, de Chaste and de Monts, who had consistently done his best to encourage the establishment of a New France, even after the abolition of the monopoly, left as his heir a little king nine years old. Once again France sank into a period of instability, which was to complicate even further the task of finding support for colonization.

Champlain returned to France. After entering into a marriage which had at least the immediate advantage of aiding him financially in the pursuit of his project,[17] he helped de Monts to prepare another voyage for the spring of 1611. He arrived at Tadoussac on May 13. This time the traders who had scrambled to get to Tadoussac before anyone else were no further ahead for their trouble; the trade was miserably poor and the Indians had become "shrewd & artful," holding back until there should be "several vessels together, so as to make better bargains."[18] The chief of the Montagnais, Batiscan, was waiting for Champlain at Quebec, but again the Indians put off for another year the exploration into the upper reaches of the St Maurice and toward Hudson Bay, on which Champlain had hoped to send one of his men. Champlain then hurried up the St Lawrence to keep the rendezvous he had made with the Algonquins, followed closely by a pack of traders hungry to take advantage of his friendship with the Indians. When he reached the St Louis Rapids, the appointed spot for the rendezvous, the Indians were not there.

For three weeks, while he waited for them, Champlain explored the region, for a great plan had begun to take form in his mind; the establishment of a settlement here, far up the St Lawrence Valley. He chose a point, later to be called Pointe Callières, at the mouth of the little Rivière St Pierre. To see how the "heavy potter's clay" would stand up to the winter, he built a wall ten yards long, four feet wide and three or four high. He had two gardens cultivated and sowed, and prepared a square, "flat & ready for building," which he called Place Royale. Square, wall and gardens; these were the first work of European hands on the island where the fort of Ville Marie was to stand, but not until thirty years later. The name Montreal appears for the first time on a map by Champlain as early as 1612.

On June 13, two hundred Hurons and some Algonquins appeared, and with them Etienne Brûlé, dressed "as a savage" and "having most excellently learned their tongue." Champlain reassured his allies that misleading rumours about him were unfounded, and was obliged to reassure them again when they complained of the behaviour of the traders who had followed him. It was during these meetings that Champlain greatly enhanced his prestige in the eyes of the Indians by shooting the St Louis Rapids with them in a canoe, although he could not even swim. The only European to have succeeded in such a feat before him was Brûlé. More Algonquins came in July, and proposed "discoveries in the North." Although the Algonquins had hitherto found every excuse to forestall such exploration, hoping to confine the French to the St Lawrence, it was now they who were inviting Champlain to go exploring in the north. With the great influx of traders in 1611, perhaps they had begun to fear for the trade relations they had established with Champlain and his followers. We shall soon see, however, that the Algonquins were only dangling a carrot. In any event, Champlain accepted the invitation and, pending the time when he himself would be able to leave for the north, he entrusted "a young boy," Nicolas de Vignau, to the care of the Algonquins, having placed in his hands "a very precise memorandum of those things which he should observe while among them."

But Champlain's first preoccupation was the establishment of a settlement beside the St Louis Rapids, provided the countryside should be found "good & fertile." The Algonquins were delighted with this plan, because it would add a measure of safety for the transport of furs, which was always perilous in the region of Lac St Pierre because of the Iroquois. It was at the St Louis Rapids, in any case, that a rendezvous was made for the following year.[19] Thus were laid down the broad lines of development for the years to follow. The Montagnais would rapidly lose their influence, for with the shift upstream of the terminus of the great fur routes, the bulk of the fur trade would no longer be carried on at Tadoussac. As a result of the shift, the French were at last to gain access to the interior of the continent.

For all the advantageous developments in the St Lawrence, it was a fragile structure on which the French establishment reposed; it could not last unless de Monts and his company could win out over their competitors in the wide-open trade conditions existing since 1609. The fur trade seemed viable, but the chances for a colony in Canada had never been slimmer. Even in Acadia, where the situation seems to have been somewhat better, the future of colonization continued to be uncertain. As it happened, the year 1612 would be a decisive one for the future of New

France, for a reorganization was to take place and the long-term monopoly was to be restored.

When he returned to France in the fall of 1611, Champlain resumed his efforts to consolidate the trade association, but the merchants were no longer interested in supporting the enterprise without a monopoly. De Monts was obliged to buy back their shares, and thus became the sole proprietor of the Habitation of Quebec. Unable to maintain it alone, however, he ceded its ownership to the merchants of La Rochelle, and for a year Quebec served as their fur-storage depot.[20] Champlain continued his search for the backing of "some high-placed person." Through the good offices of an almoner of the King, he won the ear of Prince Charles de Bourbon, Comte de Soissons, Governor of Normandy and of the Dauphiné, a close relative of the young Louis XIII, and convinced him of the importance of saving the enterprise. With this influential support, Champlain submitted his plan to the King. Admiral de Montmorency, greatuncle of Soissons, gave his approval when consulted. The result was that, on September 27, 1612, the Comte de Soissons acquired a twelve-year monopoly of the St Lawrence trade at Quebec and above. On October 8 he was named the King's Lieutenant-General "for the settlement and inhabitation of the lands of the country of New France."[21] As for de Monts, who had been Lieutenant-General since 1603, he yielded his office to a prince whose rank and influence might bring better results than hitherto in the establishment of the Laurentian colony.

A week later, the Comte de Soissons appointed Champlain to represent him in New France. Champlain was to have the broadest of powers: the construction of the necessary forts, the conclusion of treaties with the Indians or the declaration of war against them; the appointment of "such Captains & Lieutenants as shall be needed, [...] the commission of Officers for the distribution of Justice, & the enforcement of order, regulations & ordinances"; and the continuation of the search for "the easy road leading by the interior of the said country to the country of China & the East Indies."[22]

After three years of trying, Champlain had at last found a sufficiently influential sponsor to assure the execution of the King's wishes. Once Champlain was invested with the necessary powers, this still-embryonic country could be given an administrative structure; the strategic focal points of the fur trade, Cap de Victoire and the St Louis Rapids, were brought within its territorial limits; and the trade monopoly gave hope of serious and sustained efforts for the future.

No sooner had hopes been raised than they were dashed once more; the Comte de Soissons fell ill and died on November 1, 1612. A new beginning would have to be made. Taking full advantage of his new relationship with the Bourbon family, Champlain turned to a nephew of the Comte de Soissons, Henri de Bourbon, Prince de Condé, Duc d'Enghien, first-ranking prince of the blood who at one time had been heir-presumptive to the Crown. This baffling young man of twenty-four was regarded with suspicion by the Court because he had just returned from voluntary exile, during which he had had dealings with the enemies of France. When Champlain appealed to him for support he accepted at once. The Comte de Soissons had been dead only twelve days before there was a successor in the person of his nephew. On November 13, 1612, Queen Marie de Médicis, in the name of the young Louis XIII, designated the Prince de Condé as Viceroy of New France. She accorded him an exclusive trade monopoly for twelve years, at Quebec and above, and then there was an immediate modification of the eastern limits to allow the inclusion of the Tadoussac and Matane trade.[23] With a commission dated November 22, 1612, the Prince de Condé designated Champlain as his lieutenant in New France, as had the Comte de Soissons before him.[24] Champlain was now the lieutenant of a viceroy and personal representative of the first-ranking prince of the realm.

The autumn of 1612 thus saw a new beginning in the history of New France; at least, that was the hope. A high-placed authority now presided over the destiny of New France, both in Acadia and in Canada (for Condé's viceroyalty applied to both). Champlain, as his representative at Quebec, possessed all the necessary powers to give form to his colony, and along the whole length of the grande rivière de Canada (as the St Lawrence was still called) trade was controlled by a monopoly to assure the maintenance of the St Lawrence enterprise.

As an aid to his continuing efforts to put the affairs of New France in good order, Champlain produced a narrative and a number of maps. Very early in 1613, he published an important work in two books of Voyages, which recount in detail the Acadian endeavour of 1604-7, and the events of the period 1608-12. It was here that he first used the name St Lawrence when writing of the great river, thus harking back to Mercator, who had given the name to the Gulf in 1569. He published numerous small regional maps and, late in 1612 and early in 1613, two maps of the whole of New France.

It remained to be seen how the new Laurentian monopoly might be applied, essential as it was for the success of the colony, and what kind of company might be formed to exercise it. There was no great association of merchants interested in the St Lawrence trade in 1613. The Prince de Condé did no more than distribute passports to small companies. There was no co-operation between the various groups of merchants; on the contrary, so keen was the rivalry that a ship from La Rochelle was seized by competitors, complete with its cargo of beaver and other merchandise. Madame de Guercheville sent an expedition, financed from her own resources, to found a colony at St Sauveur in Acadia, but colonial plans in the St Lawrence were set aside for that year. In spite of the monopoly accorded to the Prince de Condé, and in spite of the powers vested in his representative, Quebec seemed destined to remain nothing but a warehouse for furs.

Worse still, when Champlain arrived in the St Lawrence in that year of 1613, probably accompanied by Nicolas Marsolet and Guillaume Couillart, he found that the diplomatic foundations he had been so long in laying were in peril; the Indians were disgruntled with the French and relations with them were on the point of rupture; the entire economic structure was in danger of collapse. Champlain decided then "to go into their country, so as to encourage those remaining there with the good treatment they shall receive" and "with my concern for assisting them in their wars."[25] In doing so he had another plan in mind, too; to solve the riddle of the Northern Sea. In 1611 he had sent the young Nicolas de Vignau to spend the winter among the Algonquins, so that he might study the country. Vignau, on his return to Paris in 1612, declared "with the most solemn affirmations ever heard," that he had travelled up the Ottawa River and reached the Northern Sea. He had seen, he said, "the wreckage of an English vessel," whose crew of eighty, having taken refuge on land and seeking to rob the Indians of their food, had been killed and scalped; except, Champlain notes, for "a young English boy whom they had kept for me." This report had filled Champlain with enthusiasm; this sea, "which I have sought so long," was little more than a week's journey from the St Louis rapids![26] The English had wintered in Hudson Bay in 1610 11. It must have been known that they had wintered there again in 1612-13, led by Thomas Button. New France had been invaded from the north; haste was imperative.

With a guide and two canoes obtained from the Algonquins, and accompanied by Nicolas de Vignau, the interpreter Thomas Godefroy and two other French companions, Champlain set out on May 27, 1613, on his first journey up the river that would long be known as the *route des pays d'en haut* and was at that time called Rivière des Algonquins. He met a band of Algonquins above the Long Sault rapids who wanted to take him with them on the warpath, and when he refused on the pretext of "pressing on to warn the other peoples," they told him that ahead of him "the way was bad, & that we had seen nothing until then." Champlain continued all the same, making careful observations as he went. In his journal of June 4, 1613, we find the first description of the environs of the future capital of Canada; on their right as they paddled upstream was the Gatineau River, on their left the Rideau Falls, and upstream ahead, the great Chaudière Falls. Two long portages were necessary to pass this obstacle. On June 6 the party reached a quite impassable part

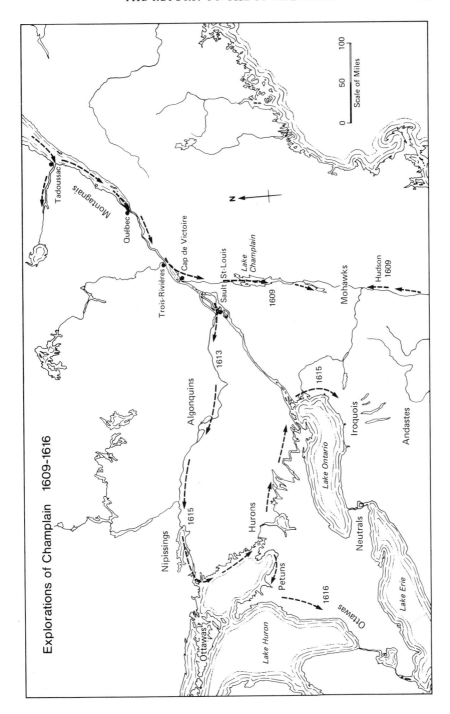

Explorations of Champlain 1609-1616

of the river and took to the land at their left, intending to regain the river at Allumette Island. Plagued by June flies and with their path repeatedly blocked by fallen trees, they made a long and exhausting portage from one lake to another and finally broke free of the woods where the Ottawa broadens into a lake below Allumette Island, then called Ile des Algonquins. This was probably June 8. Here, between an encampment on the south shore of the river and the Algonquin chief Tessoüat's dwelling on one of the small islands (perhaps Morrison Island), the fur route down the river was effectively barred.[27] All the Indians coming down the river were obliged to pay tribute, even the Hurons who in number were ten times stronger than the Algonquins. Later, it was realized that it was a matter of policy for the Algonquins to prevent the Hurons from going down to the St Lawrence and the French from going up to trade with the Hurons, in determination to "keep all the traffic to themselves."[28] The Algonquins Champlain had met above the Long Sault rapids as he toiled up the river had already done their best to discourage him, first trying to divert him to their warring expedition, then telling him that he had seen nothing yet of the difficulties of the river. These factors are essential to an understanding of later developments here among the Island Algonquins.

Indeed, as soon as Champlain began to talk about continuing up the river during the long palavers with his hosts, a multitude of objections were advanced: the great difficulty of the route; the hostility of Nipissings; and so forth. Champlain then made reference to Vignau's experience. The interpreter, he told them, had not seen all the difficulties they were making so much of, and had not found these peoples as bad as they said! The Algonquins were indignant; this Vignau had never left their village! But he had been to the Northern Sea, Champlain replied, and had seen "the wreckage of an English vessel." At this the Algonquins raised an outcry even louder than before and demanded to be allowed to put the interpreter to death. Vignau then declared that he had lied, and begged for pardon.[29]

Champlain was convinced that Vignau had played an odious trick, and heaped the most vigorous expressions of ire on the interpreter's head. And yet, was it Vignau or the Indians who had lied? The Algonquins declared the Nipissings to be their enemies and made much of the difficulties of going among these neighbours, but we know that the Algonquins and Nipissings in fact got along well together, and often went together to spend the winter in Huron country. During these palavers, moreover, the interpreter Godefroy caught the Algonquins in the act of sending out a canoe to the Nipissings! Everything holds together in Vignau's plan to lead Champlain to the Northern Sea. He had lived for a year with the Algonquins, and during this time the tribe had been continually in contact with the nations of the North, from whom they obtained furs. It was also relatively easy to travel from the Ottawa River to James Bay. But what about this "wreckage of an English vessel," the severed "80. heads" and the young Englishman? In 1611, Henry Hudson, after wintering at the mouth of the river later called the Rupert, was abandoned in a boat in the southern reaches of James Bay with eight others, among them his son John. Vignau's story does have some foundation, for these Englishmen left alone in the north might well have been captured and killed. It was customary among the Indians to spare the lives of children, and this young Englishman who was said to have been kept as a present for Champlain was quite possibly the young John Hudson. However, Champlain's text talks of "80. heads." All that is needed for these two versions to conform perfectly is to read "8." in the text. An error of this kind was committed in Champlain's publication of 1619, when a distance that Champlain intended to indicate as eight to nine leagues appeared as 89 leagues.[30] It seems quite likely, in any case, that Champlain had been duped by the Algonquins and that Vignau was the victim of their determination to preserve their monopoly in the back country.

Champlain invited the Algonquins to come down to the St Louis Rapids. He reappeared there on June 17, three weeks after his departure.[31] He had travelled only 175 miles up the pathway that had so intrigued Cartier, and he was not even the first European to do so. Moreover, he had failed to reach his objective, the Northern Sea.

At the end of August, Champlain was back in France to continue his negotiations and his publicity campaign. He published the account of his exploration of 1613 under the title of *Quatriesme voyage*, and he republished an earlier map of New France with the addition of details learned during his journey to the Algonquin country. As for his negotiations, they at last achieved happy results. On November 15, 1613, merchants of Rouen and St Malo signed a deed of association in the presence of Viceroy Condé, reserving the right to a one-third participation for merchants of La Rochelle. On November 20, the Viceroy approved the articles of agreement between Champlain and the associates. The new company obtained the exclusive right to trade in the St Lawrence for eleven years (until 1624) on both shores of the river, beginning at the Matane River. It agreed to offer a gift of a horse worth a thousand crowns (a value of three thousand livres) to the Viceroy each year, to pay allowances to Champlain as Lieutenant to the Viceroy, and to transport six families to begin the settlement of the country.[32] The new company took the official name of *Compagnie de Canada*, but in practice a number of names were used: *Compagnie de Condé*, from the name of the Viceroy; *Compagnie de Champlain*, because it was he who was its initiator; and most commonly *Compagnie de Rouen et de Saint-Malo*, because it was composed mostly of merchants from these cities from 1613 to 1618.

The establishment of this company with the issuance of letters patent in October 1614 would seem at last to have completed the reorganization that had been two years in the making. Since the autumn of 1612, there had been important changes in the administration of New France. De Monts, as Lieutenant-General with the rank of governor of a province, had been replaced by a viceroy; the Prince de Condé's rank and influence, in principle, should ensure a much stronger authority over the several parts of the colony, Canada on the one hand and on the other Acadia, which was now divided into two seigneuries, Poutrincourt's at Port Royal and Madame de Guercheville's in the rest of the Atlantic region. The Viceroy was to be represented in Canada by a lieutenant with broad administrative powers. This is an important point, for though Champlain was to be paid by the commercial company, he was not its subordinate; he was its superior in authority and in rank. The entire St Lawrence, finally, was to become the exclusive commercial reserve of the Company of Canada, which, theoretically, was to be protected against competition, and had undertaken to establish six families in the colony over eleven years. Six families was very little, but there was reason to expect, if the trade proved profitable, that the Company would go beyond its commitment, or that families would come on their own initiative, attracted by prosperity. Despite its modest scope, this reorganization of 1612-14 gave rise to hopes for more speedy development in New France. In view of the progress of the English colonies in Newfoundland and Virginia and the very recent foundation of New Holland, it could only be hoped that it was not already too late.

CHAPTER 8

Failure in Acadia

1610–1614

In New France there were now two areas of colonization, Canada and Acadia. The Habitation of Port Royal still awaited the return of the French, but the Sieur de Monts, instead of reopening it, had left to Poutrincourt the task of developing the concession that had been granted to him, while he himself undertook the establishment of a new settlement at Quebec.

Having acquired the Habitation from de Monts as of February 2, 1608,[1] Poutrincourt set to work to raise funds for his Acadian project. In 1608 he fully expected to be able to count on the support of the Lorraine family. Accordingly, he bought a ship and loaded it with cargo, but when he presented a bill of some 4,000 livres, the Lorraines declined to help him. The shipowner seized the cargo, and Poutrincourt was left owing 1,000 livres to the money-lender Fortunat du Gué. The result was that by the end of 1609 he still had not "budged from France."[2] But he set to work once again, burdened as he already was with debt and without any commercial support. He prepared a boat in his barony of Saint-Just in Champagne early in February, 1610, loaded it "with furniture, food and munitions of war," and set sail down the Seine to Dieppe.[3] There he transferred everything to his ship, the *Grâce-de-Dieu*, and left France at the end of the month with "a number of honest men and artisans."[4] Among his companions was his eldest son Charles de Biencourt, and perhaps also the young Charles Turgis de Saint-Etienne et de La Tour. They took no women with them. Poutrincourt had refused to take any Jesuits, on the pretext that he would first have to build them a lodging, but there was a secular priest on the expedition, Jessé Flesché.[5]

Three months later, the *Grâce-de-Dieu* made land at Port au Mouton on the east coast of Acadia, but as it rounded Cape Sable the ship was driven forty leagues off course, as far as the Pentagouët River. On the way back from there to Port Royal, the *Grâce-de-Dieu* made two stops; one was at Ste Croix Island, where prayers were said for the dead of the winter of 1604-5; the other, lasting several days, was at the St John River, where Poutrincourt heard the complaints of a number of Indians against Robert Gravé, son of François, though in what capacity we do not know. The accused was to undergo trial, but he escaped and took refuge among the Indians.[6]

At·long last Poutrincourt reappeared in his domain of Port Royal, after an absence of three years. The Souriquois had been visited by Angibault dit Champdoré in 1609; in 1610 they were still there to greet the French. The buildings had been respected, and each piece of furniture still stood where it had been left in 1607. The Habitation had suffered from exposure to the elements, however; roofs had to be repaired and the mill put back into working order. Because the settlement's spring was some distance away, a well was dug inside the fort. The colonists set to work to cultivate the land,[7] and it was perhaps in this year of 1610 that Poutrincourt parcelled out farms in his domain, making his grants to the colonists in deeds signed by his own hand.[8] The first page was turned in the history of settlement in Acadia.

The resumption of activity at Port Royal was shortly to be marked by a great event. Since the birth of New France in 1524, the French had not baptized a single native on American soil. On June 24, 1610, the first baptism took place. Immediately upon his return to Port Royal, Poutrincourt summoned Membertou and refreshed his memory of the meagre teachings he had already received. Barely three weeks after his arrival, Jessé Flesché baptized Membertou and twenty others of his family.[9] This mass baptism was performed with some alacrity, so that the news of it might be carried to France by the next ship to leave, and Poutrincourt was soon to draw criticism for his unseemly haste for apostolic glorification. There is no doubt that the publicity value of the ceremony had been uppermost in Poutrincourt's mind; such a spectacular and quickly-realized religious coup would, he hoped, impress the leading lights of the Church and the Court, and thus win their support. Perhaps, too, the performance of this mass baptism by a secular priest was designed to demonstrate that the Jesuits were not indispensable to New France.

On July 8, 1610, Poutrincourt's son Biencourt set sail aboard the *Grâce-de-Dieu* to carry a report to the King and find financial support, and quickly. The colony was evidently in difficult straits already. Biencourt learned of the death of Henry IV during the journey, and upon his arrival approached the Queen Mother, Marie de Médicis. Stressing the religious progress that had been made (and here Lescarbot did his bit by writing a "public narration" of the mass baptism at Port Royal), he requested the privilege of a commercial monopoly.[10]

Biencourt still made no mention of taking the Jesuits to Acadia. The Jesuits thereupon reminded the Queen Mother that Henry IV had promised to send them to Acadia with a grant of 2,000 livres; the Queen Mother's inclination was to carry out this promise. Pressure was also brought to bear by Madame de Guercheville (née Antoinette de Pons), wife of the Governor of Paris and lady-in-waiting to the Queen. Biencourt's young friend Thomas Robin de Coulogne, only a fictitious associate, it has been shown, had come with him to Paris from Acadia. When Madame de Guercheville inquired about the Jesuits, Robin de Coulogne replied that he had been put in charge of all embarkation and had no instructions regarding the Jesuits; however, he knew that Poutrincourt would be honoured to have them and would gladly consent to provide their upkeep. The Marquise replied that the King had already provided for their upkeep, and sent Robin de Coulogne to the Provincial of the Order. The Jesuits Pierre Biard and Enemond Massé received authorization to undertake the mission. Since Biencourt had been ordered to take supplies to his father for the winter, a meeting was arranged at Dieppe for the end of October.[11] In a letter that was to be carried to Poutrincourt, the Queen Mother assured the seigneur of Port Royal of her not inconsiderable protection. Father Coton, former confessor to Henry IV and confessor to Louis XIII, sent word that he would defend Poutrincourt's interests at Court. And the Jesuit Massé, who was to come to Acadia, had Father Coton's ear.[12] It behooved Poutrincourt, utterly bereft as he was, to overcome his repugnance for the Jesuits.

Fathers Biard and Massé kept the rendezvous, but to their great surprise Biencourt's ship was still in drydock and "not even repaired." Poutrincourt's son was more sorely pressed for funds than ever. He had failed in his efforts to obtain a fur-trading monopoly, which would have won him the support of seven Parisian hat-makers with an advance of a much-needed 12,000 livres. A number of wealthy godfathers and godmothers had been found for the newly baptized Christians of Port Royal, and it was hoped that the latter might thereby be showered with gifts, but the material response to this attempt, too, was disappointing. The very most Biencourt obtained was a commission, in spite of his youth, as "Vice Admiral *en la mer du Ponant* (in the Sea of the Setting Sun),"[13] a post which gave him jurisdiction over all navigation to and from Acadia and the right to endorse passports; but this was hardly a lucrative responsibility.

Biencourt and Robin de Coulogne turned then to two Huguenot shipowners, Abraham Duquesne and another by the name of Dujardin. These two were to take over the repair and outfitting of the *Grâce-de-Dieu* and would participate in the profits of the voyage. But at the news that Jesuits were to take ship, there was, it is said, "a great stir within the Reformation"; the Huguenot shipowners "wanted no more to do with the vessel, if it was going to carry Jesuits." Robin de Coulogne went to Paris and the Queen Mother ordered the Governor of Dieppe to see that the Jesuits were received aboard the ship. Once more the shipowners refused and once more there were representations in Paris. This time the Queen declared her refusal to "stoop to begging of the villains." The departure was postponed *sine die*. The Jesuits withdrew to Rouen, but Biencourt consoled them with the assurance that he would not depart without them.[14] It might be thought (and it was believed at the time) that the plan to put the missionaries aboard had been swept away by a Huguenot storm. The truth was that the Jesuits could not have departed in any case, since Biencourt was still short of money and could not outfit the *Grâce-de-Dieu*. Why then the clamour against the Jesuits? As the historian Campeau has shown, it was all a game of bluff. Biencourt had no money, while the missionaries, thanks to the Queen Mother's 1,500 livres and subscriptions solicited on their behalf, were well off, and they could count on the further generosity of benefactors, for the gracious lady de Guercheville was behind the plan of evangelism with all her heart and soul. The financial crisis might be overcome if benefactors could be persuaded to furnish enough money to get the ship into the water. The Huguenot shipowners (who had certain sums of money to recuperate) played their part by angrily refusing to outfit a ship that was to carry Jesuits (although one man's money smells just the same as another's to a merchant); Biencourt expressed distress at having to give up the Jesuits. Their performance paid off. Robin de Coulogne explained to Madame de Guercheville, as she sought a solution, that the enterprise could be rid of the shipowners with the payment of the debt of 4,000 livres. That was enough: the Marquise set to work, raised the 4,000 livres and got rid of the shipowners, who then turned about and lent 1,200 livres to Biencourt and Robin de Coulogne to enable them to transport the very Jesuits they had refused to transport themselves. The Jesuits had been the scapegoats of the whole farce, but when it was over everyone was happy; the shipowners recouped the money they had spent for the cargo; Biencourt, after having quite lost hope, had his cargo at last and collected 1,225 livres from the Jesuits for the repair of his ship; and Madame de Guercheville finally saw her missionaries on their way.[15]

When she paid the 4,000 livres for the cargo in order to be rid of the Huguenot shipowners, Madame de Guercheville laid down the condition that the missionaries should have the right to a share of the revenues of the voyage. One portion of these revenues was to be applied to the upkeep of the missionaries and another portion might be invested in the new enterprise, so that the benefactress's contribution formed the capital of a continuing fund. In order that all might be clear, or so it was hoped, a formal contract was drawn up between the Jesuits on the one hand and the Port Royal enterprise on the other. A contract of association was signed at Dieppe before a notary on January 20, 1611.[16]

It was clearly Biencourt who had the better of his partners in this contract. From an enterprise to which he contributed only a quarter of the capital, he was to receive half the profits; he charged his partners a transport fee of 1,000 livres, he borrowed from them without obligation to pay interest, and his contract did not in any way restrict the use of the money at his disposal. That same day, the shipowners Dujardin and Duquesne advanced an interest-bearing loan of 1,200 livres on stiff but normal conditions, while the Jesuits supplied three quarters of the capital, expecting only half the profits, and lent further sums, without demanding either guarantee or interest, to a partner who would not have been able to budge from France without them.[17] The Jesuits were unquestionably the losers on the deal, to such an extent that one wonders whether to call it naïveté or great generosity. It would seem, in fact, that there was a little of both; Father Biard believed that this was a good way of assuring an income for the mission, and understood that the profits to be earned would be used only for the maintenance of the French of Port Royal. In any case, he wrote later this was "the contract of association over which such a cry was raised that all were hoarse from it [...] God grant that there never be greater cause for outcry against us."[18]

Instead of leaving in mid-November, as had been planned, Biencourt did not set sail until January 26, 1611, carrying with him the two Jesuits Biard and Massé and Louis Hébert (at least, it is our belief that Hébert returned in 1611 and not 1610). The voyage lasted four months. On May 21 or 22 the ship arrived at Port Royal to find that the settlers had survived the winter only with difficulty and in much hardship. The *Grâce-de-Dieu* was a light ship (fifty or sixty tons) and the cargo she had been able to carry was not large; the provisions had diminished during the long voyage, and now there were fifty-nine mouths to feed, not counting the sagamore Membertou and his rabble.[19]

There was urgent economic business to be attended to; Poutrincourt set sail at once for the lands of the Etchemins, not even waiting long enough for the ship to be unloaded. On his arrival he called together the captains who had come there to trade, obtained their recognition of his son as Vice-Admiral, and made his peace with Robert Gravé. But ships from La Rochelle and St Malo had already garnered the available furs, and there was nothing left for Poutrincourt that spring of 1611. It was a financial disaster for the enterprise that was now the joint concern of Poutrincourt and the Jesuits. Poutrincourt was even reduced to borrowing food from the La Rochelle merchants, who thought nothing of supplying him with "spoiled & mouldy ship's biscuit." The commander of Port Royal decided thereupon to leave immediately for France, so as to organize a new shipment of supplies, leaving his young son Biencourt in charge of his colony.[20]

With him he took the priest Flesché, who gladly (it would seem) gave up his place to the Jesuits.[21] Whether by personal conviction or because Poutrincourt was anxious to hasten the conversion of the savages for publicity reasons, Flesché had baptized about eighty natives in the space of a year in both public and private ceremonies; Lescarbot, whose aim was to extol the secular priest at the expense of the Jesuits, even mentions 140 baptisms.[22] This apostolic accomplishment was a very fragile thing; some of the new Christians could not even make the sign of the cross; all they saw in their baptism was a symbol of alliance with the "Normans," as they called the French. The Jesuits might quite justifiably reproach Flesché for having acted "rashly" and of having used the sacraments wantonly; they themselves preferred, they said, to take the time to give sound instruction.

Having reached France toward the end of July 1611, Poutrincourt cast about to find help for Port Royal. Although we do not know how much he received for the few furs he had aboard his ship, we do know that the voyage had been a total financial disaster, because Poutrincourt had no money left to put into a new expedition. Gone were the 3,800 livres of which half had been borrowed from the Jesuits; vanished too were the 3,800 livres which, as the Jesuits's share in the enterprise, were to provide for the upkeep of the missionaries. But, however heavily indebted he was, Poutrincourt still had to find more money for his colony. He went to visit the Queen Mother, but obtained no help from her of a material nature, unless it was she who sent him to her lady-in-waiting, Madame de Guercheville.

The lady consented to enter into partnership with Poutrincourt. She agreed to pay out 3,000 livres for the cargo of a ship, on condition that she should have a share in the profits brought back by this ship from lands bestowed upon Poutrincourt by the King. Poutrincourt refused her any part of profits from Port Royal or "from other Seigneuries, Capes, Harbours, & Provinces" of which he declared himself to be the proprietor in New France (but for which he did not produce any proof of possession). Newly cautious as a result of the bad bargain she had made the year before, Madame de Guercheville ascertained from de Monts that Poutrincourt possessed only Port Royal and the adjacent territory; she then proceeded to obtain for herself, from de Monts, the concession of all of Acadia from the Gaspé down to the 40th parallel, except Port Royal.[23] Thus armed, she was now in a position to talk business with Poutrincourt. But still more difficulties arose. Madame de Guercheville put the 3,000 livres into the hands of the Jesuit coadjutor Gilbert Du Thet, with instructions to remit the sum direct to the merchant who was to outfit the ship.

On Poutrincourt's requisition, however, the unwary depositary paid out a draft of 1,200 livres, without demanding security; having misappropriated this large sum belonging to the company, Poutrincourt was once again in debt to his associate. All that was left for the outfitting of the ship was 1,800 livres.[24]

The Guercheville-Poutrincourt company's ship set sail from Dieppe on November 31, 1611; Poutrincourt stayed in France. When the supplies finally arrived in Acadia during the last week of January 1612, the colony was doing well despite a shortage of food. Relations between Biencourt and the Jesuits were still very strained, particularly since Biencourt, because of his rankling distrust, had refused to allow Father Biard to spend the winter with Robert Gravé on the St John River. The missionary continued nevertheless to show great consideration and tact toward Biencourt.

But a quarrel flared up over the newly-arrived cargo. Brother Du Thet expressed astonishment that Imbert, Poutrincourt's agent, had brought neither ship's roll, nor charter-party, nor memorandum of what cargo had been loaded or how the money had been spent. According to Du Thet, wheat intended for Port Royal had been sold at Dieppe and, of seven barrels of biscuit consumed during the crossing, only five should be charged to the company. Without making a formal accusation (at least from the way Father Biard tells the story), the Jesuits asked Biencourt to hold an inquiry. Instead of holding his inquiry, Biencourt transmitted this request to Imbert in the form of an accusation. The agent flew into a rage; the association with Madame de Guercheville, he said, was a plot devised by the Jesuits to expel Poutrincourt from Port Royal and from New France; he accused Du Thet of having stated during the voyage that the assassination of Henry IV had been the salvation of Christendom, and so forth. From all this, wrote Father Biard, "there arose a most unfortunate whirlwind of strife and discord." The dispute reached such a pitch that the Jesuits decided that their services were no longer of use either to the French or to the Indians, and in March 1612 resolved to return to France aboard the ship then being prepared for the return voyage.[25]

Father Biard requested Biencourt to allow one or two of the Jesuits to take ship. Biencourt refused, forbidding the captain to take anything aboard his ship from the missionaries; on March 11, he ordered the removal of a chest that Father Du Thet had already put aboard, and at the same time seized the Jesuits' mail. Since the ship was lying at anchor a quarter of a league from the settlement, the Jesuits then betook themselves to it in secret and installed themselves in the captain's cabin. When he heard of this, Biencourt held the captain on shore to prevent the departure of the ship and sent word ordering the Jesuits to disembark. They refused.

Biencourt had Father Massé forcibly removed from the ship, and then finally, after a summons brought by Louis Hébert, Father Biard agreed to return to shore. The Jesuits therefore unwillingly remained at Port Royal, but from March 13 to June 24, the Acadian colony lived under the excommunication that followed *ipso facto* from the violence done to the priests. The Fathers performed no further acts of ministry during this period and said their masses in private.[26]

Why had Biencourt been so vehemently determined to keep the Jesuits at Port Royal when he hated them so? Although he later wrote advising his father not to encumber himself with them any longer, here he was preventing them from leaving. Was it in order to keep the financial support of Madame de Guercheville, which was assured as long as the missionaries were in residence at Port Royal? He knew very well that Madame de Guercheville would be disinclined to continue her support after the way he had treated them. For the historian Campeau, who has closely studied the financial accounts of the Poutrincourts, Biencourt's conduct may be explained by the need to conceal irregularities that Father Biard intended to denounce; it was a foregone conclusion that the Marquise, who already had good reason for distrust, would have the ship seized in France and would obtain a liquidation under judicial supervision.[27]

In the wake of this drama, peace returned to Port Royal. On June 25, there was a reconciliation. The missionaries agreed to say mass for all, and they obtained permission for Brother Du Thet to go to France, there to defend himself against Imbert and to prepare a shipment of food.

The colony was already in desperate straits, that summer of 1612, for the food received in January had been quickly consumed. And the following winter had to be faced without the arrival of new supplies. At last, in mid-May 1613, sixteen months after the previous shipment of food, there appeared the *Jonas* with the announcement that Madame de Guercheville was letting Port Royal drop, having decided, as the Port Royal missionaries had hoped, to take up "the endeavour in its entirety with new forces in another location."[28]

The General of the Jesuits had been opposed to the foundation of another colony with the help of his priests; he would have preferred to bring Fathers Biard and Massé home. By the time this was learned, however, the new project was already well advanced, under the patronage of the Queen Mother and backed by the authority of the King.[29] There was no turning back. The *Jonas* set sail from Honfleur with eighty or a hundred souls, of whom thirty were to spend the winter in the new colony. Father Jacques Quentin and Brother Du Thet were on the voyage, but they were not to stay for the winter if Fathers Biard and Massé were still living. The civil and military command of the expedition had been entrusted to René

Le Cocq de La Saussaye. When the *Jonas* reached Port Royal, Fathers Biard and Massé were taken aboard and the ship set out for the Pentagouët.

It was a little way up this river, where the Kadesquit empties into it (near the present city of Bangor) that La Saussaye had been instructed to establish the new colony. This secluded spot had the advantage of being near the sea and also of offering the possibility of communication with Quebec. It seemed most suitable, both for the establishment of a colony and for the fur trade. On arrival at Mount Desert Island, however, the crew refused to go any further; as for the pilot, he would be in unfamiliar waters beyond that point and he was not inclined to take on the burden of "discovery." The Indians, moreover, were urging the Jesuits to settle in that region rather than up the river. A spot on the mainland was therefore chosen behind Mount Desert Island, where the land seemed fertile and where there was a harbour that appeared to be safe and commanded the whole coast. This spot was named St Sauveur.[30]

La Saussaye should have unloaded the *Jonas* and established a defensible position without delay, but in spite of the advice of his officers he did not see the urgency of doing so. For the time being, he sheltered his men under canvas and turned his attention to the cultivation of the land.[31] Then, on July 2, an English warship appeared and bore down on the defenceless colony. This was the *Treasurer*, commanded by Captain Samuel Argall, come to ensure undisturbed exploitation for the English in a region to which they came every year and which they considered theirs.

Argall, a member of the Council of Virginia, a shrewd trader and renowned mariner, had set sail aboard the *Treasurer* with sixty soldiers. What exactly was his mission? When he left Virginia on this first occasion, Argall's objective does not appear to have been one of destruction. The Virginians were as yet unaware that La Saussaye had come to establish a colony behind Mount Desert Island, and it was not until his second voyage that Argall attacked Port Royal. We may therefore believe, as did Father Biard, that it was pure chance that brought Argall to St Sauveur. In any case, enveloped in fog, the *Treasurer* had dropped anchor in a bay nearby. Some Indians mistook these English for French and guided them to St Sauveur. English and French waited and watched each other for a time, then, flying the English flag and with the activity on deck concealed behind a red screen, the *Treasurer* bore down to the attack. Anchored off shore and still heavy with her cargo, the *Jonas* had only ten defenders; there was no time to weigh anchor or hoist the sails. In the absence of the gunner, Brother Du Thet manned and fired the cannon, but, since he aimed hastily or not at all, the only result was a great deal of noise; then he was mortally wounded with "a musket ball in his body." As for La Saussaye, who had remained on land, he withdrew into the woods, without even taking his baggage. There was nothing left to do but to give up the ship.

Argall landed, seized La Saussaye's coffers and surreptitiously extracted the "commissions, & royal letters" found therein; when La Saussaye returned and could not produce his papers, Argall declared him a pirate and ordered the sacking of the settlement.[32]

The colonists had now to be disposed of. One group, including La Saussaye and Father Massé, left in a small boat with food supplied by Argall and finally reached the eastern coast of Acadia, where they were picked up by two French ships.[33] The rest (with the Jesuits Biard and Quentin) were taken to Virginia aboard the *Treasurer* and the *Jonas*, whose command was assumed by Argall's lieutenant.

The adventures of the Acadian deportees did not end there, however. Informed without delay of what the French had accomplished in Acadia, the Council of Virginia instructed Argall to set out again with his prisoners, to raze every French fort or settlement as far as Cape Breton, to hang La Saussaye and his men, to sack all French ships and to send the prisoners back home.[34] Argall left at once for Acadia with his warship the *Treasurer*, the *Jonas* under the command of his lieutenant Turnell, and a French pinnace built at St Sauveur that had been seized along with the *Jonas*. In October of 1613, he reappeared at St Sauveur. He razed the unfinished buildings, levelled the cross and raised another to proclaim English possession. At Ste Croix he burned the Habitation where Jean Plastrier had wintered, and destroyed everything else that smacked of France. On November 1, he appeared before the Habitation of Port Royal. It was deserted, for Biencourt and his men were at work far away. Argall ransacked it, took on board everything useful, and put the torch to the rest. Here and there he placed signs claiming Acadia for England. Bad weather then obliged him to stay at anchor for three or four days; he was still there when Biencourt returned, having heard the news from the Indians. Biencourt and Argall are said to have conferred for two hours.[35] According to the Englishman Purchas, Biencourt tried to win the protection of the English by offering to associate himself with them in the fur trade, and Argall, refusing point-blank, replied to the following effect: I am here to run you out; if I find you here again, I will treat you as an enemy.[36]

On November 9, Argall gave the orders for departure from Port Royal. He decided to take his eight Frenchmen back to Virginia instead of setting them at liberty. The next day, however, a storm scattered his little fleet; the pinnace disappeared, never to be seen again; the *Jonas*, driven toward the Azores, turned up in England in February 1614, with the Jesuits Biard and Quentin aboard; as for the *Treasurer*, it reached Virginia without further mishap.[37]

As soon as La Saussaye and Father Massé arrived in France in October

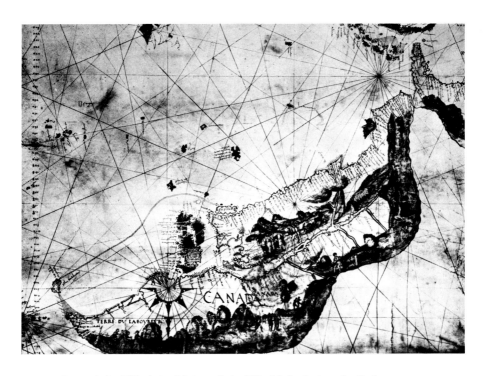

Part of the "Harleian" Map of the World depicting the St Lawrence,
about 1542. (North is at the bottom of the map.)

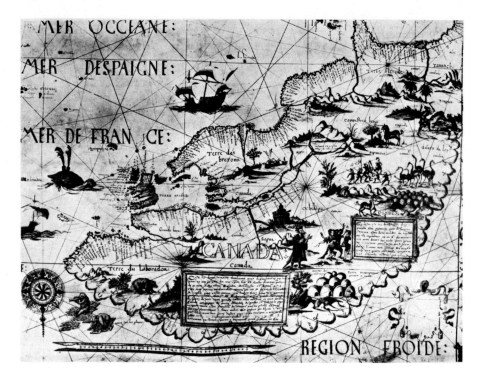

New France in 1550, by Pierre Descelliers. (North is at the bottom of the map.)

(Facing page, above) New France according to Gerardus Mercator, in 1569.

(Facing page, below) The Habitation of Chauvin at Tadoussac, 1600. (Taken from a map from Champlain's Voyages, published 1613.)

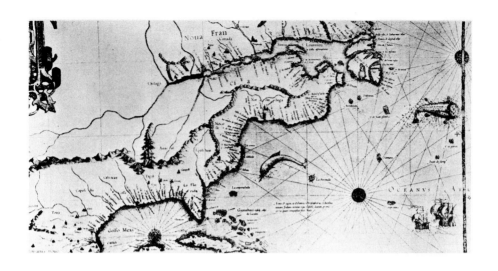

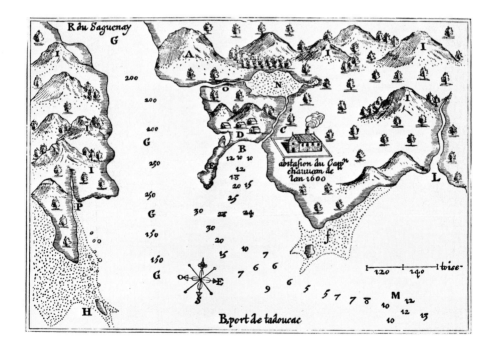

Full-sized replica of Jacques Cartier's La Grande Hermine, *as it was shown at Expo 67 in Montreal.*

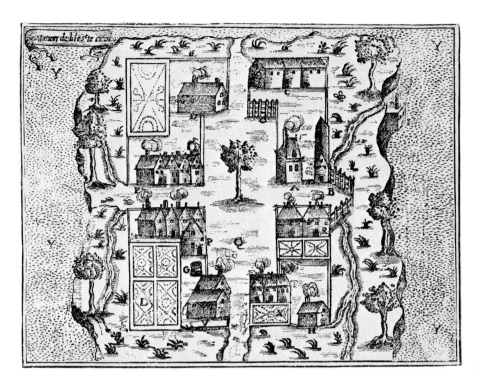

The Habitation of Ste Croix. (Reproduced from the Lavardière edition of Champlain's works.)

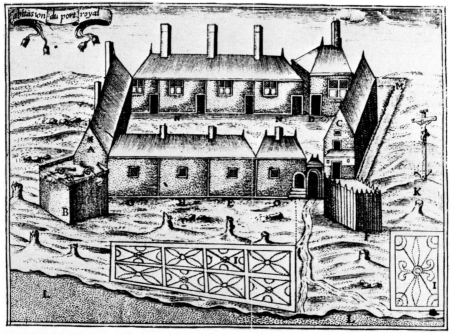

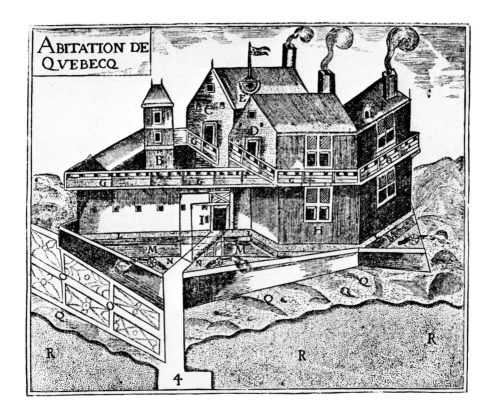

The Habitation of Quebec. *(Reproduced from the Lavardière
edition of Champlain's works.)*

*(Facing page, above) Remains of some of those who spent the winter
of 1604-1605 at Ste Croix.*

*(Facing page, below) The Habitation of Port Royal. (Reproduced from the
Lavardière edition of Champlain's works.)*

Portrait of Champlain. (Taken from an engraving representing the battle of 1609, as reproduced in Lavardière's edition of Champlain's works.)

1613, Admiral Montmorency and Madame de Guercheville had begun negotiations with England to obtain redress for the devastation wrought by Argall in time of peace. A dispute over frontiers complicated the whole affair. France claimed historic possession over eighty years; England replied that the colony of St Sauveur had been established in English territory.[38] The only redress that could be obtained from the whole disaster was the return of the *Jonas*; the surviving prisoners arrived in England in time to return to France on board the vessel.[39]

The destruction of St Sauveur brought Madame de Guercheville's colonial endeavours to an end. She remained in possession of the seigneury of Acadia until 1627, but she abstained from any further development there. As for Poutrincourt, who was still riddled with debt, in the spring of 1613 he had succeeded in entering into an association with the merchants Macain and Georges of La Rochelle, who were to receive all the beaver skins produced by the Acadian trade.[40] This had enabled him to send the *Grâce-de-Dieu* to Port Royal with supplies during the summer. Then, with Hébert, who had returned to France, he slowly prepared another expedition at La Rochelle. He set sail with all haste on December 31, however, no doubt because he had heard the news of the devastation by the English.[41] When he arrived at Port Royal on March 17, 1614, he found the Habitation in ruins; apart from the mill, which was some distance away, everything had been destroyed and the livestock had been carried off. He returned to France in the spring of 1614, leaving nothing in Acadia but the bare necessities for the operation of the fur trade under Biencourt's direction. The Poutrincourts, father and son, were henceforth no more than suppliers of furs, to the greater profit of the merchants of La Rochelle. Not for many years to come would there be anything more than a few trading posts in Acadia.

CHAPTER 9

The Rouen and St Malo Company

1614–1620

In the race among the European powers to carve out colonial empires in America, a pattern was now emerging. The Dutch were working to build their empire in the Hudson River valley, from where they might have access to the interior of the continent. The English had plans for a New England, which, as far as they were concerned, included Acadia, now that Argall had destroyed the existing French establishments there. For France there remained the great highway to the interior that she already occupied, the St Lawrence; here, with the help of the company of Rouen and St Malo merchants and their eleven-year monopoly, the foundations of a French empire might be laid.

In the spring of 1615, the company prepared and sent out three ships. After a crossing that took only a month,[1] Champlain landed once again at Tadoussac. He was accompanied by four friars in grey homespun habits, all from the Récollet Province of St Denis and belonging to the Order of Friars Minor or Franciscans, who had long been coming to America. The Friars Minor had been the first missionaries in the New World and the first to say mass on American soil; they already had some five hundred convents scattered over twenty provinces in Spanish America. The associates of Rouen and St Malo had agreed to bring six missionaries to New France each year free of charge and to feed them until such time as they should have a "Seminary." The Récollets landed in their new missionary domain in May 1615, having received from the Papal Nuncio a simple verbal permission,, which constituted the only jurisdictional tie between the Holy See and the Canadian mission.[2] No time was lost in launching the mission; a house with a chapel, whose titular saint remains unknown,[3] began to rise at once close by the cliff below Cape Diamond, near the Habitation and the storehouse; on June 24, Fathers Jamet and Le Caron sang mass beside the Rivière des Prairies on the Island of Montreal, the first mass ever celebrated above Quebec, if not in all the St Lawrence; the Laurentian Valley was divided into apostolic zones, and Father Le Caron decided to set out immediately for the far-away lands of the Hurons, so as "to be the first to proclaim the name of God in those parts," although Champlain would have greatly preferred the friars to become acclimatized first by spending the winter at Quebec.[4]

The Indians were waiting for Champlain at the St Louis Rapids. The allies were once again calling for help against the Iroquois, and Champlain and Gravé considered that such help was essential if ever the natives were to be won over, discovery to be speeded and Christianity to be spread. Champlain therefore decided to go to the Huron country for a period of, he thought, three or four months. He had already been up the Ottawa River as far as the domain of the Algonquins of Allumette Island in 1613, and in his account he wastes no words this time on a new description of the journey thus far, referring his readers to his previous publication.[5] He does not even tell us what reaction the French expedition to the Huron country aroused in the Algonquins.

Having passed beyond the Algonquin country and crossed Lake Nipissing, he entered a river which flowed out of the lake toward the west, the French River. When he came to the end of it, there before his eyes lay the great expanse of water of which he had heard in 1603 and which the natives of Hochelaga had tried to describe to Cartier: Lake Attigouautan, or Lake Huron. He gave it the name of *Mer douce* (Freshwater Sea). On August 1, after a journey of more than three and a half weeks by canoe, Champlain set foot in the land of the Hurons.[6]

In this first half of the seventeenth century, the Huron country was a small and restricted territory whose limits may be fixed by two lines, one drawn from the mouth of the Coldwater River to Lake Couchiching (two miles north of Orillia) and the other from the mouth of the Nottawasaga River to Lake Simcoe. This was Huronia as Champlain knew it, the great commercial centre of the Great Lakes, forty miles long and twenty miles wide.

Champlain had a rendezvous at Cahiagué, "the principal Village" of the Hurons, which was situated at the extreme east of their country near Lake Simcoe. There was good news; the Carantouans or Andastes, allies who dwelt to the south of the Iroquois country, could be counted on to provide five hundred men. This was a magnificent opportunity to catch the Iroquois in a flanking attack, if the plan of invasion were well co-ordinated. Brûlé, on his own suggestion, left with a dozen Indians to hasten these allies on their way.[7]

At last, on September 1, the Huron army, joined by some Algonquins, set off on the warpath. Portaging between lakes, "in easy stages" and "hunting along the way," it arrived in due course at the eastern end of another inland sea, Lake Ontario, which Champlain had never seen before and which, a few days earlier, Brûlé was perhaps the first European ever to see. The allies crossed from island to island to the south shore, and then penetrated more than thirty leagues inland. On the afternoon of October 10, six weeks after the departure from Cahiagué, they came upon an Iroquois fort, a village strongly fortified with four palisades thirty feet high and topped with galleries forming a parapet. In the village, the Iroquois had built gutters for putting out fires, fed from a nearby pond, and the galleries were stocked with stones ready for repulsing attackers.[8] It was an ingenious defence system using techniques current in Europe, and Champlain could not help but admire it. It may also have been the system that Cartier had seen at Hochelaga in 1535.

This was Iroquois country, the land of the confederation (still very loose) of tribes whose adjoining territories lay to the south of Lake Ontario. Beginning at the east, the five Iroquois nations were the Mohawks, the Oneidas, the Onondagas, the Cayugas and the Senecas. Which of these nations were the allies now confronting? Certainly not the Mohawks, because, to reach their lands, they would have to pass through Oneida territory. This village was probably Oneida or Onondaga; Champlain's account and map are not sufficiently precise to fix the exact location of the battle that was to follow. Three possibilities have been suggested; Lake Canandaigua, Lake Onondaga, and Nichols Pond, south of Lake Oneida. The last of these is the one officially accepted by the State of New York.[9]

After a first premature and unsuccessful attack launched by the Hurons, Champlain resorted to European techniques of besieging fortified towns, with a siege tower high enough to overlook the palisades, from which arquebusiers could fire down upon the galleries, and mantlets or movable wooden shelters to protect the attackers from stones and arrows as they attempted to set fire to the fortifications. Here, deep in Iroquois territory, early in the seventeenth century, a mediaeval siege was taking place. It was poorly co-ordinated, and, on October 11, after about three hours of battle, the allies were forced to fall back. They would not attempt a second assault unless the Carantouans should appear. Finally, weary of waiting, the army began to retreat on October 16. Because of a wound to his knee, Champlain was packed into a basket, "bound and pinioned on the back of one of our Savages."[10] And thus, with his crestfallen train of followers, Viceroy Condé's lieutenant returned from his military expedition in the land of the Iroquois.

This retreat in a basket and, far more still, this abortive attack on the Iroquois village signalled a sharp decline in Champlain's prestige. Until then, the French had always won out over the enemy, and in the eyes of their Indian allies they were invincible. On the other hand, the Iroquois had known nothing but defeat for half a century; first they had been forced to leave the St Lawrence and fall back south of Lake Ontario, and then they had been shut out from the flourishing commerce that the French had come to establish in the St Lawrence Valley. In 1609 and

1610, the European arquebusiers had assured the Montagnais, Algonquins and Hurons of powerful support; now the French had come with their military might to attack the Iroquois deep in their own homeland. This was a dramatic and historic event for the Iroquois: they had scored an upset victory; they had routed this army of invaders captained by a Frenchman and using tried scientific siege tactics. For them it was a turning point, from which they were to climb to a position of astonishing supremacy over the next forty years.

On October 27, upon reaching the north shore of Lake Ontario, Champlain wanted to return to Quebec. The Hurons had promised to escort him there, but although there were four volunteers, there was no canoe forthcoming. Champlain soon realized that the Hurons were deliberately keeping the French with them to protect themselves from the enemy; there was nothing for it but to "resolve to be patient."[11]

Since he was obliged to remain in the Great Lakes region, Champlain turned the situation to advantage by doing some exploration. With the Récollet Le Caron, he went in mid-January to visit the Petuns, great cultivators of tobacco and corn, who lived to the west of the Hurons between the Nottawasaga River and Lake Huron. The two Frenchmen then travelled southwest to visit the Cheveux Relevés, so called because of their elaborately upswept hair. They were Andatahouats, whose other name, Ottawas, was later to be used to designate all the Algonquians of the Great Lakes. They carried on a far-flung trade, exchanging merchandise with nations more than five hundred leagues away. After the destruction of the traditional Huron trade network by the Iroquois, it was the Cheveux Relevés who came forward to replace it, and their long acquaintance with the lands of the west made it possible for the French to penetrate far into the interior of the continent. Champlain would also have liked to push on to visit the Neutrals, who were of the Huron-Iroquois family and who lived on the shores of Lake Erie, but he was told that the Neutrals were at war with the Cheveux Relevés. (This may have been only an excuse to prevent the French from going any further, as we shall see in 1627.) Then, at long last, Champlain had hopes that a band of Nipissings visiting Huronia would lead him to the north to meet some Indians who traded with nations forty days' journey away; but this project, too, was set aside because, it would seem, a quarrel had broken out in Huronia between some Algonquins and their hosts.[12]

During that winter, Brûlé had covered a great deal more territory than had Champlain. He had left with twelve Hurons on September 8, 1615 to go to meet the Carantouans as they prepared to join the war party against the Iroquois, and returned to Huronia the following spring.[13] It seems certain, at least, that Brûlé did arrive among the Carantouans, since he had been accompanied by Hurons both going and returning, and since the Hurons had long maintained an alliance with this tribe and would continue to do so. But what of Brûlé's other adventures during this voyage? Brûlé claimed to have followed a river which emptied into the ocean in the vicinity of Florida. Was this the Susquehannah which passes through the territory inhabited by the Carantouans and flows into Chesapeake Bay? Or could it have been the Delaware, or the Hudson River, since Brûlé mentioned the Dutch? Brûlé's reference to natives who gave preferential treatment to Frenchmen raises further uncertainty, for there was no French commerce with the natives of either the Hudson River, the Delaware or Chesapeake Bay. According to his story, moreover, a miracle had saved him from torture, but if Providence had indeed intervened, as he claimed, it would have been on behalf of a man who was thoroughly contemptuous of it; and if the Indians in question (who were probably Senecas) had spared him and then showered him with kindnesses, it was because they had long been looking for an opening to talk trade with the French. Of this, Brûlé was not in a position to speak openly for fear of angering the Hurons, but in spinning a yarn about a miracle he astonished everyone, explained away the hospitality of the enemy as the result of heavenly intercession, and elevated himself in the eyes of Champlain. More astonishing still is his lack of concern for the report that he should have made to his superior. When he returned among the Hurons he stayed at Cahiagué; Champlain, after all, had sent him to Carantouan, and was only twenty-five miles away at the village of Carhagouha, but Brûlé did not take the trouble to go and recount his extraordinary adventures to his chief, nor to tell him that he had travelled far to the south and reached the Atlantic. It was not until two years later, in 1618 during trading at Trois Rivières, that Brûlé decided to speak up. One might suspect that he was afraid at that point of being recalled from among the Hurons and was using his story to prove himself indispensable. Considering the extreme vagueness of the story, the paucity of geographic information that it contains and the lapse of time that Brûlé allowed to pass before telling it, it would appear rash to accept as fact anything more than his journey to Carantouan.

After spending that winter in Huronia, Champlain was able to make the most important contribution since Cartier to what was known of the interior of the continent. The country he had seen was extensive: the lands of the Nipissings, the Hurons, the Petuns and the Cheveux Relevés, as well as a part of the lands of the Iroquois. He could place the Neutrals and he had heard tell of the Potawatomis. However, the map he drew in 1616 has many shortcomings: the upper St Lawrence is still only hypothetically represented; Lake Ontario is shown with its actual shape and location, but Lake Huron, which appears for the first time on a map, stretches lengthwise east and west; the body of water corresponding to

Lake Michigan and Lake Superior is poorly imagined; there is no Lake Erie, nor any allusion to the phenomenon of Niagara. It is very disappointing, also, not to find Huronia better represented. Indeed, it can barely be distinguished, and we can only regret that Champlain did not leave a regional map of the little country that had been his home for the winter. To the west, finally, he shows the *Mer douce* communicating with another expanse of water; does the latter open into the Asian Sea? The edge of the map comes just at this point, relieving Champlain of the need to provide an answer; in his appeal of 1618, however, he was to make much of the possibility of reaching Asia by that route. But for all the deficiencies of his map of 1616, Champlain had made a considerable addition to the geography of America.

With the coming of spring, the Hurons headed back to the St Lawrence to trade. Champlain set out with them on May 20, 1616,[14] taking the Récollet Le Caron with him, and for the next seven years the Hurons had no resident missionary. At Quebec, the winter had passed unclouded by any tragedy or epidemic. And there had been other winterers in the St Lawrence: Gabriel Picaudeau, representing a company of La Rochelle merchants, had passed the winter with four men at Matane,[15] but there seems to have been no communication between this group and the settlers at Quebec.

The missionaries' efforts in this first year had not been well rewarded. They had lived among the Indians but had been able to do little more than take cognizance of the problems confronting them. On the strength of the experience gained among the Hurons and among the Montagnais of Tadoussac, the Récollets held a study session on religious matters at Quebec in July of 1616.[16] The first conclusion borne in upon them was that before the Indians could be converted they would have to be civilized. Now to civilize them, the French would have to mix with them and, conversely, accustom the Indians to life among the French. Unfortunately the Company of Canada, for fear of weakening its monopoly, was opposed to a massive settlement of the country by the French, and did not wish to see the Indians settle in fixed locations. The Récollets also considered, apart from the fact that the Company did not maintain a sufficient number of missionaries, that the presence of Huguenots was an additional obstacle to the establishment of the faith. They therefore proposed a three-fold policy: a policy of settlement (the immigration of colonists, Huguenots excluded, who would have trading privileges and would teach the Indians to lead a settled life); a policy of missionary recruitment, with the establishment of a seminary; an information policy, to provide the associates with a source of information other than the reports of their own agents. These proposals constitute the first political and religious program ever formulated in New France. Its continuing influence in one form or another may be discerned in Champlain's memoranda of 1618, in Richelieu's policies of 1627 and in the enterprises promoted by the intendant Talon.

For the realization of the program proposed by the Récollets, steps would have to be taken immediately to promote interest in the missionary cause and to convince the associates of the importance of evangelizing and civilizing the natives. Fathers Jamet and Le Caron decided therefore to go to France. Champlain, having increased the size of the Habitation by a third, left on the same boat, taking with him some French wheat harvested at Quebec as proof of the fertility of the soil.[17] Together, they would launch a campaign to have the trading post turned into a true colony.

When they arrived at Honfleur the situation, once again, could not have been less favourable for New France, and in particular for Champlain as lieutenant to Viceroy Condé. The latter, who was second in the order of succession to the throne of France, had become the leader of a league of princes and others in opposition to the Queen Regent and her minister Concini. When civil war broke out, Condé was arrested on the order of Marie de Médicis and imprisoned in the Bastille. The following year, he was transferred to the keep of the Château de Vincennes, not to be released until October of 1619. Shortly after Condé's imprisonment in the Bastille, the Marquis de Thémines acquired the dignity of viceroy for himself. The associates, taking advantage of the situation, attempted to rid themselves of Champlain, but Champlain, in complete assurance, succeeded in postponing debate on the matter and in 1617 took ship for Quebec, where he stayed only a short time.[18]

He was accompanied by a new recruit, the apothecary Louis Hébert, who came under contract to the Company with his wife and three children and his brother-in-law Claude Rollet. By the terms of his two-year contract, for a remuneration of 300 livres a year, Hébert was to do whatever might be asked of him and would care for the sick free of charge; with the permission of the agent he might work on the land in his leisure time, but the results of such work would belong to the Company; at the end of the two years he would be freed of his obligations and would receive nothing more from the Company, but even then he would be allowed to sell his produce only to the Company and was strictly forbidden to enter into any trade with the Indians.[19] Clearly, the associates were anything but anxious to have colonists.

Champlain had based great hopes on this voyage of 1617, but the Indians failed to keep the rendezvous they had promised; and the merchants had failed him too, if it is true that a contract drawn up by de Monts with a view to increasing the scope of the Canadian enterprise was signed before the time of the voyage. De Monts was a member of the Rouen and St Malo Company and was still greatly interested in Canada. He had prevailed upon the associates to sign a number of articles envisaging a major development for Quebec, but, recalls Champlain, "all went up in smoke, by I know not what misfortunes."[20] And the Récollets' efforts in France had succeeded no better.

It was a precarious future that faced the Canadian colony. Not only did it suffer from a lack of consistent policy, but, from month to month, it was in danger of witnessing the end of the commercial company that supported it.

For all that, there were a number of voices raised, preaching the "cultivation of New France." Since Champlain's last publication in 1613, there had been several personal letters written in an attempt to counteract the colony's poor reputation; in 1615, for example, the Récollet Jamet wrote to Cardinal de Joyeuse expressing great enthusiasm.[21] These personal letters, however, reached only a small number of readers, who, generally speaking, no longer had need of being preached to.

In 1616, the public heard an appeal the like of which it had not heard for a very long time. It came from the Jesuit Biard. After defining New France in the first chapter of his *Relation*, he spent seven chapters describing the country, its climate, its products and its natives; then, after his chronological account, he devoted the last two chapters to a plea for a New France.[22] This enthusiasm for colonization matched that of Lescarbot's various publications, and Lescarbot himself heightened it with the republication of his *Histoire* in 1618. One sentence of Lescarbot's in particular sums up all these appeals: "In a New France, all of Old France may one day rejoice, with profit, glory, and honour."[23] From Acadia, too, there came a call in 1618: on September 1, Biencourt, who had succeeded his father, appealed from Port Royal to the authorities of the city of Paris for aid in the development of New France, suggesting that a haven be sought in Acadia for those unfortunate citizens who were dying of hunger in France, whereas in America they might find the means of living at ease.[24]

But the most impressive plea and the most functional program of colonization came from Champlain himself, at the end of 1617 or the beginning of 1618. It was the most coherent plan to be advanced before 1627.

Addressing himself first of all[25] to the Chamber of Commerce,[26] Champlain made an inventory of what could be drawn from the country. It may be summarized as follows:

	Value in livres per annum
Fisheries	2,000,000
Wood and by-products	1,300,000
Mines	1,000,000
Furs	400,000
Cultivation and stock-raising	1,700,000

Nor was this all; there was "that shortened road to China by way of the St Lawrence River": if the St Lawrence should prove at last to be the great highway of international commerce between Europe and Asia, what a source of riches it would be for France!

After this commercially-oriented appeal with its emphasis on glowing possibilities, Champlain presented a series of articles intended for the King but submitted first to the Chamber of Commerce.[27] This was the key document, in which he revealed his plan of colonization. What, he began by asking, would France gain from this New France? The establishment of the Christian faith "among a people of countless souls"; the possession of a land nearly 1,800 leagues long; and besides the considerable taxes to be collected on the sale of the country's products, there would be duties chargeable on merchandise coming from Asia, which should yield sums at least ten times as great as the total of all taxes then raised in France. And how were these immense benefits to be assured? By establishing a population in the country. First, three hundred families of four persons each (all capable of "hard work") would be brought to the colony, as well as three hundred men-at-arms. A city would be built in the St Charles Valley, to be called Ludovica. By the end of the first fifteen years the country would be firmly established, and there would be four cities and towns on the St Lawrence. The colony would be "buttressed" four ways: by military strength, with the three hundred men and with fortifications at Quebec and Tadoussac; by justice, requiring the presence of high authorities who would establish laws and ensure the proper conduct of business; and, third and fourth, by "trade and the tillage of the soil." Finally, Champlain estimated the cost of the first three years at 45,000 livres, but he judged that this sum could be recouped from the revenues of the country itself.

The Chamber of Commerce made a methodical study of this plan, hearing Champlain in person and consulting a number of others holding a variety of views.[28] Then, with its encouragement, Champlain presented a memorandum to the King which reiterated, but in summary form, the arguments he had advanced before the Chamber: the route to Asia which promised to bring great riches, the spread of Christianity, and the abundance of products to be yielded by New France.[29]

Unhappily, the necessary funds were not forthcoming and this magnificent plan was not put into operation. Only Champlain himself and the Récollets gained anything from these lengthy negotiations. On March 12, 1618, Louis XIII sent a letter to the merchant associates, signed by his own hand, in which he confirmed Champlain in his royally-authorized command and declared support for the proposed plan.[30] This royal gesture encouraged Champlain to apply his plan of colonization, but without giving him the means to do so; it also invited the merchant associates to co-operate, but without imposing any conditions upon them. As for the Récollets, on March 20, 1618, they obtained a charter from the Papal Nuncio giving them canonical existence and officially establishing "a mission Church." Canada was not assigned exclusively to the Récollets, however; missionaries could be sent to Canada by any Order, but if they were Récollets, they had to be Récollets from the religious province of St Denis.[31]

When Champlain reappeared at Quebec in the summer of 1618, he found that the winter there had been one of great hardship, due to a lack of food and an outbreak of scurvy (though there had been only one fatality). Furthermore, the country was in a state of agitation. Two Frenchmen, one of whom had killed an Indian, had been murdered by the Montagnais. As soon as their bodies were discovered, relations had been broken off with the Indians as a precautionary measure, and it was feared that a mass attack might be launched by eight hundred Indians who had assembled at Trois Rivières. A delegation of Montagnais then came to offer seven gifts of furs to assuage the anger of the French. The Récollets refused to allow the blood of Christians to be bartered in this way and demanded that the murderers be handed over. The French received two hostages, pending the arrival of the ships. Immediately after his arrival, Champlain went to Trois Rivières to hold consultations on the delicate situation. He agreed with Gravé to "handle the affair amicably and pass gently over these matters." The *raison d'Etat* had prevailed.[32]

Champlain noted with pleasure that the settlement at Quebec was beginning to take on an air of prosperity, with vegetables and other crops growing well. He built a furnace to test out certain powdery substances, but the experiment was inconclusive.[33] A new milestone was passed in the life of the colony that summer with the marriage of Etienne Jonquest of Normandy and Anne Hébert, daughter of Louis; it was the first marriage performed in New France. A religious milestone was passed also: in the chapel at Quebec on July 29, 1618, just after Champlain's departure, Father Dolbeau, who had stayed behind with Father Le Caron, proclaimed a jubilee for New France,[34] to correspond with that accorded to France by the Pope in June of 1617.

Champlain had told the Indians at Trois Rivières that he planned to return in 1619 with a great deal of help "in men, money and commodities" so that they might triumph over their enemies. He also planned to bring back "a goodly number of families to people this country."[35] The Company's two ships returned to France loaded with furs, but Champlain was to obtain precious little for the country, and could not even make the voyage of 1619. At the end of 1618, "by dint of entreaty," he had indeed succeeded in persuading the associates to commit themselves to a plan of settlement, the first ever accepted by a commercial company for the benefit of the St Lawrence colony. At one stroke, a population of eighty people was to be brought out and established. It was, Champlain wrote, "a gesture toward increasing the population handsomely"; but, once again, all this was to come "to naught."[36] Even Champlain's own position was more than ever in jeopardy. As he was preparing in the spring of 1619 to set sail with his young wife Hélène, he learned that the associates had decided to make a change in leadership. Gravé would command the Habitation and Champlain would be employed only at exploration. In vain Champlain produced the letter from Louis XIII confirming him in command, and his commission as Lieutenant to the Viceroy. The associates would hear none of it, and the Company's ship set sail without him. He had no choice but to return to Paris.[37]

Champlain's efforts overcame the opposition of the associates in the end, for on July 18, 1619 an edict of the Royal Council confirmed his command at Quebec and elsewhere in New France.[38] Certain difficulties were resolved by another development; on October 20, 1619, the Prince de Condé was released from prison and resumed his post of viceroy, although he did not keep it for long. For a sum of 30,000 livres, he stepped aside in favour of his brother-in-law, Henri de Montmorency et Damville, Governor of Languedoc, duke and Admiral of France. The new viceroy received his letters on February 25, 1620. On March 8 he confirmed Champlain in his office of Lieutenant to the Viceroy, and Champlain was instructed to go to Quebec and build a fort there. Looking back to the autumn of 1612, we see that after eight years the colony was still at the same stage of progress, for in 1612, too, Champlain had received an order (from the Comte de Soissons) to go and settle at Quebec, with the necessary authority to build a fort and assure the administration of justice and the enforcement of laws. Once more it was a case of starting all over again.

Armed with his lieutenancy to Viceroy Montmorency, and thus firmly ensconced over the heads of the Company of Canada, Champlain returned to New France, accompanied by his wife. He also brought with him the Récollet Georges Le Baillif, whom the Viceroy had strongly recommended he should consult.

The Habitation was in "such desolation and ruin" in 1620 that it was a pitiful sight to see. Champlain put his men to work, and "in a little while all was in proper condition to house us."[39] Then he turned to the building of the fort, on Cape Diamond some 170 feet above the Habitation. It was reached by a rough pathway, which in 1623 was made over into "a little road that led up with ease." This fort, called St Louis, was as yet only a wooden structure. By the spring of 1621 it was far enough advanced to allow Champlain to station men there in case of an alarm.[40]

CHAPTER 10

The de Caëns Take Over the St Lawrence

1620–1627

In the spring of 1621 the Laurentian colony was shaken to its core. The Viceroy's commissioner, the Sieur Guers, returned from France in May to announce to Champlain that the associates of Rouen and St Malo had lost their monopoly in November of 1620 and that a new company had taken their place, the company of the Sieurs de Caën.

What had been the situation in the Laurentian colony in that autumn of 1620? Tadoussac was still the St Lawrence seaport; ships still did not continue up the river to Quebec, in spite of Champlain's repeated requests. Quebec was the only place (except Matane, and that had been by accident) where anyone spent the winter. And what did Quebec consist of? The Habitation and storehouse of 1608, which were falling into ruins; close by, the house and chapel of the Récollets, built in 1615; on Cape Diamond, a little wooden fort in process of construction, and one house, Louis Hébert's. In the valley, on the right bank of the St Charles River, the Récollets had established their convent, and there, in June 1620, they laid the first stone of their church. As for the winter population of Quebec, statistics in contemporary documents are poor, but in 1620-21 sixty people were counted, the largest number on record up to that time. And still the colony existed only from day to day. The least delay in the arrival of supply ships reduced it to the point of famine. Upstream from Quebec there were two places where the French went every year, or almost every year, Trois Rivières and Ile St Ignace (opposite the mouth of the Richelieu), but none of them lived there. The western frontier of New France had been extended as far as the Great Lakes, thus increasing the opportunities for trade and the extent of the alliance with the Indians. But New France was still only a trading post.

Having stated in his letter to Champlain that "for several reasons" he had excluded the associates of Rouen and St Malo, Viceroy Montmorency continued: "I have chosen the Sieurs de Caën, uncle and nephew, and their associates; the one is a good merchant, and the other a good sea-

129

captain."[1] The uncle was Ezéchiel de Caën,[2] a native of Dieppe, who had been engaged in trade with distant countries since the beginning of the century at least. His son Emery, who was Catholic like his father, was soon to play an important role in this new company. The nephew was Guillaume de Caën, son of Ezéchiel's brother Guillaume and, like Champlain, a captain in the *marine du Ponant* or western fleet, who was to receive from the hands of the Viceroy a commission as *général de la flotte*. He was of the Protestant branch of the family, but, according to Dolu, the Viceroy's intendant, "such were his prospects, that there were great hopes of his becoming a Catholic."[3]

The commercial company established by the Viceroy on November 8, 1620, was officially named *Compagnie de Montmorency pour la Nouvelle-France* and, from 1625 on, *Compagnie de Vantadour*. For a period of fifteen years from January 1, 1621 until 1635, this company, generally known as the *Compagnie de Caën*, was to have exclusive right to trade in the St Lawrence Valley inside a line passing through Gaspé and extending from the 48th parallel to the 52nd, but it was forbidden to trade in munitions of war with the Indians. In return, it was to assume certain responsibilities. In the cause of settlement, the new company was to bring six families to New France in a fifteen-year period and feed and maintain them; each of these families was to consist of at least three persons. Every three years the company was to build a house of about twenty-five yards frontage, and with the expiry of the monopoly these five houses would become the property of the State, unless the associates were in occupancy themselves or had found occupants for them. The company was also to be responsible for all administrative expenses, including Champlain's emoluments as the Viceroy's Lieutenant (1,200 livres per year) and food for his family and the ten men in his service. There was also provision for other miscellaneous expenses and the transport and upkeep of six Récollets.[4] According to an estimate drawn up by the de Caëns, these settlement and administrative expenses could amount to more than 900,000 livres in silver, and that, it should be remembered, in a country completely open to illicit trade, in a colony whose very life still depended on a shuttle service of ships, and whose trade network might very well from year to year disintegrate or change according to the whims of the various Indian nations.

The associates of Rouen and St Malo, deprived of a monopoly that had been granted to them for eleven years (and should therefore not have come to an end until the autumn of 1624), protested in vain to the Viceroy. They then carried their appeal to the Royal Council, but there was no decision from the Council before the departure of their ships. This is how it happened that the associates of Rouen and St Malo set out for the St Lawrence as usual, while the de Caëns dispatched a little vessel of 35 tons to carry the news to Champlain that it was they who were now the monopoly-holders. The little vessel was the first to arrive, and the news that it carried brought great embarrassment and consternation to the authorities of Quebec. How could they deny the right to trade to the employees of the old associates, when it was they who comprised the strongest element in the colony? It was decided that they should be allowed to trade, pending the arrival of Guillaume de Caën, which would no doubt be soon.[5] But it was the large ship *Salamandre* belonging to the old associates which arrived next at Tadoussac. At Quebec there was a feeling of relief that the seizure of the old company's property ordered by the new associates had not been carried out, but there was a real danger of violent clashes between rival traders; Champlain prepared to defend his Habitation and stationed men in the new fort. The agents of the old associates were still allowed to go up the river to trade.[6] Guillaume de Caën finally arrived at Tadoussac with two ships early in the summer, after a difficult crossing, accompanied by his associate Raymond de La Ralde. De Caën had been instructed to announce an arrangement which ought to have satisfied everyone pending a final decision. On May 7, 1621, the Council of State had decided that the two companies should trade together for that year, and contribute equally to the upkeep of the residents of the Habitation.[7] However, de Caën took it upon himself to refuse recognition of the decree of May 7 and insisted on the validity of the order of seizure whose execution Champlain had deferred. De Caën moved to seize the *Salamandre* at Tadoussac; Champlain attempted to intervene by occupying the ship himself to prevent its seizure, but de Caën had been too quick for him. The next day, de Caën handed back the ship, apparently disappointed with his prize, but sent Louis Hébert to Champlain with a formal protest against the associates of Rouen and St Malo.[8]

Small wonder that in the middle of August the little colony came to the point of constituting a States-General to draw up a list of grievances. There had already been a deliberative assembly on the affairs of the colony held at Quebec in 1616, but on that occasion it had been organized by the Récollets and had been concerned primarily with religious matters. In 1621 the intention was to "advise on the most appropriate remedies against the ruin and desolation of this whole country," and to determine how the Catholic religion might be assured, as well as the authority of the King and the Viceroy. On August 18, Champlain, as Montmorency's lieutenant, and the Récollets Denis Jamet, Georges Le Baillif and Joseph Le Caron met with the leading colonists in the presence of Guers, the Viceroy's commissioner. The assembly chose the Récollet Le Baillif "as deputy representing the whole country in general." The friar, who had been pressed upon Champlain in the role of counsellor and who had had the ear of the highest authorities, was charged with the preparation of a *cahier général*, a report on the disorders afflicting the country, and with its presentation to the King.[9]

It is a matter of great regret that Sagard, who is the only one to have left an account of the assembly of 1621, did not see fit to record anything more than a summary of this report, which opened with a "remonstrance" from the Récollets. Reiterating the principles that Champlain had proposed to the King in 1618, it emphasized that religion, justice and armed strength were the "pillars & firmest foundations of a State." To assure the cause of religion, no Huguenot should be allowed to live in New France or to be maintained there; the King should found a seminary for fifty Indian children, maintain it for six years, and support the clergy with the grant of a benefice. As for justice, it would have to be "exercised with greater power the greater the size of communities established." Finally, there should be a more impressive show of armed strength in the country and broader powers for Champlain.[10]

The mission on which Le Baillif was sent to France did not end the troubles of the colony; far from it! When the members of the assembly of August 1621 had invited Le Baillif to put pen to paper on their behalf, they never dreamed how copiously he would do it. Besides preparing his report, Father Le Baillif published a violent anonymous pamphlet late in 1621 or early in 1622: *Plainte de la Nouvelle France dicte Canada, A la France sa Germaine*. In this pamphlet, New France allegorically complains to her sister, France, accusing Guillaume de Caën and his associates of crimes of every kind.[11] In support of his case against the de Caëns, Father Le Baillif shamelessly used letters, purportedly written by Champlain and other personalities of the St Lawrence colony, that were pure fabrications. Champlain and the others involved appealed to the King in protest.[12] Father Le Baillif, the chosen representative of Canada and *Eminence grise* of New France, had turned out to be a forger.

Harsh words led to blows. On January 13, 1622, Father Le Baillif, according to the complaint that he lodged with the Council of State,[13] was the victim "of attacks made against his person" by Louis Hébert, who was then in the service of the de Caëns. What decision was rendered by the Council of State is unknown.

The Récollets launched one last offensive in France, against the de Caëns; early in 1622, the Superior of the Province of St Denis requested the King to forbid Huguenots to live or even trade in New France, "in view of the trouble already stirred up" by them.[14]

Multiplying the grossest of accusations, plucking hard on all the religious strings and deliberately making use of falsehoods, the de Caëns' adversaries unleashed their wrath, but in vain. The Council of State declared its decision in favour of the de Caëns. On April 1, 1622, it adopted a "Regulation for the settlement and the trade of Canada." It had been agreed, in

1621, that the two companies would carry on trade conjointly, but the regulation of 1622 recognized only one, that of the de Caëns, to which it refers as the *Compagnie de Montmorency*. However, to compensate the associates of Rouen and St Malo, whose monopoly should have had three more years to run and who had spent a certain amount of money on the Habitation of Quebec, it was decided that they should be paid a sum of 10,000 livres and be offered individual membership in the de Caën company, and conditions were laid down for the liquidation of their possessions in the St Lawrence.[15] The bitter quarrels of the last sixteen months thereupon came to an end, and order was restored in the commerce of New France. There were still bickerings over religion, but these were mostly on questions of precedence. In the last weeks of 1622, the issue of another and final regulation completed at last the take-over by the de Caën company. Instead of receiving a payment of 10,000 livres and joining the de Caën company individually, as provided in the April 1 ruling, the old associates preferred to acquire a block of shares as a group. Ownership of the de Caën company being divided into twelve parts, it was agreed that five of these twelve should be held by the old company of Rouen and St Malo. The Council of State assigned the burden of the colony's expenses proportionately, while the fort of Quebec became the property of the King.[16]

In 1623, the little colony at Quebec entered a period of great activity in planning and construction. The Habitation, only fifteen years old, was deemed "so decrepit that at any moment it might tumble to the ground"; Champlain judged that it would be better to build anew than to be continually making repairs. Work on the fort was also a matter of urgency, as was an improvement in communications. First of all, Champlain had a road built along the St Charles River, and then he improved the path that led from the Habitation to the summit of the cape.[17] In the spring of 1624, when some work had been done on the fort, he turned to the building of a new Habitation to replace the wooden structure built in 1608. The new Habitation was to be of stone, with two wings and with turrets at the four corners. A ravelin, a semicircular fortification, would command the river, and the entire structure would be protected by moats to be crossed by a drawbridge. On May 6 the first stone was laid.[18] Quebec was entering a new era.

At Paris, where Champlain returned in 1624 with his wife, another change was in store for New France. Montmorency resigned from the viceroyalty early in 1625. Cardinal Richelieu had become Louis XIII's first and only minister, and was working to recuperate the King's authority, fragmented as it then was by the various institutions. Had he intervened against Montmorency because the Viceroy had compromised himself in the struggle between the feudal nobility and the increasingly despotic power of the throne? Or had he simply stood by and allowed the conclusion of an arrangement that weakened the influence of this man who already held three admiralties, of France, of Brittany, and of Guyenne? This, in any case, was the beginning of a rapid decline for Montmorency. In his five years as Viceroy of New France, his role had not been a negligible one. During his administration he reorganized the colony's commerce. The first fort was built on Cape Diamond and the King assumed its ownership. The Habitation was rebuilt in 1624. A court of justice was established, and the country's first ordinances were published by Champlain on September 12, 1621.[19] The first land concession in the St Lawrence Valley was executed on February 4, 1623, when Louis Hébert was granted in perpetuity the land that he occupied on the cape. It was Montmorency, moreover, who instituted the seigneurial régime in the St Lawrence. On January 3, 1624, he granted Cap Tourmente, the Isle of Orleans and other adjacent islands in fief to Guillaume de Caën, for his possession in "Seigneury & Barony."[20] In an era when so little was being done for New France, Montmorency's years as viceroy could be considered to have been well filled.

New France had long been dependent on the Montmorency family, by virtue either of the viceroyalty or of the admiralty, and so it now remained, because Henri de Montmorency sold his position and his prerogatives for 100,000 livres to a nephew, Henri de Lévy, Duc de Vantadour. There would be little point in trying to attribute Montmorency's resignation to the machinations of the Jesuits, but it was certainly the Jesuits who pressed Lévy de Vantadour to take up the succession. They were still keenly interested in New France, and their missionary efforts there would be vastly more promising if they could count on a viceroy truly fired with religious zeal and devoted to their cause. For this purpose, Lévy de Vantadour was the ideal man. This intensely devout nobleman, twenty-nine years of age, whose astonishing degree of piety was shared by his fourteen-year-old wife, had been under the spiritual direction of two Jesuits, first La Bretesche and then Noyrot. The latter, who had great hopes for the evangelization of New France, encouraged his penitent to acquire the viceroyalty.[21]

The missionary cause in Canada at this time was in no better state than the colonial. The Récollets, having spent their first years close to the Habitation, had decided in 1619 to build their convent half a league away in the St Charles Valley, where they found land suitable for agriculture. This convent was even equipped with ramparts, and was compared by Sagard to a "noble country house."[22] Its construction was closely connected with a plan for the establishment of a seminary for Indians. The Récollets had indeed recognized in 1616 that the Indians would have to be civilized before being Christianized, and that this work would be accelerated if young Indians could be suitably raised so that they might contribute later to the education of their brothers. The work was begun, but the death of Charles Des Boves in 1623 deprived the Récollets of the support they depended upon. There was no special seminary building; the Indian seminarists lived in the Récollet convent. Only eight natives in all are known to have been in residence, and of these eight, four went to France to pursue their studies, which demonstrates clearly that what was called a seminary had no regular scholastic program. Furthermore, from the fact that the four Indians went to France without even having been baptized, it may be judged to have been in reality no more than a half-way house, an antechamber, so to speak.

The Récollets were simply not up to the job they had set themselves. In 1615 and 1616, they had rejoiced in the delusion that they could be everywhere at once, but they soon came back down to earth. From 1616 to 1622, there was not a single missionary in the strategic Huron country. At Trois Rivières they stayed for only brief periods, and only in summer. Tadoussac was virtually the only place where they went more or less regularly to carry the Word during the winter. Besides, the number of Récollet priests in Canada had always been very small; never were there more than four at one time, and during the winter of 1616-17, we may note, Father Dolbeau was the only priest in all of New France. In the autumn of 1624 there were only three, two at Quebec and the other (Father Viel) in Huronia. And yet the Récollets had been here for nine years!

In view of their inadequate numbers and financial resources, and of the immense task before them, it is not surprising that they should consider seeking the help of other missionaries. In August of 1624, Father Le Caron revealed his plan to call for "new Evangelical workers."[23] He did not specify who these new workers should be. Certainly not more Récollets from the Province of St Denis, which had already proven to be too poor both in men and resources. Perhaps it was thought they should be Récollets from the Province of Aquitaine; three of these friars had been given shelter at Quebec following the closing of their mission in Acadia, and their Province had originally been considered for the Canadian mission. It would seem to be out of the question that any of the negotiations pursued by the Récollets in France had anything to do with an invitation to the Jesuits.[24] It was the Viceroy, Vantadour, who proposed the Jesuits. Legalistically speaking, it was not necessary to obtain the consent of the Récollets, because the missionary exclusivity stipulated in 1618 was valid only against Récollets from Provinces other than that of St Denis, and not against other religious orders. Nevertheless, so that the best possible conditions of co-operation might be assured, it was proper that the Jesuits should first have the agreement of the Récollets, and all was arranged in the friendliest of atmospheres.

Three Jesuit priests, Fathers Charles Lalemant, Enemond Massé and Jean de Brébeuf, arrived in Quebec in June of 1625. They had come at the expense of Viceroy Lévy de Vantadour and had set out with only a verbal permission from the King. They carried no formal letters, and no order had been issued to anyone to give them lodging. The Catholic Emery de Caën was in command at Quebec at the time, but Guillaume de Caën, his Huguenot cousin, informed the Jesuits that he could not give them shelter either in the Habitation or the fort.[25] There was no solution for them but the unimaginable one (unimaginable because they had come with the support of the Viceroy and the approval of the King) of return-ing to France. The Récollets then entered the scene and arranged that the Jesuits should take shelter in the St Charles convent, without cost "to the country."[26] There they were to stay until the summer of 1627.

With the same zeal shown by the Récollet Le Caron in 1615, Father Brébeuf was anxious to set out for Huronia immediately upon his arrival, in company with the Récollet La Roche d'Aillon, also newly come from France. It was necessary, however, to wait for the Récollet Viel, who was returning from the Huron country, so that they might consult with him. He was coming down to Quebec that year with a young Frenchman whom we know only by his Huron nickname, Auhaitsique,[27] but both perished in the Rivière des Prairies, in the very last of the rapids they had to pass. The death of Father Viel, which seems indeed to have been no more than an accident,[28] was a cruel blow for the Jesuits as well as for the Récollets. The Jesuit Brébeuf and the Récollet d'Aillon, both newcomers to the coun-try, had counted on the benefit of his experience among the Hurons and his knowledge of their language. They were obliged to postpone their departure until the following year. The Récollets had already been reduced to three priests in New France, and now there were only two.

That winter of 1625-26 there was no mission to distant parts, either for the Récollets or for the Jesuits. The important mission to the Hurons was suspended for the second time. The year 1626, however, was one of great progress in the establishment of the Jesuits. In the spring, some eight hundred paces from the Récollet convent but on the other side of the St Charles, they completed the first building of their own convent, which they called Notre Dame des Anges[29] in recognition of the service rendered them by the Récollets. Immediately upon his return to the country, Cham-plain chose Father Lalemant as "director of his conscience."[30] But still the Jesuits felt their position in New France to be somewhat insecure; even in France, from their own colleagues, the Quebec Jesuits were encountering resistance, and for this reason Father Noyrot, having just arrived, turned about and went immediately back to Paris.[31] The Récollets, for their part, received no reinforcement whatever; Father Le Caron returned to Canada alone, without a single recruit.

The accession of Vantadour to the viceroyalty in 1625 had brought no immediate change for the Huguenot Guillaume de Caën, but it was foreseeable that, under the pious Viceroy and with Jesuit influence now lending weight to that of the Récollets, de Caën's adversaries would win out in the end. Since the spring of 1621, moreover, de Caën had been encountering endless trouble. Every year he had to contend with the activities of illicit traders, which gobbled up a portion of his profits, for La Rochelle, Basque and other independents made continual incursions upon the fur trade. And then there were difficulties between de Caën and the old associates of Rouen and St Malo who had joined his company. The company's accounting had been complicated by the apportionment of the expenses of the enterprise, and had led to the preparation of a lawsuit involving a sum of 78,500 livres 18 sols.[32] These difficulties led not to rupture within the company but to a most curious settlement. The old associates of Rouen and St Malo decided in early 1626 to take no further active part in the operations of the company; they would leave the actual trading entirely to the de Caëns and would simply participate in the company's profits, receiving forty per cent interest on an investment of 60,000 livres per voyage. However, they got the better of the man who had ostensibly eased them out of the picture, by requiring (with the powerful backing of the Viceroy) that the company's fleet henceforth be commanded by a Catholic.[33] In other words, the Huguenot Guillaume de Caën would no longer come to New France.

While Guillaume de Caën was defending his position before the associates and the Council of State, the Récollet Joseph Le Caron had a pamphlet printed that amounted to a condemnation of de Caën and his monopoly, an *Advis* addressed to Louis XIII under the title *Au Roy sur La Nouvelle France*.[34] Father Le Caron had published a disputatious work in 1600 and had taught the young Louis XIII the "primary elements of the Faith." Like Father Le Baillif four years earlier, he was using every ounce of his influence to destroy de Caën and the Huguenots. Although he exaggerated and in certain cases stooped to half-truths, the dossier he presented had the effect of a devastating indictment.

This attack from Father Le Caron was the latest of a succession of protestations to issue from New France against the presence of the Huguenots: the complaints contained in the report on the country in 1621; the allegorical pamphlet by the Récollet Le Baillif in 1622; warnings addressed to the Viceroy in 1624. There was also the stipulation laid down in January 1626 by the associates of Rouen and St Malo to the effect that the fleet should henceforth be under Catholic command. Such an accumulation could not fail to have its effect on Lévy de Vantadour, who, after all, had acquired his viceroyalty for religious purposes. Cardinal Richelieu could even less afford to turn a deaf ear. The Peace of Montpellier in October

1622 had been only a partial victory for the crown; Richelieu had resumed the struggle against the power of the Protestants in France, but in February 1626 he had signed, albeit grudgingly, the Peace of La Rochelle, which pledged that the commercial activities of that Protestant city would not be disturbed. Without immediately cutting out the Huguenots as a whole, nor effecting any change whatever in the company or the monopoly, Richelieu decided that the fleet should be under Catholic command, and that Guillaume de Caën should not only be deprived of his right to the title *général de la flotte*, but should no longer even be allowed to set foot in New France. With the agreement of the Viceroy, de Caën designated his Catholic brother-in-law, Raymond de La Ralde, to replace him.[35]

From then on, de Caën redoubled his efforts to bring a degree of consolidation to New France. Although he would henceforth be absent from the country for good, he set to work through Champlain to put his barony of Cap Tourmente to good use, at his own expense. He had visited his domain with Champlain in 1623 and judged the cape, with its broad meadows stretching to the foot of the mountain, to be "suitable for the feeding of livestock," and that summer Champlain had had two thousand bales of hay harvested there and transported by water to Quebec.[36] However, using Cap Tourmente as a source of forage in this way proved to be a great inconvenience because of the distance involved. A more practical solution was to take the livestock to the food. And so Cap Tourmente became a stock-raising centre; by this means, it was hoped, the colony would be assured of a permanent supply of meat. It was only in 1626 that the plan to build on the site could be realized. In the course of that summer, Champlain had a stable built measuring sixty feet by twenty, and two wings, each eighteen feet by fifteen, using "wood and earth" throughout, Norman fashion. From the unfortunately vague description by Champlain and Sagard, we may picture lodgings and stable in a single unit, roofed with thatch, as was common in Normandy. It contained a chapel, according to Sagard, which was in use at least in the spring of 1628. Eight people were left to spend the winter there, including a woman and a little girl.[37]

The development of de Caën's barony was well launched. This Habitation was the first on the St Lawrence outside of Quebec; it had taken eighteen years to realize such an addition to the colony. A second addition should be noted, in another area also belonging to the de Caën company. During the summer of 1626, a dwelling was built at a cost of 6,000 livres on Miscou Island, at the de Caëns' expense.[38] The de Caëns therefore built three Habitations within six years, one at Quebec (which replaced that of 1608), another at Cap Tourmente, and a third at Miscou. Since they had been bound to build five houses over a period of fifteen years, they were in this respect well advanced in the program that had been laid out for them.

On February 28, 1626, the Viceroy raised the domain of Louis Hébert on Cape Diamond to the status of noble fief and accorded him another noble fief on the St Charles River upstream from the Récollet convent. On March 10, he made a grant of land to the Jesuits: one league by four, with frontage on the St Lawrence and the left bank of the St Charles and including a point of land on the right bank of the St Charles.[39] And in the spring of 1627, de Caën sent a shipment of livestock for the colony to add to the flocks and herds of Cap Tourmente.[40] It must have been on this occasion that the first plough arrived, because in the following spring the soil was turned with ploughshare and oxen for the first time in the St Lawrence since Roberval's day.[41] Louis Hébert, however, was no longer there to receive this plough, for he had died in January 1627.

CHAPTER 11

Problems of Indian Policy

1604–1627

To assure themselves of the unswerving commercial loyalty of their Indian allies, the French soon realized that it was not enough to have permanent settlements, nor even missionaries striving to civilize the natives through Christianity. It was political control that they would have to aim for, and, because of the nature of the Indian trade network, control not only of one nation but of a whole complex of nations. This, far more than colonization or evangelization, appears to have been the overriding immediate goal of the French in the period 1604-1627.

On the north shore of the Gulf, at the gateway to Canada, there was a nation that lived perpetually at war with everyone — the Eskimos. It was the Montagnais who contemptuously gave them this name, which meant "eaters of raw meat." The Eskimos' name for themselves was *Inuit*, meaning "men."[1] They had war on all sides: war against the Montagnais, their neighbours to the west; war against the Souriquois, who descended upon them from the Baie de Chaleur and Gaspé; war for many a year against the Basques and then against the French in general. According to Champlain, "they make war on the fishermen, who for their own safety arm small vessels to watch over their boats at sea as they fish for cod"; at their hands many citizens of St Malo had perished, and the St Malo fishermen had often "paid them back twofold." In 1632, Champlain admitted that he had still been unable to "make any peace with them."[2] So it was to be until the eighteenth century. For the French of 1627, the Eskimo domain remained inaccessible, a forbidden world.

The Montagnais, sometimes called Montagnards and particularly Canadiens, but calling themselves *Ilnut*, "the people,"[3] belonged to the Algonquian linguistic family. The name Montagnais meant in those days all the natives living on the north shore from Sept Iles to Trois Rivières: Betsiamites, Naskapis, Papinachois, Chekoutimis, Canadiens (the Montagnais of Tadoussac and Quebec), and even the Attikamegas who lived on the upper reaches of the St Maurice. The principal centre of the Montagnais was

Tadoussac, where they had a fortified village on Pointe aux Vaches. They also had an encampment in a pine grove a league or two above Quebec, which would correspond to present-day Sillery. They were to be found, too, at Trois Rivières for the annual trading, and it seems that they sometimes camped there for the winter.

Champlain, who had been in contact with them almost every year since 1608, declared in 1624 that "we have no greater enemies." The French indeed lived in constant fear of them. Champlain even imagines them saying to themselves, "if we kill the French, soon other trading ships will come and we will be the better off, for we will have goods more cheaply from the La Rochelle and Basque merchants."[4]

The little French population of fifty souls that spent each winter cut off from all contact with other Europeans may have tended to exaggerate the danger that they faced. Be that as it may, the Montagnais kept watch over their own interests like the most sagacious of tradesmen. They were already highly reputed for their long trading journeys into the interior of the continent, and they had no intention of letting their furs go for a pittance; they were the middlemen between the French and the nations of the interior, and were determined above all to keep the French from going directly to the source of supply. Here we touch upon one of the major reasons why the French were slow to make discoveries to the north and to the west. Various tribes had thrown up barriers across the principal waterways leading to the St Lawrence, and they found any number of excuses for preventing the French from passing beyond them. The Montagnais had their share in the blockade; in 1608, Champlain had hoped to go exploring up the Saguenay, but, as he writes, the Indians "did not wish that I should go with them, nor any of our people," and covered up with a vague promise; in 1610, the Montagnais said, they would lead Champlain by way of Trois Rivières as far as Hudson Bay, returning by the Saguenay. They were careful not to keep their promise. Champlain believed that the time would come at last in 1611,[5] but still he was to wait. The Montagnais, Sagard assures us, in order to keep the trade with the interior for themselves, simply did not wish to take lay Frenchmen to the Saguenay.[6]

If effective control was ever to be exercised over these difficult allies, it seemed that they would first have to be pinned down to some precise spot, near the French, and gradually turned into farmers. French merchants, however, were as much opposed to that policy as to French colonization, because they foresaw that if the Montagnais ceased to be nomads, and consequently ceased to be hunters, the fur market would suffer. A Catholic of rank is even reported to have told the Récollets Viel and Sagard that if the missionaries turned these Indians into "sedentary neighbours," he and his kind would take sticks and drive them out.[7]

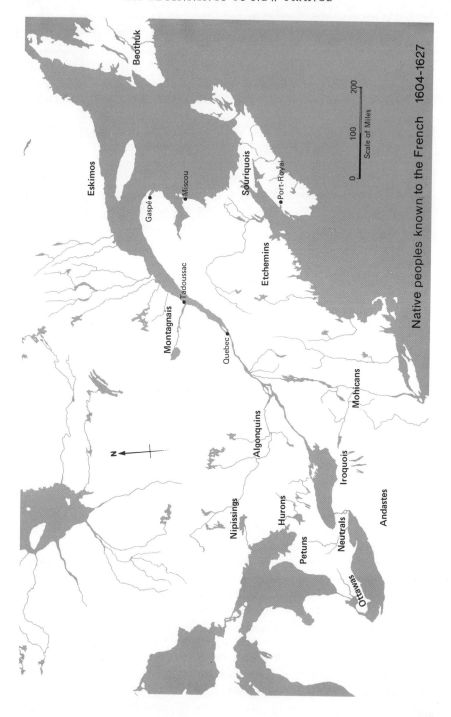

Native peoples known to the French   1604-1627

It was in the autumn of 1621 that Champlain saw an opportunity to intervene in the domestic and political affairs of the Montagnais. Miristou, also called Mahigan Aticq Ouche, wanted to become chief of his tribe, with Champlain's help. Champlain said to him, "If the French should choose to help you, it would be on condition that you settle near Quebec with thirty of your Montagnais." The candidate complied, and in the spring of 1622, with some of his tribesmen, began to clear the land at a place consequently known for a time as the *désert des Sauvages*. Champlain was satisfied and promised Mahigan Aticq that he would ensure his election over the two or three other candidates. The election took place; Mahigan Aticq became chief, and was officially recognized by the French with the presentation of a sword. The same was done for another Montagnais, who wished to become sub-chief. Champlain's plan had succeeded: the Montagnais had lost their political independence. "In this we showed the other savages that in future, when they desired to elect a chief, it would be with the consent of the French," wrote Champlain with satisfaction. Then the French would "begin to win some governance over them, and be better able to instruct them in our belief."[8]

If Champlain had succeeded in imposing his control over the internal affairs of the Montagnais, the plan for settling these people on the land was, for all that, never to be a great success. Turning them into a sedentary people and teaching them to live from the cultivation of the soil would have taken resources that Champlain did not have. In 1627, when the Récollet Le Caron exhorted the Indians to settle down so that they might learn the faith and accustom themselves to government by the French, the Montagnais asked to be supplied with food for a year or two, the time it would take to "prepare the land"; the ships of 1627 had not yet arrived, however, and there was no food to give them.[9]

Some Indians did settle down, but very few; in all, three or four families.[10] It was a very modest beginning, but these wandering hunters could hardly be transformed completely in two or three years. When the necessary means became available (for they would have to be supplied with everything if they were to be turned into farmers), the plan would be attempted again on a larger scale; this was to be the Sillery reserve experiment.

Westward from the territory of the Montagnais or Canadiens were the Algonquins, ensconced on the upper Ottawa River. The first of these were the Ouescharini, or Algonquins of the Petite Nation, who lived back from the river (behind the present town of Montebello) and who did not seem to play any important role in the movement of furs. Upstream, on what is now called Allumette Island and in the immediate surroundings, were the Honqueronons, better known as the Island Algonquins. Among the Indians, writes Sagard, these Algonquins were "the merchant class, in that they do much trade and as good merchants undertake long journeys"; they were "the harshest, proudest and least courteous of all those with whom I have conversed in all the lands of Canada."[11]

The Island Algonquins held a strategic and very important position on the river, because they had absolute control over a long series of rapids and over the portage that led around it, and any who passed that way were obliged to pay tribute. So as to keep their position as middlemen between the French and the nations of the interior, they did their utmost to bar this route. They did not, in fact, dare refuse passage to the French, nor even exact tribute from them, but they did try to discourage them. It will be remembered that in 1613 they did everything possible to prevent Champlain from travelling up the river. The barrier was to remain intact for many years; the Jesuit Le Jeune refers to it in 1633 and again in 1636.[12] It disappeared only when the Iroquois scattered the Algonquins in the wake of their victory over the Hurons in 1649-50.

Between Allumette Island and Lake Huron there was another barrier, but a much less formidable one. This was posed by the Nipissings, called Squekaneronons by the Hurons and Sorciers by the French because of their habit of consulting "the devil in time of necessity."[13] The Nipissings, like the Island Algonquins, traded afar. According to Sagard, they even had commercial relations with a nation to whose shores came a certain people by sea "with large boats of wood bearing many kinds of merchandise, such as axes shaped like a partridge's tail, and long leggings with shoes attached," all articles which they exchanged with the Nipissings for furs.[14] Although the Nipissings did not seem to make much trouble for other Indians passing through their country on their way to the St Lawrence, they fully intended to keep their distant trade relations to themselves and were unwilling to take lay Frenchmen on their journeys.

While the Montagnais and the Island Algonquins could be counted on, in spite of all, since they needed the trading posts of the St Lawrence to provide a market for their goods, it was very difficult to keep the Hurons in the alliance, because of their situation in the interior of the continent. It was they, first and foremost, who were the masters of the commerce of the Great Lakes. Their tiny domain was the terminus of the great trade routes. The Hurons were the exclusive buyers of the produce of their immediate neighbours, the Petuns; they denied the French access to the Neutrals; they provided the principal outlet for the far-roving Nipissings; it was to them that the Cheveux Relevés (the future Ottawas) brought furs from the far-away nations of the west.[15] In the interior of the continent, the Hurons played the role that the little city of Venice played in the Mediterranean, or the Dutch in international commerce. Like the Italians of the sixteenth century, who had made their language the international language of commerce, and as the English made theirs in the nineteenth century, the Hurons had no need to speak other languages than their own. They knew only Huron, and Huron was the language of commerce for the Island Algonquins, the Nipissings, the Petuns, the Neutrals, the Cheveux Relevés, and even for the Potawatomis (beyond Detroit) and the distant Winnebagos of the western shore of Lake Michigan.[16]

The alliance of the French with the Hurons was very recent, dating only from 1609, and it was still very fragile. At first there had been only one European outlet for furs, through the French of the St Lawrence, but this was no longer so from 1613 on, as the Dutch strove to channel the fur trade toward the Hudson River. How long could the Hurons be expected to remain faithful to the St Lawrence market, which required a journey of almost six hundred miles, when they were only three hundred miles away from the Dutch trading posts? Only the Iroquois, to whom they were racially and culturally related, stood between them and the Dutch, and the Iroquois were working to make a place for themselves in the mainstream of the fur trade even before achieving political unity; by 1626 they were to succeed in acquiring access to the Hudson River and the Dutch markets. It would have been natural for trade to flow from Huronia to the Iroquois country and thence to the Hudson, and this would have meant that all the furs of the Great Lakes would be channelled toward New Amsterdam, the St Lawrence market thereby losing most of its profitability. To prevent this natural orientation, the French constantly maintained interpreters among the Hurons from 1610 on. Their role was essentially to persuade the Hurons each spring to come down to the St Lawrence to trade. Etienne Brûlé, for his part, received 100 pistoles a year "to urge the savages to come to trade." But the poor behaviour of most of these Frenchmen did little to strengthen the alliance, and even less to make French culture and Christianity attractive to the Hurons.[17] In 1623 it was feared that the latter were thinking of disassociating themselves from the French and joining with the Iroquois; because of an imminent meeting between the two, a special French mission was sent to the Hurons. This was a political mission, consisting of eleven laymen and three Récollets, its purpose being to rekindle the Hurons' enthusiasm for the French and to ensure that they would not "make alliance with our enemies."[18]

While making every effort to preserve the Huron alliance, the French also considered opening a new commercial route to reach beyond Huronia. If, for example, trade relations could be established with the Neutrals, and if they could be brought to the French trading posts by way of the upper St Lawrence, the Huron monopoly would have been breached and French influence on the Great Lakes would no longer depend on the Hurons alone. This, in short, was the real object of the mission of the

Récollet La Roche d'Aillon in 1626-27. On an order from Father Le Caron, the Récollet went in October 1626 to the land of the Neutrals, a territory extending some eighty leagues along the Niagara River and the north shore of Lake Erie, where they raised very good tobacco. At first he was received cordially and was even declared a "citizen and child of the country." Three months later, however, there was an outburst of antagonism against him.

During this time, and this was the purpose of his journey, Father d'Aillon had set about learning what he could of the flow of waters from Lake Ontario, so that he might lead the Neutrals by this route to the trading posts of the St Lawrence; if the outlet of this lake could be found, ten days would be all it would take to paddle down the river to trade, while the route from Huronia by way of Nipissing and Algonquin territory took at least three weeks. Such a change of route would undoubtedly have had the effect of shifting the commercial pivot of the Great Lakes to the Niagara country, to the benefit of the Neutrals. It was also reasonable to suppose that the Iroquois, situated conveniently on this new highway, would have immediately thrown in their lot with the St Lawrence trade, or else played both fields at once, as in fact they did after the general peace of 1701.

The Neutrals, it would seem, knew very little about paddling canoes and nothing at all about the proposed route, but they were nevertheless ready to send four canoes in an attempt to initiate it. The first and most obdurate adversaries of this plan could be no other than the Hurons, for it would jeopardize both their political predominance and their Great Lakes monopoly. They kept a weather eye open, and when they learned what was happening they spread a rumour among the Neutrals that Father d'Aillon was nothing but a weaver of spells. Things deteriorated to the point where the Récollet had his baggage ransacked and was slapped and punched; an attempt was even made on his life. The Jesuits in Huronia sent a Frenchman to bring him away.[19] The whole affair had hardly enhanced the missionary cause; in the eyes of the Indians, the missionary had become a commercial agent acting in the interests of a competitor. This may perhaps explain the increasingly numerous difficulties encountered by the missionaries among the Hurons.

The French fared no better in solving the Iroquois problem. It should first be noted that, since the establishment of the French in the St Lawrence, the war against the Iroquois had never been more than a minor one of skirmishes between small groups, and it was only in the 1640's that it took on the scale of a general conflict between the Iroquois and the French. In the first thirty years of the seventeenth century, the two sides had not yet come to a confrontation. Nor was the Five Nations Confederacy as yet in existence; each Iroquois nation was still fending for itself. Once the Mohawks had vanquished the Mohicans and taken over the Dutch trade, they denied passage to their Iroquois neighbours, who in turn denied the Mohawks passage to the west and southwest. Champlain, it will be remembered, means the Mohawks when he speaks of the Iroquois, not all the five nations. It was the Mohawks that he defeated in 1609 and 1610, and it was probably also the Mohawks that he intended to attack in 1615. But even among the Mohawks there was no general mobilization against the allies of the St Lawrence; it was only small bands of them who came to make war, just as the Montagnais went in small bands to make war on the Mohawks.

After the battle of 1610 on the Richelieu there was no large-scale invasion of the St Lawrence by the Iroquois in this period. At least, neither Champlain nor Sagard mentions any. The Récollet Le Clercq, in a work of 1691,[20] speaks of two surprise attacks from the Iroquois, one in 1621 when the Récollet Poullain was captured on his way to visit the Nipissings (and was released soon after), and the other about 1622, when the Iroquois attacked the Habitation of Quebec and the convent of the Récollets. Champlain's and Sagard's silence with respect to these attacks, however, particularly the second, casts considerable doubt on these reports.

When there was talk of peace, again it was a matter of small groups exchanging visits; these were not official diplomatic missions. Such was the case when, on June 9, 1622, two Iroquois turned up at Quebec, at the hut of the chief Mahigan Aticq. Champlain went to meet them, then feasted them at the Habitation the following day. These Iroquois offered to put an end to the war that had been going on "for more than fifty years," but they had not been sent by their tribe; they had come on their own initiative to see some friends and relatives held in captivity by the Montagnais. It was therefore as friends that they were received, but since Champlain was hopeful that such a peace might bring an increase in trade and facilitate exploration, it was decided that a mission should be sent to invite the Iroquois to come to Quebec on an official visit. The emissaries were given merchandise worth thirty-eight beaver skins, to be presented as a gift at their destination.[21]

We do not know what reply the Iroquois gave to this overture of 1622. We know only that in 1623 it was necessary to send Father Le Caron in all haste to Huronia with a French party to prevent a commercial alliance between the Hurons and the Iroquois. Such an alliance would have been fatal to the St Lawrence trade. Peace with the Iroquois was hoped for, but on condition that it should be favourable to the St Lawrence. In the spring of 1624, the peace was still at the stage of preliminary talks. It was a most delicate stage; in April of 1624, Champlain was obliged to resort to threats to keep a party of Montagnais from going on the warpath. He succeeded in sending a party of Montagnais as ambassadors instead. The Iroquois received the mission very well, but on the return journey one of the ambassadors, the Montagnais Simon, could not resist the temptation to kill an Iroquois, and the French were hard put to "repair this mistake." For all that, it was learned in Quebec on July 25, 1624 that six Iroquois were coming to confirm the friendship treaty. According to Le Clercq, Champlain called a meeting of the Indian nations at Trois Rivières, and, that summer of 1624, a general peace was signed with the Iroquois. Champlain had the making of peace very much at heart, but since he makes no mention of this solemn ceremony at Trois Rivières in 1624, we may conclude that there was no such ceremony, but only a simple confirmation of the friendship treaty. In any case, it seems that, on the occasion of this peace, some Iroquois came and settled near Quebec alongside the Montagnais.[22]

The *petite guerre* was to be resumed, nevertheless. In 1626 the Mohicans, who had enjoyed the mastery of the upper Hudson River, were defeated decisively by the Mohawks, whose access to the Dutch trading posts they had been blocking. From then on, the Mohicans were pushed back to the Connecticut River region, leaving the Mohawks the undisputed masters of the Dutch fur market. The Mohicans were allies of the Montagnais, and when the Montagnais visited them in the course of the following winter the Mohicans asked them to take the warpath against the Iroquois. Whether it was to maintain this alliance or to avenge their own losses, the Montagnais accepted, and during the trading season of 1627 they returned with Iroquois prisoners. They began to exercise their vengeance on the prisoners, despite efforts by the Jesuit Lalemant and the Récollet brother Mohier to intervene. Champlain stepped in at this point and persuaded them that the prisoners should be sent home along with a party of ambassadors who would go to talk peace. Several Frenchmen offered to go, but their offers had to be declined because the conditions they asked were excessive. Only the offer of Pierre Magnan was accepted; he was to receive twelve crowns and the profit from any beaver he might bring back. As companions he was given two Montagnais (Simon, and another known as Le Réconcilié), and two Iroquois prisoners, one of whom had been adopted at any early age by the Montagnais.

It was indeed a curiously-composed ambassadorial mission: the sole Frenchman was this Pierre Magnan who, for having beaten a man to death at home, had been constrained to "betake himself to New France"; the Reconciled was a Montagnais who had killed two Frenchmen at Cap Tourmente in 1617 and had been pardoned in 1623; it was he who was to be the indirect cause of the mission's failure. When it became known, recounts Champlain, that the Reconciled would be part of the mission, an Algonquin who detested him went to the Mohawks and told them that this man was coming as a spy. The Mohawks, who were anxious to avenge certain of their losses on the allies of the Mohicans, took the Algonquin's story for the truth, and the Reconciled was taken prisoner upon his arrival. He was made to eat of his own flesh, "pieces from his thighs and other parts of his body." As for Magnan, he was burned slowly and agonizingly to death. A third ambassador was killed with a tomahawk as he tried to escape, but the life of the Iroquois who had been adopted by the Montagnais was spared. Champlain had little regret for the death of Magnan and the Reconciled; as far as he was concerned, they were murderers whom God had undertaken to punish through the Iroquois: "Thus does God sometimes punish men who think to escape His Justice by one road and are caught by another."[23] Magnan was the only Frenchman to fall victim to the Iroquois during this period of 1604-27.

The attempt to bring about peace between the Mohawks and Montagnais had failed once again. If they were not to lose face in the eyes of their allies, the French had no choice but to resort to war. In anticipation, the Montagnais seized a little Iroquois hostage; they tortured him and passed around his flesh among themselves to be eaten. Once again it was the traditional vicious circle; one side always had deaths to revenge on the other. So the *petite guerre* continued, as the occasion arose.

CHAPTER 12

The Meeting of Cultures

In the sixteenth century, European presence in North America can hardly be said to have been anything more than occasional and fleeting. When Europeans came to spend the winter, they lived on the fringe of the native society; those engaged in the drying of fish came only in summer. This presence had already brought about certain changes in the way of life of some groups of natives, but its influence had as yet touched only the coastal regions. Europe was still only on the threshold of the new continent.

It was in the first quarter of the seventeenth century that Europeans and natives began to have a real and profound influence on each other. This may be considered the period when the natives began, in many respects, to be Europeanized. The French, for their part, having made attempts to gain a foothold in widely differing areas and climates (the St Lawrence Valley, Brazil and Florida) without finding a lasting place for themselves, finally settled down and began to adapt to their new environment. Between 1604 and 1627 appeared the first generation of French Americans.

For Europeans of the preceding century, the Newfoundland cod fishermen aside, the Atlantic crossing had been an almost superhuman undertaking. In the seventeenth century, such crossings were still fraught with danger and hardship, to be sure, but were no longer out of the ordinary. The fact that crossings were made every year was new, too; ships were now virtually shuttling back and forth between Europe and America, and what was out of the ordinary was not that they came so regularly, but that on occasion they did not come.

The voyage was a slow one until the nineteenth century. The long detour by way of the West Indies was abandoned, but the far-away Azores still sometimes served as port of call, as in 1606 and 1611, or else, which seems to have been habitual practice, ships would head for Brouage in Saintonge from Havre de Grâce or Honfleur to take on a shipment of salt, for the Atlantic crossing was still tied to the economics of fishing. The voyage would sometimes take up to three months, though most often it could be done in two. In 1615 and again in 1618, it was even completed in a single month. The duration of the return to France, as far as we can tell, was usually shorter, ordinarily less than two months, and we may note that in 1613 it was only two weeks. Not insignificantly, Champlain carefully notes the dates of departure and arrival on his first voyages, then, as if these details ceased to be of interest, he lets them drop.

Once established, the French quickly adapted themselves to the new conditions of transport in the American interior. Apart from a few footpaths around Port Royal and Quebec, there was no way of going from one point to another except by boat and, more generally, in the birchbark canoes used by the natives of Acadia and the St Lawrence Valley. The French were soon excellent canoeists. In winter, like the Indians they took to snowshoes and to toboggans for the transport of heavy loads over the snow. In the seventeenth century they thus acquired a mobility that their predecessors of the sixteenth never had.

The winter of 1535-36 had been a miserable failure, the two of 1541-42 and 1542-43 might be considered so too, and even the winter of 1600-1601, leading to the possible conclusion that the St Lawrence was uninhabitable the year round. In the beginning, each winter had been a new ordeal that tried the limits of human endurance, but the French learned to live with winter and became so accustomed to it that, in time, Champlain ceases even to mention it. They now knew how to build a house that would hold the heat and minimize the effect of the wind, having learned since the days of Ste Croix Island to dig a cellar first, and not build directly on the ground. They knew enough, too, to bring in a provision of wood before the winter and thus spare themselves unnecessarily fatiguing toil.

The greatest obstacle of the earliest days was the scourge that had ruined Ste Croix in 1536 and Tadoussac in 1600, the scurvy. In this respect, progress was slow. Of the seventy-nine persons wintering at Ste Croix Island in 1604-5, thirty-five or thirty-six died. Thereafter, the malady declined: the following year at Port Royal there were between six and twelve deaths out of a population of forty; in 1606-7 there were only four or perhaps seven victims, and subsequently, for many years, there is no mention of scurvy in the Acadian peninsula. In the St Lawrence Valley, 1608-9 was another disaster; of the twenty-eight who spent that first winter at Quebec, thirteen died of scurvy, not counting seven dysentery victims, but in 1609-10 there was little sickness, and there was none at all in 1610-11. After that there is no mention of a serious incidence of sickness until the first winter spent at Miscou in 1626-27, during which everyone fell ill and "all came close to dying from the land sickness." The scourge was not yet vanquished for good: in 1629-30, another dozen died in Cape Breton; in the winter of 1634-35, almost everyone at Trois Rivières suffered from scurvy and a number died.[1] But these, we believe, were exceptional crises; the obstacle of scurvy appears to have been surmounted.

This was not because of a rediscovery of the wonderful *annedda* of Cartier's day (neither the natives of the St Lawrence nor those of Acadia knew of the Stadacona remedy), but because of the adoption of appropriate living and eating habits, and in particular the use of foods containing vitamin C. It had been known in Europe since the beginning of the century that both land and sea scurvy must be warded off by the consumption of potatoes, oranges and lemons. And so we see antiscorbutic foods appearing on the French menu.

Naturally enough, the French tried to eat and drink as they did in France. They had salt and salted meats, flour for bread and biscuits, hams, spices, sugar, small fruits like raisins and prunes, nuts such as almonds, and, in general, other foods suitable for export, and they grew a variety of old-world vegetables. They also had cod, the American fish which had been a European staple since time immemorial, but, curiously enough, the cod they ate had travelled all the way from America to Europe and back to Quebec; as Father Le Jeune wrote in 1636, they did not go to catch this fish that was "at our door so to speak [. . .] because there are not yet enough men here to go down to do this fishing."[2]

As for drinking as they would in Europe, they did their best. According to Sagard, wine was very scarce in the St Lawrence Valley; when sacramental wine was in short supply, the men would make some from local wild grapes. There were distilled spirits which led to drunkenness here as elsewhere, and, to Champlain's annoyance, the men of the Habitation used a trap door inside the storehouse to get to the cellar and "drink our beverages, quite unconscionably." But spirits were also a source of comfort during the rigours of winter, and when Brother Sagard made his journey to the Huron country in 1623 he found that one or two bottles of spirits "were most necessary to strengthen one's courage on the way."[3] A common drink was cider, and there was also locally-made beer.

They found some new gastronomic items in America. First of all there was maize or Indian corn, the Indians' principal staple, from which they made a preparation that they called *migan*. They would grind it and boil it with fish, or else they would take dried corn, roast it in the ashes, and then reduce it to meal. It was preferably with corn meal that they made their *sagamité*, although this word signified "every sort of soup, gruel, & similar things," into which they would throw, with great abandon, anything edible that happened to be at hand. The French were obliged to get used to corn, whether prepared as *migan*, *sagamité* or any other way. Brother Sagard, for his part, declined to partake of *sagamité* at two successive meals that consisted of that and nothing else; at the third meal, he ate it only from desperation.[4] It would seem that when the French did take to corn, in most cases it was as a last resort. They even grew it themselves.

Also new for the French were a number of meats; moose, which was hunted in winter, bear, whose flesh was "very good and tender, and similar to beef," and even dog, which was greatly relished by the Indians and to which the French accustomed themselves in spite of their initial repugnance. Feathered game was new as well, and very abundant. In the spring of 1627, after three days of hunting at Cap Tourmente, fifty-six *outardes* or wild geese, thirty ducks, twenty teal and some other birds were assembled for a baptismal feast. There were also *tourtres* or *tourtes* (wild carrier-pigeons), of which there was an extraordinary profusion until the nineteenth century, and of which, as early as 1607, the French made "excellent pies."[5]

For Fridays and Saturdays ("on Friday flesh thou shalt not eat nor Saturday likewise") and for the very numerous days of abstinence, there were fish from the river, particularly eel. Among the food that could be eaten on such days (and this too was a new dish) was beaver, whose flesh was "very good, almost like mutton"; the tail, "the best and most delicate of the beast" and the feet were considered "as fish & the rest meat."[6]

Among the fruits and vegetables to which the Indians introduced the French were "local pumpkins," which were eaten "cooked in water, or else under hot cinders," and which Sagard found "very good." There were also blueberries, which were found in abundance in the country of the Algonquins and Hurons. These were dried for the winter, along with raspberries and other small fruits, "as we do with prunes in France, for Lent." The Indians used them "as preserves, salt & spices, to give taste to their *sagamité*, & to put in their little cakes which they cook under the ashes."[7]

In those early days, thanks to the Indians, the French discovered maple sap. Since he came back to the St Lawrence from the upper country after the spring run of sap and returned at once to France, Sagard did not have an opportunity to taste it, but he heard it talked of: "a certain tree that the Montagnais call Michian, in which they make a cut in Springtime to draw from it a juice as sweet as honey, but in very small quantity, otherwise this tree could not be too highly esteemed. I have not tasted of this liquor as I have of the juice of the beech tree, but believe it to be very good to taste."[8] From documentary evidence, it seems that the process for making syrup, taffy or sugar had not as yet been found.

Among these new pleasures was a very important one that the French were quick to adopt from the Indians: tobacco. This had made a vivid if unfavourable impression on Cartier in the sixteenth century, but in the seventeenth the French acquired quite a taste for it. They accepted a present of some from the Indians in 1605. Champlain used it at least during the long palavers. On his return from Huronia in 1624, Brûlé brought back a bag of it, which he lost during a quarrel with the Indians just before arriving at Quebec. In this tobacco, the Indians found "a taste most excellent" and were enlivened by it as if with wine. The French sought the same pleasure in it for themselves. Some of them, writes Lescarbot, were so addicted "to this tobacco intoxication that they can no more do without it than without food and drink." To "drink of this smoke, they would sell their shirts from their backs," according to the Jesuit Biard. The habit once acquired, observes Sagard, "one cannot be rid of it except with great difficulty," and he heard men "curse the hour that they had ever acquired it."[9]

Lescarbot wrote in 1610 that he judged that it was "beyond our power" to live in this country as the natives lived, but in fact the French quickly accustomed themselves to the Indian way of life, so quickly that Sagard, after his stay of 1623-24, stated that "The French themselves, better educated & raised in the School of the Faith, are becoming Savages for no better reason than that they live with the Savages."[10]

Besides Indian food, the French adopted many other features of native life in this new continent. A number of Indian techniques soon became their own; forced germination, for example. Huron women soaked pumpkin seeds in water, sowed them in boxes of bark and kept them in a warm place; the seeds would germinate in a matter of days and were then transplanted in the fields.[11] There was also the transport of wood in winter. The Indians, writes Sagard, had contrived "a means of gathering it in Winter time, over the snow, most conveniently tied to certain toboggans or planks of cedar." This, we believe, is the method that Champlain used during the winter of 1623-24, when, with the help of the Indians, he had wood for the reconstruction of the fort dragged to the site over the snow.[12] From the Indians, the French also quickly adopted the practice of "sweating." Hot stones were laid under a low round tent, and the men would assemble inside, "quite naked, sitting on the ground, crowded together in a circle one against the next"; to further stimulate sweating they would drink "great draughts of cold water"; then, after having sweated a great deal, they would "go and throw themselves into the river, or if not, wash themselves in cold water."[13]

There was another aspect of Indian influence which was even more beguiling. The French, who in Europe were subjected to restrictions at every turn, found here a race of men who lived without any restrictions whatever, in what might appear to be absolute freedom. At Port Royal and at Quebec there was indeed an embryonic European society, but a man had only to step outside the settlement to escape from it. When the

French lived among the Souriquois, the Montagnais, the Algonquins or the Hurons, they were free of all the social and religious constraints hitherto imposed on them, and had no one to answer to but themselves. The younger they were, the more readily they succumbed to the pleasures of this life of liberty; the young La Tour came to Acadia at the age of fourteen, and Brûlé and Marsolet arrived as "little boys." Suddenly they found themselves let loose in a world where there were no longer any curbs on their desires. These Frenchmen, wrote the Récollet Le Caron, "set a scandalous example & for the most part are there only to do so, & are better fitted to blaspheme the name of Christ than to do honour to His memory, committing abuses and a thousand kinds of vile deeds, even more than these poor miserable Savages."[14] Indeed, the native women, Souriquois, Montagnais, Algonquins or Hurons, went about naked in summertime, and offered themselves without hesitation to whomever they pleased. It would seem that even the Hurons, for whom the flesh was a permissible pleasure and therefore not a particularly sensual attraction, were shocked at the behaviour of the French.

For some of the French, certainly, an Indian woman was nothing more than an object of pleasure. Robert Gravé (son of François) was accused by the Indians of having abused and raped one of their women. About 1626, the young La Tour fathered his first daughter (for he was to have two others) by a Souriquois woman; this is the first métis child mentioned in the history of French America. But there were also Frenchmen who were just as captivated but more serious of mind, and who from the earliest days sought wives among the Indians. Referring to events previous to January 1628, Champlain writes that Robert Giffard, "some time before," wished to have a young Indian woman "to educate her & marry her," but her people would not give her up to him, "whatever offers he made."[15] And if we rightly understand a statement by Le Clercq, it was during this same period that two Frenchmen married "Savage women who had learned our Language & our customs, & who have since persevered in great understanding, peace & union with their husbands."[16]

Fortunately for the natives, the meeting and mingling of cultures was slowed by the language barrier. Between the Amerindian languages and French there was no relationship of any kind; no point of comparison, no parallel, nothing in common whatever. The French had been trying to overcome this obstacle since the sixteenth century. If rapid progress were to be made, it was essential that one group, either the French or the Indians, should systematically learn the language of the other. Cartier decided that it should be the Indians, and he kidnapped Domagaya and Taignoagny and took them to France. There, it would seem, they learned enough French to assist in the preparation of a Franco-Iroquois lexicon of at least fifty words. When Cartier again brought interpreters back to

France it was possible to draw up a more substantial lexicon: 168 words or expressions. On his third voyage in 1541, he came without interpreters, and then he initiated the system which was to be much in vogue in the seventeenth century, entrusting two boys to the chief of Achelacy so that they might learn the language by living with the Indians. Alas, two days later he discovered that the boys' teacher had gone to hatch plots at Stadacona, and relations between the French and the Iroquois soon deteriorated to the point of war.

When the French returned to the St Lawrence at the beginning of the seventeenth century, the meagre knowledge of Iroquois that they had been able to garner was no longer of any value. With the ethnic revolution in the St Lawrence Valley, the former masters of the river had departed; the vocabulary from the preceding century was useless. A new beginning would have to be made.

The linguistic barrier was a formidable one. In Acadia, in a relatively small territory, the French had three languages to cope with, Micmac or Souriquois in the peninsula, Etchemin or Malecite on the St John and Penobscot rivers, and Almouchiquois on the Kennebec River. Even though these languages were of common Algonquian origin and very closely related, they still represented three distinct barriers. In the St Lawrence region there was Montagnais; another obstacle. Further inland there were more still; counting only the peoples with whom the French were in contact in this period, there was the language of the Island and Petite-Nation Algonquins (on the Ottawa River), that of the Nipissings (between the Algonquin territory and the Great Lakes), and the Huron-Iroquois tongue.

Sagard writes that between Montagnais, Algonquin and Nipissing, all of the Algonquian linguistic family, there was "no more difference than between Gascon or Provençal and French," and he groups the three of them under the general name *Canadien*.[17] Without any overriding control, however, these linguistic offshoots tended to develop freely and, since there was no grammar, each evolved quickly and unpredictably; it was therefore essential to have an interpreter for Montagnais, another for Algonquin and a third for Nipissing.

As for Huron-Iroquois (so-called because the Hurons and Iroquois spoke essentially the same language), its origin was altogether different, and a knowledge of Algonquian was of no help in learning it. On the other hand, since it had become the common language of commerce between nations, it was a most useful tool and an open-sesame to the entire Great Lakes region.

If there had been hope of using French for communicating with the Indians, or at least with those in regular contact with the French (Montagnais, Algonquins and Hurons), this hope proved to be an empty one. The situation had not even changed by 1667, when Colbert complained to the intendant Talon that the Indians had not been obliged to "learn our language, instead of our French traders being obliged to learn theirs in order to have some small commerce with them."[18] All the more so for the French of these earlier years; they simply had to learn the language of the natives.

It could have been otherwise. True, it would have required a considerable intellectual effort on the part of the Indians to learn French, but many of them were passable linguists already, and were capable of making such an effort. If they did not do so, it was because they did not need to; it was the Indians, not the French, who had the upper hand economically, for they were the suppliers of the precious furs. Sometimes they almost had to be begged to come to trade. Why should they learn the language of a client over whom they had such a hold?

French and the native languages therefore coexisted without either giving way to the other, but if there was a degree of penetration of one by the other, it would seem that it was easily French which was the more heavily penetrated. The natives did sometimes adopt French names (for instance, among the Montagnais, Mecabau called Martin, Chief Choumin nicknamed le cadet, and the chief's newborn son given the name "Père-Joseph"), but it was usually they who gave Indian names to the French. In the first quarter of the seventeenth century, Amerindian terms began to appear in French to designate things which did not exist in Europe; caribou, for example, oüaraon for "green toads" or frogs which were "green, & two or three times larger than the common ones," Mekezin, for the Indian footware, and toca for the red berries "resembling our cornioles,"[19] which became atocas (cranberries). French was becoming Americanized, if ever so slightly.

To overcome the linguistic obstacle, the French resorted to the twofold technique already tried in Cartier's day, learning from the Indians themselves on the one hand and on the other attempting to gallicize a few Indians who would then serve as interpreters.

This second technique, as we have seen, was put to the test by the Récollets, but of the total of six Indians that they sent to France only two returned, and only one of those two persevered and proved to be of service. The first technique was the more common. In 1605 a Frenchman was entrusted by de Monts to the Indians of Casco Bay, the first to live with the natives as one of them in order to learn the language. From then on there were always to be some Frenchmen living with the Indians, both in Acadia and in the St Lawrence Valley.

The missionaries, both Récollets and Jesuits, in order to pursue their work of evangelism, had no choice but to buckle down and learn the native languages. Whom might they count on to teach them? Not yet on those rootless waifs, the few little Indian boys that they were striving to gallicize. As for the interpreters who already knew these languages, turning teacher did not appeal to them.

The missionaries could only follow the example of the novice inter- preters and learn directly from the Indians. They found that they could obtain the services of an Indian who would live with them as "master of the Woodland language," giving private lessons at home. The makeshift master, however, tended to lack intellectual discipline. "I learned," writes the Jesuit Le Jeune, "conjugations, declensions, a little syntax, vocabulary, with unbelievable toil, for I must sometimes ask twenty questions to have cognizance of a single word, so much would my unschooled master vacil- late." To induce his master to be more attentive, the pupil had from time to time to ply him with tobacco; or else the teacher, conscious of the dignity of his position, would not speak until a well-filled platter had been set before him; and when the pupil could press no more of the most precious provender upon his guest, from whose mouth only a few pearls of the native language had as yet fallen, the lesson would come to an end. What was more, these teachers were known to indulge in a little personal amusement as an aid to digestion; thus, complains the Jesuit Biard, the master would slip obscenities into the missionaries' translations, "which we would innocently go about preaching as inspiring maxims of the Gospel."[20]

The most effective method was still to go and live among the Indians. This is what the Jesuit Massé did in 1612, when he went to the St John River to study the language, and this is what the Récollets and Jesuits of the St Lawrence were also to do. It was workable enough when the natives were sedentary, like the Hurons, but it was a source of much hardship for the missionaries to the Montagnais, for example, who had to follow the Indians in their winter hunting and live in conditions beyond normal endurance for a European. Nor did they all have the Jesuit Brébeuf's extraordinary talent for languages. Champlain writes that Brébeuf learned in two or three years "what others might learn in twenty."[21]

There were great technical difficulties in language study. The Montagnais had no sounds equivalent to f, l or v, and in their language l became r and v became p. The Hurons had no labials; our f would mutate to s, m to n, and p to t. Another difficulty was the absence of grammar, or, at least, of a written literature which might have stabilized the language; there was no such thing among the Indians with whom the French were in contact. Language was therefore in a state of constant and rapid evolu- tion, and whatever one managed to learn might shortly be of no further use. Yet another problem was the lack of abstract terms in the Indian languages, making it virtually impossible to convey such concepts as virtue, vice, faith and temptation.

In order to make it possible to cope with these languages, lexicons were drawn up which were scrutinized carefully and added to and corrected according to the experience of the missionaries. The study of the Huron tongue, the common language of the Great Lakes, resulted in a work of great importance; in 1632 the Récollet Sagard published a Huron dictionary of 132 pages. A work of such magnitude on a North American native language had never before been realized; nor, as far as Huron was concerned, was it ever to be equalled.

It may be safely said that there was mutual enthusiasm for the meeting of cultures; if the French found much that was attractive in the life of the Indians, there were a number of aspects of French life that entranced the Indians. While they were somewhat negatively impressed by the bearded faces of the newcomers, most were dazzled by the French manner of dress, and took to it themselves at the earliest opportunity.

The article of clothing most unreservedly admired was the hat, which became something of a status symbol among them, and in gestures of courtesy it came to play the same role for them as it did in France. The Indians "seldom visit us without a hat," writes Lescarbot, "so that they may greet us with more solemnity." The Montagnais Mecabau would try out "little reverences, hoping to do them in the French manner." Salutations, at least those of departure, were quite a new phenomenon for the Indians; they themselves had "no salutation for taking leave," and it was from the French that they learned the custom of farewells. When the chief of Tadoussac appeared at the 1636 assembly at Quebec to speak before it, "he took off his hat, & bowed gracefully enough in the French manner, then addressed himself to the Captains, in particular to Monsieur du Plessis, whom he called his younger brother: 'You see,' said he, 'that I am French; you know, my brother, that my Nation takes me for such.' "[22] With his hat and his bowing and scraping, he felt sure of having achieved a degree of refinement which raised him to the dignity of a Frenchman.

To realize the pervasiveness of European influence in this period, we need only observe that the *matachiaz* (referred to also as wampum, strings and belts of "porcelain," or *rassade* beads) were already being replaced by glassware from France. Traditionally, from certain far-away nations by the sea, the Indians would obtain "great whelk shells, which they broke into small pieces & polished on sandstone or some other hard stone." They would make the pieces into squares, each "as big as a walnut," or else into balls as big as chick-peas, which they pierced and made into chains and bracelets. According to a later description, these beads were threaded on leather strips, making strings of "porcelain"; several strings would make up a belt, and it was these belts that were wampum. These strings and belts were "the universal currency among the savages; they served them as money, jewelry, decoration, annals and registers; the bond between nations and individuals"; riches and archives that were closely guarded. They were both the most sacred and the most familiar possessions of the Indians, as well as being uniquely theirs. All too soon, the beads traditionally made from shells were supplanted by materials of French fabrication. The Indians wanted nothing to do with "ivory for porcelain," but were willing to accept the "Matachiaz brought from France," little tubular beads of glass mixed with tin or copper which, since there was no other standard, were measured out to them by the fathom.[23] The substitution of French glassware for American shellware in such a personal tradition clearly shows the extent and rapidity of the encroachment of European influence on Indian culture.

In these early years of the seventeenth century, European and particularly French customs began to have an effect on the eating habits of the Indians.

Among the Souriquois of Acadia, pottery of domestic fabrication was gradually replaced by French cooking pots acquired by barter. The Montagnais also made use of these vessels; at least, they did so in 1623, and it would seem that by then this was already customary. Naturally enough, when the French entertained the Indians, it was French containers that were used; at the banquet for the Iroquois ambassadors in 1622, the cooking was done "in a cauldron for the brewing of beer, which held more than a hogshead"; for the feast of the spring of 1627, everything was thrown together to cook "in Mistress Hébert's great brewing cauldron."[24]

The influence of French cuisine went further than the use of utensils. The Indians were served with wine in 1623. When they first beheld it, they believed the liquid to be blood. They quickly adopted French drinking habits. Spirits were popular; to what extent in the first quarter of the seventeenth century it is difficult to determine, but in 1632 the Jesuit Le Jeune spoke of drunkenness among the Indians, as if it were a common occurrence among men and women alike.[25]

The Indians very soon acquired a liking for a number of items of French food. According to Lescarbot, instead of continuing to work the soil to feed themselves, the Souriquois came to the French to beg "beans, peas, biscuits, and other edibles," and became "lazy." In the St Lawrence Valley, the French provided the natives with peas, prunes and figs.

Of these new foods that the French introduced, it was bread for which the Indians developed the most pressing need. As early as 1534-35, the Iroquois Domagaya and Taignoagny, having acquired a taste for bread in France, could no longer do without it on their return to Stadacona. In March 1605, some Acadian Indians were given bread in exchange for game. The Souriquois of 1606 clamoured for bread in exchange for meat. In the St Lawrence Valley, the Montagnais discovered a similar liking.

This desire for bread was even to be at the root of a double murder, when a Montagnais killed two Frenchmen in 1627. Murder was thus committed for bread in the St Lawrence before ever it was committed for alcohol.

The confrontation between Europe and America was gradually taking shape in the sphere of religion, for the meeting of cultures could not fail to have an influence on the religious life of the Indians. The French were very slow in coming to understand something of the Indians' religious behaviour; they hardly had a glimmer of comprehension before 1632. Observers, both priests and laymen, wrote at first, as did Champlain, that the Indians "recognize no Divinity," that they "neither worship nor believe in any God, nor anything whatever," living "like brute beasts."[26] Finding no European-style religious organization or expression among the natives, the French could not see that the Indian did nevertheless have a religion of his own. They did not understand that, if the native chose to impart only vague and scant information, it was not because he had nothing to say, but rather that he was reluctant to reveal more; it becomes increasingly apparent that he kept his religious life to himself as soon as he realized that the French were turning it to ridicule.

About the only feature of this native religion recognized by European priests (at least, in the early years) was its agent, called Aoutmoin among the Souriquois, Manitou among the Montagnais and Algonquins, and Oki by the Hurons. Besides being responsible for communication with the spirit world, as its chosen representative, this agent served as doctor.

The Christian priest and the *shaman*, to use the generic term, engaged in a silent contest of strength as soon as the native realized that the priest had come among his people to replace the indigenous theology with a foreign one. Between the shaman and the priest, it was the more powerful who would win the Indians to his side. History has recorded a number of specific tests of strength. At St Mary's Bay, the Jesuit Biard placed a cross about the neck of a dying woman, and the next day she was cured. At St Sauveur in 1613, Biard baptized a dying child, and, to the great astonishment of the Indians, the child was immediately restored to health. In Huronia in 1623, in spite of all the efforts of the Oki, it rained and rained, and the Hurons finally appealed to the missionaries. "Barely had we commenced our little prayers, & were walking in procession around our little hut (Father Joseph in vestments) saying Litanies & other fitting prayers, when our most good & merciful Lord forthwith caused the rains to cease," and good weather then prevailed for three weeks: a spectacular victory which earned for the missionaries the venerable title of Arondiouane.[27] Once again, the priest had had the better of the shaman.

Although continual contact between the French and the Indians was still a recent phenomenon, the Indians were already noticing an increase in mortality among their number. "They are astonished and complain often," writes Father Biard, "that since the French are among them & have commerce with them, many of them die & their population is decreasing. For they assure us that before this presence, & frequentation, all their lands were most populous," and that "they have been more ravaged with sickness" with the increase in contacts with the French. Father Biard attributes the cause to an over-indulgence in "unaccustomed meats," as well as in wine and spirits.[28] But the explanation current among the Indians laid the blame on religion. It was, said the Montagnais La Forière, "that the priests who prayed to God, with the ceremony they devised, were causing many of their [Indian] companions to die, which had never been before."[29]

Neither the Indians nor the French yet understood that the depopulation crisis was being caused by European diseases, against which the Indians were completely defenceless; even the mildest influenza could bring death to the Amerindian. Appalled to see so many of their people die since the French had come, the Indians looked for an explanation in the spirit world; for them, the evil was born of that mysterious religion brought by priests who at times were more powerful than the Aoutmoin, the Manitou and the Oki.

Once the missionaries had destroyed the confidence of the Indians in their shamans there would follow the disintegration of the Indian culture, the disruption of a traditional conception of the world, and the acceptance of a new theology. "But a religion, whatever it may be, must be based upon a corresponding civilization. On what could the Indian base his new faith, he who, in theory at least, had newly renounced his own civilization?"[30] In this meeting of two cultures, the one sophisticated and exerting powerful attractions, the other primitive and almost defenceless, we can already foresee that the one will destroy the other.

CHAPTER 13

Tribulations of the Hundred Associates

1627–1632

When Verrazano conceived the name *Nova Gallia* in 1524, he envisaged
a New France that would embrace the entire North American continent
from Spanish Florida to the far north. This was what France claimed in
1627 for the Company of the Hundred Associates. From this continental
New France, however, some considerable portions had already been sliced
away. In Verrazano's Arcadia, the English colony of Virginia had developed rapidly; by 1627 it already counted a population of two thousand
and was the most successful European colony in North America, a rich
tobacco-producer that attracted an abundance of capital and a heavy flow
of immigrants; New France, by comparison, needed only Indian labour
for the operation of its fur trade. Another European colony, less populous
than Virginia and much less prosperous, had been established by the
Dutch in the Hudson River valley; even with its mere two hundred
inhabitants in 1625, New Holland already surpassed the population of
New France by a good hundred. In the country between the Kennebec
River and Cape Cod, where de Monts and Poutrincourt had searched in
vain for an ideal site for colonization, religious dissenters from Great
Britain were at work building their New England. This New England
still consisted only of two small colonies separated by some fifty miles, but
its population was nevertheless three times as great as that of the whole
of New France. And there was yet another European colonial venture in
Verrazano's New France, English once again, in the Avalon Peninsula of
Newfoundland, the little colony of Ferryland headed by George Calvert,
and it alone was numerically as strong as all of New France. In the far
northern regions, France had been totally absent since the second quarter
of the preceding century, and it was now only the English and the Danes
who continued to explore along the coasts of Labrador and Ungava and
into Hudson Bay.

And so in 1627 all that remained of Verrazano's New France were those
regions that France had been labouring painfully to colonize for twenty

years, Acadia and the St Lawrence, completely isolated one from the other, and totalling together some hundred inhabitants.

Acadia, as far as England was concerned, had been British since 1621 and was called Nova Scotia. For the French it was no longer anything more than a trading area, where Biencourt had succeeded his father, Poutrincourt, in 1615. In the pursuit of his fur-trading activities, Biencourt had entered into an association with some Huguenots of La Rochelle, and each year a ship came to Acadia from that city to take on a cargo of furs. From 1619 to 1627, there is no mention of any activity other than the fur trade. There was a period when this trade seemed to have enough cohesion to justify the establishment of a mission by the Récollets of the Province of Aquitaine; in 1620, four Récollets established their principal post on the St John River (probably on Emenenic Island), and resumed the missionary work abandoned seven years earlier. The Provincial of Aquitaine closed the mission in 1624, however. Upon Biencourt's death in 1623, his brother Jacques inherited the Acadian enterprise,[1] whose direction he left to Biencourt's associate, Charles de La Tour. Like Biencourt, La Tour encountered endless difficulties, difficulties created by the English in the trade on the Kennebec and Pentagouët rivers, difficulties with the French of the St Lawrence, too, which worsened with the advent of the de Caëns because of the vagueness of the bounds of their commercial monopoly. In 1627, La Tour made proposals to the King and to Richelieu for the reorganization of Acadia,[2] and these were carried to France by his father. Richelieu was then founding the Company of the Hundred Associates, whose monopoly was to cover the whole of New France. To facilitate this foundation, the Marquise de Guercheville had renounced her Acadian seigneury (that is to say, Acadia less Port Royal), and this no doubt is why the La Tours were able to obtain a concession of five leagues by ten on the St John River.[3] But the Acadia of 1627 was tenuous indeed, and its total French population was about twenty.

Outside Acadia, the nearest French settlement with an Habitation was on Miscou Island. De Caën had left a few men to spend the winter there in 1626-27 and the building was still standing, but it does not appear to have been occupied in the following winter. There was no building at Gaspé, although this was a regular port of call for ships bound for Canada from France. And what of the occupation of the St Lawrence, the great waterway that the French had known and travelled for a century past? Matane had been inhabited for only one winter, in 1615-16, and then only by poachers from La Rochelle. At Tadoussac there was a house (with galleries and moats) for the use of the company,[4] but, as far as we can see, no one had spent the winter there since Chauvin's experiment of 1600, even though the Récollets lived for more or less long periods at the Montagnais village nearby. Besides, the Tadoussac fur trade was diminishing, to the benefit of Cap de Victoire (above Sorel) and Trois Rivières. Tadoussac had remained the seaport of the Laurentian colony, despite Champlain's objections, but once the trading ships had left, the port was deserted.

A hundred miles upstream, at Cap Tourmente in Guillaume de Caën's barony, the French did live the year round, but only since 1626. There, a tiny French population of seven or eight were preparing to spend a second winter, to watch over forty or fifty head of livestock.

Thirty miles above Cap Tourmente was the capital, the only centre of population in the New France of 1627, the one place that supported anything approaching an organized French community. At the foot of Cape Diamond, between the river and the cliff, was a little cluster of buildings: the Habitation, rebuilt in stone in 1624, complete with turrets; the Company's storehouse, dating from 1608; the house built for the Récollets in 1615, and a few other small houses. High on the cliff, directly above the Habitation, rose Fort St Louis, flanked by two demi-bastions; it had been constructed of wood in 1626 on the site of the first fort of 1620, but its ramparts had not yet been completed. Near the fort was Louis Hébert's "enclosure," which had been raised to the status of noble fief the year before. Far below in the valley of the St Charles where, in 1618, Champlain had dreamed of building the city of Ludovica, the only buildings were those of the Jesuit and Récollet establishments, one on either side of the river. The clearing of land had progressed very little: a total of eighteen or twenty acres, according to Father Lalemant. The population of this capital, the largest French population that New France could boast, consisted of no more than seventy-two people.[5]

Above Quebec there was a total absence of French occupation, and even (generally speaking, during the winter) of Montagnais occupation.

In all of New France there were only 107 people in 1627, a total which appears quite absurd when compared with the other European colonies in North America:

Virginia	2,000
New Holland	200
New England	310
Newfoundland	100
English and Dutch population	2,610

In 1627, then, New France was pitifully weak numerically. Even more disappointing is a count of those who had settled for good in the country or appeared to have done so: a total of twenty people.

This tiny population, even the most closely-knit group at Quebec, was no better provided for than it would have been in the preceding century.

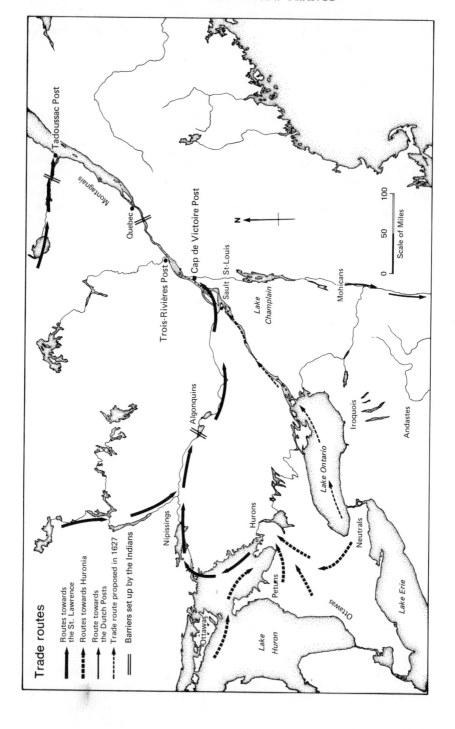

Trade routes

Routes towards
the St. Lawrence

Routes towards Huronia

Route towards
the Dutch Posts

Trade route proposed in 1627

Barriers set up by the Indians

Tadoussac Post

Montagnais

Quebec

Cap de Victoire Post

Trois-Rivières Post

Sault St-Louis

Lake Champlain

Mohicans

N

Scale of Miles

0   50   100

Algonquins

Nipissings

Iroquois

Andastes

Lake Ontario

Hurons

Neutrals

Petuns

Ottawas

Ottawas

Lake Huron

Lake Erie

From November until April it was completely cut off from Europe, and during the navigable months it was often enough left without a single boat; if, perchance, it was found necessary to go down-river to Gaspé, a boat would have to be built first. As for food, only enough for a winter was provided, in the certainty that the ships would be returning the following spring; should the returning ships be the least delayed, however, the winterers of Quebec would cry famine.

The community was organized only in very summary fashion. In 1621, administrative machinery of a sort had been established. On September 12, 1621, Champlain published his first ordinances (of whose content or application we know nothing), and in 1625 a lieutenant and an ensign were appointed as his assistants. By 1627 there was little of this institutional structure still in evidence.

The seigneurial régime had been established, but as yet there was no seigneurial community or way of life.

There was no parish life either. The Church as yet had no formal structure; in Acadia there was no longer a single priest, and in Canada the priests, in point of fact, served only as chaplains to the French population. As for the missionary effort, in 1615 there seems to have been serious intent to push ahead, but by 1627 it had brought about only dubious results. Of the fifty-four converts claimed in those twelve years, thirty-nine died after baptism and two more did not persevere in their new-found faith. There remained therefore, from the St Lawrence to the Great Lakes, only thirteen native Christians!

At this time New France still had no teaching institution of any kind, even though the Récollets were initiating a few Indians to the French way of life before sending them to study and be baptized in France. There is no known text to show that the Récollets served as schoolmasters for the French population before 1629, and in fact only one boy, Eustache Martin, reached school age during this period.

The greatest accomplishment for New France had been the development of the fur-trade network; by 1627 it was immense and far-reaching. In Acadia, the French had made a firm alliance with the Indians, thereby gaining access to the trade routes of the St John River, the Ste Croix River, the Pentagouët and (although in competition with the English) the Kennebec. The compass of these routes was fairly narrow, but in the St Lawrence the extent of the network was practically unlimited. Furs arrived at Tadoussac through the Montagnais from the nations of the north, and there was as yet no one in the upper reaches of the continent to draw off this supply; at Trois Rivières and at Cap de Victoire (the more important of the two meeting-places) the great trading nations kept an annual rendezvous, Montagnais of the St Lawrence, Algonquins of the Ottawa River, Nipissings and Hurons. Through the Hurons in particular, with their position on the Great Lakes at the hub of the commercial routes of the interior, the French could count on a virtually inexhaustible supply of furs.

But the establishment of this great trade network and its consolidation through the relations maintained with the Indians who were strongest at the time cannot hide the numerical insignificance of French settlement nor its instability. Would the returns from the fur trade have made it possible for the de Caëns to do more for the cause of colonization? We do know that the margin of profit between the buying and selling price was considerable; a beaver skin was worth some 30 sols in the hands of the Indian in 1631; it was resold in France for about 300 sols[6] and, according to Father Lalemant, 12,000 or 15,000 beaver pelts were gathered per year.[7] However, there were not inconsiderable expenses to be met: the chartering of two ships, a hundred crewmen to be fed and paid, Champlain's salary and the pay and upkeep of his men. De Caën evaluated his annual expenses at 46,000 livres.[8] Out of a possible profit of 100,000 livres, 24,000 livres were payable to the old associates of Rouen and St Malo, and the rest de Caën had to share with his own associates. For all that, the business was certainly profitable, since de Caën fought to the bitter end to keep it.

Whether a company of modest proportions could give rise in any case to a powerful colony is another question, and France herself had no such expectations; all she had asked of the monopolists was that they should build five houses and settle six families, of three people each, over fifteen years. The entire system encouraged indifference toward the establishment of a colony. How could settlements be developed when their existence was bound to the fur-trade network? Indian labour sufficed amply for its operation, and there was no other economic activity in the country to attract European labour.

But there were changes afoot, for Richelieu had plans for a sweeping reform.

In a world transformed by the Renaissance, gold had become the principal vehicle of exchange between nations, and because gold was a rare commodity to be accumulated and laid by in the greatest possible quantities, nationalism in commercial matters was imperative for any state seeking to prosper. This was mercantilism, the management of a state's economy by keeping the importation of manufactured goods to a minimum and acquiring a maximum of raw materials from abroad for the supply of its own industry. Colonies became an essential factor in such a system; they supplied raw materials which otherwise would have to be bought from foreign powers and, theoretically, they would absorb a portion of the mother country's production, thus stimulating its export trade.

In this first quarter of the seventeenth century, while Spain, Portugal, England and even the Netherlands had acquired possessions in the far corners of the world in the pursuit of their mercantile policies, France still had no colonial economy and did not even have the means of acquiring one. England had established her East India Company in 1600, and the Netherlands had had a similar company since 1602. These companies embodied a system which, through close ties between company and state, assured riches for the merchant classes and power for the state through maritime commerce. France, in comparison, still had only the seasonal fur trade of New France, which, moreover, she left to the exploitation of small private companies. The little island of St Christophe in the West Indies, occupied in 1625, was her only other colonial possession.

Yet there was no dearth of men close to Richelieu who were ready and anxious to demonstrate the immense possibilities open to France in North America, should she seek to found her power upon a colonial economy. Champlain had done so in his pleas for New France in 1618, when Richelieu was initially a member of the Royal Council. Early in 1626, the Récollet Le Caron, former tutor at Court, had written his long memorandum charging lack of good faith or inefficiency on the part of the small companies. In November of the same year, Isaac de Razilly, Knight of Malta, addressed a memorandum to Richelieu demonstrating "the importance of trade by sea" and colonial development for the prosperity of France;[9] this memorandum would appear to have had a decisive influence on France's foreign policy.

Richelieu had been appointed to the Royal Council for the second time in April 1624, and in August of that year he became *Chef du Conseil*. In 1626 he had himself appointed Grand Master and Superintendent General of the Navigation and Commerce of France, and in January 1627 he abolished the post of Admiral of France.[10] Now he had absolute control over all voyages afar. In the spring of 1627, he signed the act of association of a new company, determining the conditions under which the establishment of a powerful French colony in North America would be undertaken.[11] This was the Company of the Hundred Associates. When Madame de Guercheville renounced her claim to Acadia in favour of the Associates, and Vantadour sold them his post as Viceroy of New France and his share of the colony's commerce for 100,000 livres,[12] Richelieu was free to establish a new régime.

The new company, with the official title of *Compagnie de la Nouvelle-France*, would have its headquarters at Paris and would be composed of a hundred associates and more. Its capital was to be 300,000 livres, each member contributing 3,000 livres. The profits of the enterprise would not be distributed for the first three years but would be added to the capital of each member, and thereafter, until otherwise decided, each member might withdraw only a third of the sums accruing to him, the other two thirds being added to his capital. Thus it was hoped that the permanence of the enterprise would be assured, with increasingly abundant funds at its disposal, at least in its early stages.

Never before had a French company been accorded so much. Besides the fort and Habitation of Quebec, two fully-equipped warships and four cannon, the Hundred Associates were granted all of New France, and this grant was no longer bounded to the south by the 40th parallel as it had been for de Monts, but, reverting to the explorations of the sixteenth century, extended from Florida to the Arctic Circle, and from Newfoundland to the Great Lakes and "beyond, so far as they may be enabled to broadcast and make known His Majesty's Name." In short, this was the New France dreamed of since Verrazano's day; all of North America known or yet to be known. This immense domain was to be the Company's property in fief and seigneury, and could be subdivided into fiefs.

The Hundred Associates were also granted the monopoly of all commerce in New France for the first fifteen years, with the exception of fisheries; at the end of the fifteen years the monopoly would cover only hides, skins and pelts. The French living in New France would be permitted to "trade freely in pelts with the savages," but on condition that these pelts should be turned over to the Company, which would buy them for 40 sols apiece.

The King, moreover, introduced four exceptional concessions. Until then nobles and ecclesiastics could not, on pain of losing their rank, become shareholders in a commercial company; at most they were allowed to collect the income from capital sums which, once committed, they renounced the right to recuperate. Now, however, noble or clerical members of the Company of the Hundred Associates might engage in commercial activities on an equal footing with the merchants without losing their privileges, and of even greater import was the King's promise to accord letters of nobility to twelve members of the Company who were commoners, the twelve to be chosen by the Company, demonstrating that henceforth commerce, like military service, might lead to advancement in the social hierarchy. Secondly, the King would grant that any immigrant who wished to return to France after practising his craft for six years in New France would be accorded the dignity of "master craftsman" and might hold "open shop." This provision was intended to facilitate settlement and the establishment of industry by making it relatively easy for artisans in New France to obtain the coveted recognition of skill that was so difficult to obtain in France. Thirdly, to encourage emigration and hasten the formation of a European society in America, the descendants of Frenchmen who settled in the colony, and even Amerindians who had been baptized, would be "deemed to be French-born" without further formality; if they came to France, they would enjoy the same privileges as those born in the mother country. Finally, for the encouragement of commerce, for the first fifteen years merchandise shipped either way between France and New France would be exempt from all taxes.

For their part, the Hundred Associates undertook to settle four thousand colonists in New France, all French and Catholic, over the first fifteen years (ending December 1643), to ensure their subsistence during the first three years and, when the time came to be freed of that charge, to grant them cleared land and the wheat they would need for the first sowing. During this same fifteen-year period, the Company would house and maintain three ecclesiastics at each Habitation (that is to say, each centre of settlement), or else provide them with cleared land; in addition to the settlement and administration of the country, then, the Company would assume the cost of fifteen years' spiritual ministry.

This great company was launched with all speed. Cardinal Richelieu himself became one of its members, committing himself personally to the work he was so anxious to accomplish. Among the Company's first members, we find a number who had already been closely associated with New France: Isaac de Razilly and Champlain; Louis Houël de Petit-Pré, who had come to the assistance of the Récollets in the colony; Captain Charles Daniel, an associate of the de Caëns; the merchants Simon Le Maistre and Jean Rozée. The list of May 17, 1629 totalled 107 members, of whom twenty-six stated that they were merchants or business men, twelve being from Paris; the other members were for the most part officers of the upper levels of civil, judicial or military administration.[13] The predominance of these officers and the large number of Parisian merchants had the effect of changing the commercial orientation of New France; no longer was its commerce centred on Brittany and Normandy, as it had long been, but on the French capital.

It was on May 6, 1628, outside La Rochelle, to which he was then laying siege, that Louis XIII affixed his signature to the agreements of April 29 and May 7, 1627. The wish expressed by Razilly had been realized; France had adopted a massive colonial policy, and, like England and the Netherlands, she had forged a superb instrument of maritime power. In the new context of mercantilism, she was preparing to occupy a country that she hoped would embrace the whole of North America and should greatly strengthen her commerce and manufacturing industries. The New France that she intended to establish would be founded upon commerce and crafts and should be able to support a society whose social hierarchy would be the same as her own. But the Huguenots, against whom such a bitter struggle had been waged to preserve the unity of the State, would be excluded from that society. In short, for the enhancement of her pros-

perity and power, France intended to create in America a French and
Catholic society.

Unhappily, the launching of the project was attended by an unpropitious
set of circumstances. In the spring of 1627, when the Associates reached
agreement on these articles, Louis XIII and Richelieu were not only
striving to reduce La Rochelle, the last Protestant stronghold, but they also
came to grips with England under Charles I and Buckingham. Using as
their pretext the recent Treaty of Monçon which allied France with their
traditional enemy, Spain, the English took sides with La Rochelle, and
Buckingham himself set out to break the blockade. Their invading army
came to grief on the Ile de Ré, despite the 13,000 men they had thrown
into the battle. But this victory for the French brought an end neither to
the siege of La Rochelle nor to the war between the two countries. It was
in the midst of conflict, therefore, that the Hundred Associates would
have to undertake an enterprise whose success depended above all on
safety at sea. Worse still, on the initiative of Gervase Kirke, a company
was then being formed in London whose intention was the same as the
Hundred Associates', to wit, the occupation of the key regions of New
France and the monopolization of its commerce. In association with London
merchants, Kirke financed and prepared his initial expedition,[14] instructing
his eldest son David first of all to drive the French from the St Lawrence.

Faced with this situation, the Hundred Associates requested that they
be allowed to suspend the departure of their first expedition, planned for
1628. Confident of support from Spain and jubilant over Buckingham's
defeat, the King was convinced that the war would soon come to an end
and refused to countenance any delay. The Hundred Associates set to work.

But the English were already launching their first invasion of the St
Lawrence River. In the spring of 1628, Gervase Kirke's company sent out
three ships. Aboard were David Kirke, who was in command, his brothers
Louis and Thomas, and Captain Jacques Michel; all four had been born
at Dieppe.[15] David Kirke carried official letters from Charles I which
authorized him to take possession of Canada and Acadia.

It was the Kirkes who arrived first. They seized the Habitation of Miscou;
they captured a Basque ship come to trade at Ile Perçée, and then the
Hundred Associates' first supply ship bound for Quebec under the command of Captain Norot. Then they sailed up the river and occupied the
port of Tadoussac. Informed of the existence of a settlement at Cap Tourmente, David Kirke sent fifteen men there early in July. These men pre-
tended at first to have been sent by the Hundred Associates, but when
they found how few Frenchmen were there they seized the place, killed
the livestock (of which only six cows survived), set fire to the buildings,
and hastily re-embarked after releasing their prisoners, who made their
way to Quebec to announce the disaster.[16] A few days later, Kirke sent

some Basques to Champlain with a letter demanding the surrender of Quebec. From this letter Champlain learned of the extent of Kirke's operations and the determination of the English to prevent the arrival of help. Pretending to be better supplied than he was, he rejected Kirke's demand.[17]

Quebec was, in fact, already facing starvation. As far back as June 18, Champlain had recorded that food was running short and that only fifty pounds of gunpowder remained. But good news came before long, to reassure him as to the wisdom of his refusal: Desdames, an agent of the Hundred Associates, arrived in a shallop to announce that a fleet had reached Gaspé, carrying "all necessary commodities & quantities of workmen & families coming to inhabit & clear the land [and] build & prepare the necessary lodgings."[18] With an investment of 164,720 livres, the Hundred Associates had dispatched a fleet of four ships in April 1628, commanded by Claude Roquemont de Brison, one of the founding members of the Company. Four hundred people had embarked, most of them colonists. A small ship chartered and equipped by the Jesuit Noyrot, bursar of the missions of New France, had joined the fleet.[19] Soon after its departure the expedition had survived a violent storm and then had escaped from two heavily-armed ships from La Rochelle. After a crossing of a month and a half, the fleet had stopped at Anticosti Island to raise a cross as an act of official taking of possession, and then went to drop anchor in Gaspé Bay, from where word was sent to Champlain. This, for Champlain, meant salvation, provided that the French fleet carried the day against the Kirkes. Desdames himself had narrowly escaped them, but shortly after his departure from St Barnabas Island he had heard cannon fire, which led him to suppose that the battle had begun.

Although he had been informed of the presence of the Kirkes in the St Lawrence, Roquemont ventured up the river under cover of fog. Kirke sighted him opposite Tadoussac on July 17, and sailed out to meet him. Until the afternoon of the next day there were fired "on both sides more than twelve hundred cannon shots," then, since the English had the upper hand, Roquemont was obliged to "ask for terms."[20]

He had been more brave than wise, says Champlain reproachfully, in not waiting at Gaspé until the Kirkes had departed; he had lost everything and left "all the country in ruin, & nearly a hunderd men, women & children to die of hunger, and these would be forced, for lack of succour, to abandon the fort & habitation to the first enemy who might come."[21] The Hundred Associates' first expedition had been completely wiped out: a loss of 164,720 livres!

The English, fortunately, retired without following up their success. Apart from destroying the Habitation at Miscou, they had engaged in no large-scale operations in Acadia, where the young La Tour's means of resistance were even slimmer than Champlain's. Despite the damage done at Miscou, Tadoussac and Cap Tourmente, Acadia and Canada were still occupied only by the French, since the Scottish colonists that Alexander had planned to establish in Acadia had not arrived at their destination. There was still hope that the following year's supplies might set everything back to rights.

The colony of Quebec, desperately short of food since the spring, faced the prospect of spending a winter without having received any supplies. The winter proved to be exceptionally long, and was passed in the direst hardship. The remaining food was painfully eked out, but by May of 1629 all was gone.[22] How could the colonists survive until the arrival of the ships from France? First, the number of mouths to be fed might be reduced by sending as many people as possible to Gaspé, where, with furs, they might buy their passage to France on fishing vessels, but for this purpose there was only one small boat, and that would first have to be repaired. Or else a party might go to the lands of the Iroquois and stay there by force of arms, subsisting on the enemy's food. Then it was heard that some Abenakis, seven or eight days' journey to the south, wished to make an alliance with the French; perhaps some food could be had from them. A man was delegated to go out to meet them, and he left on May 16, 1629 with some Indian guides. Finally, Champlain sent Desdames to the Gulf with a party in an attempt to obtain food from fishermen.[23]

Meanwhile, the situation was becoming increasingly desperate. There on the shores of a river full of fish, the French could not even resort to fishing: "without nets, lines & hooks, we could do but little." Hoping that the ten or twenty acres of cultivated land would produce at least some grain, the colonists took to the woods in the meantime to gather food but could find only roots, in particular Solomon's Seal.[24]

On the morning of July 19, 1629, the French were surprised and dismayed to learn that three English ships had arrived behind Pointe Lévy.[25] Not since the days of Roberval had ships of this size been known to sail up the river as far as Quebec. Once again, it was the Kirkes invading the St Lawrence.

The expedition that Gervase Kirke had sent to New France in 1628 had been highly profitable, for the English fleet had captured the Hundred Associates' fleet loaded with food and goods for barter, and nineteen fishing boats to boot. It was well worth their while coming back in 1629. There had been quarrels in England over the possession of the St Lawrence, however, with William Alexander the elder laying claim to a seigneury a hundred leagues wide in the Laurentian Valley from the Gulf all the way to the Asian Sea. A settlement was arrived at by which William Alexander the younger agreed to enter into association with the Kirkes. The King granted them the St Lawrence trade monopoly (the Gulf included), with authorization to drive out the French and to found colonies.[26]

The Anglo-Scotch Company set to work in the spring of 1629, dispatching a second expedition against Quebec and also founding two Scottish colonies in Acadia, one at Port Royal, the other on Cape Breton. Acadia, it will be remembered, had been a New Scotland in the eyes of the English since 1621. William Alexander's feudal fief included Sable Island, the Acadian peninsula (then called New Caledonia), Cape Breton, New Brunswick (called Alexandria), and the Gaspé peninsula. It was not until 1629, however, that plans for the founding of settlements could be realized. In the spring of that year, William Alexander junior left England with two shiploads of colonists and soldiers. He landed at Port Royal and, very close to the site of the earlier French settlement of 1605-13, he established Fort Charles. That same spring another Scot, James Stewart, Lord Ochiltree, duly commissioned by Nova Scotia's proprietor, settled on Cape Breton with some sixty compatriots. At Port aux Baleines, near the future site of Louisbourg, he began to build Fort Rosemar. From there, on the strength of his commission, he exacted a tithe on the catch of all fishermen in the region.

With their second expedition to the St Lawrence, piloted by Jacques Michel, the Kirkes intended to dislodge Champlain and finally have the fur-trade monopoly for themselves. David Kirke, as Admiral of the Anglo-Scotch Company's fleet, sent his brothers Louis and Thomas with three ships to attack Quebec. Being "without food, powder, or match, & without succour," Champlain and his people decided that there was nothing left to do but to give up the fort and Habitation, after negotiating the "most advantageous terms." On July 19, a boat appeared on the river bearing a white flag; it brought a letter from the Kirkes demanding surrender. Efforts on the part of the Récollet Le Caron to gain time were fruitless, and Champlain was obliged to reply that he would submit on certain conditions. The terms finally agreed upon were less advantageous than he had asked. The French would be repatriated, however, and were authorized to take certain of their belongings with them.[27]

On July 20, Louis Kirke came ashore with 150 soldiers and a Protestant minister to take possession of the fort and the Habitation, and the next day, accompanied by the firing of salvos, the English flag was raised on a bastion.[28] Thus began the first English occupation of the St Lawrence.

In the wake of this capitulation, should all the French take ship for Europe? There was much hesitation. The widow Hébert and the Couillart family, who after all had nothing in France, finally decided to remain. Louis Kirke promised them freedom to harvest their grain and to trade with the Indians. The English even undertook to pay them four livres for each of their beaver pelts.[29]

At last, on July 24, the first group set out for Tadoussac under the direction of Thomas Kirke. Champlain, who was impatient to meet David

Kirke, was aboard. And from far out in the river as they passed La Mal-baie, what should they see but a ship hugging the shore in an attempt to slip past the English; it was Emery de Caën arriving with the long-awaited help.[30]

What had happened was that, on April 24, peace had returned to Europe. Richelieu, happy with his triumph over the Huguenots, had also got the better of Savoy despite the Spaniards. England had then signed the Treaty of Susa. The Hundred Associates at once prepared a second fleet of four ships, at a cost of 103,976 livres, which Isaac de Razilly was ordered to escort to the St Lawrence in safety. The Jesuits again equipped a small ship to go to the aid of their confrères in Canada. This fleet lost almost two months waiting at La Rochelle for Razilly, only to learn finally that he had been sent to Morocco.[31]

Emery de Caën, however, had been instructed to go ahead with the supplies that Quebec had been awaiting for two years, take aboard the furs belonging to the de Caën Company, and barter his remaining merchandise. He arrived somewhat late at Gaspé, having been delayed by bad weather. There he found Boullé, who was watching for ships from France and who assured him that the St Lawrence was still free. Boullé then hurried back up the river to announce to Champlain that help was arriving at last, but he was captured on the way and held prisoner at Tadoussac. Word of the arrival of help from France had sent the English post-haste up the river to occupy Quebec. De Caën, undeterred by having met Indians with English merchandise, also headed for Quebec. Under cover of fog he passed Tadous-sac unseen, but ran aground. David Kirke discovered him at last, but was certain that he could not escape and made no haste to attack him. De Caën freed his ship and continued up the river, and so it was that he met Thomas Kirke at La Malbaie coming down. After an exchange of cannon fire, Thomas Kirke proceeded to board the other vessel and obliged Cham-plain to act as mediator. De Caën submitted, and it was then that Cham-plain and Kirke learned that peace had been signed between France and England.[32]

The Hundred Associates' fleet had no better luck than Emery de Caën's supply ship. The four vessels, joined by the Jesuits' ship, had not been able to leave La Rochelle until June 26, sailing under the command of Captain Charles Daniel. Among other things, Daniel was bringing a new commis-sion to Champlain, dated March 21, 1629, giving him command in New France in the absence of Cardinal Richelieu. The Jesuits' ship had been forced to turn back the year before, but this time it was lost completely; carrying twenty-four people, including Fathers Lalemant, Noyrot and Vieuxpont and Brother Louis Malot, it broke up on August 24 on the rocks off Canso. Father Noyrot and Brother Malot perished and a Basque ship picked up the survivors. Father Vieuxpont went to Cape Breton and

Father Lalemant took to sea again, but was shipwrecked on the coast of Spain.[33] As for Daniel, he landed on Cape Breton on August 28 in the Grand Cibou (Bras-d'Or Bay), where he learned that Quebec was under English occupation. He decided not to continue further, but in order at least to assert the rights of the Hundred Associates, and to protect French fishermen, he launched an attack with fifty men on the Scottish settlement of Fort Rosemar at Port aux Baleines. He forced the evacuation of the settlement and then returned to the Grand Cibou, where he built Fort Ste Anne. Leaving forty men there, well supplied, under the command of a certain Sieur Claude, and two Jesuits, Fathers Vieuxpont and Vimont, he headed back to France on November 5. Another ship of the Hundred Associates' fleet, commanded by Joubert, had reached Gaspé. Joubert, when he was informed of the situation in the St Lawrence, decided to return to France, but his ship was wrecked off the coast of Brittany.[34]

Meanwhile, the French of Quebec had completed their evacuation. The last to depart left on September 9, including Gravé and the Récollets, who had taken care to hide their liturgical articles here and there in the woods. Having made sure that their men at Quebec were well supplied for the winter, the Kirkes set sail from Tadoussac on September 14. With them they took Champlain, his lieutenant Boullé, de Caën, the agent Gravé and his assistants, the Jesuits Massé, Brébeuf and de Noüe, and the Récollets Le Caron and La Roche d'Aillon, all to be repatriated. On October 27, the prisoners were landed at Dover, from where they crossed over to France. Champlain, Boullé and de Caën remained in England for a time, however, to lay complaints with the authorities over the military operations carried out by the Kirkes in time of peace.[35]

For the second consecutive year, the Hundred Associates had suffered a total loss. Besides having been deprived once again of the profits of the fur trade, they had lost the entire sum of 103,976 livres that they had invested in the second voyage.[36] France and the Hundred Associates were left with only two posts, and insignificant ones at that: Fort Ste Anne on Cape Breton, with forty men and the only two priests in all of New France that winter, and Fort St Louis or Lomeron on Cape Sable, with the young La Tour in command. True, the French had wiped out the Scot Ochiltree's Fort Rosemar, but Alexander had maintained his position at Port Royal.

As soon as it was known in Europe what had happened in America, France set out to regain both Canada and Acadia. Aided by Champlain and André Daniel, both members of the Company of the Hundred Associates, the French ambassador to England began negotiations toward the end of 1629. With five memoranda dated February 11, 1630, and invoking the Treaty of Susa which predated the English occupation of New France, he asked that Alexander give up Port Royal and Cape Breton and that the Kirkes do likewise with Quebec. The reply was that the King of England was favourably disposed to the return of Quebec and all that had been taken with it, and that a search would be made for the furs which, according to de Caën, the merchants of London had hidden to avoid giving back.[37] The reply made no mention whatsoever of Acadia; while it was recognized that the French had been improperly dispossessed of the place they had occupied, it was maintained that Port Royal and Cape Breton had not at the time been occupied by the French, and that the English were therefore under no obligation to give them back.[38] The King of England was reluctant to return them for two other reasons: Acadia (or Nova Scotia, since 1621), had been formally granted to William Alexander, who had worked toward its development; and then there was the dowry that France had not yet paid out for the marriage of Princess Henrietta, sister of Louis XIII, to Charles I.

With the intention of forcing England's consent, the Hundred Associates equipped another fleet in 1630 at a cost of 77,092 livres and placed it under the command of Razilly, but Louis XIII and Richelieu were preoccupied with the Italian wars, and the fleet did not sail. Nor did the Company send any large expedition the following year, "because so many losses had crushed its spirit."[39]

In 1630 and 1631, only supply ships went to New France. One of the Company's directors, the merchant Jean Tuffet of Bordeaux, sent two ships commanded by the Basque Bernard Marot in 1630 with aid for the young La Tour at Fort St Louis. The following spring another ship arrived with supplies, and this same ship returned in October with a good number of artisans and some Récollets.[40] The little colony on Cape Breton also received help; in spite of the loss of a dozen men from scurvy, Fort Ste Anne had survived its first winter. In the spring of 1631, Captain Daniel returned to find that the commandant, Claude, was being held prisoner by his men for having murdered his lieutenant. Daniel delegated his brother to command in Claude's place and returned to France at the end of 1631, with "but little in furs and fish."[41]

For all the attempts made in high places to obtain its restitution, the St Lawrence remained closed to the French for three years, and this meant another series of heavy losses for the Hundred Associates. Besides having acquired a fort at Quebec which gave it exclusive access to the great fur-trade network of the interior, the Anglo-Scotch Company of Alexander and Kirke had confiscated in 1629 some 1,700 beaver pelts belonging to the de Caëns and had obtained another 5,000 pelts by barter in the same year. In 1630, two more of its ships were sent to Quebec, where they had the trade all to themselves and returned, it is said, with furs worth 300,000 livres. What was more, in 1630 any ship that ventured into the gulf and river without a trade or fishing permit from the company was confiscated.[42]

As compensation for the losses he had suffered through the suppression of his monopoly, Guillaume de Caën had obtained the trade monopoly of Quebec from Richelieu for the year 1631. Emery de Caën therefore set sail for the St Lawrence aboard the *Don-de-Dieu*. The English intercepted him at Tadoussac. He invoked the Treaty of Susa and the King of England's promise to return the St Lawrence to France, and the English agreed at first to share the fur trade with him, on condition that he produce the necessary documents at Quebec. However, at Quebec, pleading first the paucity of the trade that year and then, when the Hurons arrived laden with beaver, claiming that the monopoly belonged to England, they forbade him to trade at all with the Indians. In spite of his formal protest of August 22, 1631, the most he was allowed was to store his merchandise until the following year under the care of his men. The Hundred Associates sent a ship that year to try to trade at Tadoussac, but her captain dared not venture into the river when he saw the English ships there, and had to be satisfied with a little trading at Miscou. In 1631, therefore, the fur trade was no more profitable for the Hundred Associates than for the de Caëns.[43]

Discussions between France and England dragged on and on. In order to force the issue, early in 1632, France considered resorting to the same show of strength as in 1630, by preparing a great fleet under Razilly's command to proceed with reoccupation *manu militari*. The King of England decided not to prolong his opposition; by the Treaty of St Germain en Laye of March 29, 1632, England agreed to evacuate "all the places occupied in New France, la Cadie and Canada," leaving them in the same condition in which they had been found. Both sides agreed to return vessels and other property taken in time of peace. For his part, Guillaume de Caën was to receive, among other things, a sum of 82,700 livres.[44] And England was at last to get a part, at least, of Queen Henrietta's dowry.

It was not the Hundred Associates, however, who were to profit immediately from the recovery of New France and the fur trade. Since Guillaume de Caën had borne the costs of a fruitless voyage in 1631 and, above all, since he claimed to have been sorely wronged in the whole affair and was demanding 266,000 livres in compensation, Richelieu granted him the fur-trade monopoly for 1632 and a vessel worth 10,000 livres so that he might go to Quebec and receive its official restitution while Isaac de Razilly went to reoccupy Acadia in the name of the King. Emery de Caën was appointed commandant at Quebec for the following winter. He arrived at Tadoussac on June 18, and on June 29 he called upon the English to withdraw from Quebec. All this time the English were continuing to trade in furs, to the detriment of the new monopolist. On July 6, de Caën confronted Thomas Kirke with the original of his commissions authorizing the French to retake possession of the establishment. The English put off their departure for another week, and finally left Quebec on July 13, having had ample time to get their hands on all the available furs.[45] And so in 1632 the monopoly proved as useless to de Caën as it had to the Hundred Associates. But in any event, New France had been recovered; the English evacuated the St Lawrence, and the Scots turned over Port Royal to Razilly. The Hundred Associates could now resume the program laid down for them in 1627, and in 1633 could at last, and indeed for the first time, count on the profits of their fur-trade monopoly.

This face, perhaps his own,
appears on Champlain's 1632 map
of New France.

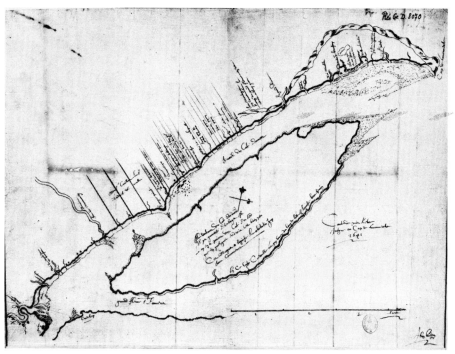

The Côte de Beaupré and the Isle of Orleans, in 1641, according to
Jean Bourdon. (The Isle of Orleans is not yet inhabited.)

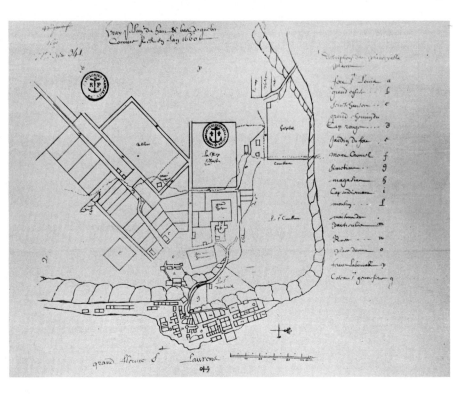

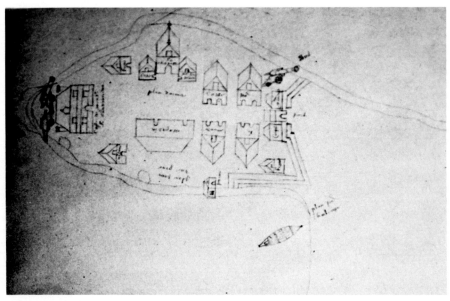

Modern reconstruction of Fort Ste Marie.

(Facing page, above) Quebec in 1660, according to Jean Bourdon.

(Facing page, below) The first representation of Montreal, 1642.
(Population was confined to the interior of the fort, at the confluence
of the St Lawrence and St Pierre rivers.)

The taking of Quebec by the English, 1629, as later depicted
in A New Discovery of a Vast Country in America, by
Louis Hennepin (1699).

(Facing page, above) Plan of the fort at Quebec on Cape
Diamond (Fort St Louis) in 1635, by Jean Bourdon.

(Facing page, below) Plan of the Habitation of Quebec,
around 1635, by Jean Bourdon.

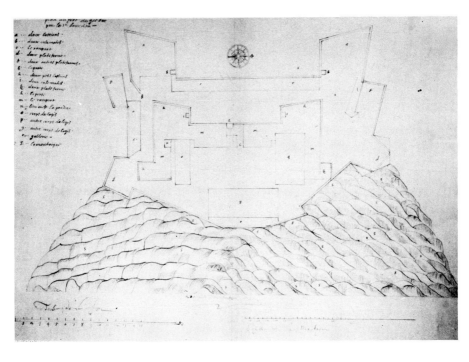

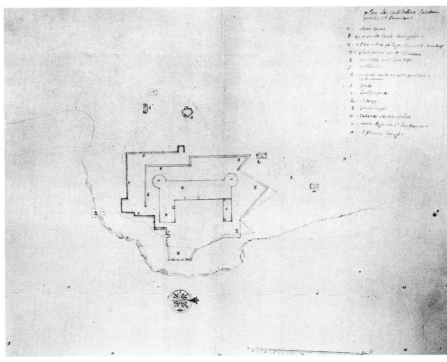

1

The first entries in the registry book of Notre Dame Church in Montreal.

Monseigneur de Laval,
engraving from a portrait by
the Récollet Brother Luc.

Marie de l'Incarnation,
engraving from a portrait
painted shortly after her death.

*Marguerite Bourgeoys, painted immediately after her death
by the artist Pierre Le Ber.*

CHAPTER 14

New Colonists for the St Lawrence

1632–1645

"The great losses suffered by these Gentlemen in the early infancy of their Company," wrote Father Le Jeune, "are indeed like a very dense night, which covered all these lands with horror"; it seemed at the time that New France would never be anything more than "a storehouse for the skins of dead beasts."[1] At last, in 1632, there was reason to hope for a great effort at colonization, but the relaunching of the 1627 project was not to begin that year. When Emery de Caën arrived at Quebec on July 5, accompanied by his lieutenant Du Plessis-Bochart and two Jesuits, Paul Le Jeune and Anne de Noüe, his function was simply to repossess the country for France.[2]

Father Le Jeune's image of a "very dense night" was well chosen. When the English sailed away on July 13, 1632, they left Canada in a most lamentable state. On Miscou Island, they had burned the Habitation of 1626. Of the establishment at Cap Tourmente nothing was left, after the 1628 raid, and the few remaining animals had scattered. Burned too was the Habitation of Quebec, so recently rebuilt between Cape Diamond and the river; nothing remained of it but "walls of tumbling stones." On the cape, Fort St Louis, at least, was still standing, and the English had even added a wooden parapet and filled in two platforms. The Jesuit and Récollet convents had been abandoned for three years and were very much run down. Half of one of the Jesuits' buildings had been burned by the English, the doors and windows of the principal living quarters had been removed or broken, and no furniture was left but two wooden tables; and, adds Father Le Jeune, "it is even worse in the Récollet fathers' house." This convent was to deteriorate still further, when some families who were installed in it kept "cows in the lower chambers." There had been no new clearing of land during the three years of occupation; the English had been content with sowing only the land already cultivated.[3]

Missionary work was about to be resumed, but just at this time the St Lawrence colony lost an important source of spiritual strength: the Récollets. They had already returned to Acadia in 1630 and were preparing to return to the St Lawrence when it was decided that they should be replaced by Capuchins. In his instructions from Richelieu in 1632, Razilly was ordered to take three Capuchins with him to Acadia; Richelieu had also instructed de Caën to take three Capuchins to Quebec in 1632, but de Caën arrived with Jesuits only. The Récollets appealed to Lauson, Intendant of the Hundred Associates, "on whom they relied," but Lauson gave them only vague replies, "putting them off from year to year, without effect."[4] They were not to reappear until 1670. And yet they had been the first missionaries in the St Lawrence, ten years before the Jesuits! They had long missionary experience among the Montagnais and the Hurons. They had a well-built convent at Quebec and had been granted large tracts of land. The motives behind the opposition they encountered from Lauson and the Hundred Associates are open to conjecture. Whatever the case, the Jesuits were to remain the sole spiritual masters of the Laurentian colony until 1657. The result, within this exclusively Catholic community guided by priests of a single order, was a large measure of religious uniformity and peace; there was an equally large measure of bitterness on the part of the Récollets, who were to accuse the Jesuits of having ousted them from the St Lawrence. For the moment, in any event, the work of the missionaries was resumed with diminished forces.

There was at least one thing that did not have to be rebuilt, and that was the fur trade; however, if the trade network was intact, thanks to the French interpreters who had stayed in the country, the French still had to protect their trade against poachers. The English had so effectively won the Indians over by trading alcohol and fire-arms for furs that when English ships came to poach at Tadoussac and even "far up the river" in 1633, the Indians, in spite of their alliance with the French, did not fail to take advantage of the bargains they offered.[5] Each year, too, the Algonquins had to be dealt with. "These Island People wished to prevent the Hurons from coming to the French, & the French from going to the Hurons, so as to keep all the traffic to themselves." They would stop at nothing to "block the road." The French had therefore to be constantly vigilant lest the Hurons should be discouraged for good. In 1634, very few Hurons came to trade, because most of them were kept at home by the war with the Iroquois, but in 1636 their passage was completely cut off by the Algonquins. In this period it was the Algonquins, not the Iroquois, who were the greatest obstacle for the French in their trade with the interior.[6]

In 1637, a new nation of Indians appeared on the scene to jeopardize the fur-trade network, the Abenakis, who lived on the upper reaches of the Kennebec River and maintained relations with the trading posts of New England. That year a dozen of them turned up in the St Lawrence, and the French foresaw a possible danger to "the interests of Messieurs les

Associez" because the Abenakis could well "take the Beaver away from these parts and trade them elsewhere." Governor Montmagny, vexed to see these Indians come and "traffic inside our French preserves," threatened to cut off food supplies from the storehouse to the Montagnais as long as the Abenakis were about. The chief of the Montagnais tried to stop the visitors at Quebec, but they skirted the blockade and went to Trois Rivières to meet the Algonquins who were trading there. Informed of this by the Governor, Commander Chasteaufort had the Abenakis brought before him. They had not come to trade, they said, but to bring help to their allies. Their baggage was inspected and found to consist of nothing but arque-buses, which were promptly confiscated, whereupon they returned home.[7] In 1640, they were found again at Sillery, having even brought with them from the Kennebec an Englishman who planned to reach the Northern Sea by way of the Saguenay River. Montmagny forbade the Englishman to come to Quebec and put him under surveillance until such time as he could make the return journey with his guides. However, the explorer decided to give himself up to the French instead, since the Abenakis had fallen ill and the rivers had dried up; Montmagny had him taken to Tad-oussac, "to go back to England by way of France."[8]

These attempts after 1632 to maintain the immense trade network for the benefit of the French gave rise to a long voyage westward, the only exploration undertaken between Brûlé's day and Radisson's. Since Brûlé's journey of about 1623 to Lake Superior there had been no important addi-tion to geographical knowledge, because the Indians persistently barred access to the interior to prevent the French from going to the source of supply for furs. The Hurons, like the Algonquins, would open the way to the French only if it might be useful for themselves; in 1634 such an occasion arose, and they called upon the French for help. It had become necessary for them to restore peace between themselves and another nation, the People of the Sea, or Winnebagos (or again, Puants), who dwelt on the western shore of a "second freshwater sea" adjoining Lake Huron. The Winnebagos occupied a strategic position on the great fur-supply route. For the accomplishment of this mission, a man was chosen who had lived for some dozen years on the Great Lakes since his arrival in 1618; this was Jean Nicollet, who knew the Indians well and stood high in their esteem. Since there was still hope of finding the Asian Sea and Nicollet cherished the dream of reaching Cathay, he took with him a mandarin robe, "a great robe of Chinese damask, with flowers over all & birds of various colours." It was from Huronia, with Huron companions, that he undertook his long journey in 1634-35. He was the first European to penetrate as far as Lake Michigan (called at first Lac des Puants, Lac des Illinois, Lac St Joseph and Lac Dauphin). He made contact with the Menominees, sedentary Win-nebagos on the western shore of the lake; he met or heard of the Sioux,

Assiniboines and Potawatomis. From the Baie des Puants (Green Bay to-day), he is said to have travelled by way of the Fox River as far as the land of the Mascoutens, and even to have reached the Wisconsin River which empties into the Mississippi, although the Jesuit Marquette speaks of the village of the Mascoutens as being "the furthest of the discoveries made by the French" at that time. In any case, Nicollet did not discover the Asian Sea nor appear before the Chinese mandarins in the splendour of his mandarin robe, but he accomplished some very important exploration, making it possible to add to the map of the continent Lake Michigan and the area whence the exploration of the Mississippi would be launched forty years later. He also attained the immediate objective of his journey, the re-establishment of a peace that was essential to the maintenace of the trade network.[9]

The stability of this network was indeed necessary to the life of the colony, but settlement was no less so, and the Hundred Associates were taking steps to provide it. In 1633 the Company sent three ships carrying two hundred people, but evidently this expedition launched no large-scale settlement, since in 1634 the Jesuit Le Jeune still refers to "the family that is here."[10] Settlement did not begin in earnest until 1634, with the arrival of Giffard, the Juchereau brothers, and other recruits who were destined to make their mark on the future of New France. This influx brought the first new colonists since 1617.

Robert Giffard, apothecary and surgeon from Mortagne in Perche, had already been to Quebec, perhaps as early as 1625. In 1628, soon after his marriage to Marie Regnouard, he had set out again for New France, but had been captured by the Kirkes. On January 15, 1634, at the age of forty-three or forty-four, he secured the grant of a seigneury near Quebec, signed a commercial partnership agreement with a gentleman from Perche (Pierre Le Bouyer de Saint-Gervais, lieutenant-general of the bailliage of Perche), then set sail with "all his family [and] a number of persons that he took with him to live in the country." It was quite a colony in itself that he led from Mortagne and its environs, including Jean Guyon, master mason, with his wife and six children, Zacharie Cloutier, master carpenter, with his wife and five children, Gaspard Boucher, farmer and carpenter, with his wife and four children (one of whom was the young Pierre, future governor of Trois Rivières), Marin Boucher, a relative, with his wife and three children, Thomas Giroux, François Bélanger, Claire Morin, Jeanne Mercier, and Henry Pinguet, a prosperous merchant from Tourouvre, who brought his wife and three children.[11]

Another group from Perche had gathered about the Juchereaus. Jean Juchereau de Maur (born at Tourouvre in 1592) brought his wife and his four children, among them Jean Juchereau de La Ferté and Nicolas Juchereau de Saint-Denys. His brother, Noël Juchereau des Chatelets (born in 1593), a bachelor with a degree in law, joined the group. The Juchereaus were well-to-do people in France who occupied positions of responsibility and headed business enterprises.[12] They were joined by Noël Langlois, Charles Pierre, François Baugy and three Gagnons from Tourouvre. Among other important recruits who stepped ashore at Quebec, we note Jean Bourdon from Rouen, a bachelor who was to play an important role as an engineer, and his friend, the priest Jean Le Sueur dit de Saint-Sauveur, the only secular priest during the first years of this period and the first to come to the St Lawrence since the chaplains of Cartier's day (if in fact there were any).

In 1635, other families answered Giffard's call: François Auber, Philippe Amyot, Robert Drouin, Jean Côté and Martin Grouvel, who were the progenitors of some of the most prominent families of French Canada. In 1636, a whole family complex arrived from Normandy, the Legardeurs and the Leneufs, who were soon to found a dynasty in the fur trade: Pierre Legardeur de Repentigny with his wife and three children; his brother, Charles Legardeur de Tilly, who was a bachelor; Jacques Leneuf de La Poterie, their brother-in-law; Michel Leneuf du Hérisson, his mother and his sisters, Marie and Madeleine.

These early waves of immigants, made up of nobles, merchants, skilled workers, professional men and soldiers, accounted for the sudden advance of population up-river from Quebec, until then the furthest point of French settlement. Two posts were established above Quebec in 1634. The first, referred to by Champlain as an "Habitation," was built on a small rocky island opposite the present village of Grondines, where navigation became difficult because of rock shoals covering great stretches of the river bed. It consisted of "a platform, on which were placed Cannon, in order to command the whole river"; the artillery was still there in 1636.[13]

The second post founded on Champlain's initiative, far more deserving of the name *habitation*, was at Trois Rivières. Even when most of the trading was done at Cap de Victoire, or at Ile St Ignace opposite the mouth of the Richelieu, this was a traditional meeting place because of its situation and its sandy beaches, so convenient for the landing of canoes. After the return of the French in 1632, it was the site of regular meetings for fur trading; fortifications there would afford protection for Quebec and, most important, for the Indian allies against the Mohawks who invaded the St Lawrence from the Richelieu River. Moreover, as Champlain wrote, at this spot "the temperature of the air is much more moderate, the land more fertile, the fishing and hunting more abundant than at Quebec."[14] On July 4, 1634, Laviolette was sent by Champlain to build a few houses and a palisade "on a natural platform, which overlooks the great river."[15]

By 1636, the progress being made in the Laurentian colony was heartening indeed for anyone who had known it all but deserted. The excitement was further heightened not only by the large number of soldiers guarding the fort at Quebec, "like a place of importance in the heat of war," and by so many officers who had come with their families,[16] but above all by the presence of three Knights of Malta. This was not the first time that the military order of St John of Jerusalem (or of Malta) had played a part in the affairs of New France; first there had been Commander Aymar de Chaste in 1603, then the Comte de Soissons in 1612 and, more recently, Isaac de Razilly, commandant of Acadia, whose death preceded that of Champlain late in 1635. In the St Lawrence colony of 1636, all authority was in the hands of Knights of Malta: at Quebec, Governor Montmagny and his lieutenant Bréhaut de Lisle, and at Trois Rivières, Bras-de-fer de Chasteaufort. It may even be that Richelieu systematically chose members of the knightly religious order to assure New France of men of high moral calibre so that, in its remoteness, it might not become a resort for pirates, like Newfoundland.[17] This may also explain the close religious supervision exercised over the population and the severity with which prohibitions were enforced and punishments administered; an iron collar or the stocks were common penalties for blasphemy, drunkenness or the trading of spirits to the Indians.[18] In any case, the St Lawrence colony under the leadership of a number of Knights of Malta might present a front to the world as a strong bastion of French power.

Whether this military strength was real or illusory at the time, the colony was on the threshold of a great period of organized land settlement. The seigneurial régime was already an established institution, though not systematized. This was the era when certain patterns began to emerge, with the establishment of a group of great landowners. The Hundred Associates, seigneurs of New France since 1627, did not begin to grant fiefs until 1633 within their Laurentian domain. On December 3, Jacques Hertel was the first to receive a fief under the new régime, two hundred arpents at Trois Rivières, later reduced to fifty. More grants were to follow.* Thanks to Jean Bourdon's map, the oldest seigneurial map of the country, we can see that the geographic pattern was already set by 1641: since the river flows from southwest to northeast, and the lands bordering on the river were the first to be granted, the fiefs tended to take the form of narrow rectangles whose lateral boundaries ran northwest and southeast, although geographic accidents gave rise to a good many exceptions. Similarly, land granted to settlers within a fief was divided into narrower rectangles whose lateral boundaries paralleled those of the fief. Another feature strongly characteristic of the French régime, the *rang*, had its inception in these early days: in the first stage, as Bourdon's map

---

*The reader will find in Chapter 18, on the settling of New France up to 1663, a more detailed treatment of the establishing of the seigneurial régime.

shows, the settlers' holdings were located at the water's edge; later on, in the eighteenth century, a second row of holdings appearing behind the first completed the pattern. Whether this arrangement was the result of the custom in some French provinces of establishing farms one behind the other in rows,[19] or whether the initial occupation of the river frontage was simply a matter of necessity, French Canada's traditional mode of settlement first becomes apparent in this period.

The Hundred Associates, then, had brought about the first vigorous recruitment of population for the colony and provided the framework of the seigneurial régime. For all that, the settlement they promoted was not a spectacular success. After 1636, the spark given it by Giffard, the Juchereaus and the Legardeurs faded. In 1641, nine years after the reoccupation of the St Lawrence, the colony still numbered only about two hundred settlers, although, according to the contract of 1627, there should by then have been more than three thousand.

Trois Rivières, Sillery, Quebec, and a few settlers at Beauport and on the Côte de Beaupré: that, in 1641, was the extent of French colonization along the St Lawrence. The administrative structure was still rudimentary; both civil and military authority rested with Governor Montmagny, who, on occasion, called together a Council composed of the Superior of the Jesuits, the High Seneschal (seigneurial judge) and a few notables. As far as the Church was concerned, the St Lawrence was still only a mission, under the spiritual authority of the Superior of the Jesuits.[20]

But suddenly, beyond this little country in which only two hundred people had been settled along a two-hundred-mile stretch of the river, there appeared a new Habitation a hundred miles upstream: Ville Marie. Like some earlier French establishments in America, it represented, far more than a natural outgrowth of the colonizing process, a dispersion of available resources.

A post at Montreal had, it is true, been long awaited. As early as 1611, Champlain had planned to build one at this place where navigation of the river was brought to a halt, but there had never been sufficient funds available. When the project was revived in 1635, resources were still lacking; nor had there been sufficient progress in the colony to warrant an establishment at Montreal. On the contrary, development at Quebec and consolidation at Trois Rivières would have been much more to the point. Particular circumstances, however, were to upset the logical plan of colonization. The project for a settlement at Montreal was, this time, of purely religious motivation; it began in the mind of a pious layman, Jérôme Le Royer de La Dauversière, tax collector at La Flèche in Anjou and former pupil of the Jesuits, who was ardently devoted to the religious revival in France. It was in 1635, it would seem, on the occasion of a visit to Paris on behalf of the Compagnie du Saint-Sacrement, that La Dauversière conceived the plan of establishing a centre of evangelization for the Indians on the Island of Montreal. He was already engaged in founding the Institut des Hospitalières de Saint-Joseph. His Jesuit confessor, Father François Chauveau, kept a rein on his enthusiasm for a certain time, and then in 1638, when the Institut des Hospitalières was well launched, encouraged him to pursue the Montreal project and brought forward one of his penitents, Pierre Chevrier, Baron de Fancamp, to assist him. Having met Father Lalemant, who had returned from Canada, La Dauversière and Fancamp went to the house of Chancellor Séguier in February 1639 to make the acquaintance of the young priest Jean-Jacques Olier, who at the time was occupied with rural missions in France. With the help of Baron Gaston de Renty, Superior of the Compagnie du Saint-Sacrement, it was decided later in 1639 to found a society to be named officially *Les Messieurs et Dames de la Société de Notre-Dame de Montréal pour la conversion des Sauvages de la Nouvelle France.*[21]

The Society would have to begin by acquiring the Island of Montreal. But it had already been conceded in 1636 to Jean de Lauson, who seemed bent on cornering as much land as possible in New France. La Dauversière met with refusal at first, but when he and Father Lalemant tried again, Lauson agreed to give up the island to the Society on August 7, 1640. Then came a new hitch. The Hundred Associates annulled the concession of the island, giving as their reason that Lauson had forfeited his rights by failing to develop his fief. Finally, the following December 17, the Hundred Associates agreed to grant the entire Island of Montreal to the Society, with the exception of the mountain and an area to the southwest. To this concession they added another, a seigneury of two leagues by six which was to be known as St Sulpice.[22] In 1641, thanks to the influence of Father Lalemant, others rallied to the cause. Among them was Paul Chomedey de Maisonneuve, a career soldier from Champagne who, at the age of twenty-nine, had already retired from active service and was living a quiet life of devotion. Another was Jeanne Mance, aged thirty-five, also from Champagne,[23] who stepped forward to offer her services as housekeeper and nurse. Maisonneuve accepted the command of the Montrealists, as they were called.

This band of colonists, consisting of some forty people, did not arrive at Quebec until the end of August 1641, too late to undertake the establishment of Ville Marie that year. Maisonneuve had been warned that "he must be prepared to be less well received by certain persons than he might have hoped: which he saw soon afterward," and indeed he was obliged to "swallow some doses of wormwood." Adversaries of the scheme had persuaded Montmagny to oppose it, on grounds of the danger of Iroquois incursions; "the design of this new Company," they said, "was so absurd that there could be no better name for it than the 'Insane Enterprise.'"

Governor Montmagny suggested to Maisonneuve that he would do better to establish his colony on the Isle of Orleans, but finally gave way before the courage and determination of the Montrealists' leader and agreed to support the foundation of the new colony. In October, 1641, he and Maisonneuve, accompanied by the Jesuit Vimont and persons "well-versed in the knowledge of the country," travelled up the river to the spot "chosen for the first dwelling." On October 15, the official taking of possession was enacted.[24]

The Montrealists spent the winter at Sillery, near Quebec, attending to "carpentry and other useful and necessary preparatives for a new habitation and colony." Among other things, boats had to be built to take the colonists to Montreal. At last, in the spring of 1642, the party set out, accompanied by Governor Montmagny, and reached Montreal on May 17. Tents were raised, and the men built "a redoubt of heavy stakes," a temporary chapel of bark, and a small hospital on the point of land, later named Callières, that Champlain had chosen more than thirty years before.[25]

There remained on the island for the winter a little population of fifty-five people, "from diverse places, of different humours, of diverse conditions, & all of one heart." There was, it would seem, "no cause for complaint in the space of ten whole months, to the great satisfaction of the commandant." The new colony lived through its first winter without being afflicted by any sickness, and this, adds the Jesuit *Relation* of 1643, "has never before been observed in any new settlement"; everywhere else, the first winter had almost ruined each new establishment.[26]

In 1643 the colonists rebuilt their Habitation, for they had been poorly housed until then. The news that arrived was encouraging: Governor Montmagny sent word that the King had approved the expenditures necessary for the construction of a fort and had made a gift to the Society of a ship of five hundred tons called the *Notre-Dame*. A foundation yielding 2,000 livres a year had just been established for the maintenance of a hospital, and the Society was giving 12,000 livres for its construction.[27]

The initial burst of enthusiasm was not to last for long, although in 1644 there was much rejoicing over the first harvest of French wheat (an experiment recommended by the Sieur d'Ailleboust) and over the arrival of a detachment of soldiers. Already, undesirable elements were mingling with the devout first-comers.[28] For a number of years, moreover, the colony ceased to develop: recruitment was at a standstill and the rate of natural increase was negligible. There was not a single French marriage until November 3, 1647, and between 1642 and 1652 there were only ten in all. The first French birth occurred in 1648; for the whole ten-year period of 1642-52 there were only twenty-two births, and during the same period there were twenty-three burials. For those who had come to settle on the land, the first concessions were not made until 1648.[29] In 1653, the arrival of about a hundred colonists brought new blood to reanimate the community, and then the little settlement of Ville Marie returned to the doldrums.

Seemingly there were two factors behind this state of affairs: the instability of the backers of this new enterprise, and the incursions of the Iroquois.

The attacks of the Iroquois (almost always the Mohawks) were at first only isolated forays carried out by small, elusive groups; nothing compared to what they would be a few years later: "little wars," Father Vimont calls them, "because [the Iroquois] come in parties," making war "only in the manner of robbers who lie in wait near highways without revealing themselves unless they see their advantage." But, he adds, all this was most tiresome. Each year there were peace talks and exchanges of wampum belts between the Mohawks and the Algonquins, but on both sides there were always deaths to be avenged. Since the new colony was situated above the mouth of the Richelieu River, the Mohawk invasion route, it was threatened with total isolation. In addition to this, the Iroquois "block all the approaches to our great River, prevent the commerce of these Gentlemen [the Hundred Associates] & threaten to ruin the whole country."[30] In order to maintain contact with Montreal, protect Trois Rivières and contain the Mohawks, Governor Montmagny decided to "raise fortifications on the avenues of the Hiroquois." As soon as he received word that France was sending "a powerful reinforcement," he went to the Richelieu and, on August 13, 1642, chose "a place suitable for building a Fortress which shall command the mouth" of the river. He had been directing work on the palisade for a week when three hundred Iroquois appeared, armed with arquebuses, and mounted an assault. They were repulsed, but only after a lengthy battle. Unhappily, since France never sent the promised reinforcements, this fort was not to prove as useful as had been hoped; in 1643, the Iroquois began to skirt the fort and block the St Lawrence by occupying Lac St Pierre. By the autumn of 1645, the strength of the garrison was almost nil; the commandant (Senneterre, at the time) had taken ship for France, the Jesuits in residence had withdrawn, and only eight or ten soldiers were left there for the winter. It would seem that French occupation of the fort ceased entirely in 1646.[31] Under such conditions, the remote colony of Montreal was once more doomed to isolation; the difficulty of maintaining contact in order to ensure the arrival of supplies was sufficient to make further progress impossible.

There was also the fact that the settlement, launched in the heat of missionary fervour, was not yet soundly based. This devout community was inspired by absolute confidence in God, and certain of its members' acts of devotion had brought forth truly astonishing results, which served to excite their faith still further. But these pious people did not, generally speaking, have a very realistic view of things, and would launch blindly upon hazardous undertakings despite the advice of those with more experience. Furthermore, their benefactors tended to be temperamental. The rich and aging Pierre de Puiseaux, with his prosperous establishment at Sillery, had given all his worldly goods to the work of Ville Marie and had gone to Montreal in 1642, but the following year he changed his mind, returned to Quebec, and took back what had originally belonged to him. Madame de La Peltrie, brimming with zeal for the conversion of the Indians, had founded the Ursuline convent at Quebec in 1639. Then, unsatisfied, she had withdrawn her support from the Ursulines, although it was vital to them, and had thrown herself, with all she owned, into the Montreal venture. She spent the winter of 1642-43 at Ville Marie, but her zeal was still unassuaged and she prepared to set out for Huronia. A returning missionary persuaded her of the uselessness of such a move, but she still deprived the Montrealists of the support they had come to depend on, for she decided to go back to her Ursulines.[32] The benefactors in France showed the same kind of instability in their support, giving more or less liberally as their zeal at the moment dictated, or, like La Dauversière, engaging in shaky financial operations, or else vanishing from the scene without replacement.

Despite the founding of Trois Rivières (which was still no more than the tiny post it had been in 1634), despite the construction of Fort Richelieu (which stood deserted after 1645), and despite the addition of the colony of Montreal (which had only some fifty inhabitants in 1645), it can be said that the Laurentian colony had not progressed in ten years. True, from almost nothing when the Hundred Associates were at last able to set to work, the population figure had risen to about three hundred by 1645, but this was a far cry from the objective of fifteen thousand set by Richelieu. The principal architects of the revival of 1627 (Louis XIII, Richelieu, Razilly, Champlain) were dead, and no great figures dedicated to the colonial cause had as yet replaced them. It was in this state of stagnation that the colony was taken over by a new body, the *Communauté des Habitants*.

CHAPTER 15

Acadia: Lost Again

1632–1654

While in 1645 the New France of the St Lawrence was attempting to apply a new formula that might rescue it from stagnation, the New France of Acadia was still beset by quarrels that threatened to open the door once again for the New Englanders.

And yet, after the Treaty of St Germain en Laye in 1632, it was Acadia whose prospects had looked the more promising. It was here, far more than in the St Lawrence, that France had concentrated her efforts at colonization. Moreover, the English occupation had not had as disruptive an effect in Acadia as in the St Lawrence, where the English in occupying Quebec had controlled the entire valley and were masters of the immense fur-trade network. In Cape Breton the French had made short work of a Scottish colony in 1629 and had built a solidly-entrenched settlement in Grand Cibou Bay. On the peninsula, Charles de La Tour ("the young La Tour") had continued his operations at Cape Sable in his Fort St Louis, regularly supplied from La Rochelle and provided with artisans and Récollets. He had even been able, in 1631, to establish Fort Ste Marie at the mouth of the St John River,[1] thereby gaining access to Acadia's richest source of furs. In the great domains granted him at Cape Sable and on the St John River La Tour's authority had been unchallenged, and since 1631 he had borne the title of King's Lieutenant-General for Acadia. After the peace of 1632 there was no new start to be made here, only a continuation.

Spurred by Commander Isaac de Razilly, the King's Lieutenant-General in New France, the French were about to launch the most vigorous colonial effort in Acadian history, or so it appeared from the importance of its leader and the systematic way in which it was carried out. Razilly was the key figure in Richelieu's colonial policy; if his attention was to be focused on Acadia rather than on the St Lawrence, it was because, as a distinguished career soldier, he was in a much better position than Champlain to protect the outposts of New France and turn Acadia into a great defensive bulwark against New England, which since 1630 had been enjoying an extraordinary development. Richelieu, when he ordered Razilly to clear Port Royal, had given him a fully-equipped warship, the *Espérance-en-Dieu*, and a sum of 10,000 livres. The Company of the Hundred Associates, besides, had granted him in fief and seigneury the river and bay of Ste Croix, a domain of twelve leagues frontage and twenty leagues depth.[2]

Razilly brought three men into association with him in this venture, all of whom were long to play leading roles in Acadia: his brother Claude de Launay-Razilly, who financed the enterprise, his cousin Charles de Menou d'Aulnay-Charnizé, a man of about twenty-eight who had been serving as the Commander's lieutenant for a number of years, and a La Rochelle merchant of thirty-four, Nicolas Denys, who had been the Hundred Associates' representative in Acadia since 1631.

Razilly's fleet of three ships took to sea on July 23, 1632 and arrived at La Hève on the east coast of the peninsula on September 8. Here Razilly decided to stop; he built Fort Ste Marie de Grâce, with a chapel for the Capuchins who had sailed with him and buildings in which to lodge his three hundred men.[3] Then, firmly installed at La Hève, he set out to fulfil the special mission entrusted to him by Richelieu, the retaking of Port Royal, where Fort Charles was still occupied by William Alexander's Scots under the command of Captain Andrew Forrester. Meanwhile, Forrester had crossed the Bay of Fundy on September 18 (in time of peace, therefore) and attacked La Tour's fort on the St John River. He had taken from it 1,500 pelts and also food and munitions, toppled the French coat of arms, carried off the men of the garrison to an island in the Pentagouët region, and then returned to Port Royal. Some time later, La Tour was able to recover part of his merchandise by force at Machias, where a Saco merchant kept a trading post.[4]

In December of 1632, Razilly finally went to Port Royal and demanded the evacuation of the Scottish colony. Forrester made no trouble. Some forty colonists went aboard the *Saint-Jehan*, which was returning to France, and were put ashore on the coast of England with their furs and other valuable belongings. When, on July 4, 1631, the King of England had ordered Alexander to evacuate Port Royal, he had enjoined him to destroy what the Scots had built there and to leave the site "completely deserted & depopulated," as it had been when Alexander had taken over. It would seem that Forrester carried out this order to the letter, since the new French fort of Port Royal was built further up the bay. In any event, the Scots had been well supplied, for they sold Razilly 15,000 livres' worth of food and munitions.[5] In spite of speculation, it is not at all certain that a number of the Scots stayed at Port Royal and became integrated with the French population; it is more likely that French or Flemish colonists were mistaken for Scots.[6]

The *Saint-Jehan* returned in 1633 with new provisions for Razilly's settlements, but the Company of the Hundred Associates, after the losses it had suffered, was not able to support the Acadian enterprise by itself. The Company had spent 150,000 livres on the voyages of 1632 and 1633, but even this sum had been insufficient, since in 1632 Commander Razilly already owed 53,200 livres to his brother Launay-Razilly and his associate, Jean Condonnier. The Hundred Associates therefore agreed to turn over their business to a private company, the Razilly-Condonnier company. In repayment of sums already expended by the Razillys, and because they were taking charge of settlement, the Hundred Associates conceded to Claude Launay-Razilly in 1634 the fort and Habitation of La Hève, with ten leagues square of land, Port Royal, also with ten leagues square, and Sable Island. They also granted the monopoly of trade, from Canso all the way to Virginia, for a period of ten years, but this monopoly was to be shared equally between the Razillys and La Tour.[7]

For his part, La Tour had officially assumed responsibility for the upkeep and settlement of the Habitations of Cape Sable and the St John River in January 1633. In 1635 he acquired or obtained confirmation of extensive possessions in Acadia: Fort St Louis on Cape Sable, with a domain ten leagues square, and another domain five leagues by ten on the St John River (the 1627 concession).[8] The Pentagouët River was added to his seigneuries upon its return to the French; on that river the French of Acadia and the English of New England had been in conflict for several years, and in 1632 the English of Plymouth had seized the post built there some time before by La Tour, holding on to it in spite of an attack by men from La Rochelle. Menou d'Aulnay was sent by Razilly in August of 1635 to put an end to this occupation. He accomplished his mission, seized the merchandise and threatened, it would seem, to drive back the English, not just to Pemaquid, but as far as the 40th parallel. The French were thereafter to remain in the Pentagouët country until 1654; it was formally conceded, however, not to Menou d'Aulnay, who had captured it, but to La Tour. The latter retook possession of it at the end of 1635 and on January 5, 1636, the Hundred Associates granted him a seigneury there of ten leagues square.[9]

By the end of 1635, then, Acadia was divided into two parts. The first, belonging to the Razillys, comprised Sable Island, the fort of La Hève with its seigneury, Port Royal with its seigneury (these three regions being the personal property of Launay-Razilly), and the seigneury of the Ste Croix River, which was the property of Commander Razilly. The second, belonging to La Tour, comprised Fort St Louis on Cape Sable, with its seigneury, Fort Ste Marie at the mouth of the St John River, with its seigneury, and a seigneury on the Pentagouët River. As in the time of Poutrincourt and Madame de Guercheville, the government of Acadia had two heads: La Tour, "Lieutenant-General for the King on the coasts of Acadia" (the title given to him by the Hundred Associates in the concession of January 1635), and Commander Razilly, styled Lieutenant-General for the King in the concession of 1632; each dealt separately with the Hundred Associates, the seigneurs of New France. If this system had the inconvenience of permitting less unity of action, it does not seem to have hindered the French enterprise in Acadia: La Tour and the Razillys worked by common consent under the immediate authority of Richelieu and the Hundred Associates.

However, as far as the Razillys were concerned, the seigneuries and trade monopoly granted them brought no immediate relief to the already heavily-endebted enterprise. In July 1634, Commander Razilly declared that he and his friends had spent some 150,000 livres over the past two years without receiving any return, and he called for help from Richelieu, proposing a plan which would cost the State nothing but would be to France's entire advantage. According to this plan, 150,000 livres would put five of the King's ships at his disposal for trade and fishing in the first year, eight in the second, ten in the third, and twelve in the fourth. This build-up of shipping would require no increase in investment, since it would be effected only out of profits. The benefits, moreover, would be fourfold: along with the settlement of the country, the conversion of the Indians; the establishment of major maritime commerce; relief for the State's treasury (since these twelve ships would no longer be a charge upon it); and greater security at sea. In other words, Razilly was asking for massive support from the State, with the intention that control of the whole endeavour should pass into the hands of the King or Richelieu. In fact, he was asking for a revival of the plan of 1627, which, because of their successive reversals, the Hundred Associates were no longer able to carry out themselves. Richelieu did not consider it expedient or even possible to tie up the State's funds or the King's ships in the Acadian enterprise in this way, but, since the Razillys foresaw the necessity of abandoning the enterprise altogether, he entered personally into association with them on January 16, 1635. In return for a sum of 17,000 livres, he assumed ownership of a fifth of the property and rights of the Razillys. Shortly afterward, two other associates acquired shares for a total sum of 20,000 livres. With this new influx of capital, the Razillys were able to continue their work.[10]

In this period, the bustle of activity throughout Acadia, from Cape Breton to the Pentagouët, justified hopes for the greatest success. On Cape Breton, Captain Charles Daniel had withdrawn from his Fort Ste Anne in the Grand Cibou, but on February 26, 1633, the Hundred Associates conceded the whole island to a new company formed by Pierre Desportes and Jean Belleteste, members of the Hundred Associates, who at once sent a shipment worth 6,200 livres to Fort Ste Anne. Late in 1633, Desportes and Belleteste formed another new company with a capital of 45,000 livres; this company obtained the Cape Breton trade monopoly for a period of four years, and, although it was a trading concern, it set about recruiting colonists and clearing the land for settlement.[11] At Canso, frequented since time immemorial by fishing boats, Razilly built Fort St François and put his lieutenant, Nicolas Le Creux du Breuil, in command. At La Hève, in what Nicolas Denys calls "a very fine and very excellent countryside," Razilly lived in a house a league from the river's mouth, and around him were some forty settlers who were already harvesting "quantities of wheat." Not far away, on a little river that emptied into the La Hève River, Nicolas Denys built himself a house and employed a dozen men, "some of them labourers, others coopers making staves for barrels, carpenters, & others for hunting." Denys counted on the fur trade only "as an accessory," preferring to rely on sedentary fishing and on the cultivation of the land. In association with Razilly, he established a fishery which succeeded so well at first that he saw fit to buy a 200-ton ship to take cargoes of cod for sale in Portugal, under the command of his brother, Denys de Vitray. Unfortunately, a war between Portugal and France put an end to this enterprise. With Razilly's backing, Denys also started a business in lumber, drawing on great stands of oak near his house. Razilly allowed him to ship his wood aboard the vessels which came with supplies for the colony.[12]

On Cape Sable, the young La Tour too had organized an embryonic colony about his fort; nearby, his father had set up house complete with his wife and servants. About 1635, Denys saw flourishing vegetable gardens there, including one kept by a Récollet, but, as Denys observed, Fort St Louis was a "habitation for trading in pelts."[13] In the bay of Port Royal, a new colony seems to have taken root immediately after the departure of the Scots in December 1632, for in that same month a Capuchin establishment was noted there.[14] La Tour's Fort Ste Marie, across the Bay of Fundy, was a "habitation for trading" like the fort at Cape Sable. Its situation was highly advantageous, since the St John River drew a flow of furs from an extensive reservoir and also caught a certain spill-over from Laurentian hunting; as many as three thousand moose hides a year were traded there, besides beaver and otter furs.[15] In the Ste Croix River country, Commander Isaac de Razilly's personal domain, there seems to have been no post as yet, but the Pentagouët country, which was La Tour's fief and was protected by a fort, was a centre of very active trade after the English were forced out.

Although La Tour continued to conduct his own affairs in his usual energetic way, it is Commander Razilly who appears to have been the driving force in the Acadian enterprise; and, as he wrote to Richelieu in 1634, he was well able to defend "the Cross and Lilies" in Acadia.[16] The period of progress was to come abruptly to an end when Razilly died at La Hève in December 1635. Between the two leaders of Acadia, co-operation and mutual understanding had reigned until then; Razilly and La Tour, sharing the trade monopoly, had run their respective domains without interference from each other. After Razilly's death the frame-work remained as it had been, but between La Tour and Razilly's suc-cessor there soon arose conflicts that were to lead to a long civil war.

Commander Razilly's heir was his brother, Claude de Launay-Razilly, who was already the proprietor of La Hève and Port Royal. He now took over Razilly's domains, but since he was detained in France he delegated his authority to his cousin, Charles Menou d'Aulnay-Charnizé, who had been Razilly's lieutenant. "This brought much change in the country," writes Nicolas Denys; Razilly had "wished only to make known the virtues [of Acadia] and to populate it," but Menou d'Aulnay "on the contrary feared that it would become inhabited, and [...] brought no one in."[17] This change in attitude was probably not due solely to Menou d'Aulnay, who was at the time Launay-Razilly's lieutenant and was dependent upon him in all things, particularly from a financial point of view; the Com-mander's death seems to have deprived the association of the all-important backing of high-placed authorities (in particular Richelieu and the Hun-dred Associates). The accumulation of debt obliged Launay-Razilly not only to concern himself more with the fur trade than with settlement, but even to effect a cutback, abandoning La Hève in order to concentrate on Port Royal. In any event, Menou d'Aulnay's first important move was to evacuate the colony of La Hève in 1636 and regroup everyone at Port Royal. This meant a waste of three years of colonization and also weak-ened the defence of the coast, but Port Royal lent itself much better to the sound establishment of a colony because of its excellent soil and port facilities.

With the turn of events, unfortunately, one of Isaac de Razilly's foremost associates found his interests sacrificed: Nicolas Denys. In 1637 Denys was still recruiting woodcutters at La Rochelle for five-year service, promising them half the profits of his lumber operation, but it would seem that Menou d'Aulnay, although he had been offered a share of the profits, would never agree to allow Denys to load his wood on board the ships returning empty to France. Denys was therefore obliged to abandon his business and depart, leaving, according to his statement, 20,000 livres' worth of finished wood where it lay.[18] He did not return to Acadia for some ten years.

Similarly, the mutual understanding that had existed between Commander Razilly and La Tour was conspicuously absent between La Tour and Menou d'Aulnay; in fact, between these two men who were supposed to share equally in the trade monopoly of Acadia, a struggle began that was to be pursued without quarter until one of them should be crushed. La Tour initially had the advantage in this commercial rivalry. His business seemed to be doing excellently, with his La Rochelle connection providing regular supplies and a market for his furs.[19] Although he, too, was engaged in settlement, he had no other costs to bear than the pay of his agents and workmen. The Hundred Associates, who were to support him in preference to Menou d'Aulnay, had just granted him, in 1636, the Pentagouët River and post. In the St John River, where from this time onwards he kept his principal dwelling, he possessed the fur route that, after the St Lawrence, was the richest of all. On the other hand, the Razilly company represented by Menou d'Aulnay was in a difficult position financially, and although it had heavy expenses to bear in maintaining the Port Royal colony it had rights to only half the profits of the Acadian fur trade. Finally, if one observes the behaviour of Menou d'Aulnay in the ensuing years, one cannot help seeing in him an ambition-driven man reaching for power at all costs. As Denys writes (although it was an adversary's judgement), Menou d'Aulnay's disposition "& that of his council was to reign."[20]

It was in 1638 that Menou d'Aulnay was first officially invested with authority by the King. Louis XIII then put him on an equal footing with La Tour, as Razilly had been, and it was reiterated that the fur-trade monopoly should still be divided equally between the two leaders. Through ignorance of Acadian geography, however, the King gave Menou d'Aulnay authority over territory belonging to La Tour, and gave La Tour authority over domains held by Menou d'Aulnay; thus the latter became Lieutenant-General of the "Etchemin coast," that is to say from the Bay of Fundy to New England, and La Tour was named Lieutenant-General of the Acadian Peninsula, whereas the peninsula, less Cape Sable, should have been assigned to Menou d'Aulnay, and Cape Sable, the St John River and the Pentagouët River should have been left to La Tour.[21] As if there were not already enough to squabble over!

Nevertheless, the basic and constant cause of strife between the two lieutenants-general of Acadia seems indeed to have been the trade monopoly that they were supposed to share equally. A violent quarrel flared at Port Royal in 1639 between Menou d'Aulnay and La Tour, probably over the profits to be divided; then, in 1640, La Tour imprisoned some men that Menou d'Aulnay had sent to Pentagouët. Menou d'Aulnay set out himself for Pentagouët, then returned to Port Royal to find La Tour there; La Tour attacked him, although it is not known exactly why or in what circumstances. The affair ended to Menou d'Aulnay's advantage; he seized La

Tour, releasing him later upon agreement between the two to carry their grievances to France.[22]

There also, Menou d'Aulnay emerged the victor. He went to France in the autumn of 1640 with the Capuchin Pascal de Troyes, who supported him at every turn as he argued his case all the way up to the Queen herself. He was instructed to transmit an order to La Tour to go to France and explain his behaviour and, in case of La Tour's refusal, to place him under arrest. "You shall use all means and forces at your command," wrote the King to Menou d'Aulnay, "and shall place the forts which are now in his hands into those of faithful persons devoted to my service, who shall be responsible for them." Furthermore, through an edict issued on February 1, 1641, the King's Council annulled the concession of Fort Pentagouët by the Hundred Associates in 1636 and confirmed Menou d'Aulnay's possession of it. On February 24, the King went even further, naming Menou d'Aulnay commandant of Fort St Louis on Cape Sable in place of La Tour, who was nevertheless still seigneur of that part of the peninsula.[23]

Having been summoned during the summer of 1641 to comply with the King's edicts, La Tour withdrew with his family and his Récollets to Fort Ste Marie on the St John River, the last domain left to him. Menou d'Aulnay betook himself to Cape Sable and razed the entire settlement, fort, Habitation, chapel and missionary convent. Then he sent a message to the St John River summoning La Tour to submit to his authority, but in vain. At the end of 1641, Menou d'Aulnay went once more to France. With the steadfast support of the Capuchins (who, it may be noted, were shareholders in his company), he reaped another victory: La Tour's business agent was emprisoned in France, Menou d'Aulnay obtained the means for effecting La Tour's arrest, and all and sundry were forbidden to carry aid to the St John River fort in any form, whether food, men or munitions.[24]

Menou d'Aulnay also took advantage of this voyage to consolidate his financial situation. In recognition of services rendered to Commander Razilly and his company, he obtained on January 15, 1642 the gift of a seventh of the 17,000 livres' capital invested by Launay-Razilly and Le Tardif. The following day, he bought Launay-Razilly's four shares for 14,000 livres. On February 9, he was named administrator of the "part and portion" of the Capuchins, the share of 20,000 livres that Richelieu had held in the company and had subsequently turned over to the Capuchins for the benefit of their missions and schools in Acadia. On February 19, Menou d'Aulnay received from Launay-Razilly another gift of gratitude, a sum of 4,000 livres from Commander Razilly's estate, with which he purchased from the estate the Ste Croix River seigneury. Finally, on May 16, 1642, he signed an agreement at La Rochelle with the merchant Emmanuel Le Borgne, who immediately advanced him 16,000 livres and agreed to keep Acadia supplied with provisions in return for its furs.[25]

With his back to the wall and deprived of all help from France, La Tour turned to New England as a last resort. Soon after the loss of Cape Sable and Menou d'Aulnay's demand for his submission at the St John River fort, he sent a certain Sieur Rochette to Boston in September 1641 to try to make some commercial arrangements with Massachusetts and obtain help against Menou d'Aulnay. The Puritans accepted the offer of trade in principle without committing themselves further, on the pretext that La Tour's emissary did not carry the proper credentials. In October 1642, once more blockaded in the St John River, La Tour dispatched another representative to approach the Puritans, who, this time, sent a ship to buy La Tour's furs.[26] This commercial liaison with New England was used by Menou d'Aulnay to incriminate La Tour still further, even though there was no reason why La Tour should not carry on such trade; as Governor and the King's Lieutenant-General (titles to which the Hundred Associates still recognized his claim), La Tour had the right to conclude commercial treaties with foreign colonies, a right which was to be exercised by Menou d'Aulnay himself in 1644 and would also be exercised by Governor d'Ailleboust in 1651.

Help was also on the way from France. La Tour's wife, Françoise-Marie Jacquelin, whom he had married at Port Royal in 1640, had gone to France to plead her husband's cause. Armand de Maillé, Duc de Fronsac, Richelieu's successor as Superintendent of Navigation, still considered La Tour as "Governor and Lieutenant-General for the King on the coast of Acadia," and he looked the other way when, in the spring of 1643, the Hundred Associates sent La Tour the Saint-Clément, "equipped for war," carrying soldiers and provisions. Although the St John River was under blockade, La Tour managed to reach the Saint-Clément and, judging his force too weak to drive off Menou d'Aulnay, he headed for New England to request reinforcements. Having examined the official commissions which showed that La Tour was still vested with authority, the Puritans allowed him to lease ships and enlist volunteers, but their colony as such refused to take sides in the conflict. La Tour hired four fully-equipped ships and seventy volunteers for a period of two months. Upon the arrival of this fleet in August, Menou d'Aulnay was obliged to retire to Port Royal. La Tour pursued him there and demanded reparation for the damages he had suffered, which Menou d'Aulnay refused. Since his English mercenaries hung back from launching an assault, La Tour made do with sowing destruction here and there and, upon his return to the St John River, he seized three boatloads of furs that Menou d'Aulnay had left behind. With the expiry of their contract the Bostonians went home, and the Saint-Clément returned to France.[27]

The treatment he had received at the hands of La Tour and the English gave Menou d'Aulnay further cause to raise the cry of treason, and this he did not fail to do during his 1643-44 visit to France. The Capuchins, who were in a position to lend him powerful backing at Court, gave him a memorandum bitterly accusing La Tour of a variety of crimes, including heresy. Menou d'Aulnay himself presented a long indictment of his rival covering the period 1624-43.[28]

In 1644, Menou d'Aulnay returned from France with reinforcements and resumed his blockade of the St John River fort. For La Tour, this time, no help was forthcoming from Boston. Quite the contrary, in fact, for in September of that year Menou d'Aulnay signed a treaty with Boston through the good offices of a man named Marie, who is thought to have been a Capuchin in lay clothing. The Puritans did, indeed, reserve the right to trade with either Menou d'Aulnay or La Tour, but the advantage of the treaty for Menou d'Aulnay was that it would prevent any military alliance between Boston and his adversary. La Tour would therefore receive no aid and, with sufficient forces now at his command, Menou d'Aulnay was to emerge triumphant. He took the St John River fort of Ste Marie on April 16, 1645. La Tour was then at Boston, still trying to get help, and there was only a small garrison of forty-five men to defend the fort. La Tour's wife resisted nevertheless for three days and three nights; then the defenders were overwhelmed by an assault on Easter Monday. According to Nicolas Denys, Menou d'Aulnay hanged a number of the survivors and threw Madame de La Tour into prison. She died shortly after.

At Boston, on May 13, La Tour mortgaged his St John River fort, unaware that he no longer possessed anything. Alone now in the enjoyment of the trade monopoly in Acadia, Menou d'Aulnay built himself another fort not far from the old Fort Ste Marie and left a lieutenant to command there in his place. Determined to enforce his exclusive privilege throughout the region, he arrested fur traders operating near Richibucto (on the east coast of New Brunswick) and, even further up the coast, some men of the Miscou Company; in this region, as on the St John River, he was collecting furs.[29]

Royal authority now carried Menou d'Aulnay to the height of his power. La Tour was judged guilty of open rebellion and of conspiring with the enemy. The Queen Regent, Anne of Austria, expressed her gratitude to Menou d'Aulnay on September 27, 1645, for the zeal he had displayed. The following day the young Louis XIV promised him a fully-equipped vessel and congratulated him on his struggle against the rascally La Tour who, wrote the King, had been plotting "with a number of foreigners" to "put the fort that he commanded into their hands, which would not only have caused injury to my service through the loss of all these coasts, but also the loss of the cod fisheries." At the governor's château at Quebec, where he had taken refuge in August 1646, La Tour learned in 1647 that Menou d'Aulnay had officially become absolute master of all Acadia. Indeed, in letters patent of February 1647, in which the King invoked reasons obviously based on the submissions that had been made to the Court, very sweeping powers were accorded to Menou d'Aulnay as Governor and Lieutenant-General of Acadia. For the upkeep of the colony that he had "begun to form," he obtained the monopoly of the trade in furs with the Indians, along with the possession in seigneury of all Acadia. This Acadia, moreover, was not restricted to the combined territories granted originally to Razilly and La Tour, that is to say, from New England in the south to Canso in the north; Menou d'Aulnay's Acadia extended far beyond Canso, as far as the St Lawrence River. The country of which he was now the sole seigneur and governor, and whose trade monopoly was to be his alone, embraced the same territory as Sir William Alexander's Nova Scotia of 1621. Never since 1603 had France accorded so much territory to a single individual; as the historian Baudry writes, "none of our Canadian governors ever received such hyperbolic appointments or privileges, [...] a veritable delegation of viceregal powers."[30]

This immense Acadia was at last reunited under a single authority, and at last a period of tranquillity appeared to be in store. But Menou d'Aulnay was faced with antagonism or rivalry from every side. The Company of the Hundred Associates was, of course, the first to be dissatisfied with the decision of 1647. With the exception of the command of a vessel in 1633, Menou d'Aulnay had never received any responsibility from the Hundred Associates, and never, even when he had acquired the rights of the Razilly brothers, had they presented him to the King as governor, as it was their right to do in their seigneury of New France. As early as 1638 and 1641, however, in official documents emanating from the King, Menou d'Aulnay had borne the title of Governor in complete disregard for the position and rights of the Hundred Associates. The Associates had consistently backed La Tour against Menou d'Aulnay, and as far as they were concerned, even after he had been condemned by royal letters, La Tour was still "Governor and Lieutenant-General for the King on the coast of Acadia." Moreover, the four years that La Tour spent at the governor's château at Quebec, when he was officially considered a rebel, could only have been spent there under the protection of the Hundred Associates. Understandably, then, the Company was not a little displeased with these letters of 1647, which not only named Menou d'Aulnay governor but also bestowed on him the seigneury of all Acadia when, in accordance with its well-established right, the Company had already conceded certain parts to other persons: Cape Breton, for instance.[31]

Cape Breton had been conceded by the Hundred Associates in February 1633 to two of their members, Pierre Desportes and Jean Belleteste, together with the trade monopoly for a four-year period. Desportes continued to maintain Fort Ste Anne in Grand Cibou Bay and entered into partnership with two members of the Hundred Associates, Charles Daniel and Nicolas Libert Le Jeune. The Cape Breton Company was reorganized in 1636 but continued to be directed by two shareholders of the Hundred Associates, Pierre Desportes and Jean Tuffet; fur trading and fishing were carried on from Fort Ste Anne and from a new fort called St Pierre in the bay of the same name on the east coast of the Strait of Canso. After Tuffet's death in 1642, his son André maintained the association until 1645, when the greater part of the company's interests passed into the hands of Gilles Guignard de La Fontaine, who became holder of the sub-fiefs of Ste Anne and St Pierre, still under the authority of the Hundred Associates. It was therefore between him and Menou d'Aulnay that difficulties arose. Menou d'Aulnay seized a ship from him in 1645; then, in September 1647, on the strength of his letters, he took the Cape Breton domains by force.[32]

To the north of his immense Acadian fief, Menou d'Aulnay saw another rival continuing to fish and trade with authority from the Hundred Associates: Nicolas Denys. About 1645, Denys had obtained Miscou Island from the Company. He had built an Habitation there, and had extended his operations to the bay of Nipisiguit (Bathurst today), in the Baie de Chaleur. In 1647, Menou d'Aulnay went to Miscou and to Nipisiguit and seized Denys's posts, promising to reimburse him the following year in "merchandise & victuals"; Denys was to await the reimbursement in vain.[33]

Menou d'Aulnay's grasping domination of the whole of Acadia gave no new impetus to the colony; he was simply not able to develop such a vast domain. By 1648, he was already more than 200,000 livres in debt. His La Rochelle supplier, Emmanuel Le Borgne, came to Port Royal to demand payment, but to no avail; his only recourse was to the courts. Menou d'Aulnay had eliminated all those who might have served the cause of Acadia, and had been unable to replace them.

His sudden death in 1650, in the waters of the bay of Port Royal, led to a revival of the disputes that had raged before 1647. From Quebec, La Tour went immediately to France to lay claim to his rights. He was imprisoned for a short time at La Rochelle, probably because of legal action for the settlement of debts, but rose quickly to favour in the eyes of Louis XIV. An edict of February 16, 1651 declared him absolved of the accusations against him. .He was confirmed in his functions of

Governor and King's Lieutenant-General "in all the lands, territories, coasts and confines of Acadia" and was accorded the same powers and the same monopoly that had been given to Menou d'Aulnay. When he returned to Port Royal the following September he presented the King's letters to Menou d'Aulnay's widow, Jeanne Motin, resumed possession of the domains of Cape Sable and the St John River, and took over the government of Acadia.[34]

Meanwhile, Emmanuel Le Borgne was taking steps to recover the 260,000 livres now owing to him. On November 9, 1650, he obtained recognition of the debt from the late Menou d'Aulnay's father and gained rights not only to the Menou d'Aulnay assets in France but to "all the habitations of La Hève, Port Roial, Pentagouette, the Rivière Saint-Jean and also of Miscou, the isle of Cap Breton and other dependencies."[35] Le Borgne was thus setting himself up as the heir to Menou d'Aulnay's vast domain and entering into conflict with La Tour and with those in Cape Breton and at Miscou who held their rights from the Hundred Associates. In the spring of 1651 he sent his men to seize the widow Menou d'Aulnay's assets at Port Royal, and it was in her name that these men set out to expel all those who had returned to pursue their former activities in Acadia. Nicolas Denys had come back in 1651 with his brother Simon Denys de La Trinité and had resumed trading and fishing at Fort Ste Anne and Fort St Pierre. They were expelled from both places once more and were sent to Quebec.[36]

The widow Menou d'Aulnay sent her steward, Brice de Sainte-Croix, to seek protection in France against Le Borgne and to save what remained of her possessions there. Brice de Sainte-Croix approached the King's uncle, César de Vendôme, Superintendent of Navigation, and concluded an agreement in February 1652, by which the widow ceded half of her possessions in Acadia to Vendôme plus the St John River fort and Fort St Pierre, to which she still laid claim. The following November, without the assent of the Hundred Associates, Vendôme was named Governor and Lieutenant-General for the King in all of Acadia.[37] And so in 1652 confusion was rampant. La Tour was governor and seigneur of Acadia, the Duc de Vendôme had just been named governor and co-seigneur (with the widow Menou d'Aulnay), while Le Borgne claimed the assets of the Menou d'Aulnay estate in their entirety, or in other words, once again all of Acadia.

But the Duc de Vendôme sent no help to the widow Menou d'Aulnay with her eight small children, and the widow finally accepted the most unexpected of compromises; in February 1653 she signed a contract of marriage with La Tour, for "the peace and tranquillity of the country and concord and union between the two families." They agreed to remain in separation of property until such time as the widow had paid her debts.

The *douaire* or marriage settlement was to consist of the enjoyment and possession of the St John River fort and 30,000 livres besides, whose source was to be the revenue of this fort. La Tour undertook to support the Menou d'Aulnay children in their claims to their just rights.[38] This astonishing marriage took place the following summer.

That year Le Borgne deemed it necessary to come to Acadia himself at the head of impressive forces. He arrived at Port Royal in La Tour's absence and prevailed upon La Tour's bride to sign an acknowledgement of 200,000 livres of debt; he seized merchandise belonging to La Tour and went on from there to spread his domination over the rest of Acadia. He seized the Pentagoüet post and levelled the entire settlement at La Hève, causing a loss of 100,000 livres. On Cape Breton, he captured Forts St Pierre and Ste Anne, to which Denys had returned again in 1652, and threw Denys into a cell. The Nipisiguit post on the Baie de Chaleur was also ravaged. Only the St John River fort escaped attack.[39]

In 1654 confusion continued to reign for all except Nicolas Denys, who had returned to France and won his case against Le Borgne. On December 3, 1653, the Miscou Company having renounced its rights, the Hundred Associates granted Denys, in ownership and seigneury, all the country between Canso and Cap des Rosiers in Gaspé, along with the trade monopoly, on condition that he establish at least two settlements of forty families each over the next six years. Moreover, upon his presentation by the Hundred Associates on January 30, 1654, the King named him Governor and King's Lieutenant-General not only in his immense seigneury but also in Ile St Jean (Prince Edward Island), the Magdalen Islands and Newfoundland. The fur trade was reserved to him exclusively throughout the extent of this region, and he alone was authorized to establish a company for sedentary fishing in the whole of the northeast of the continent, from Newfoundland to Massachusetts.[40] As seigneur of Cape Breton and the Baie de Chaleur, governor of a country extending from Canso to Newfoundland, monopoly-holder for both the fur trade and fishing, Nicolas Denys returned in 1654 to continue his work at Fort St Pierre on Cape Breton.

South of the Strait of Canso, disputes over possession continued to rage. Le Borgne, leaning heavily upon his rights over Menou d'Aulnay's estate in claiming possession of all of Acadia, concluded an agreement of association with the Duc de Vendôme, who had been made Governor of Acadia and who himself claimed possession of all of Acadia in partnership with the widow Menou d'Aulnay. Thus united, Vendôme and Le Borgne prepared to drive out the trespassers, La Tour on the St John River and Denys in Cape Breton. Aboard the *Châteaufort*, which carried 75,000 livres' worth of merchandise, Le Borgne returned to Acadia in 1654. After an abortive attempt to take La Tour unawares on the St

John River, he prepared to attack Cape Breton. Thereupon another set of claimants arrived on the scene: the English.[41]

They came 170 strong aboard three ships under the command of Robert Sedgwick, who had received a commission from Cromwell as Admiral of the Fleet and Commander-in-Chief of New England for the purpose of securing the defeat of New Holland. Peace had been restored between England and the Netherlands, however, and Sedgwick, then working to base the economy of New England on the fishing industry, resolved to attack Acadia. France and England were not at war (France, moreover, had recognized Cromwell's republic in 1652), but skirmishes between ships of the two nations were frequent. In mid-July, La Tour capitulated and was held prisoner, having turned over to the English merchandise worth 200,000 livres. Sedgwick then went to Port Royal where Le Borgne capitulated in his turn on August 16, after putting up a brief resistance. The Pentagouët fort, occupied by the French since 1635, fell to the English on September 2. Major John Leverett became the military governor of occupied Acadia and Sedgwick returned to England, taking La Tour with him.

The French population was not evacuated. By virtue of the terms of the capitulation of Port Royal, the inhabitants retained ownership of their property, and Jeanne Motin continued to cultivate her farms on the upper reaches of the river above Port Royal with her children about her, the eldest being fifteen. Even the Capuchins were permitted to remain in the country, on condition that they should live two or three leagues from the fort.[42]

The quarrel over jurisdiction by no means came to an end with the loss of Acadia's principal centres in 1654. It continued, in fact, into the eighteenth century. Having been detained in England for a year, and no longer hoping to see his rights prevail in France, La Tour obtained recognition of a barony granted him by William Alexander in 1630, covering the south and east coast of the Acadian peninsula as far as La Hève. In 1656, all of Acadia from La Hève to the frontier of New England became the domain of an association composed of La Tour and the Englishmen Temple and Crowne. On his eventual return to the country, however, La Tour sold his rights to his two associates and retired with his family to Cape Sable, never again to take part in the affairs of Acadia.[43] For Temple and Crowne there was little tranquillity, since, apart from disagreements between them over their respective domains, their possession was disputed by a number of their compatriots: Thomas Elliot, the Kirke brothers, William Alexander's heirs. And then, of course, they still had to defend themselves against the claims of the French. On November 20, 1657, the Hundred Associates conceded all of Acadia to Le Borgne, from the Rivière Verte (St Mary's River) to New England, with the exception of the part belonging personally to La Tour, and on December 10, Le Borgne became its governor and Lieutenant-General for the King. From that moment, he worked with the Duc de Vendôme toward recovering possession of his territory. He went to England in 1658 to negotiate for the restitution of Acadia, while his son, Alexandre Le Borgne de Belle-Isle, occupied La Hève in May and seized furs belonging to Temple. Temple then recaptured La Hève and took Le Borgne de Belle-Isle to England. The Le Borgnes had no choice but to await a settlement that was not forthcoming until 1667.[44]

Throughout the dramas that were Acadia's lot, there had been little new settlement. Some twenty people were living with La Tour in 1627, but no trace has been found of them after that date. To this precarious population were added the three hundred hand-picked men brought to La Hève in 1632 by Razilly, but these were perhaps as yet only artisans who had come without their families, since the first birth to a French couple occurred only in 1636. The sole document available for the study of Acadian immigration during this period is the passenger roll of the ship Saint-Jehan, which left La Rochelle on April 1, 1636, with seventy-eight people aboard. This may have been the first large group to come to Acadia as settlers since the time of the Sieur de Monts. Many of them were to return to France, however; of the nine households of 1636, only four remained in Acadia, and of the fifty-four ploughmen, carpenters and others, not more than five or six chose to remain permanently. A very frail beginning, all the more so since these people dispersed, some going to Port Royal and others to Canso. But in any event, along with La Tour, these were the forefathers of the Acadian population, who were to leave duly identified descendants.[45]

In spite of the quarrels that developed after Razilly's death, the leaders of Acadia recruited each year a number of *engagés* who came on contract for a limited time, but it is difficult to discover what became of them. Menou d'Aulnay brought a contingent of twenty-five men and five women in 1640, and in 1643 he claimed credit for having brought twenty French households to Acadia. It seems that in 1644 he was maintaining two hundred soldiers, ploughmen and artisans, not counting women and children. Of La Tour's accomplishment we know even less: from lists of contracts with *engagés* it is known that he recruited forty-five men for his fort on the St John River, but that was at a time when disaster was already imminent; later, he recruited *engagés* for his Cape Sable seigneury, to which he was to bring Mius d'Entremont. For Cape Breton, recruitment was steady but on a very small scale.[46]

From an estimated French population of 120 in Acadia in 1641, the figure rose to four hundred in 1643, but it seems likely that there were no longer more than three hundred, or some fifty families, in 1650. The population must have been much the same in 1654, when most of Acadia passed into the hands of the English, and growth was subsequently to be very slow, since in 1671 there were only four hundred inhabitants.[47]

Little is known of the social institutions of this small and scattered population. As in the St Lawrence, the seigneurial régime was relied upon to provide a hierarchical and community structure, but most of the Acadian seigneuries in this period served only to promote fishing and fur trading. Except perhaps at Cape Sable and at Port Royal, there seems to have been no organized seigneurial life. What little we know about social activities in this Acadian colony is related mainly to the religious life of the people.

If one considers only the small number of inhabitants, taking no account of their dispersion, the colony was well provided with priests: Récollets, Jesuits and, above all, Capuchins. In 1630, not having set eyes upon a priest since 1624, the colonists were sent three Récollets from Guyenne, to whom La Tour gave lodging in his Cape Sable fort. Commander Razilly introduced some Capuchins to Acadia in 1632, and in 1633 Louis XIII wrote to La Tour instructing him to dismiss the "clergy, both secular and regular, who may be there" and to replace them with Capuchins, "to avert those inconveniences which may arise from the variety of persons and diverse conditions in that country."[48] The two Jesuits who had maintained a mission on Cape Breton may also have received an order to depart; in any case they left the Grand Cibou in 1633 and went to Quebec. Soon, however, the "variety of clergy" was back. The Jesuits returned to Cape Breton in 1634, opened a mission at Miscou in 1635, and from then on were to be found regularly in Acadia (on Cape Breton, at Miscou and at Nipisiguit) until 1647, when they appear to have been expelled by Menou d'Aulnay. Although the Récollets went back to France after the 1633 order, their absence from Acadia was only temporary. They followed La Tour when he settled on the St John River in 1641 and Menou d'Aulnay burned their house at Cape Sable; in 1643, two of them accompanied La Tour to Boston. The Récollets finally withdrew from the St John River fort in January 1645 after a dispute with Madame de La Tour, and took refuge at Port Royal with the Capuchins; the following summer, they returned to France.[49]

As for the Capuchins, their fate was closely tied to the unending quarrels that followed one upon the other after 1635. Having been brought to Acadia by Commander Razilly, they continued in association with his successor, Menou d'Aulnay. For the maintenance of their missions and their schools of "little savages," Richelieu turned over to them in 1640 a sum of 20,000 livres, which represented his share in the Razilly company. They could hardly do otherwise than take sides with Menou d'Aulnay, and they did all they could to ensure his success. Certain Capuchins there were who did not agree, and who accused Menou d'Aulnay of misappropriating the 20,000 livres for his own benefit, but the dissenters were sent back to France and those remaining drew together in solid support of the Governor.[50]

When Menou d'Aulnay died in 1650 the Capuchins remained faithful to him; one of them, Ignace, wrote so eulogistically of the last period of Menou d'Aulnay's life that an enthusiastic historian was inspired to depict this governor as the saint of Acadia. They declared themselves against his creditor, Le Borgne, and they backed the association that the widow Menou d'Aulnay established with the Duc de Vendôme through her steward Brice de Sainte-Croix. This no doubt would explain the rough treatment they received at the hands of Le Borgne's men in 1652. The English occupation of Acadia brought a quick end to the Capuchins' stay; the last of them left for France in 1655. The results of this mission of more than twenty years seem rather disappointing, and indeed as early as 1641, official reports to the Propaganda were very pessimistic regarding the chances for success in Acadia: in reference perhaps to Port Royal alone, it was said that only five or six souls had been baptized in ten years. Elsewhere it was stated that one Capuchin had converted more Indians than all his confrères, but that amounted to only a score of families and a number of individuals baptized at the point of death.[51]

The "seminary" for Indians, founded not at La Hève in 1632, as has been mistakenly stated, but at Port Royal about 1644, might have produced some interesting results if only it had appeared in more propitious circumstances. In 1644, thanks to a gift from the Queen, Madame de Brice was brought to Port Royal. She was the mother of two Acadian missionaries, and came despite her advanced age to take on the direction of the "Abenaki college"; she taught a dozen pupils, both boys and girls. After a brief existence of eight years, the school closed in 1652 when Madame de Brice and the Capuchins were expelled from the country by Le Borgne's men. Its accomplishment therefore appears to have been negligible, but the Jesuit institution of Notre Dame des Anges founded at Quebec for the same purpose, with more considerable resources and in much more favourable circumstances, was hardly more productive.

Missionary efforts in Acadia ceased completely in 1655 with the departure of the last of the Capuchins and did not resume until 1659, when some Jesuits reappeared at Nipisiguit and at Miscou.[52] If the ferocious struggles waged interminably since the death of Commander Razilly had created a climate unfavourable to the work of evangelization, they had also impeded the progress of settlement and reduced Acadia, once again, to a state of confusion and disorder. In 1664, Nicolas Denys wrote: "There is no one but the King capable of turning it to account, and I was given to understand that he wished to have the whole country"; but it was not until 1667 that Acadia was restored to France by the Treaty of Breda, and not until 1670 that the French reoccupation became effective.

CHAPTER 16

The Habitants' Company

1645–1658

In his journal of 1645, Father Jérôme Lalemant notes with pleasure some great news brought by the ships that arrived in August: the Hundred Associates had "ceded the fur trade to the Habitans [. . .] agente regina & nobis impellentibus."[1] While the victories of Menou d'Aulnay were reunifying Acadia, an important change was occurring in the St Lawrence colony through the intervention of the Queen Regent and the Jesuits: the Communauté des Habitants was about to take over the management of commercial affairs and assume administrative responsibility.

Trade had fallen off greatly over the past few years. The colony was making little progress, and, in response to popular request, Father Le Jeune had been sent to France to present the grievances of the habitants. Before a change in the state of affairs could be brought about, however, further steps had to be taken in 1644, this time by two Canadian delegates, Pierre Legardeur de Repentigny and Jean-Paul Godefroy, who went to France with concrete proposals. The Hundred Associates deliberated for a month and finally, by a "treaty" of January 14, 1645, approved by the Queen on March 6, they agreed to relinquish their fur-trade monopoly in favour of the colony.[2]

After having spent 1,200,000 livres on New France since 1627, the Company of the Hundred Associates was left with a debt of more than 400,000 livres, and this burden it must now distribute among all its members. The Company declared that, at a time when it was hoping to enjoy at last "the fruits of its labours" and to recoup the enormous sums it had spent, it nevertheless preferred to act "for the glory of God, the service of the King, and the establishment of his Colonies": a noble way indeed of washing its hands.

To be sure, the Hundred Associates reserved their rights of ownership over all of New France; they alone were empowered to grant seigneuries, to choose the governor and to dispense justice; as seigneurs, they would be assured of annual dues to be paid in kind: a thousand pounds in weight

of beaver pelts. What they were ceding to the habitants was "all rights
and powers relating to the trade in Pelts" throughout the lands of the
St Lawrence as far as its mouth, which consequently did not include the
Baie de Chaleur nor Acadia. Since the Hundred Associates had already
ceded the Island of Montreal to the Society of Notre Dame, the treaty
of January 1645 did not, in principle, apply to the territory of the
Montrealists, but since the fur trade was to become the business of the
habitants of New France it seemed only natural that those of Montreal
should participate under the same conditions as those of Trois Rivières
and Quebec. The Montrealists therefore agreed to join the new trading
company.

When the fur monopoly was ceded to the habitants it was not ceded
to them as individuals but "only jointly," *en communauté*; hence the
name *la Communauté des Habitants*. In accepting the monopoly, the
Communauté also assumed the Hundred Associates' obligations: it would
cover the costs, both in France and in Canada, of "the administration of
the Colony"; it would see to the payment of the governor and military
officers, to the maintenance of the forts and garrisons and the upkeep of
the ecclesiastics, to whom it would pay the same annual allowances they
had received from the Hundred Associates; it would have the same responsibility for settlement, being bound to bring twenty persons of either
sex to the colony each year; and then, since the lands of the St Lawrence
still belonged to the Hundred Associates, the Communauté would report
annually on the state of their defences. The treaty was to take effect in
1645, on the day the first ship belonging to the Communauté arrived in
Tadoussac from France.

The Communauté was to be composed of those "recognized as *habitants
du pays*" and qualified thereby for membership in the company, but in
fact it comprised only a small group of business men, fifteen at most according to a 1646 petition.[3] They were the same men who, before 1645,
had succeeded in supplanting a subsidiary company established by the
Hundred Associates for the St Lawrence trade; Noël Juchereau des Chatelets had been its representative at Quebec and he turns up again in
1645 as *commis général* or general manager of the Communauté. These
business men soon formed a powerful consortium in the colony, reinforced by the ties of kinship: Pierre Legardeur de Repentigny, director of
the Communauté and admiral of the fleet, was assisted by his brother,
Charles Legardeur de Tilly, who commanded a Communauté ship; in
1646 a daughter of de Repentigny's married Jean-Paul Godefroy, likewise
a ship's captain for the Communauté, who soon became controller-general
of the company and then admiral of the fleet upon his father-in-law's
death; the two Legardeurs acquired as a brother-in-law Jacques Leneuf
de La Poterie, also a member of the Communauté, as was his brother

Michel Leneuf du Hérisson, who was the brother-in-law of yet another member, Jean Godefroy de Lintot; Noël Juchereau des Chatelets was the brother of Jean Juchereau de Maur, whose sons Jean Juchereau de La Ferté and Nicolas Juchereau de Saint-Denys became sons-in-law of another influential member, Robert Giffard.[4] These were the gentlemen, all inter-related by blood or marriage, who had charge of the new commercial enterprise in the St Lawrence colony.

This important event, the acquisition of the fur-trade monopoly by a group of settlers, marks a great step forward in the history of the colony; the essential element of the economy was now to be in the hands of an indigenous body. Not that this was entirely a novelty in North America: in 1624 the English company that had supported the colony of Plymouth withdrew, and it was a group of colonists who acquired its shares in 1627, in much the same way that the business interests of the Hundred Associates in the St Lawrence were being taken over in 1645.

The formation of the Communauté des Habitants came at a most propitious moment, when furs long accumulated in the interior were at last beginning to reach the St Lawrence. In 1644 there had been much bewailing of the feeble trickle to which the arrival of furs had dwindled, communications between the Huron country and the St Lawrence having been completely disrupted in 1643. Then, in September 1645, just after the Communauté had taken charge, Governor Montmagny succeeded in bringing about a solemn peace between the Mohawks on the one hand and the Algonquin and Huron allies on the other. An uneasy peace, to be sure, but it did reopen the trade routes. So it was that furs arrived to a value of 196,000 livres; five ships set sail from New France loaded with beaver worth 300,000 livres, two thirds of which belonged to the Communauté. And 1646 brought still greater prosperity, for the peace, confirmed in the spring, made possible even larger deliveries: in addition to moose hides, the Communauté received beaver worth 320,000 livres and could have obtained even more had it not run short of trade goods, so that the Hurons were obliged to return home with a dozen bundles of furs.[5]

Alas, this happy state of peace was not to last; in the spring of 1647, war was openly declared and communications were severed again between Huronia and the St Lawrence. The Hurons did not come down to trade that year. Only once more, in fact, would a fleet of Huron canoes laden with furs be seen descending the river, for the renewal of war was to lead to the total destruction of Huronia.[6]

Within the St Lawrence colony the economic and social situation was deteriorating also, and not solely on account of the Iroquois wars. In the fall of 1645, Governor Montmagny had posted the colony's first general order prohibiting individuals from trading in beaver or other furs with the

Indians.[7] This ruling ran counter to everyone's interests, and in January of 1646 the common people appeared to be on the brink of revolt. Among other things, there were accusations that the general manager, Juchereau des Chatelets, was living too high. The malcontents found themselves a spokesman in the person of René Robineau de Bécancour, a young man twenty years of age who was on the Governor's staff. There was "much vexation and talk and discontent," and satirical tracts appeared. Finally, Montmagny punished the leaders of the uprising and put an end to the tempestuous affair.[8]

The Jesuits, who had not been fairly compensated by the Communauté for what they had supplied to the soldiers in Huronia, also had cause for complaint. For them, as for everyone else, furs were the currency with which to purchase the necessities of life. When Father Vimont asked the general manager whether they were to be worse off now than under the Hundred Associates, his reply was that things would go along as usual, "but let us be discreet about it."[9] The prohibition against fur trading was maintained throughout 1646 and 1647, and for the Jesuits it posed a question of conscience about which they conferred in July 1647. They concluded that they themselves should abstain from fur trading, but that if the warehouse was not being "reasonable" one could "in conscience dissimulate, the habitants having the right by natural law, and from the King, to trade."[10]

Opposition to the Communauté's small group of business men continued unabated. The behaviour of certain young relatives of theirs, in particular, gave rise to scandal: three young men, the sons of Legardeur de Repentigny, Guillaume Couillart and Robert Giffard, together with the nephews of Juchereau des Chatelets, were generally considered "rogues" who "had played a thousand tricks" with the fur shipment of 1645. Moreover, persons in managerial positions "had their salaries and the rewards for their services greatly augmented," to the point where Governor Maisonneuve refused his signature. All this confusion led "to the drafting of memoranda" with a view to changes in regulations.[11]

Montmagny's secretary, Governor Maisonneuve and Robert Giffard went to France in an attempt to obtain a reform. Meanwhile, Bourdon was chosen as procurator syndic, and in July 1647, in the name of those habitants who had taken exception to the directors, he placed the administration of the Communauté in the hands of Montmagny. New regulations arrived from France with the ships of the following month.[12]

On February 22, 1647, in response to a petition charging that "abuses and malversations" were being committed in Canada in the fur trade and elsewhere, three commissioners had been appointed by the Queen Regent to study the representations submitted by the Hundred Associates and by the habitants of Canada. On March 27, the commissioners having made their report, the King's Council decreed a new administrative structure.[13]

This regulation of 1647 established a Council of three: the Governor of Quebec, the Superior of the Jesuits (until such time as there should be a bishop), and the Governor of Montreal. It was this body that was to choose by majority vote the officials of the Communauté, to serve for a period of not more than three consecutive years: a commodore of the fleet and the officers of its vessels, the clerks of the fur trade, and a secretary. The secretary would have charge of records and serve as notary, and would be required to send each year to the commissioners in France a copy of the annual rendering of accounts and a brief summary of the state of affairs in the country. Besides naming the officials of the Communauté, the Council was charged with examining its accounts, establishing regulations to govern the fur trade, and adopting all rules necessary for the good of the country; it was also directed to see that officers and clerks should receive nothing more than their approved salaries.

When the affairs of the Communauté were to be studied, the Council would admit to its sittings, in a consultative capacity only, the commodore of the fleet and the syndics whom the people of Quebec, Trois Rivières and Montreal were to elect annually by ballot.

The King's Council adopted two other provisions which the Queen Regent thought appropriate for the restoration of order in the country. First, it set forth in detail the financial charges to be borne in future by the Communauté: annual sums payable to the governors of Quebec and Montreal for their own remuneration and their lieutenants' and the maintenance of forts and garrisons, and to the Jesuits for the support of missionaries; free transport of a certain tonnage of goods for the two governors and the Jesuits and of supplies for the Ursulines and Hospitalières; for new settlers, free transport of food and personal effects during their first two years. Secondly, in a return to the policy of the Hundred Associates, an unpopular rule imposed in 1645 was reversed: all the habitants could henceforth trade with the Indians, on condition that the pelts be eventually brought to the warehouses of the Communauté, which would buy them at a price fixed in advance by the Council of Quebec.

There were several important innovations in this regulation of 1647. For the first time Canada was to be administered by a Council, and within this council the Governor would have only one vote. Also for the first time, the Church's role in the administration was to become official, and the vote of the Church's representative would carry as much weight as the Governor's. Another innovation was the inclusion of elected syndics in the governing council, even if only in a consultative capacity and only when the fur trade was to be under discussion. Finally, while the Communauté had been virtually a law unto itself since 1645, the Council of

Quebec must now answer for it to the three Royal Commissioners (Laisné, de Morangis and de Mesmes), who would propose new measures as the need arose. In short, all-powerful as it had been from 1645 to 1647, the Communauté was now under double tutelage. Thus an entirely different administrative structure was established: under royal authority, three Commissioners to supervise the affairs of the country; and a Council, embodying military and religious authority, to be responsible for the sound functioning of the Communauté.

This regulation was put into effect immediately following its arrival in Quebec early in August 1647. If, however, a change had been hoped for in the management of the Communauté, there was reason for disappointment, for the same officials remained in their respective capacities. Legardeur de Repentigny was reappointed admiral of the fleet for another year, Jean-Paul Godefroy remained as controller-general, and Noël Juchereau des Chatelets was still general manager.

The habitants had even more important reasons for complaint. The Council was far from properly representative of the population; the Governor of Trois Rivières had been passed over and the syndics had no vote in the Council. The Communauté had been burdened with heavy expenses, a total of 40,000 livres annually plus the free conveyance of 130 tons of goods for the various authorities of the country. Nothing had been decided upon for the relief of the Communauté's warehouse, which was saddled with sidelines of business having nothing to do with the fur trade. Finally, military defence was still limited to the posts of Quebec, Trois Rivières and Montreal; there was no provision whatever for the defence of the countryside, and Fort Richelieu, which had been abandoned the year before, was no longer even mentioned, despite its strategic importance on the water route.

Once again the Royal Commissioners heard the grievances of the habitants, and on the basis of their new report the King's Council issued another edict on March 5, 1648 to modify that of 1647.[14]

By the terms of this edict, the Council of Quebec would consist of seven members: the Governor General (whose three-year mandate could be renewed only once), the Superior of the Jesuits (still pending the creation of a bishop), the former Governor General, the Governors of Trois Rivières and Montreal (when they were in Quebec), and two habitants, who would be elected every three years by the Council members and by the syndics of the towns and who would have the right, this time, to speak and vote at Council meetings. If there were no former governor-general, a third habitant would be elected in similar fashion. For the first year, however, since a new régime was in the making, and there being no former governor-general, it was more convenient for the King's Council to appoint three habitant members, rather than await elections;

these three, who represented only Quebec and Trois Rivières, were François Chavigny de Berchereau, Jean-Paul Godefroy and Robert Giffard.

In further response to popular complaint, the costs to be borne by the Communauté were redistributed. From now on, the governors and their garrisons would receive only 16,000 livres instead of 35,000; the sum of 19,000 livres thus saved would be used to purchase arms and munitions, to raise fortifications at Sillery,[15] and, most important of all, to maintain a *camp volant* of forty men. In summer, this mobile force would serve to keep open "the passages by water and by land," and in winter to "patrol and reconnoitre the countryside."

The edict of 1648 also laid down rules for commercial activity. The warehouse of the Communauté would in future deal only in furs, and the Communauté alone would be permitted to import goods for barter. However, since the habitants would be in need of articles for their own use (articles hitherto obtained through the Communauté), those wishing to take the initiative could henceforth import such merchandise themselves and would be free to carry on both wholesale and retail business. This freedom of import trade, an entirely new departure in the history of the colony, was later to extend also to the export of the country's products other than furs, specifically fish, wood and minerals.

Finally, the 1648 edict made two other important provisions. First, all legal disputes involving the Communauté would be heard by the King's Council, in order to ensure that "quarrels" should not paralyse so vital an organism. Second, both Canadian-born Frenchmen and Christian Indians would be empowered to will and inherit property and to accept legacies and gifts; churches, monasteries, and hospitals for "poor savages" were likewise empowered to accept pious bequests and endowments in France and in Canada. Thus was enacted a necessary adjunct to Article 17 of the Charter of the Hundred Associates.[16]

Because it gave the representatives of the people the right to speak and vote within the ruling council of the land, the regulation of 1648 has been accorded great importance: the new arrangements have indeed been acclaimed in our own time as "the admission of the people to the Council" and seen as the beginning of a Parliament. In point of fact, these representatives were not the choice of the people. First, the syndics were chosen by a very small segment of the population; in 1647, Hertel had been elected by fifteen people in Trois Rivières, and in 1648 the Quebec syndic was elected by some twenty.[17] Then these syndics and the sitting members of the Council together elected the two or three representatives of the people. This was neither universal suffrage nor even election by a large proportion of the populace. Still, the most influential of the habitants were now able, through the Council, to play some role in the administration of the colony.

The 1648 regulation takes on far more importance when we appreciate that for the first time an attempt was being made to organize the country as a social entity, whereas the 1647 regulation had been concerned mainly with the fur trade. The Council of Quebec was now more representative of the colony as a whole, defence was no longer limited to the garrisons, and individuals could henceforth engage in general commercial activities, an innovation that benefited the Communauté as well, since it was thereby relieved of a burden. The Communauté itself was now on a sounder base and would be subject to closer supervision. No one, for example, could borrow in its name without prior permission from the Council of Quebec, and this stipulation was enforced: in 1650, Father Jérome Lalemant was requested by the Council to scrutinize the Communauté's operations in France; not only was he to "look to the inspection of beaver pelts in France that had been shipped without the instruction of the warehouse," but he alone was empowered to authorize the borrowing of money in France in the name of the Communauté.[18] Finally, in case of dispute, the court of first and last instance would be the King's Council.

But just at the time when sound and effective administration of the Communauté appeared to have been ensured by this reorganization, total war broke out between the Iroquois and the allies of the St Lawrence, and this war would not only paralyse commerce but create a turmoil among the tribes of the Great Lakes that was to disrupt the entire network of the fur trade.

Before 1634, the French had been little inconvenienced by the skirmishing that went on between the Mohawks and the Montagnais, but as first one fort was established at Trois Rivières and then another at Montreal, the French had become more and more involved in the conflict. What the Mohawks sought, by their incursions and their frequent truces alike, was to induce the Montagnais to take sides against the Hurons, or else, more directly, to "divert the Hurons [from the] commerce that they have with our French traders" and prevail upon them to trade with the Iroquois.[19] In short, it was the Great Lakes fur monopoly that was at stake.

In the region of the Great Lakes there had been no peace since 1609, the year the Hurons made their alliance with the French and became their suppliers. Until about 1640, the Hurons had been fairly successful at beating off the Iroquois attacks. This was because the nations known collectively as Iroquois had taken a long time to consolidate against their competitors in the fur trade and to find means of establishing their supremacy.

Throughout the first quarter of the seventeenth century, the Iroquois were excluded from the biggest fur market, the St Lawrence, by the alliance of the Hurons, Algonquins and Montagnais, and from the Hudson

River market by the alliance between the Mohicans and the Dutch. Then, in 1626, despite the help of the Dutch, the Mohicans were crushed and the Mohawks became the sole suppliers for New Holland. But little by little the Iroquois source of pelts was drying up, while through Huronia, small though it was, an abundance of furs continued to pour from the Great Lakes down to the St Lawrence. The Iroquois must either see their flourishing Hudson River trade decline, or else compel the Hurons to link up with them, a solution which seemed natural enough, since the Hurons and Iroquois were of the same culture.

After 1640, moreover, the Iroquois acquired greater cohesion. In 1646, Father Lalemant was already using the term "Confederated Nations" to designate the Mohawks, Oneidas, Onondagas and Senecas; he adds "and others," for with this group were the Cayugas, the Sokoquis and also the Mohicans, who, since their defeat twenty years previously, had been obliged to take sides with the Iroquois.[20]

The position of the Iroquois was strengthened even more by the arquebuses with which the Dutch supplied them. Time and again, reference is made in the *Relations* to the fire-arms in the hands of most of the Iroquois while the Hurons had practically none. One of the allied Indians was to complain that "the Dutch of these shores are causing us to die, supplying fire-arms, & in abundance, & at a good price, to the Hiroquois our enemies." For the Dutch, fire-arms were in fact a means of ensuring the allegiance of their fur suppliers. The French, on the other hand, steadfastly refused to barter fire-arms, in compliance with a rule which dated from the time of Champlain (in those days there was good reason to mistrust the Montagnais), and which remained in force throughout the period under study; thus an order of 1644 reiterated that it was forbidden to barter "arquebuses, pistols and other fire-arms" with the Indians, whether they were Christian or not, and the order was subsequently renewed.[21] At each encounter with the Iroquois, the native allies of the French therefore found themselves seriously handicapped. Thanks to his arquebuses, Champlain had easily had the better of the Iroquois in 1609; now it was the Iroquois who had the arquebuses and would proceed in short order to the annihilation of the Hurons.

In 1647 the Iroquois made incursions everywhere. At Trois Rivières and Montreal, anyone leaving the forts might fall into an ambush. The route to the upper country, the *pays d'en haut*, was blocked once more; the Hurons did not come down to trade, and all contact with Huronia was lost. Then, in 1648, confidence returned, and it was said that the Iroquois had "lost more than they had won." In any case, 250 Hurons succeeded in piercing the blockade and came to trade at Trois Rivières, and twenty or thirty Frenchmen set off for Huronia to provide an escort.[22]

Although the furs from the upper country were few indeed, the Tadoussac trade had brought in at least 250,000 livres' worth.[23] The situation was therefore not yet desperate in the St Lawrence colony. In 1648 it was the Hurons who suffered the harshest blows. Never, it was written, had they been "more sorely afflicted."

While the Iroquois were still striking only at the Huron borders, there had been a surge of hope for peace. The Onondagas, who had just suffered a crushing defeat and were as much afraid of the Mohawks as of the Hurons, entered into serious peace talks. The Cayugas, too, showed an interest in making peace. The Senecas and Mohawks remained implacably hostile, going even to the point of massacring ambassadors, but the Andastes, who dwelt to the south of the Iroquois, were preparing to enter the war on the side of their old allies the Hurons, and this, it was hoped, would bring "great assistance and great relief."[24]

But it was already too late. One of the Neutral tribes, whose lands bordered on Huronia and had served as a kind of buffer zone, was wiped out by the Iroquois. The Hurons of the Cahiagué region in the east were forced to leave it and take refuge among neighbouring tribes. Unable to withstand the Iroquois assault, the other Hurons fell back toward Fort Ste Marie, which found itself on the firing line despite its extreme northerly position in the Huron country; and at the fort there were only eight French soldiers to help them. In June 1649, sixty Frenchmen were sent from Montreal with munitions, to reinforce Huronia: by the time they arrived, there would be no more Fort Ste Marie and no more Huronia either.[25]

In March of that year an army of twelve hundred Iroquois had invaded the Huron country. They destroyed the town of St Ignace, where they tortured to death the Jesuit Fathers Jean de Brébeuf and Gabriel Lalemant. They destroyed the town of St Louis as well. Fort Ste Marie, the last stronghold, brought them to a stop, but around the fort there remained only a vast wasteland, and the Hurons who survived had to endure the worst famine known in half a century. The Jesuits resolved to evacuate the country. They planned at first to reassemble the Hurons on Manitoulin Island at the northern end of Lake Huron and create there a new centre for the upper country, but they finally opted for the Hurons' choice, Ile St Joseph (today Christian Island) in Nottawasaga Bay, only twenty miles from Fort Ste Marie. In May of 1649, having first set fire to the fort, they repaired to the island with three hundred families and began to build fortifications there.[26]

It was in July that the St Lawrence colony heard "the sad news of the destruction of the Hurons", "the ruin & desolation of those poor nations of the upper country." The unhappy event coincided with a grain-crop failure, and the volume of furs coming down from the Lakes was of course very meagre. To make matters worse, the wreck of a ship bound for Canada, the *Saint-Sauveur*, brought "considerable loss" to everyone. But there was still hope of saving Huronia, and early in the summer of 1650 forty well-armed Frenchmen were sent out. On their way up the river they met the broken remnants of the Huron nation coming to take refuge in the Laurentian colony.[27]

The Hurons who had reassembled on Ile St Joseph had passed the winter of 1649-50 in extreme hardship, ravaged by sickness and famine and by their perpetual fear of the Iroquois who, flushed with their triumphs of the summer of 1649, continued their orgy of destruction. Late in 1649 they annihilated the Petuns. They destroyed the Nipissings, and scattered the Algonquins afar. In the spring of 1650 they fell upon a group of Hurons who had left Ile St Joseph in search of food and massacred them all. Of the Hurons who survived the ruin of their country, some decided to take refuge with the Andastes, others with the nations of the west. Still others gave themselves up to the Iroquois, "among whom they had many relatives, who wished to have them"; this was what the Iroquois most desired, reduced as they were by their wars and accustomed to absorbing other nations, a practice which they carried to the point where it could be said that they counted more strangers among them than pure Iroquois. And finally, the few remaining Hurons asked the Jesuits to take them to Quebec.[28]

On June 10, 1650, the missionaries set out on the return journey with three hundred Hurons, "sad relics of a nation once so numerous," arriving at last in Montreal in mid-July. This might have been "an advantageous place for the settlement of the Savages," but Montreal, too, seemed to them a "frontier of the Iroquois." They stayed for only two days, reluctant to "start their Colony" there, and finally reached Quebec on July 28. They had succeeded in making their journey without the Iroquois falling upon them, but many others attempting to join them were cut to pieces on the way. In the autumn of 1650 there were about four hundred Hurons encamped near the Hôtel Dieu. The following year the Jesuits led them to the Isle of Orleans, called for the time Ste Marie (the third Huron mission to bear this name).[29]

The Iroquois pursued their devastation of the Great Lakes region with as much success as ever. In the autumn of 1650 and the spring of 1651, they broke up and completely dispersed the Neutrals and those Hurons who had taken refuge with them. Having made themselves masters of the Ottawa River, they invaded another route which had become important to the fur trade as a by-pass, one leading overland from the Ottawa River to the St Maurice; here the Attikamegas in their turn became their victims.[30] They showed themselves more and more aggressive toward the settlements of the St Lawrence. Marie de l'Incarnation wrote in 1650 that the Iroquois had done "what they had never before dared to do"; while ordinarily they kept their distance some forty leagues from Quebec, now "at this one stroke, they have come within three leagues of here." And in this year of 1650, Marie de l'Incarnation interpreted the views of "the most judicious": if France sent no help, "either we must die," she wrote, "or we must return to France." Certainly her first thought was for the Ursuline mission, and on October 14 the Ursulines and Madame de La Peltrie agreed on what should be done if, "in view of the continual incursions of the barbarians," they were forced to leave Canada. But Marie de l'Incarnation did not exclude the possibility of a general evacuation of the colony; should the enemy pursue "their conquests and victories, there will no longer be a place here for the French. Commerce will be impossible; without commerce, no more ships will come; without ships, we shall have none of the necessities of life."[31]

If the Dutch of New Holland had a vested interest in bolstering the power of the Iroquois, New France was not alone in suffering the consequences of their policy. New England, too, was engaged in the fur trade, though to a lesser extent. Its principal suppliers were the Abenakis of the Kennebec River, from where, according to the Jesuit Druillettes, the Plymouth colony derived a sixth of its revenues. If the Iroquois were to extend their domination to the natives of the Kennebec, or disperse them, the English of Plymouth would suffer commercially, and so would those of Boston, who also had a certain interest in the fur trade. Moreover, since the English colonies of America were divided amongst themselves on the question of the monarchy, some having remained loyal to the King while others enthusiastically supported the republic, New England's trade with Virginia and the English West Indies was on the point of rupture. What it was in danger of losing elsewhere, New England might gain in the St Lawrence. Finally, without yet having come to the point of open warfare, New England and New Holland were continually engaged in border skirmishes. All of this might lead the New England colonies, confederated since 1643 in an offensive and defensive alliance, to adopt a policy which would force the Dutch to diminish the pressure exerted by the Iroquois. Confronted with New England's population of thirty thousand, New Holland, with only two thousand, would surely be obliged to give way. For that matter, New England would be quite able to subdue the Iroquois itself if it chose to: "the way into the Iroquois country is very short and very easy," wrote the Jesuit Druillettes, "and the New Englanders could very well eliminate the savage nations."[32] It was for these reasons that the authorities of the Laurentian colony decided in 1650 to seek a military alliance with New England against the Iroquois, along with a commercial treaty.

Father Gabriel Druillettes, who was entrusted with this diplomatic mission, had often travelled the route to New England since 1646, and knew it well. In that year, he had gone to do missionary work among the Abenakis, travelling by way of the Chaudière River, and it seems that the presence of a Jesuit among the Abenakis was regarded favourably in New England.[33] Following this mission, Boston may even have taken the initiative in writing to the Council of Quebec in 1647 to propose a commercial treaty between the two colonies. The Council of Quebec was still studying the possibility in 1648, and in 1649 New England let it be known that it was ready to conclude an alliance, regardless of the chance of war between England and France.[34]

Up to that time the Council of Quebec had been in no particular hurry to execute this project, but in 1650 the situation was such that it felt an urgent need for the alliance, counting heavily on it to put a stop to Iroquois expansion. On September 1, accompanied by a native chief from Sillery, Druillettes set out once again for Kennebec, carrying credentials and authorized to speak in the name of Governor d'Ailleboust de Coulonge. When he arrived in Boston on December 8, 1650, he was gratified to be received most cordially by Governor Dudley, as he was also by Bradford, Governor of Plymouth. Both showed themselves enthusiastic, and they assured Druillettes that the Governor of Connecticut would also be in favour of the alliance since he, too, had an Indian nation to protect against the Iroquois. Governor Bradford sent a written proposal to Connecticut suggesting this alliance, and it seems that he even requested New Holland to cease trading arms to the Iroquois. The representatives of the four confederated colonies were to meet shortly and it was expected that New England would join in a compact against the Iroquois, or, at the very least, that Boston would organize an expedition of volunteers.[35]

Upon the Jesuit's return to Quebec in June 1651, the Council decided to take immediate advantage of such a favourable prospect. On the 20th of that month, Jean-Paul Godefroy was sent to New England with Druillettes to press for the signing of a treaty. They were empowered, so the Canadian authorities wrote, "both to establish an effective commercial link between us and you, and to lighten the expenses" that would have to be met in the war against the Iroquois. But this mission did not bring the expected results. Godefroy returned in October to announce that the colony of Plymouth did not care to engage in open warfare with the Iroquois and that it had persuaded the other confederated colonies to accept only a commercial treaty.[36] There was no question of sending a force of volunteers against the Iroquois. It would appear that the possibility of a war with the Dutch had had much to do with this decision; the 1651 Navigation Act was, in fact, to trigger hostilities between England and the Netherlands the following year. Governor d'Ailleboust de Coulonge had not even won as much help from Boston as had La Tour in 1643. As for help from France, there was precious little hope of it; metropolitan France was beset by the Princes' Fronde at that time, civil war was spreading, and the frontier provinces were transformed into battlefields. Thus it was that the author of the 1652 *Relation* spoke of Old France as being "torn apart by her own children."[37] New France therefore found herself quite alone, face to face with the ever more powerful Iroquois.

There was still hope that a war between Indians of the Great Lakes might divert the Iroquois from their attacks on the St Lawrence settlements. In the east, the Mohawks had come to grips with the Sokoquis; in the west the Andastes and the Neutrals had joined forces and beaten the Senecas. But the Senecas called the Mohawks to their aid and, thus allied, the Iroquois emerged victorious. Once again loomed the menace of a massive attack by the Iroquois nations against the Laurentian colony.

Economic activity was now at its lowest ebb. Since the destruction of Huronia, no more fleets of Huron canoes had been coming down. The Algonquins of the Ottawa River had been dispersed. The nations of the upper St Maurice no longer dared come to trade. Only the Tadoussac route remained open, and there, too, the Iroquois made incursions from time to time. Financially, the Communauté des Habitants had reached a lamentable state. It had accumulated a heavy burden of debt in 1649: some 45,000 livres at 25 per cent interest. The following year, the shipment of beaver furs to France amounted to only 28,800 pounds in weight, of which nearly a third was sold at a loss. The Communauté was unable to pay what it owed and was obliged to borrow anew from the merchants of La Rochelle. In 1651 its debts rose to 90,785 livres. But that was another bad year for the fur trade; having waited in vain until the end of November for "the beaver from Montreal," the Communauté was able to ship out only 13,131 pounds of furs. It was reduced to borrowing once again, this time pledging to the La Rochelle merchants in advance all the beaver that could be collected in 1652. This loan of 1651, a sum of 132,000 livres, was used to equip four vessels. Of these, on their return voyage in 1652, one got no further than the Azores and a second was confiscated at La Rochelle by rebels. The cargoes of the other two brought only 10,326 livres. Never again would the Communauté be able to honour its debts, not even after they had been reduced to 80,000 livres by the creditors in 1655.[38]

During this time the Communauté's warehouses were almost empty. At Quebec, it was written in 1653, "there is nothing but poverty." At Trois Rivières, what furs could be obtained were used immediately to defray the cost of defence. The Montreal warehouse had not received a single beaver pelt for a whole year.[39] Under these conditions, the Communauté could no longer meet even the most necessary expenses of the country. First the mobile force was disbanded. Then the defences at Trois Rivières were reduced; the fort, "which was going to ruin and would have caused much expense," was levelled to the ground; the people of Trois Rivières accepted the withdrawal of the garrison and resolved to protect their position by volunteer service, "knowing full well the lack of funds at present weighing upon the Communauté."[40]

The year 1652 had been an extremely hard one for the French and their allies. The Iroquois ravaged the country of the Attikamegas, through which furs had continued to arrive from the upper country. They prowled "all Spring & all Summer around the French settlements." The list of the dead and captured grew longer and longer; the Governor of Trois Rivières himself, Du Plessis-Kerbodot, was cut down by the Iroquois on August 19 with fifteen of his men. The massive attack that was expected with such dread did not materialize in the course of the winter, but as soon as spring came in 1653 the Mohawks resumed their total war, and in the month of August they succeeded in cutting off Trois Rivières completely.[41]

Then suddenly, in the autumn of 1653, there was peace. Overtures were forthcoming from the Onondagas and even from the Mohawks, "the proudest & most arrogant," still "puffed up with their victories."[42] Initially, the Iroquois were perhaps interested in making peace solely in order to persuade the Hurons to join them and so replenish their decimated ranks. But this peace, which was to prove of some duration, seems to have been mainly the consequence of a new development that was becoming increasingly evident in the Great Lakes region: with the Ottawas as prime movers, the Algonquin nations were working toward the formation of a powerful league with the surviving Petuns and Neutrals to oppose the Iroquois nations. The Iroquois, moreover, were now faced on their western frontiers by harsh adversaries, the Eries, who were soon to set all "afire among the upper four nations of the Iroquois." In any case, the author of the 1653 *Relation* breathes a great sigh of relief: "At last we have peace."[43]

And so the Iroquois suddenly became most ingratiating. In 1653 the Onondagas invited the French, both lay and missionary, to come and settle in their country, and when the Jesuit Simon Le Moyne was chosen as envoy, the Iroquois nations vied among themselves for the honour of receiving him. In the course of the summer of 1654, the Jesuit went with several French companions to the Iroquois country, where he was surprised to find a Christian community of a thousand Hurons. On the return of the ambassadors it was decided that an establishment should be founded at Onondaga in 1655.[44]

This peace gave promise of very favourable consequences. Lake Ontario was more quickly and easily accessible than Huronia had been, and with an end to the war with the Iroquois it might become the centre of an extensive commerce with the most distant nations.[45]

With the word of peace came some other heartening news. A hundred and fifty leagues beyond Huronia, two thousand natives were preparing to come down in the spring of 1654 with quantities of furs, hoping to obtain fire-arms and ammunition "to make themselves more formidable to their enemies."[46] The Ottawas were taking over the role of the Hurons on the Great Lakes.

But in 1653, when these new suppliers of furs were not expected until the following year and the normal channels of trade had been disrupted by the incursions of the Iroquois, some attempt had to be made to obtain the furs that had been accumulating for three years in the upper country. There was only one thing to do; the French must go out and get the furs for themselves. Up to this time, apart from a few interpreters who acted as go-betweens and promoters among the natives, the French had never gone in search of furs; the delivery of pelts to the trading posts of the St Lawrence was the exclusive domain of the Indians. The year 1653, then, saw the first excursion or *course* into the woods for furs, and the *coureurs de bois* came into being. (Only later did the term acquire a pejorative sense.) The author of the 1653 *Relation* writes that "all our young Frenchmen intend to go trading, to find the Nations scattered here & there, & they hope to come back laden with the Beaver of several years." The massive departure was to provoke the intervention of the authorities in April 1654. So that the "number and character" of those persons setting out in quest of furs might be known, Governor Lauson forbade anyone's departure "without first obtaining leave," and imposed fines for transgressors. In this we see the origin of the trading permits which were later to be the source of many a problem.[47]

The "coureurs de bois" returned in 1654 with their cargoes, and at Montreal that year there was a spectacle that had not been seen for a long time, the arrival of a fleet of fur-laden canoes. But a new misfortune awaited the Communauté. One of its ships, "richly freighted with skins of the Beaver of the country," was captured by the English in sight of the coast of France; everything was confiscated, even to the clothes of the passengers. The loss amounted to 300,000 livres.[48]

The fur trade prospered again in 1655, and once more it was on the high seas that misfortune struck. Of the five vessels that set sail for New France with cargoes of trade goods and food, only two arrived. The three others were lost, the first to the English, the second to the Spaniards, and the third to the sea. "Not only have the merchants with interests in these vessels borne great losses, but also the whole country has suffered grievously."[49]

Things were to improve in 1656, thanks to a series of fortunate events. With the end of the Fronde in France, external trade returned to normal. It was with great satisfaction that the Jesuit de Quen wrote, in 1656:

"Not for twenty years had vessels been seen arriving so early in this country, nor in greater number. We saw five or six of them drop anchor all at the same time in the roads of Kebec, and that at the very beginning of June." Two months later, the peace with the Iroquois still holding, another event brought "universal joy to the whole Country"; this was the arrival of a band of Ottawas from the western Great Lakes region with a fleet of fur-laden canoes. These Ottawas were accompanied by a Frenchman who was destined for great celebrity, Médard Chouart des Groseilliers, and by another Frenchman, unidentified, who cannot at that date have been Pierre-Esprit Radisson as has been thought.[50]

Thirty young French adventurers set out with the Ottawas for the upper country (this represented a massive departure in those days), but a change in the tide of events forced them to turn back and postpone their journey indefinitely; relations had deteriorated again between the French and the Iroquois.

The state of peace had in fact been resting on opportune but unstable circumstances. In the face of ferocious attacks by the Eries on their left flank, the Iroquois nations had found it expedient to make peace with the French. For the Onondagas in particular, trading at the St Lawrence posts was more attractive than continued dependence on the Dutch trade, which obliged them to pass through the Mohawk country. Moreover, being "engaged in great wars with the many Nations they had provoked," they were anxious to obtain Huron reinforcements to bolster their ranks, and they even entertained the hope of a military alliance with the French. They visualized a "great fort" that the French would build for them, in which they could take refuge if their enemies pressed too hard. In 1655 the Onondagas therefore came to Quebec to call not only for military aid but also for the establishment of a French settlement in their country. The Jesuit Le Moyne undertook a second ambassadorial mission that year, and three Jesuits and a number of other Frenchmen spent the winter of 1655-56 at Onondaga. In July 1656, fifty soldiers, under the command of Zacharie Dupuy, built "a strong Redoubt" and a chapel on a promontory overlooking Lake Gannentaha. This French establishment, the first ever built in Iroquois country, was named Ste Marie. Since it was hoped that the French presence there would be permanent, Governor Lauson granted to the Jesuits, on April 12, 1656, a seigneury ten leagues square at a location of their own choice in the territory of the Onondagas. The latter had offered to receive the French and to give them the necessary space for their settlement, but it would seem that they were not consulted on the concession of what amounted to three quarters of their country. Be that as it may, the Jesuits took up residence at Ste Marie des Iroquois and went forth from there to preach the faith to all the Iroquois, with the exception of the still intractable Mohawks.[51]

It was indeed the Mohawks who were to ruin the state of peace. Thanks to the existence of Ste Marie, they enjoyed a measure of security from the Eries, but the peace threatened to spoil their commerce. Oneidas, Onondagas, Cayugas and Senecas alike were obliged to pass through their country to trade with New Holland, and therein lay a lucrative source of revenue. Now that the other Iroquois had found a more convenient outlet on the St Lawrence, however, the Mohawks were in danger of being isolated again.[52] They therefore did everything possible to disrupt the peace, by intrigue and persistent harassment of the French and their native allies; and since, like all the Iroquois, they were still bent on persuading or forcing the Hurons to join them, they went down to Quebec in May of 1656, reached the Isle of Orleans under cover of night, and massacred or carried off scores of Hurons. Obliged to choose between being killed and joining the Iroquois, a number of Huron families left the island in 1657 and gave themselves up, some to the Mohawks, others to the Onondagas.[53]

By 1658 the conditions on which the peace of 1653 had rested were entirely dissipated. Launching an all-out offensive, seven hundred Mohawks had besieged and vanquished two thousand Eries, thus eliminating the principal danger that menaced the Iroquois nations from the west, and so the balance of power was tipped. On hearing of this Iroquois triumph, and having been informed also of a plan for the massive invasion of the St Lawrence, the French of Ste Marie des Iroquois realized that Onondaga could well prove to be their "tomb." On March 20, 1658, through an elaborate manoeuvre executed in the greatest secrecy, they abandoned their fort and were already far away by the time the Onondaga townsmen became aware of their disappearance. They arrived safe and sound in Quebec a month later.[54] Once again there was to be total war between the Iroquois nations and the Laurentian colony, and once again the way was blocked for the fur trade.

Meanwhile the affairs of the Communauté had continued to deteriorate until, overwhelmed by debt and unable to meet the expenses of the colony, it offered to turn back the fur-trade monopoly and its obligations to the Hundred Associates. But the Hundred Associates' experience had been too bitter for them to wish to repeat it, and they declined the invitation.[55]

In the course of the winter of 1656-57, the King was therefore asked to follow up the reforms of 1647 and 1648 with another amendment to the administrative structure of the Communauté. This he did by the edict of March 7, 1657.[56]

The fur trade was henceforth to be governed by a council called the *Conseil de la traite*, composed of the Governor General, a director appointed for a three-year term by the Hundred Associates, and four councillors who would have the right to speak and vote and who would be chosen by election, two by the colonists of Quebec, a third by those of Trois Rivières and the fourth by those of Montreal. The Hundred Associates' financial agent would also have a seat on the council to see that the Communauté fulfilled its normal annual obligations. This council was to have no power to modify any emoluments or obligations already fixed, "whether for the Governor, religious communities, or other persons," but would supervise the fulfilment of obligations and the payment of expenses, decisions being made by majority vote. The Communauté was to submit an annual rendering of receipts and expenditures, together with a proposal for the application of funds generated by the *droit du quart*, a tax of 25 per cent on the value of furs traded by the habitants; a copy of this proposal was to be forwarded to the Hundred Associates for approval.

This first provision for control of the Communauté's operations was followed by a second, intended to ensure more regular revenues. Payment to the Communauté of the 25-per-cent tax on trading by individuals would be enforced, and the Communauté would henceforth have the monopoly of all trade goods. Merchants importing such goods from France would be required to consign them to the Communauté's agents, and the *Conseil de la traite*, on presentation of bills of lading, was to fix their value. This merchandise was then to be divided among the warehouses of the Communauté, and only half of it would be sold to the habitants, payable in cash; the other half would be bartered by the Communauté itself.

The effect of this 1657 regulation was to bring the Hundred Associates back into the administration they had turned over to the Communauté in 1645. In view of the failure of the Communauté in the management of the fur trade and the dissatisfaction of the creditors, it was incumbent upon the Company of the Hundred Associates, in its continuing capacity as seigneur of the country with responsibility for the administration of justice, to exercise the closest supervision over the conduct of the trade. The Communauté was therefore being placed under the direct tutelage of the Hundred Associates.

This *Conseil de la traite* did not take the place of the Council established in 1648 for the country as a whole. The Jesuit *Journal*, which carefully notes all important events, makes no mention of any change in the government of the colony. The task of government was still carried out by a Council on which sat the Governor General, the Superior of the Jesuits, the Governors of Trois Rivières and Montreal, and the representatives of the habitants. The *Conseil de la traite* was simply an addition to the administrative structure; under the authority of the general council, its responsibility was the supervision of the fur trade.

If this 1657 reform had come about in the good years of the fur trade it might perhaps have been of benefit to the Communauté. As things were, it came at a time of disaster. The supply of furs continued to fall off deplorably and the whole country suffered a crisis of "very great poverty." The Communauté was so short of funds that its new director, d'Ailleboust de Coulonge, convinced that the 1657 reform could have no effect and despairing even of being able to draw his own pay, left his post and withdrew to Montreal. Governor d'Argenson, too, was much concerned for his salary, but, as he wrote, if he had sought to get it paid in France from the proceeds of the beaver sold there, he would have had to take all the funds of the warehouse for himself alone. The Communauté could not even pay its seigneurial dues in 1658, and was not sure of being able to do so the following year either.[57]

The resumption of total war paralysed the entire country. When Governor d'Argenson arrived at Percé in 1658, he was forced to wait there a whole month because the boats were immobilized at Quebec on account of the Iroquois.[58] The last survivors of the once-powerful Huron nation were no longer safe on the Isle of Orleans; they came to take refuge in the upper town of Quebec, in a little fort built for them near the Château St Louis. Colonists who had been settled on distant seigneuries abandoned their farms and sought protection in the towns. The whole colony, in 1658, was bracing itself for a long, hard siege.

CHAPTER 17

The Jesuits at the Helm

1632–1659

When the French reoccupied the St Lawrence in 1632 they did not need to reconstruct the fur-trade network; it had remained intact during the English occupation. In the religious domain, on the contrary, all the work had to be begun again: the Canadian Church had to be built and given its essential institutions, and missions to the Indians had to be established. These great tasks fell to the Jesuits, until the time of Monseigneur de Laval's arrival; between 1632 and 1659, the history of the Canadian Church was the history of the Jesuits.

The first missionaries had arrived in 1615, but in 1633 the Jesuit Le Jeune could only remark: "Some are astonished that after so many years in New France there has been no word of the conversion of the Savages. It is necessary to clear, till, & sow, before harvesting."[1] Missionary work was still in the land-clearance stage.

As before, the Indians were followed as they hunted afar, in the hope of winning at least a few to Christianity, but these terrible journeys through the bush exhausted the missionaries and did nothing for the establishment of a Christian community. It became apparent that the roving Montagnais would never be Christianized unless they could first be induced to settle down. It was believed, moreover, that the new religion would be more easily accepted by Montagnais, Algonquins and Hurons alike if they could be persuaded to live in the French manner, and the missionaries were convinced that the surest means of achieving this end was first of all to give young Indians a French upbringing. The Récollets had applied this method as early as 1617, but with scant resources; the Jesuits now went about the task much more systematically at their seminary of Notre Dame des Anges.

The house was repaired and enlarged and in December 1632 was ready to receive two boys of seven and ten years of age. Besides the two boarders there were small day-pupils from the neighbourhood, whom Father Le Jeune called to class by ringing a bell. That first year, however, funds were still lacking to provide for the establishment as planned, and in June 1633 the Jesuits were obliged to send one of the boarders home. But Father Le Jeune did not lose sight of his plans for a seminary, particularly since there appeared to be no difficulty in recruitment.[2]

In 1636, his goal of bringing Huron boys to Quebec for instruction seemed on the point of realization. A missionary was preparing to bring down from Huronia twelve "little boys, most pleasing, & most happy" to come. Alas, at the moment of departure, seeing their mothers' tears, nine changed their minds. Upon reaching the St Lawrence, it was the fathers who could not face the separation, and in the end only one Huron boy remained out of the original twelve, and he was "already rather old." But two others were found, then Jean Nicollet brought three more, and that year Father Le Jeune could write, "Already, by the grace of God, a Huron Seminary is begun."[3] It was to prove difficult to keep up. First, one Huron boy left; then two died, "the two best minds," both of the same sickness. Convinced that this sickness was the result of "the change of air & exercise & notably of food," the Jesuits began to feed the three who remained "partly in the Huron manner, partly in the French," and on this diet they improved. But one of them decided to return home, and two new boys were captured by the Iroquois on their way to Quebec; then three young recruits came to join the two already there, but, "one fine morning" in the spring of 1638, the three newcomers vanished, taking with them everything they could carry. So there was the seminary, reduced to the scale of its beginnings. Seven Montagnais and Algonquin boys were recruited subsequently, but the Jesuits began to feel that the seminary of Notre Dame des Anges was located too far away from the French and that it should be moved into Quebec.[4] In 1640, disappointed with their indifferent success, the loss of their house in the upper town by fire, and other misfortunes, they abandoned the seminary completely.[5] For a time, however, they continued to try to gallicize some little Indian boys by having them mingle with the French boys of their school .

The Jesuits had in fact found it necessary to provide for the needs of the French society that was then beginning to take form. Their project for the instruction of French boys had become a definite plan by 1635, if not earlier; according to the *Relation* of that year, they proposed "to establish a college for the instruction of the children of families which are constantly increasing," and they intended to begin "to teach a number of children" in the autumn.[6]

For the support of this work a sizable endowment was essential. Such an endowment was forthcoming in 1635 when the Marquis Rohault de Gamache, whose son René had joined the Jesuits the preceding year, made them a gift of 48,000 livres and an annuity of 3,000 livres. On August 15, 1635, the General of the Jesuits at Rome signed letters authorizing the foundation of the school.[7] The new institution also received a gift of land; twelve arpents were conceded to the Jesuits on March 18, 1637, "for the emplacement of their house and college in the upper town"; when this concession was reduced to six arpents, the Jesuits received eighteen in compensation at the site called La Vacherie.[8] Since some thirty pupils were expected for the autumn of 1636, work was begun at once on a school building, a wooden structure attached to the presbytery and the church of Notre Dame de Recouvrance. This was the building that was destroyed by fire in 1640; the college was temporarily installed in a house belonging to the Hundred Associates, and reconstruction was begun during the winter of 1647-48.[9]

Like Harvard College, which had its beginnings in 1636, the Quebec college was devoted to spiritual ends. In the articles of foundation the Jesuits undertook to provide religious instruction, "pro spirituali Canadensium auxilio et institutione," but teaching was very soon extended to reading and writing. At the request of parents Latin was added next, and then, little by little, the other subjects taught by the colleges of France, which, in New France, only the College of Quebec was in a position to teach. In 1651, in order to accommodate pupils from outside Quebec, a "Seminary" was opened for the lodging of boarders, "under a gentleman who undertook to care for them"; twelve years later it was housing some twenty schoolboys. In 1655 the number of teachers at the college was increased to four, thanks to an endowment from the King, and then the program of study was the same as that of the colleges of France: grammar, literature, rhetoric and philosophy. The Quebec schoolboys were soon able to demonstrate in public what they had learned. On October 18, 1651, for example, they greeted the new governor, Lauson, with "latinâ oratione & versibus Gallicis."[10]

In their plans for settling and gallicizing the Indians, the Jesuits had counted in vain on their "little savages." They then tried a new approach, this time with "persons older & more capable of instruction," at the Sillery reserve, which was regarded "as a new kind of Seminary."[11] This project did not really begin to take form until they had abandoned the experiment of Notre Dame des Anges.

While the notion of persuading nomadic Indians to settle down in order to convert them more easily was of long standing, the idea of a reserve where they would find all the essentials upon their arrival was of more recent date. In 1634 Father Le Jeune proposed, as a means of inducing the Indians "to receive our Holy Faith," that they should be "confined to a kind of Town"; there they should be "helped to clear & cultivate the land, & to build for themselves." It was hoped that the nomads of the St Lawrence would in this way become accustomed "little by little to deriving something themselves from the land"; their wanderings might thus be "arrested," provided that the initial work were done by French workmen.[12]

The first financial contribution for this enterprise came in 1637 from the priest Noël Brûlart de Sillery, Commander of the Order of Malta and formerly a minister and ambassador of the King, who sent workmen that year "to begin a building, & to clear some land." A site was chosen at the foot of the cliff of Cape Diamond, a league and a half above Quebec; it was a place long frequented by the Montagnais because of its sandy bay. The first concessionnaire of the land there, François Derré de Gand, gave it up for the missionary cause and even supplied some workmen at his own expense.[13]

By 1641 the Sillery reserve contained some thirty families, and by 1645 there were 167 baptized converts. Besides the houses built for them they had a church called St Michel, a hospital run by the Hospitalières from 1640 to 1644, a windmill, an oven, and even a brewery. In 1649 a stone wall was built around the settlement, flanked by four turrets. On March 13, 1651, the reserve, measuring one league by four, was granted in seigneury and freehold to the neophytes, under the guardianship of the Jesuits.[14]

The first years had been a success. Nomads had been led to settle down and even to clear land for farming; in 1646, for example, they brought more than fifteen arpents under cultivation. The Jesuits saw their hopes realized, for the Montagnais, with the Algonquin converts from Trois Rivières who had joined them, soon formed a community leading an intensely religious life under Christian chiefs who imposed rigorous discipline on drunkards and on Christians who married pagans or associated with them; indeed the Jesuits were obliged to intervene from time to time, to temper excesses of zeal.[15]

But the atmosphere of the reserve slowly changed with the years. Both the Montagnais and the Algonquins took to roaming the woods again, until in the winters Sillery was all but deserted. Drunkenness, so severely punished in the early years, gradually became common. As for the lands of the seigneury, they were increasingly occupied by the French, because of their proximity to Quebec; by 1663 there were seventy French concessions in the seigneury. The reserve nevertheless continued to hold its own up to that time, even though a fire in 1657 destroyed the chapel, the Jesuits' residence and buildings of the fort, and brought development temporarily to a halt.[16] In spite of these difficulties, the Jesuits still had reason to believe that the Sillery reserve would be a lasting contribution to the work of evangelization.

In their great program of work, the Jesuits had not forgotten that the Indians must be cared for in a hospital in time of sickness, and that instruction for Indian girls must also be provided. To realize these aims, women had to be found, and Father Le Jeune's appeals for volunteers and funds were answered sooner than had been hoped. In 1636 Madame de Combalet, future Duchesse d'Aiguillon and niece of Richelieu, promised to send workmen to prepare a lodging for the nuns who had offered to come and devote themselves to the care of the sick, and in 1637 she signed the articles of foundation for a hospital to be entrusted to the Hospitalières of Dieppe. The hospital was duly endowed and provided with land: seven and a half arpents in Quebec itself, sixty just outside, and a seigneury of one league by ten in the region of Les Grondines. On August 12, 1638, the foundations were laid and the hospital was dedicated "to the Blood of the Son of God."[17]

Meanwhile an anonymous gentleman, "seeing that a hospital was being prepared for the poor Savages, undertook the founding of a seminary for girls" and expressed a wish to endow a convent for nuns at Quebec. On January 15, 1637, the Hundred Associates therefore granted to these nuns, as yet unnamed, twelve arpents in the upper town of Quebec, where they and "the daughters of the Savages and of the French" might be housed. (This concession in the town itself was later reduced, and the reduction compensated by another concession just outside.) On the same date, a seigneury measuring one league by ten was granted to them; this was to be the seigneury of Ste Croix.[18]

The nuns being considered were the Ursulines, in particular an Ursuline from Tours, Mother Marie de l'Incarnation, a widow turned nun who since 1635 had often expressed her desire to respond to Father Le Jeune's appeal. A benefactress came forward to help the Ursulines; this was Madame Chauvigny de La Peltrie, like Madame de Combalet a devout widow, who had heard the call of the *Relations* and longed to come to New France. The Jesuits put her in touch with Marie de l'Incarnation and she at once placed a portion of her wealth at the disposal of the Ursulines.[19]

And so the Hospitalières and the Ursulines were ready at the same time. On August 1, 1639, the little population of Quebec saw two groups of nuns disembark. The first group consisted of three young Hospitalières from Dieppe (their average age was hardly more than 26) accompanied by a servant who aspired to become a lay sister. The second was led by Madame de La Peltrie and was composed of three Ursulines, including Marie de l'Incarnation; they had brought with them a girl of nineteen, Charlotte Barré, who intended to enter religious life.[20]

With the nuns there arrived six Jesuits, and Father Le Jeune could therefore hail the arrival of a vessel bearing "a College of Jesuits, a house of Hospitalières, & a Convent of Ursulines."

The hospital, although it had been begun in 1638, was not ready, and neither was the convent. The Hôtel Dieu was in fact advanced only as far as its first beams; the Hospitalières were therefore lodged in the Hundred Associates' warehouse (on the present Place d'Armes of Quebec). As for the Ursulines, whose convent was not even begun, they were installed in "a small house at the water's edge," which Madame de La Peltrie had rented from Noël Juchereau des Chatelets.[21]

The Hospitalières at first stayed in Quebec for only one winter. Since the Hôtel Dieu showed little progress, and no water had been found "in all this property," they decided to "abandon this place and all the work begun here" and, with permission from their benefactress, to go and settle at Sillery with the Indians. They remained there, however, only until May 29, 1644, when the danger of Iroquois attacks obliged them to follow the Indians back to Quebec. Completion of the Hôtel Dieu was hastened and they moved into it early in the winter of 1644-45. It was a poor and inadequate building, but the Hospitalières were to stay permanently in Quebec and in 1658 they would have a new and much bigger convent of stone, with a chapel.[22]

In spite of its fumbling beginnings, the Hôtel Dieu became a firmly established institution, thanks to Madame d'Aiguillon's generous gifts and to effective recruitment. Its personnel, from the original three choir nuns of 1639, had increased by 1659 to twelve, with a novice and three lay sisters as well. The vacancies left by four deaths over these twenty years and the return to France of two of the nuns had been amply filled. Some of the recruits were sought locally, not only among French immigrants but also among girls of Canadian birth. There was even a Huron girl, Geneviève Skannudharoi, who was permitted to take the veil after eight months as a postulant; the only Indian nun to take vows under the French régime, she fell dangerously ill and was at the point of death when admitted to the profession. Assured of a good supply of recruits, the Hôtel Dieu of Quebec constituted a religious community that was remarkably young; in 1659, the average age of its twelve choir nuns was only 34.2 years. This establishment, brought into existence by the Jesuits, could well be considered a success.

The Ursulines' beginnings had been even more eventful and more difficult. The diminutive and ramshackle abode that they had acquired upon their arrival, supposedly only a pied-à-terre, was to be their convent for three long years. Although the household already numbered five, five Indian girls were taken in immediately, and later even some toddlers two or three years old. In the course of the winter the little house found room for more Indian girls and two French girls, to say nothing of day pupils. In 1640, two more Ursulines arrived from Paris. The school had forty-eight pupils in 1640-41, although most were day pupils. At last, in 1642, the school was able to move into the convent in the upper town, a spacious three-storey building of stone measuring ninety-two feet by twenty-eight, heated by four fireplaces and surrounded by a palisade of massive stakes. This building, which included a chapel twenty-eight feet by seventeen, was "the most handsome and the biggest in Canada."[23]

Trials awaited the Ursulines in their new convent. The first of these originated with their foundress, Madame de La Peltrie. A woman of unstable character, and a perfectionist in her own rather childish way, she yearned for greater action in spreading the faith, and in the spring of 1642 decided to join the Montrealists as they prepared to found their colony. She took away all the belongings she had given to the Ursulines, "her furniture and numerous other things used in the church and school," leaving them so little that they could house only three of their pupils. And at the very time when she was almost wrecking this newly launched work, she talked of founding a second Ursuline convent at Montreal. Fortunately, the Ville Marie adventure was only a passing fancy for Madame de La Peltrie. After eighteen months she came back and once more put all her belongings at the disposal of the Ursulines.[24]

Then, just as the work was beginning to prosper, the fine building was destroyed by fire on December 30, 1650, through the carelessness of a lay sister. On the advice of the Governor and of the Jesuits, who lent 8,000 livres, construction of a new convent was begun in the summer of 1651. This building was bigger than its predecessor, and cost some 30,000 livres to build and furnish, but gifts were forthcoming in abundance. Soon the Ursulines were left with a debt of only 4,000 livres.[25]

Another trial, a less painful one, though difficult to measure, came from within the community itself. The nuns had come from two different convents in France, one at Tours and the other at Paris, which had different vows, different rules, and different costumes. It was essential to achieve a certain uniformity, but this was not done without friction. In the end, Marie de l'Incarnation's devotion and the Jesuit Lalemant's counsel overcame the ticklish problem. The Tours Ursulines took the Paris Ursulines' additional vow and the Paris Ursulines adopted the habit of Tours, and in 1647 Father Lalemant drew up "our rules, our regulations, and generally all we need for living a life of order." Ten years later, Marie de l'Incarnation wrote: "And although we are thus assembled from different places, we live together as if we had taken our vows in one and the same Congregation and one and the same convent."[26] The Jesuits, then, had not only persuaded the Ursulines of France to undertake the Canadian vocation and assisted their establishment in New France, but had also helped them achieve an internal readjustment that ensured harmony within their community.

That community had grown despite its trials, but slowly. Death had struck only once as yet, but two nuns (one from Tours, the other from Brittany) returned to France after some twelve years in Canada and their departure left "great crosses" for Marie de l'Incarnation to bear. An attempt was made at local recruitment, although the Mother Superior considered it too slow and too uncertain: a noviciate was opened at the end of 1646, but the first novice, Madame de La Peltrie herself, soon returned to secular life. During the first twenty years, only three nuns entered the Order at Quebec; one of these was Geneviève Bourdon, the first Canadian to become an Ursuline. General insecurity and financial losses delayed recruitment from France; although the number of Quebec Ursulines had risen to eight by 1644, there were still only nine in 1659, and their average age was 43.6 years. Nevertheless, in 1654 and again in 1659 they were urged to found a convent in Montreal, but each time Marie de l'Incarnation declined on the ground that the Order was not in a position to do so.[27]

In spite of all their difficulties, the Ursulines had done a great deal for education. In 1640-41, they had forty-eight pupils, all baptized, "not to speak of more than eight hundred visits from the Savages, whom we have helped as best we could. We are established at Quebec as being the safest place for ourselves, and the most advantageous for teaching." The Ursulines also tried to further the Jesuits' plans for inducing nomadic Indians to settle down or for integrating Indians with French, by encouraging their gallicized charges to marry. "We have Huron girls," writes Marie de l'Incarnation, "whom the Reverend Fathers have thought it suitable for us to raise in the French manner: for since all the Hurons are now converted, and are living near the French, it is expected that they may in time intermarry, and this cannot happen unless the girls become French in language and in customs." There are no statistics available on the results of the Ursulines' efforts to educate Indian girls, but although the work was destined for ultimate failure it was still flourishing in 1659, and at that time there was every reason to believe that it would endure. As for French day pupils, their exact number is unknown; it is believed that there were about twenty each year, before 1650.[28] In any event, the Ursulines continued to fulfil the objective originally proposed by Father Le Jeune: the education of both French and Indian girls.

But the Jesuits' most spectacular effort, and indeed the most spectacular phase of the entire religious history of New France, was their work in Huronia. It will be remembered that missionaries were convinced that the Indians must live a sedentary life in order to be Christianized; despite the Notre Dame des Anges seminary and the Sillery reserve, work with the Montagnais and Algonquins of the St Lawrence had met with little success. However, on the Great Lakes dwelt the naturally sedentary Hurons; their country was densely populated, supporting some 30,000 inhabitants in the early days, and was moreover the great commercial hub of the upper country. By establishing themselves there, the missionaries might win a great many souls for Christianity. At the same time, owing to the close association between Church and State, they would be ensuring to the French of the St Lawrence a permanent alliance with the principal suppliers of beaver.

The Jesuits were therefore to launch a prodigious undertaking among the Hurons, devoting, it could be said, the best of their strength to the task. Lack of enthusiasm on the part of the Indians had delayed the return of missionaries to Huronia until 1634. That year, three Jesuits went in, but by 1638 there were ten and by 1649 as many as eighteen, with four coadjutors, twenty-two lay volunteers and eleven servants. In the missionary work of the Jesuits, the resources mobilized for this tiny area equalled those for all of New France.

In the autumn of 1639, the missionaries decided that it would be convenient to have, instead of a number of small stations, "but a single house, firm and stable" as "the heart of all our missions," and they withdrew from their establishments at Teanaustaiaé and Ossossané to take up their abode together at Ste Marie.[29] At the northern edge of the Huron territory, "on the bank of a beautiful river" between a small lake and Georgian Bay, Ste Marie thus became the missionary centre of the Great Lakes, serving "for the retreat & meditation of our evangelical workers." It was also the supply depot for the missionaries, restocked annually from Quebec, and a prayer centre for Christian Hurons in search of tranquillity for their devotions. The mission, which was to become a fortified post, soon grew into an impressive establishment with its residence and chapel, a small hospital and various other services, and even some domestic animals, imported from Quebec: oxen, cows, pigs and chickens.[30]

In 1639 there was begun at Ste Marie an institution that would provide the Jesuits with invaluable assistance over the next ten years: donnés, those "young men who give themselves to us to provide temporal care, and to serve us as would coadjutors."[31] From six in 1640 their number increased rapidly, to eleven in 1644 and twenty-four in 1648, and when Fort Ste Marie was evacuated there were still twenty-two of them. Among these dedicated young men who served the Jesuits were Pierre Boucher and Charles Le Moyne, both of whom were to enter the ranks of the nobility, and also René Goupil and Jean de La Lande, who died as martyrs.

The life of the missionaries in Huronia was always one of hardship, and particularly so in the early years. The Indians despised these men who were neither hunters nor traders and who never took up arms, could not paddle or carry burdens on portages, and had no women. On the return journeys to their country they readily accepted the interpreters because they served as agents of the fur trade and were economically useful, but the missionaries were taken into their canoes only with the greatest reluctance. They were coming only to preach a foreign theology, unfamiliar customs, restrictive and vexing laws, and the Hurons found every imaginable pretext for refusing to take along these useless men who would have to be given transport, food and lodging on the month-long journey.

Once in Huron territory, after a gruelling journey with surly and inconsiderate guides, the missionaries had no more than enough to keep body and soul together, and even then the Hurons were more disposed to rob them than help them. They lived as did the Indians: a wretched existence, by European standards. And in addition to hardship there was isolation. Usually the missionaries' letters were carried down to the St Lawrence in the spring, and they received letters from Quebec late in the summer – their only news in twelve months. However, many things could happen to interrupt these communications. In 1642, the Iroquois intercepted the letters and supplies that the Jesuits of Quebec had sent. The following spring, the Iroquois again seized letters, coming this time from Huronia; in the summer, letters and provisions fell into their hands once more. In 1644 it was the same story; and again in 1649.[32]

As for evangelization, great and persistent obstacles loomed. It meant persuading the Indians to accept a new religion that was in conflict with the most intimate aspects of their culture and their most sacred customs, and they could see no necessity for doing so. For the Hurons, becoming Christian meant adopting, as well as new beliefs, a mode of behaviour that was French, and this too was little to their liking. Another obstacle was the "libertinism" or complete freedom permitted to the children, who were "so incapable of order & of discipline" that the missionaries decided they would have to begin in the more difficult way, with the conversion of adults. With them, an especially hard rule to impose was the stability of marriage, and in such a new and slowly-developing Christian community, whom might the first Christians marry? The first converts had in fact to marry pagan women, since they "could find no baptized women who wished to wed them." But the Church did not permit such marriages! The situation of the first Christians was therefore most irregular; in the circumstances, they were permitted to come to prayers, but they could not receive the sacraments.[33]

The introduction of Christianity was made far more difficult still by a series of epidemics that struck the Hurons. European diseases hitherto unknown to the Amerindians broke out among them and the mortality rate was extremely high. Since the French suffered little or not at all, the Hurons concluded that the French were wilfully causing these afflictions, and they blamed the missionaries in particular. Of all the religious ceremonies, it was baptism that was regarded with the greatest suspicion. In the early years, since they were as yet having no success in converting adults, the missionaries concentrated on baptizing all those, whether adults or children, who were at the point of death. At first they did so openly and with the consent of relatives, who expected the ceremony to effect a cure, but when death followed baptism the Hurons came to believe that baptism was the cause of death. From then on, the Jesuits resorted to every kind of subterfuge in order to administer baptism secretly to the dying.[34]

Baptisms became numerous from 1636-37 on, but nearly every year the missionaries had to admit that most of those they had baptized were at the point of death. Thus in 1639-40, when they mention a total of a thousand persons baptized, the Jesuits add that there were not even twenty who were not close to death, and that it was "to augment the Church triumphant rather than the Church militant" that they were labouring. Of those who returned to health, moreover, a number renounced their new faith. So in 1640-41, in this country where the missionaries had been at work since 1634 and had performed more than eighteen hundred baptisms, there were still only fifty Hurons who were professed Christians. Later on, there was a spectacular increase in the number of baptisms as the Hurons, broken by famine, sickness and war, put themselves into the hands of the missionaries. Mass baptisms were performed during the years in which Huronia was being destroyed, and the *Relations* give these extremely high totals: in 1647-48, thirteen hundred; in 1648-49, twenty-seven hundred; in 1649-50, three thousand. Father Ragueneau wrote, in 1648: "I might say that never has this country been more sorely afflicted than we see it now, & never has the Faith appeared at greater advantage"; but, he adds, God "has chosen to plant his holy Name there amid their ruins."[35]

It was indeed amid the ruins of a nation that the missionaries continued their work, with hardly a hope of establishing a lasting Christian community. The little Huron Church, consisting of the few converts who survived the epidemics, was continually disrupted by the attacking Iroquois. Father Jogues, on his way to Huronia in August 1642, was captured with the *donné* Goupil and twenty-three Huron converts and neophytes; in 1643, a hundred Christians were massacred; in 1644, three canoe fleets of Hurons, most of them Christians, were routed. In July 1648, Father Daniel was killed at Teanaustaiaé; in March 1649, Fathers Brébeuf and Lalemant were martyred; in December, Father Garnier was killed by the Iroquois and Father Chabanel by a Huron turncoat. Of the thirteen Jesuits who brought the last survivors of Huronia to Quebec in 1650, eight returned immediately to France since the St Lawrence colony could neither maintain nor usefully employ so many missionaries.[36]

Not long afterwards, however, another field for missionary work was opened up to the Jesuits, in the territory of the very Iroquois who had destroyed Huronia and among whom the missionaries now found a large number of Christian Hurons. Following Father Simon Le Moyne's ambassadorial visit to the Iroquois, a Jesuit mission was begun in 1655: while Father Le Moyne tried again to persuade the Mohawks to make peace, Fathers Dablon and Chaumonot went to the Onondaga country. There they built the first Iroquois chapel and set to work "to restore the old foundations of the Huron Church" and at the same time introduce Christianity to the Iroquois. Father Dablon went to Quebec seeking reinforcements and returned to Onondaga in 1656 with more missionaries and colonists under the leadership of Dupuy. The Jesuit missionaries to the Iroquois now numbered five. As they had done in Huronia, they turned their mission of Ste Marie into "the base & the Seminary of all the other missions." In 1657 they wrote with enthusiasm: "More Iroquois have turned Christian in two months than there were Hurons converted in several years." Among the new Christians were five of the most important Onondagas, and the lasting friendship of Chief Garakontié dates from this time. The missionaries' work with the captives living among the Iroquois was even more encouraging. But war broke out anew between the Iroquois and the French colony of the St Lawrence; Garakontié gave warning of the peril facing both the missionaries and the laymen; and the Jesuits, "seeing that their death would be useless to a poor captive Church" and would do more harm than good to New France, evacuated their Iroquois mission with all haste in March 1658.[37]

This was also the period when the Jesuits consolidated their political influence in the Laurentian colony, to such a point that the Church was soon in a position to impose its will on the State. Canada in this period has been justifiably described by English-Canadian historians as a "mission colony."

The political power of the missionaries had become apparent well before 1632. As early as 1620, Champlain had been strongly urged to consult the Récollet Le Baillif in all matters. In 1621, it was Le Baillif who was chosen "as deputy representing the whole country in general," to draw up and present a memorandum of "remonstrances" to the King. The Jesuits began to show their political strength with the part they played in Vantadour's accession to the viceroyalty of New France and in the organization of the Company of the Hundred Associates. When Champlain died in December of 1635, it was the Jesuit Le Jeune who was entrusted by the Hundred Associates with letters designating the provisional commandant, and it was he who read these letters to the assembled people in the church at Quebec.[38] The Jesuits were, moreover, well placed to influence the destiny of the colony in that since 1632 its spiritual guidance had been their monopoly, not only at Quebec, but also at Trois Rivières and Montreal. Their role was decisive in the establishment and support of the Ursulines and the Hospitalières at Quebec and in the formation of the Society of Notre Dame of Montreal. And they were now the only missionaries to the Indians in the St Lawrence and in the Great Lakes region, where their fortified mission was the sole French fort in the interior of the continent.

Their decisive political influence can readily be seen at work in the formation of the Communauté des Habitants, and the predominance of the Church was swiftly confirmed in 1647 when the Superior of the Jesuits became the second of the three members of the Council of Quebec, a body charged not only with the appointing of directors of the Communauté and the supervision of its accounts but with the administration of the entire country. The Superior of the Jesuits continued to be an ex-officio member of the Council of Quebec until 1659, ranking next to the Governor. And this was no mere honorific appointment; in 1650, Father Jérôme Lalemant was given the responsibility of supervising the operations of the Communauté in France, and he alone could authorize borrowings on its behalf. The first ambassadors to New England (1650) and to the Iroquois (1654 and succeeding years) were Jesuits. But of all these ecclesiastics, it was the Jesuit Ragueneau who, during his term as Superior (1650-53) and later, played the strongest political role, provoking much angry resentment toward Jesuits in general. Father Poncet declared in 1655 that Governor Lauson was completely "ad manum Patris," in Father Ragueneau's hands; and Father de Quen, when he became Superior, felt that Father Ragueneau should leave the scene, since he had become far more deeply involved in temporal affairs than was proper for the Society of Jesus, and had brought upon the Jesuits more than enough strife and jealousy.[39]

It was in 1657 that the Jesuits' pre-eminence began to be challenged The breach was opened by the Sulpicians, who, when the time came, were to find a staunch supporter in the Governor.

The Society of St Sulpice, founded in the same period as Ville Marie, was closely allied through its founder, Olier, to the Society of Notre Dame of Montreal. The Montrealists, who viewed the decisions taken by the Council of Quebec as being constantly detrimental to them, were striving to build an increasingly autonomous colony in New France, and this desire for independence was soon felt with regard to the Jesuits, although the latter had contributed to the founding of Ville Marie and had been its religious mentors since 1642. In the autumn of 1656, Maisonneuve went to France intending to recruit priests, on the pretext that the Jesuits were "pressed on all sides for missions" to the Indians.[40] The priests he hoped to obtain were of course Olier's. Olier approved the plan to install his priests at Montreal and, since New France had been asking for a bishop for so many years, the Abbé de Queylus, their chosen Superior, was proposed for the bishopric.

As early as 1631, the Secretary of the Congregation of the Propaganda had taken steps toward the creation of a bishopric for New France, and in

1634 he proposed a Récollet from Guyenne, Father Pons. This choice encountered opposition from Richelieu and fell by the wayside. In 1641, the Secretary found another candidate, Camus du Peron of Lyons, a member of the Society of Notre Dame, but he, too, was set aside.[41] In 1645, the Society proposed another of its members, Thomas Le Gauffre. Mazarin and the Jesuits supported this proposal and the project reached the very threshold of success, but Le Gauffre died suddenly while in retreat at a Jesuit establishment where he had gone to make his decision. So there was still no bishop, and Marie de l'Incarnation thought it only right that the Jesuits, who had "planted Christianity" in Canada, "should cultivate it yet a while longer, without there coming anyone who might prove contrary to their designs."[42] In 1650, the Hundred Associates came forward in their turn to propose that a Jesuit (Lalemant, Ragueneau or Le Jeune) should be the first bishop of New France,[43] but, either because the Jesuits did not normally have access to ecclesiastical dignities, or perhaps because of France's internal troubles, the plan went no further. If it had succeeded, it would have carried the Jesuits to a pinnacle of absolute power, because this was the period when Governor Lauson was under the domination of Father Ragueneau.

When the project was revived in January 1657 it posed a very real threat to the Jesuits' influence by putting forward one of the Sulpicians whom the Society of Notre Dame had designated for Montreal. At the instigation of the Society, the Abbé de Queylus was proposed as bishop by Monseigneur Godeau, Bishop of Vence, to the General Assembly of the Clergy of France. But the Jesuits had foreseen the move and, in the same month, they recommended to the King a 36-year-old priest, François de Laval, who had been one of their students at La Flèche and Clermont. A member since 1650 of the Society of Good Friends, of which the Jesuit Bagot was the director, Laval was a regular visitor at the Hermitage of Caën established by Bernières-Louvigny under the direction of the Jesuits. For four years he had been expecting to leave for Tonkin, with the title of Vicar Apostolic. The Jesuits' candidate was immediately approved by the King and proposed to Rome.[44]

The Jesuits had triumphed in the choice of the future bishop, but the battle for religious supremacy was still not won. The Abbé de Queylus took the lead once again on April 22, 1657 by having himself named Grand Vicar and canonical judge by the Archbishop of Rouen, Monseigneur de Harlay, who claimed New France as part of his diocese. While Laval remained in France, waiting in vain for his bulls and his consecration, the Abbé de Queylus disembarked at Quebec in the course of the summer. The new Grand Vicar of the Archbishop of Rouen presented his letters to the Superior of the Jesuits. It happened that the Jesuits, too, held letters of grand-vicarship from the same archbishop, letters which they had accepted without much discussion in 1649 and had not made public until 1653. Neither their letters nor those of de Queylus were valid in the eyes of the Pope, but, for the moment, the Jesuits dared not cross the would-be Grand Vicar and submitted to his jurisdiction pending further inquiry.[45]

For the Jesuits, who had been the undisputed masters of the spiritual domain since 1632, being placed in tutelage in 1657 was a cruel blow. It was not to be the last. De Queylus proceeded to send his brother Sulpicians, Gabriel Soüart, Dominique Galinier and Antoine d'Allet (the last-named still a deacon) to serve the French and Indians of Ville Marie in place of the Jesuits. On September 12, he took over the parish of Quebec, which had been theirs for twenty-five years. He threatened to turn them out of the house they occupied and had built at their own expense. He forbade them to perform any ministry outside their own chapel. He wrote a long memorandum of accusations against them to their General. In September he preached a sermon against them. In October he delivered a speech satirizing (without mentioning by name) those who, for the last thirty or forty years, had controlled "the state and Religion."[46]

Barred from parish duties in both Montreal and Quebec, threatened in their own house, sniped at by a triumphant adversary, the Jesuits could no longer even turn to the Governor for protection. Lauson had left in 1656, to be replaced by his son, Charles de Lauson-Charny, but in September 1657 he, too, returned to France. The interim governor was Louis d'Ailleboust de Coulonge, a member of the Society of Notre Dame, who took sides with the Abbé de Queylus. Then at last, in the summer of 1658, the Jesuits registered a victory: new letters from the Archbishop of Rouen restricted the jurisdiction of de Queylus to Montreal alone. The Grand Vicar was therefore obliged to leave Quebec, which he did on August 21, and the Jesuits once more took over the parish.[47]

The two sides held to their positions, the Jesuits at Quebec and Trois Rivières and the Sulpicians at Montreal. At least the Jesuits had some peace after the departure of de Queylus, but the situation was still precarious. Indeed, the new governor, d'Argenson, who arrived in July, was a friend of de Queylus and he was to create a good many difficulties for them; "he is not our friend," wrote the Superior, adding that there was everything to fear from an association between the Governor and de Queylus. It was not open warfare, but the Jesuits were being discreetly undermined at Quebec and at Trois Rivières. They could see only one solution: "the appointment of a bishop who would not be the enemy of the Society [of Jesus]."[48]

Although he had been approved by the King and proposed to Rome early in 1657, that bishop was still awaited. The arrangements dragged on at length, despite the best efforts of the Jesuits. The French court was anxious to establish a bishopric at Quebec, so that the incumbent would be dependent on the King "and swear allegiance to him, like the others of France," while the Pope, claiming "some particular right in foreign parts," had no intention of issuing bulls to any but a vicar apostolic, with the title of Bishop *in partibus*. Toward the end of 1657, the King yielded and gave instructions to request a bishop *in partibus*; Rome signed the bulls in June 1657, but, since the Archbishop of Rouen continued his opposition, invoking defects in the formalities, Laval's consecration was performed in the greatest secrecy on December 8 in the Church of St Germain des Prés. The Archbishop of Rouen was still opposed, but on March 27, 1659, the King ordered that François de Laval, now titular bishop of Petrea in Arabia, should be recognized throughout the length and breadth of New France "in his episcopal functions." The King added, however, that, pending the establishment of a bishopric under the jurisdiction of Rouen, he did not mean to deny the rights of the Archbishop – which left Monseigneur de Harlay free to do what he would, and he promptly renewed the letters appointing the Abbé de Queylus as Grand Vicar, thus setting him up in competition with Monseigneur de Laval.[49]

The Vicar Apostolic finally arrived at Quebec in June 1659. He was accompanied by three secular priests (one of whom was Charles de Lauson-Charny, the former interim governor who had been a friend of the Jesuits), and also Father Jérome Lalemant, whom he had obtained despite the Court's disapproval. The Abbé de Queylus first came forward to declare his submission, and then, having learned that the Archbishop of Rouen was renewing his credentials as Grand Vicar, insisted on being recognized as such. Monseigneur de Laval thereupon produced an order from the King which stated that Monseigneur de Harlay could no longer intervene in New France until such time as Rome had decided otherwise. De Queylus withdrew, and set out for France the following month determined to appeal the order. For the moment (for the conflict was not yet over), Laval was free to "dispose all things [at Montreal as well as at Quebec] without appeal, in spiritual matters."[50]

That was the situation in the autumn of 1659. The parish of Quebec would henceforth be in the charge of secular priests, but with the full agreement of the Jesuits. The Vicar Apostolic now exercised the complete spiritual jurisdiction in New France that had for so long been the Jesuits', and he inherited the political influence that they had acquired over a quarter of a century; but this bishop had studied under the Jesuits, had been guided toward the episcopate by them, and had bestowed letters of grandvicarship upon their Superior. Henceforth the Jesuits, while continuing their parish duties at Trois Rivières, could apply themselves to their tasks of education and evangelization without any longer feeling too much concern about their relegation to second place.

CHAPTER 18

Land Tenure and Population

1663

No evaluation of the Hundred Associates' accomplishments could properly be made without first examining the state of land settlement by the end of their tenure, for while their fortunes ebbed and flowed, a permanent population took root on the shores of the St Lawrence, in that part of New France called Canada. In 1663, apart from Acadia (which was now under English rule) and the minuscule establishment founded in 1662 in Placentia Bay, Newfoundland, Canada was the only French colony in North America worth considering. Its population was 3,035.

The Hundred Associates' charter of 1627 empowered them to distribute the land of New France in the form of fiefs. They were therefore authorized to create a "feudal" régime, the term being understood to mean simply land tenure by fief, not the politico-military social system that the French monarchy had finally succeeded in liquidating at the dawn of the modern era. This tenure is called seigneurial because the fief was generally a seigneury, that is, its holder enjoyed seigneurial rank in the social hierarchy.

This feudal régime did in fact share a number of features with mediaeval feudalism. Thus, the unit of land distribution was the fief, which was divisible into sub-fiefs and even sub-sub-fiefs. The holder of a fief was obliged to swear *foi et hommage*, or fealty and homage, and to submit an *aveu et dénombrement*, which included a general plan of the seigneury and a detailed description or census, with a statement of dues received from settlers. Another token of vassalage was the payment of a tax when the seigneury changed hands. This was very onerous indeed if imposed strictly as provided by the Coutume du Vexin-le-François, the codified customary law of Normandy, to which 81% of seigneurial lands in New France were subject prior to 1663. Besides these obligations, the seigneur also had rights inherited from the feudal era. Among others, he might have judicial rights within his seigneury, even to dispensing *la haute justice*, which is to say, judgement and punishment of all crimes; theoretically he could order limbs broken and impose the death sentence. Since "haute justice" was in force over 96.8% of seigneurial lands in 1663, the Hundred Associates had dispensed this right with a liberal hand when granting seigneuries. When the seigneur conceded land to the habitants, who thereby became his *censitaires*, he remained the dominant proprietor; he collected a token annual cash payment signifying his domination, and certain other dues as rent for the land conceded; he could also impose *corvées* or compulsory days of work for the development of his personal domain.

However, if the framework and trappings belonged to mediaeval feudalism, the system bore an unmistakable seventeenth-century stamp. The State took pains to deny the seigneur anything that might smack of the militarism of mediaeval fiefdoms (armed defence was not his responsibility in any event), and to preclude any possible interference with the freedom of the great waterway flowing past the seigneuries. "Foi et hommage" had become a formality, no longer a solemn statement of vassalage binding one man to another, and the "aveu et dénombrement" was looked on as a purely administrative matter. The powers of "haute justice" were really no more than honorary, for the seigneurs were simply not equipped to exercise them and in practice it was the Hundred Associates' own court that tried all civil and criminal cases. Finally, no seigneur could bind his censitaires to his person or to his fief; they were free to move, if they chose, from one seigneury to another.

The seigneurial régime established in 1627 had therefore retained only the framework of the system that had made France a prosperous country through the distribution and methodical cultivation of land under seigneurial authority. In the seventeenth century, the State, having emerged the victor in its struggles with feudalism, found it convenient to strengthen the seigneurial system in its rights and privileges, in order to make it an "instrument of good order" in the rural areas. This was the system that was established also in New France. Without it, the fledgeling society would have been different from its parent and would have lacked the traditional scale of values for measuring one man's dignity against another's, and for rewarding meritorious service. The Hundred Associates were careful to perpetuate this scale of values by soliciting the participation of "persons of consequence" and by granting them lands "with some honorific title," as shown by the many expressions to that effect found in their deeds of grant. And participation it was indeed, for the grantee undertook to bring a stipulated number of colonists to New France and settle them on his lands. From 1626 until 1656 at least, every new seigneur's deeds spelled out what was expected of him. Land settlement was the goal, and the entire system was intended to attract as many participants as possible in order to achieve it.

The land of New France, then, was to be divided into fiefs, and from the earliest days the fiefs took the form of elongated rectangles projecting inland from the river. The first to take this form was the St Joseph fief (later called Lespinay), conceded on the St Charles River in 1626 but surveyed in the time of the Hundred Associates. In 1663, island grants apart, three quarters of the fiefs were in this form of elongated rectangles, which gave each seigneur frontage on the St Lawrence waterway. These rectangles were laid out side by side with their long axes roughly at right angles to the river, which gave them a common lie of northwest-southeast. This pattern was established when the seigneurs took possession, though no official instructions to that effect have been found. In any event, this was the pattern that was followed from 1637 on, and is shown on Jean Bourdon's map of 1641.

Two seigneurial fiefs were granted before 1627. The Hundred Associates began to add others only in 1633 and 1634, and these were relatively small. The three-year period 1635-37 saw fourteen seigneuries granted, covering in all 7,938,334 arpents (a square arpent equalling roughly five sixths of an acre), of which 69.9% went to the Lauson family. Never to be surpassed were these three years, when the founding members of the Hundred Associates were working most actively, despite heavy losses, and when the Company was pursuing its task most effectively. This productive period was followed by fourteen years when grants were few; 1647 was exceptional, with 474,516 arpents granted. In 1652 there was another peak of 3,950,772 arpents, but most of this total was accounted for by a single fief, the seigneury of Gaspésie, 30 leagues by 18, granted to a group of eleven associates. After that, except for 1656, with the concession of the Onondaga seigneury of ten leagues square, which was never developed, enfeoffment came to a halt for this period ending in 1663. The Company had lost its cohesion and New France was suffering from warfare, poverty and internal squabbles.

In 1663 the amount of seigneurial land was immense: 13,298,041¼ arpents in 104 seigneuries, in fiefs, sub-fiefs and sub-sub-fiefs.[1] On the north shore of the St Lawrence, from Trinity Bay to Lake St Francis, there were 4,594 linear arpents of seigneurial frontage (1 linear arpent equalling 192 feet), or 39.2% of total frontage; on the south shore, from Lake St Francis to Cap Chat, 3,348 arpents of seigneurial frontage, or 24% of total frontage. This was accomplished over 36 years, but, interestingly enough, represents a third of seigneurial frontage as it stood in 1760. The scant progress in seigneurial development can therefore hardly be laid to indifference on the part of the Hundred Associates. There were other reasons for it.

The Hundred Associates, in any event, achieved the first step by grant-

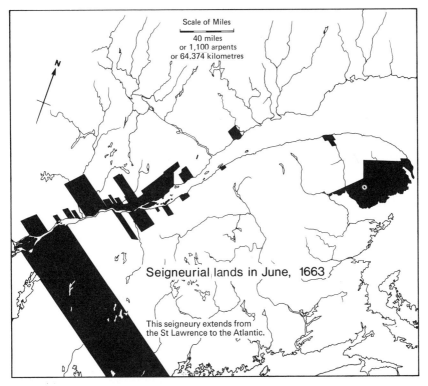

Scale of Miles

40 miles
or 1,100 arpents
or 64.374 kilometres

N

Seigneurial lands in June, 1663

This seigneury extends from
the St Lawrence to the Atlantic.

ing seigneuries. It was then up to the seigneurs to take the second step with the settlement of censitaires.

Who were these seigneurs? In 1663 they were 69 in number, 62 individuals and seven religious institutions (the Jesuits, Sulpicians and Ursulines, the Hospitalières of Quebec and of Montreal, the Fabrique or parish council of Quebec, and the Christian Indians of Sillery). The religious institutions, which were responsible for missionary works, education and medical care, held 10.7% of the seigneurial land, which was very little more than in 1645. The situation of their lands was more important than their size, however, for one quarter of seigneurial river frontage was in their hands. Donations from individuals, two in particular, accounted for 15.6% of their land. The secular Sisters of the Congregation of Notre Dame, a Montreal teaching order, had yet to be granted a single arpent, and the Hôtel-Dieu of Montreal held only 512½ arpents, and in sub-fief at that. The Jesuits had the lion's share with 60.3% of all land held by religious institutions.

It was the 62 individuals who had most of the seigneurial land; 89.3% of the total. In 1663, few seigneuries had changed hands since their concession. There had of course been some changes, nineteen due to deaths and ten to gifts *inter vivos*, but the records show only a single sale, and that was to prevent the seigneury of Rivière-du-Sud from falling into mortmain, since the seigneur, Montmagny, was preparing to enter the Order of St John of Jerusalem. Even counting sales of shares between members of the Compagnie de Beaupré, only 2.3% of all seigneurial land had changed hands by sale. This shows the stability of the seigneurs in this early period when there might well have been a certain amount of speculation.

Seigneurial land was *terre de qualité*, and as such was to be granted to persons of quality, which is why, in 1663, 84.3% was held by the nobility (10,009,312 arpents), though only 32 of the 62 individual seigneurs were nobles; only 3.3% of that was held by Canadian nobles. In 1645 the nobles had held a greater proportion (90.8%), but the bourgeois class was making increasing inroads on the formerly noble preserve, and its share rose from 5.5% in 1645 to 14% in 1663.

Already more than a third of the population of New France was Canadian-born, and nearly half (48.2%) of the seigneurial land was held by 13 Canadian-born seigneurs. Of the 62 individual seigneurs, moreover, 51 were domiciled in Canada. Of the land held by these, 80.2% was in the hands of 35 seigneurs of the Quebec region, the oldest and most accessible to the seat of power; among Montrealers, who still held aloof from the rest of the St Lawrence colony, there were four seigneurs, holding only 7.1%.

Another interesting fact is that in 1663 more than half the seigneurial land was held by women (54.5%), in comparison with 2.7% in 1645. The importance of women in this respect was due not so much to the women's religious communities as to the twelve widows, remarried or not, who had control of land inherited from their former husbands or in tutorship for a son of minor age. This was not brought about by any concerted effort on the part of women, but by a series of chance circumstances. Furthermore, of land held in the name of minors, 48% was attributable to children under sixteen years of age, and seigneuries had been granted to eight of less than six years of age.

Herein was one of the abuses of land distribution. And there were worse abuses. In 1663, almost half of all seigneurial land (47.2%) was held by a single seigneur, the widow of Jean de Lauson the younger; 45.5% was held by another 14 seigneurs, and the remaining 7.3% by 47 seigneurs. There was a powerful oligarchy in landholdings, besides; 9½ million arpents were in the hands of seven families (d'Ailleboust, Bourdon, Giffard, Godefroy, Lauson, Legardeur and Leneuf). Four of these families (Lauson, Giffard, Legardeur and Leneuf) were related by blood or marriage and formed a closely-knit group. Family relationship therefore created a veritable family empire in seigneurial landholdings, so that, of 51 seigneurs domiciled in Canada, 23 belonged to a single family clan which controlled 72.1% of the land held by the 62 individual seigneurs. In other words, two thirds of all seigneurial land (institutional and individual) was in the hands of twenty-three related persons.[2]

Had the 69 seigneurs that the Hundred Associates had recruited by 1663 taken the trouble to fulfil their obligations with regard to settlement? Within their seigneuries, did they in fact create *censives*?

The Quebec region, the oldest and the first to receive immigrants, was the most developed, with 100,581.15 arpents conceded, divided into 494 farms (plus 4 farms of unknown size). In the countryside about Quebec, only nine seigneuries were inhabited, with settlement on the north shore of the St Lawrence from Cap Tourmente to Cap Rouge, the northern half of the Isle of Orleans and, on the south shore, part of the river front called the Côte de Lauson. In the Trois Rivières region, there were only 8,604.09 arpents conceded, in 119 farms (plus 11 farms of unknown size) at Cap de la Madeleine, on the islands at the mouth of the St Maurice River, and around the town of Trois Rivières. The Montreal region was the least advanced: 2,387.8 arpents in 95 farms (plus four farms of unknown size). In June 1663, an estimated total of 111,573.04 arpents had been conceded, representing a very small percentage of all

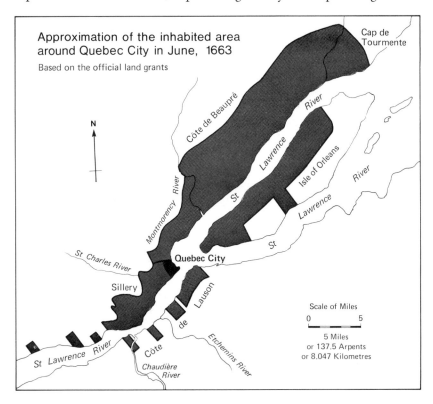

Approximation of the inhabited area around Quebec City in June, 1663

Based on the official land grants

Scale of Miles

0 — 5

5 Miles
or 137.5 Arpents
or 8.047 Kilometres

seigneurial land, 0.87%; not much more than the 0.3% of 1645. This was because the distribution of seigneuries had advanced much more quickly than immigration, and because the Iroquois wars had paralysed rural expansion around Trois Rivières and Montreal. Moreover, seigneurs who had tried to establish settlements at the northeast end of the Isle of Orleans, as well as half way between Quebec and Trois Rivières and half way between Trois Rivières and Montreal, had been forced by the Indian incursions to fall back on those areas already settled.

It must also be added that the concession of land to censitaires began in earnest only in 1644, spurred, as we believe, by Governor Montmagny, or perhaps by the Communauté des Habitants. However, the most productive years in the concession of censives (1651, 1652, 1654 and 1655) were during the administration of Jean de Lauson the elder; 45.1% of the hundred thousand arpents of 1663 were conceded during his governorship.

The Lausons, who held immense lands, had worked very effectively at settlement; Jean de Lauson the younger had settled a large part of the Côte de Lauson, his brother Lauson-Charny had settled almost half the Isle of Orleans, and Lauson de la Citière, another brother, had settled the river frontage of his seigneury of Gaudarville and taken the initiative of providing for the defence of his censitaires. The Compagnie de Beaupré, formed originally of members of the Hundred Associates and in which the Lausons were active partners, had been consistently energetic; it had settled habitants along 469 arpents of river frontage, from Cap Tourmente to the Montmorency River, and had besides granted sub-fiefs to other seigneurs on the Isle of Orleans for settlement. By 1663, 11.2% of the seigneury of Beaupré had been conceded, which was a very high proportion at that time.

Last but not least among the active seigneurs were the Jesuits. The seigneury of Notre Dame des Anges was not very advanced at this point, since large-scale distribution of land began there only in 1652, but the 75 arpents of frontage were already almost completely occupied. At Sillery, which the Jesuits administered for the Christian Indians, the creation of censives had been going on apace; all the frontage (less the part reserved) had been conceded since 1652, and in the first six months of 1663 another 2,040 arpents were conceded with the opening of a second and then a third range, which was most exceptional in this period of seigneurial history. By June 1663, a third of this seigneury of 10,584 arpents had been conceded! While many seigneurs lacked the will or the means to settle their seigneuries, at least the Lausons, the Compagnie de Beaupré and the Jesuits had accomplished what could be expected of them, given the difficult conditions they had to contend with.

Three centres of population had been established in the St Lawrence, Quebec, Trois Rivières and Montreal, but only Quebec could really be called a town. It was during the régime of the Hundred Associates that Quebec began to take definite shape; around 1638-40, the Company decided to establish it on Cape Diamond rather than in the valley of the St Charles River where land had been set aside for the municipality. Some 59 arpents of conceded land on the Cape were recuperated for the purpose, and were then subdivided into building lots. The year 1655 appears to have been a decisive one in the history of Quebec, second only to 1608, the year of its foundation. By 1663 the physical characteristics of the city were already well defined; the French régime established an urban pattern that was to remain unchanged. Between the river and the Cape there was the lower town, also called Quai de Québec or Quai de Champlain, with 90 lots, all small in order to accommodate as many people as possible. Seven streets had been laid out,[3] and all were lined with houses since people liked to live near the water. There were two significant buildings, the new warehouse built by the Communauté des Habitants and, on the site of the future church of Notre Dame des Victoires, the old warehouse (Champlain's), which was crumbling in ruins. There was also a platform with cannon pointing out over the harbour roads and, on Rue Sous-le-Fort, a brewery and a bakery. The upper town was reached by a steep, winding road, the Côte de la Montagne. The upper town of 1663 was virtually the same as the walled city of Quebec today. On the west it was closed by a line of earthworks slightly east of the present ramparts. There were already a number of paths and streets; among others, a path leading from the church to the hospital (later the Côte de la Fabrique), a street leading to the Jesuits' house, or Rue Ste Anne, one leading to the Ursuline convent (the future Rue des Jardins), and Rue St Louis, also called Grande Allée. From the top of the winding Côte de la Montagne, beyond a cemetery and a brick oven, one could see the parish church and presbytery; immediately to the left, the Huron fort and the sites of Champlain's chapel and the church of Notre Dame de Recouvrance (both burned down in 1640); straight ahead, the Jesuit College with its two buildings but as yet no outside chapel; to the north and lower down, the Hôtel Dieu which housed sixteen cloistered nuns; then, moving toward the south, one would come upon Fort St Louis with its enclosing wall and Rue St Louis with the convent and outside chapel of the seventeen cloistered Ursulines; to the left of Rue St Louis, the gardens of the fort and the Mont Carmel bastion. On the Cape behind was a windmill belonging to Denys de La Trinité, and at the highest point, where the citadel is today, there were farms conceded to habitants. From the edge of the upper town, one could see Jean Bourdon's fort and windmill toward the west and, down in the valley on the right bank of the St Charles River, a windmill belonging to the Jesuits and the ruins of the

Récollet convent. In the upper town there were 52 lots covering a total of 128 arpents. Only some thirty arpents remained to be occupied.

In the surrounding countryside there were certain features basically important to the socio-economic life of the region, from Cap Rouge above Quebec to Cap Tourmente down-river. At Cap Rouge there was a walled redoubt on a small island and the fort of the Gaudarville seigneury on the cliff. In the Sillery seigneury there were two forts: on the cliff St François Xavier with its bastions and village (a municipality of 18 inhabitants), and on the river bank the Sillery fort, with four turrets and a chapel, and its windmill on the cliff behind. East of Sillery there was another mill on a rivulet called St Denys. On the north slope of the Cape a village was beginning to take form in the St François seigneury. Beyond the St Charles River, on the right bank of the Lairet, the Jesuits had built a windmill on their farmland of Notre Dame des Anges. In the Beauport seigneury there was the village of Fargy, with some twenty building lots, a flour mill, a chapel and a cemetery. The neighbouring Beaupré seigneury had two villages, Château Richer with a fort, a dozen building lots, a church and a windmill, and Ste Anne, where the people had been building a church for two years. At the northeast tip of the Isle of Orleans were the ruined buildings and mill of Argentenay, and, working around the end of the island and back upstream, Fort St Pierre in Charny-Lirec, the beginnings of a village at the southeast tip in the Beaulieu sub-fief and, on the Champigny farm, a "retreat" with a wooden palisade enclosing a building which served as a chapel. On the south shore, the Lauson seigneury had no church as yet, but Bissot dit Larivière was operating a flour mill there.

In the Trois Rivières region there had been some development too. There were three forts to protect the inhabitants; one was in the Ste Marie sub-fief (Pierre Boucher's seigneury) with the beginnings of a village; the second, on the Faverel River (site of the present Marian sanctuary), was Fort St François, a palisaded village with a chapel and hospital; the third was at the mouth of the St Maurice River, where there was a windmill which gave the fort its name, and an embryonic village. On Ile St Christophe at the mouth of the St Maurice, there was a redoubt. The town of Trois Rivières was enclosed in a four-sided palisade, fortified by a redoubt at the north corner. Its streets were laid out with chequerboard regularity.[4] A church stood at the main gate, and at the south corner the Jesuits had built an outside chapel on some land overlooking the St Lawrence. There were some fifty building lots in the town, of which one belonging to the Algonquin Pachiriny had been subdivided into thirteen small lots. On the plateau outside the town were the ruins of the fort of 1634; on its northwest part, Leneuf de La Poterie had built a windmill by the road leading from the town to the common pastureland. Below the

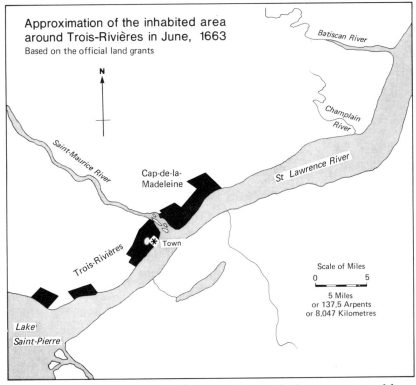

Approximation of the inhabited area
around Trois-Rivières in June, 1663
Based on the official land grants

N

Batiscan River

Champlain River

Saint-Maurice River

Cap-de-la-
Madeleine

St Lawrence River

Town

Trois-Rivières

Scale of Miles

0   5

5 Miles
or 137.5 Arpents
or 8.047 Kilometres

Lake
Saint-Pierre

plateau the town was extended by several lots, which were protected by a redoubt.

As for Montreal, the site was still commonly referred to in documents as "place reserved for the town," since all that existed as yet were two streets, Chemin de la Commune (later Rue St Paul) and Rue Notre-Dame, joined by some pathways. There was neither wall nor palisade, and the town was developing rather haphazardly between Fort Ville-Marie, which was surrounded by four bastions, and a rise of land called the Côteau St Louis[5] which was topped by a redoubt and a windmill. Another redoubt had been built in the vicinity of today's Rue St François Xavier. Inside the town was the Hôtel Dieu with its chapel and cemetery, and the school run by the Sisters of the Congregation of Notre Dame. Town and country were almost indistinguishable, for the fields pressed close about the buildings; in terms of the city of today, there were fields between Iberville and Metcalfe Streets, from Place Royale to Rue d'Argenson, and on Point St Charles. There was protection at the two extremities, upstream at the St Gabriel farm and downstream at the Ste Marie farm, each having a redoubt. Records for 1663 show 38 building lots in the town.

Each of the regions of the St Lawrence was thus organized to be self-sufficient, for the bare necessities at least. The Quebec region was the best equipped; three churches, two outside chapels, five inside chapels, a college, a convent school for girls, a hospital, nine mills and, in the country-side about, five or six forts. The Trois Rivières region had a church and two outside chapels, a hospital and two mills; the main town was protected by a strong palisade and two redoubts, and at Cap de la Madeleine there were three forts. Montreal had a bastioned fort, redoubts, two mills (if the old fort mill was still working), an outside chapel, a hospital, and a school for girls. Altogether, the spiritual welfare of the people was amply provided for, and each region had a hospital; defences, at least of a passive kind, were well distributed, and the total of a dozen mills is quite remarkable.[6]

These material facilities served a population of 3,035, as far as we can determine, though the presence of 221 (7.3%) is uncertain. This population was distributed over three regions isolated from one another by distance, the Quebec region being the most populous:

Quebec region	1,976	65.1%
Trois Rivières region	462	15.2%
Montreal region	597	19.7%

The fragmentary nature of the documentation and the vagueness of the

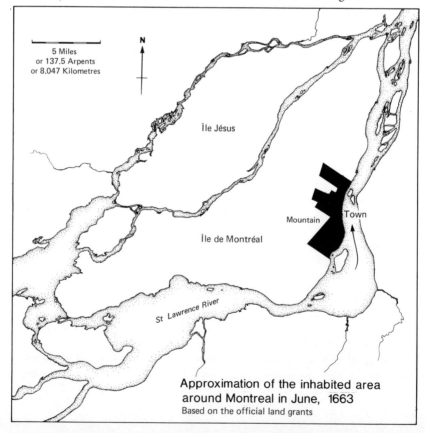

Approximation of the inhabited area
around Montreal in June, 1663
Based on the official land grants

Growth of the population of Canada, 1627 to 1663

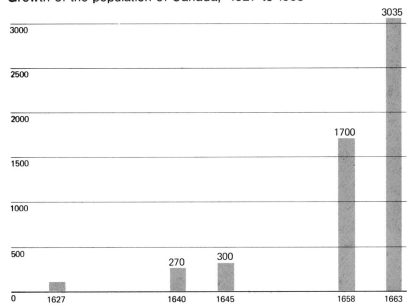

This graph does not include the population of Acadia.

data make it difficult to know precisely how many were townspeople and how many were country-dwellers living off the land. However, we can make an estimation with a different approach. What proportion of the colonists of 1663 were urban- or rural-based economically? Taking together the seigneurs whose seigneuries were uninhabited, who had conceded no land and had no town lot, those with uninhabited seigneuries but with town lots, and persons with town lots only or with no land of any kind, we find 996 persons (32.8%) with no rural base; a second group of 851 had both land and town lots and were rural-based economically; a third group of 1,188 lived entirely on a rural base. Combining the last two, we find that two thirds of the population (2,039 persons) were rural-based economically, whether they were town- or country-dwellers. The greatest proportion in this category was in the Quebec region: 72.2%, compared with only 59.5% for Trois Rivières and 56.6% for Montreal.

More than a third of the population was Canadian-born; including four Amerindians integrated by marriage, there were 1,175 Canadians by birth, or 38.7% of the total population. The proportions were more or less equal in the three regions; 40.6% for Quebec, 36.4% for Trois Rivières and 34.5% for Montreal. There were even two generations of Canadians, 1,030 first- and 145 second-generation. In sex these Canadians were fairly evenly balanced; 52.3% male and 47.7% female. The oldest of them was a woman of 43, but the average age was very young, only 7.6 years, and only eight were 30 or over. There were already a number of métis in the population. Four Amerindian women and one métis had married Frenchmen (Martin Provost, Laurent Duboct, Jean Durand, Pierre Couc and Elie Dusceau), and nine métis children of these marriages were still living in 1663, making a total of 10 métis including Dusceau's wife – a minute proportion of 0.3% of the population. But since these métis were to have descendants (those of Provost were particularly numerous), it would remain to be calculated what this 0.3% could amount to in the French-speaking population of the twentieth century.

The rest of the population were immigrants. Leaving aside the 607 about whom there is little information (though most must have come from Europe), 1,253 known persons came from France, 1,246 of French birth and 7 of other origin.[7]

Certain French provinces (eight eastern provinces, plus Roussillon on the Mediterranean) were not represented at all among the immigrant population of 1663. A total of 72, including 14 Church men and women, came from sixteen other provinces. Twenty-five provinces, then, had as yet taken little or no part in the St Lawrence venture. Fourteen provinces had provided more than 20 immigrants each, for a total of 1,174 or 93.7% of the non-Canadians in 1663. Six of these fourteen were maritime provinces and five more bordered on maritime provinces; four fifths of the immigrant population came from these eleven provinces. There were two distinct Atlantic regions of origin; one north of the mouth of the Loire, with its Norman and Breton ports, from whence came 56.1% of the im-

Contribution of Paris and the provinces of France to the population of 1663

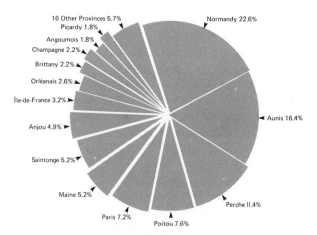

16 Other Provinces 5.7%
Picardy 1.8%
Angoumois 1.8%
Champagne 2.2%
Brittany 2.2%
Orléanais 2.6%
Île-de-France 3.2%
Anjou 4.9%
Saintonge 5.2%
Maine 5.2%
Paris 7.2%
Poitou 7.6%
Perche 11.4%
Aunis 16.4%
Normandy 22.6%

Of the 1,860 inhabitants in June, 1663 who were not born in Canada, we know the provincial origins of 1,253. The chart is based on this second figure.

migrants; the other to the south, with the ports of Aunis, Saintonge and Guyenne, representing 38.9%. It was, then, the provinces more or less directly involved in the sphere of Atlantic activity, particularly those of the north, that contributed most to the immigrant population.[8] By far the most immigrants came from Normandy (282), Aunis (204) and Perche (142). That Normandy and Aunis should head the list is hardly surprising, for both had been in contact with the St Lawrence since the earliest days, and both were maritime by vocation. But why Perche, a little province squeezed between Normandy, Maine and Orléanais, without direct access to the sea and away from the main routes leading to it? Clearly, the importance of any particular province as a source of immigrants depended not only on economic conditions but also on the activities of recruiting agents, particularly those of the Legardeurs and Le Moynes in Normandy, the Giffards and Juchereaus in Perche, and the Society of Notre Dame all the way up the Loire and into Champagne, as well as the recruiting done by the Jesuits in a number of areas.

The order of importance of the provinces in immigration was not the same in all three St Lawrence regions. Normandy came first both for the Quebec region and the colony as a whole, followed by Aunis and Perche; for Trois Rivières, however, Aunis came first, before Normandy and Perche; for Montreal, Normandy was again in first place, but barely, with Anjou second and then Aunis. But to determine the provincial origin for the entire population, we must add back the Canadians by birth, counting

French origins of the population of 1663 by province

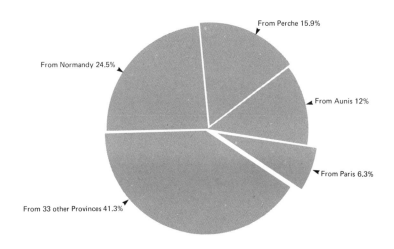

From Perche 15.9%

From Normandy 24.5%

From Aunis 12%

From Paris 6.3%

From 33 other Provinces 41.3%

Of the 3,035 inhabitants in June, 1663, we know the province of origin of 2,428 (immigrants and Canadian-born).

their origin as that of the father. On this basis, of 2,428 people (or four fifths of the population, omitting the 607 of obscure origin) 24.5% were from Normandy by birth or parentage, 15.9% from Perche, 12% from Aunis; 6.3% were of Parisian origin, and the remaining 41.3% were of 33 different origins. Most of the population of 1663, then, originated in Normandy, Perche, Aunis, and Paris, in order of proportional importance. Perche moves to second place here by virtue of the fact that immigrants from that province had more than doubled their number, from 142 to 388, through their birth-rate, far outstripping all others, even those from Normandy. Regionally, this order of provincial origin prevailed only at Quebec, with Normandy first, then Perche, Aunis, and Paris. For Trois Rivières, the order was Normandy, Aunis, Saintonge, and Perche. For Montreal, it was Normandy, Anjou, Aunis, Maine and Paris (equal proportions), and last of all Perche.

People of Norman origin were not only the most numerous among both immigrants and Canadians by birth; they were the most energetic in obtaining land concessions. Normans occupied 24.5% of conceded land, followed by people from Perche with 18.8%. In third place came Canadians by birth, with a considerable drop to 8.3%, though this group held 48.2% of seigneurial land in the hands of individuals. The other provinces that provided high proportions of the immigrant population came far behind; Aunis, second in immigration, was only sixth in land occupation with 5.4%; Poitou, fourth in immigration, was tenth with 3.9%. Brittany, however, which was eleventh in immigration, jumped to fourth in land occupation with 7.4%.

Immigrants from a single province do not seem to have clustered together in any of the seigneuries. Though, for example, Normans settled on the land often had other Normans for immediate neighbours, just as often their immediate neighbours were of other origins. From this point of view the pattern of land settlement was very mixed. It cannot be said that there were pockets of Norman settlement, or pockets of any other origin.

Since systematic settlement only began in 1633, the population was young. The average age, calculated from 84.2% of the male and 96.1% of the female population was only 20.6 years, 22.2 for men and 18.2 for women; it was lowest in the Trois Rivières region, where the average man was 21.7 years old and the average woman a mere adolescent of 16.8 years. Half the population was under twenty! If one could make a pyramid of the known ages one could see at once how the population was constituted from its two sources, with immigration as the more important, followed by births. At its apex there would be only one octogenarian, fifteen septuagenarians, and eight persons between 65 and 69; in its midsection it would bulge with the concentration of immigrants in the 20-44 age group; then it would narrow again at the 15-19 age group, which contained only 173 persons, and widen with the birth-rate toward its broad base of 581 children aged four years and under.

It was a young population and very predominantly a male one. In this country only newly-opened to European settlement it was natural that women should come in large numbers only when the groundwork had been laid. After more than half a century (if one counts from 1608), Canada still had a large surplus of men over women; in June 1663, 62.9% of the total population was male and only 37.1% female, and the proportions were much the same in each of the three regions, except that at Trois Rivières only a third were female.

Men predominated in number in all age groups, including the 20-49 range, that is to say the ages when people are most likely to marry. There was a shortage of women, and particularly women of marriageable age, or twelve and over. Today we find it difficult to envisage marriage at the age of twelve, and yet, at Montreal, 6 out of 74 wives in 1663 had married at twelve, and 11 more at thirteen or fourteen. Marie Pontonier, at eighteen, was already on her third husband! It was customary, in any event, for girls to be sought in marriage as soon as they were twelve. But in 1663, while there was a natural balance between the sexes under the age of puberty, there were twice the number of men of marriageable age (14 years and over) as women.

But the problem was more serious than that, for the proportion of available marriageable women relative to the number of marriageable men was far less. In calculating the number of marriageable women, we must first set aside the 41 women of the religious communities and the 470 who were already married, which leaves 108, or 71 single women and 37 widows.[9] The single women of marriageable age were all very young, the average age being 15.1 years. In the Quebec region there was not one over 24 years; in the Trois Rivières region, twelve of the fourteen single women were under 15 years. Out of the total 71 who were single, all but one were under thirty, and two thirds were under fifteen. For the 37 widows, on the other hand, age or family responsibilities were often very real obstacles to remarriage; eight of them were 60 or over, and the average age of thirty of them was 46.9; more than two thirds of the 37 had child dependents. We might therefore set aside 27 of these widows whose attraction was minimal by virtue either of advanced age or their dependent children. But by all means let us be generous and consider them marriageable. Nevertheless, there were hardly more than a hundred marriageable women, while the marriageable men numbered 769. The civil status of 348 of these men is unknown, but it seems probable that most were single. In any event, it is no exaggeration to state that for every six men in search of wives in 1663, there was only one available woman. The imbalance was particularly serious in the 20-34 age bracket, where there was only one marriageable woman for twenty-four men! Since the balance was more or less normal in children under the age of puberty, the situation would have righted itself in due course, but it is understandable that in the meantime the State should try to hasten the arrival of women in Canada, which it did immediately after 1663.

For all that, there were 957 married people: 470 couples, and 17 men who had come without their wives. The average age of the husband was 37.9, and of the wife 29.9, but, as a reflection of the custom for girls to be sought in marriage as soon as they reached marriageable age, there were 65 wives who were not yet twenty. The youngest wife was 12 years and 9 months old and was married to a man of thirty-one. A considerable disparity indeed; but among couples in 1663, disparity was the general rule. Among 436 couples whose age is known, only in 17 cases were man and wife of the same age. In more than half of all couples, the spread was from one to 10 years, and in a quarter it was from 11 to 15 years. There were also disparities of 20, 25 and even 34 years. The man was of course almost always the older; only 49 couples are known in which the woman was the older.

There was also disparity of origin, in couples. To all appearances, immigrants who married after their arrival in New France did not seek spouses of the same province of origin. In only 79 couples out of 302 (one quarter) had husband and wife come from the same province; in the rest (three quarters), the marital partners had come from neighbouring or distant provinces. Already, too, there had been 72 marriages between immigrants and Canadians by birth. Finally, we know of only 4 couples where both man and wife were Canadians. And so the marriages of this period contributed largely to the fusion of origins that was one of the manifestations of social change in seventeenth-century Canada.

Another disparity in couples was in literacy. We have information on this subject for only 280 couples, but we must make do with what we have. Two thirds of these couples were equal in the sense that both man and wife could sign their names or could not. In the other 99, either only the husband could sign his name (71 couples) or only the wife (28 couples). Illiteracy, then, was more frequent in the wife.

There were a good many remarried persons among the couples of Canada. Of the 940 husbands and wives in June 1663, 101 or 10.8% had been married once or twice before. Remarried women were the more numerous; for 66, this was their second marriage; for 6, their third. When they remarried, half of these 101 persons had dependent children, so that some families were composed of the children of two or even three successive marriages. We know of 39 such families (7.4% of the 525 families) with a total of 228 unmarried children (17.5% of the 1,306 unmarried children).

Children were already impressively numerous. Counting only those under the age of puberty, there were 1,107, more than a third of the population, fairly equally balanced between 615 boys and 492 girls. Counting all children, married or not, there were 1,497, or nearly half the population, an average of 3.2 children per family. Four fifths of the families of Canada had from one to 6 children; 8.4% had 7 or more; ten families had 8, eight had 9, and three had 10; one family had 11 children, another 12, and there was even one family with 13. The last two were families of first and second marriages, but the thirteen children in one family all had the same mother. Little wonder that she should be chosen as the local midwife.

Although this society did not as yet have the kind of structure that makes it easy to classify individuals according to trade or profession, and although in Canada a man's trade or profession was not necessarily his usual occupation, we have attempted to form some picture of this aspect of the society of 1663. Unfortunately, available documentation is enlightening on only 680 men of marriageable age, or about half the total. First there were 37 churchmen: 27 Jesuits (15 of them priests), 2 Sulpician priests, 5 other secular priests, and 3 tonsured clerics. The average age of the Jesuits was high, 47.9 years, compared to 37.8 for the secular clergy. There were few Canadians among these churchmen; one was a *donné* with the Jesuits and three were aspiring secular priests.

The public service, civil and military, comprised only 44 men, or 3.4%

Trades and professions of the male population as of June, 1663

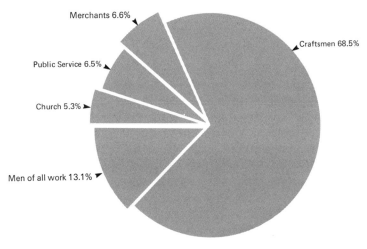

Merchants 6.6%

Craftsmen 68.5%

Public Service 6.5%

Church 5.3%

Men of all work 13.1%

Of the 1,293 adult males, we know the professions of 680.

of all men of marriageable age. This seems very few; one wonders whether the incomplete documentation gives a realistic picture on this score, but the rudimentary nature of the administrative structure is most probably the explanation. Quebec, being the seat of colonial government, was best supplied with public servants, while at Montreal they were practically non-existent, civil, judicial and military authority being concentrated almost entirely in the hands of a single man, the commandant. Well placed, of course, to profit from land distribution, this small number of officials held 11.7% of the seigneurial land granted to individuals as well as 9.2% of conceded land. None of them were Canadians.

There were not only very few public servants, but very few men whose principal occupation was commerce, which is astonishing in a colony whose economy was supposed to be founded on the fur trade: only 45, in fact, or 3.5% of men of marriageable age. They, too, were concentrated in the Quebec region, where alone there were 33 merchants. This small group of men engaged in commerce had only just begun to have a share in seigneurial landholdings; so far, they had 7.4%, which was much less than the percentage held by public servants. Among the 45 merchants, only three were Canadians by birth.

Those who claimed a trade numbered 465, or 36% of men or marriageable age. We distinguish nine categories:

military trades	71
marine trades	32
agriculture	97
health services	17
food trades	39
clothing trades	36
construction trades	125
toolmaking	39
other trades	9

The most numerous were men in construction trades, of whom there were 125, or 26.9% of all those listed; they included 75 carpenters and joiners. In a population like that of the St Lawrence, where three hundred building lots had been conceded over a few years, particularly since 1655, and where settlement on conceded farmland was increasing steadily, it was natural that there should be a good number of men engaged in these trades. Most tradesmen, 53.8%, had no land; five of them (including three master tradesmen) were seigneurs, but together they held only 2% of the seigneurial land. Finally there were 89 of no particular trade, men of all work who had no education, no land, and generally speaking no homes, four fifths of them being unmarried. Among them there were 61 domestics, the most deprived of all.

We have not mentioned women in this context. They were excluded from the public service, had no place in commerce, and were in fact, according to our documentation, almost totally absent from the work force, in which we find only 7 women out of a total of 635 of marriageable age. Apart from two midwives, they were all domestics. Women were best represented in the four religious communities at Quebec and Montreal, where altogether there were 41 women engaged in the education of girls and in hospital care. Among them were 5 Canadians.

In general, then, the population of Canada seems to have been well served spiritually, in education, and in nursing, but the public service was inadequately organized, particularly at Montreal, and there were very few merchants for the size of the population. The largest identifiable group were the tradesmen, and more of these were in the building trades than in any other category. A large number of tradesmen were engaged in. farming, however, and it could even be that 40.4% of all the men claiming trades belonged in fact more to the agricultural classification than to any other.

Was there much illiteracy in the population of 1663? In the religious communities, as one might expect, there was none; the 30 churchmen and 22 churchwomen on whom we have full information all signed their names. Similarly, there was none among the public servants. Among the merchants, none of whom should have been illiterate, there were 4 out of 42 who declared themselves unable to sign their names. In the trades category, 42.6% could not sign their names. This was still less than half, but in the construction trades, where one would think reading and writing were necessary, fully half were illiterate. What is particularly astonishing is that more than a third of the master tradesmen in this category could not sign their names. Two thirds of the men referred to as men of all work were illiterate. However, among the military, four fifths were able to sign their names and it was their literacy that made it possible for so many soldiers to move to administration or to trades and professions where it was essential. In France in the same period, 80% of the population was illiterate, so that one might expect a similar proportion in Canada. It is surprising to say the least, therefore, to find that out of 1,244 people of marriageable age, only 44.3% could not sign their names. Illiteracy was more common among women than men, 53.8 for women and 40.6% for men.

Though more than a third of the population was Canadian born, settlement had not been going on long enough for Canadians to be represented proportionately in all the society's segments studied here. True enough, Canadians held 48.2% of seigneurial lands distributed to individuals and 7.4% of conceded land. Elsewhere their representation was small: 4 out of 37 churchmen and 5 out of 41 churchwomen, no public servants, none among the 109 master tradesmen, only 3 of the 45 merchants and 3 of the tradesmen.

In 1663 the standards of the French social hierarchy were still fresh in the minds of immigrants from France, and these were the standards used by Talon in 1667 and by Frontenac in 1672. According to these standards as applied in Canada, at the top of the social pyramid was the Church with its 78 members or 2.5% of the population, of whom as yet only 8 were Canadian born. The Church held 10.7% of seigneurial land and 4.3% of conceded land. Second in rank were the 96 nobles (women and children included), or 3.2% of the population, slightly more than half of them Canadians. The nobles domiciled in Canada held 70.8% of seigneurial land, or six times the Church holdings and seven and a half times the holdings of the bourgeois class. Among them as among the Church members there was no illiteracy.

At the bottom of the social pyramid was the third estate, comprising 94.3% of the population. Heading this class were the 192 bourgeois, only 4 of whom were Canadian born. They were public servants (including military officers who were not nobles), merchants, seigneurs without rank, and master tradesmen. Eight of these bourgeois had married noblewomen and five bourgeois families had married their daughters to noblemen, which, it was considered, raised them a notch above their kind and a step closer to the nobility. Of these 192 bourgeois, only 41 were engaged in commerce as their principal activity, and more than half were master tradesmen. The bourgeoisie as a whole, then, almost a quarter of whom were illiterate,[10] bore far more the characteristics of tradesmen than of merchants. The bourgeois of Canada held only 9.9% of the seigneurial land in the hands of individuals, but within the seigneuries they held 25% of conceded land. Including women and children, they totalled 796, or 26.3% of the population, compared with 3.2% for the nobility and 2.5% for members of the Church. Finally, on the lowest level of the third estate were the common folk: men with or without a trade and "men of all work," the latter including domestics who were mostly young men in search of a career. These common folk with their families numbered 2,065 or 68% of the population.

It remained to be seen how this theoretical division of society into classes might be reflected in the reality of colonial life; it was not, after all, a social group as such that was transplanted to North America, nor even a regional group from a particular province. In Canada, half way through the seventeenth century, society was undergoing a remarkable realignment in its relationships, and this was to continue until the end of the century. In 1663, here was a population composed largely of immigrants from thirty French provinces; even though half of them had come from three provinces alone, these immigrants had nevertheless come from widely varying places and climates, and they had widely varying attitudes to life. The statistics show that they did not attempt to cluster together according to their places of origin, and that when they married they did not care what provinces their spouses had come from. There was realignment in the professions and trades as well. There were public servants from eleven different provinces who engaged in commerce, were seigneurs, and lived from the land. There were merchants from thirteen provinces who also were seigneurs or farmers, and tradesmen from many provinces who were perhaps more farmers than artisans, even the master tradesmen. There was family realignment through second and third marriages involving a tenth of the 940 husbands and wives, with the result that there were 56 couples out of 470 in which one of the marital partners was not the parent of all of the children, and 17.5% of all unmarried children had brothers and sisters who were the issue of two or even three successive marriages. And finally there was social realignment. This is seen very clearly in the fact that noblemen who were engaged in commerce associated on an equal footing with common folk of the humblest order. Fourteen out of twenty noble couples were formed of a noble and a commoner. It is further seen in the rapid elevation to the nobility of a surgeon (Robert Giffard), a former sailor (Guillaume Couillart), and a man who had once been a domestic, as had Pierre Boucher. Boucher's noble children could talk of "our grandfather the joiner."

A very mixed society, in many ways. It is not even easy to identify it as urban or rural. Since the population seems to have gathered to a large extent in the towns (though we have not been able to determine this with any precision), the tendency is to conclude that it was an urban society. But at Trois Rivières and Montreal in particular, it was the necessity of defence that forced the country people to fall back on the towns. Furthermore, the percentage of full-time merchants was minute, and we know of no important industry, even of the cottage kind, capable of supporting the considerable body of workmen. We do know that almost half the tradesmen had farms and cultivated them, and we have seen that two thirds of the total population was rural-based economically. On the basis of the only demographic data obtainable for 1663, the more valid conclusion is that settlement during the period of the Hundred Associates created an essentially rural society.

New France at the Threshold of a New Era

France in North America was still far from her objectives. According to the plan of the Hundred Associates, New France should have had fifteen thousand inhabitants by 1645, but it had only three hundred. At the planned rate of increase it should have had thirty thousand by 1663, but by that date there were only slightly more than three thousand.

Meanwhile, the other European colonies were continuing to increase their numerical superiority and had already enjoyed twenty years of dynamic expansion. Newfoundland had been at a standstill, it is true, but what spectacular progress had been made in others! New England had been confederated since 1643; with the encouragement of a Puritan Parliament in England and benefiting particularly from the Navigation Act of 1651, it had enjoyed an astonishing degree of political and economic freedom under Cromwell and continued to behave like an independent colony under Charles II. Already sufficiently strong in 1654 to overrun French Acadia, by 1660 it had attained a population of forty thousand. In the Hudson River valley and on the Delaware (where they had taken over New Sweden), the Dutch had a population of ten thousand. Maryland, torn by politico-religious strife, had made little progress, but its neighbour, Virginia, had grown from a population of two thousand to thirty thousand, its parliamentary institutions were established and functioning and its colonists were growing rich on tobacco. These English colonies had already passed the trial stage; they formed a European society successfully transplanted to America. They were self-supporting and rapidly becoming a source of economic strength to the mother country.

In comparison with these ninety thousand inhabitants of the English and the Dutch colonies, what of New France, which had aspired to possession of all the land from Florida to the Pole in 1627, but counted only around three thousand inhabitants in 1663?

New France had even lost some territory. The Acadian peninsula, the oldest part, had been under English rule since 1654. On Cape Breton there were only the few men maintained by Nicolas Denys, and there were a few others at Miscou and Nipisiguit. Apart from the tiny new colony founded in 1662 in Placentia Bay, Newfoundland, only in the St Lawrence should we look for French settlement, and this settlement was centred about three points, Quebec, Trois Rivières and Montreal, each isolated from the others. Attempts to expand outside these points had not succeeded; seigneurs who had begun work in fiefs between Quebec and Trois Rivières, for example, had been forced by the Iroquois to abandon their efforts.[1] Immigration, too, had fallen to a trickle. In 1653 some hundred people had immigrated, all destined for Montreal. Thirty-two *filles à marier* had arrived in 1659, but only another three followed over the next two years. Between 1654 and 1661, there were only two or three hundred immigrants, that is to say, thirty or forty per year. In 1662, however, there was an influx of two hundred colonists and a hundred soldiers.

Sparsely populated as it was, New France had expanded very little geographically. The French now had access to Lac St Jean, since the Indians had seen fit at long last to lift their barriers, and this had become the terminus of the great commercial routes of the interior. The Jesuit de Quen was the first of the French to arrive there, in 1647. In May 1661, the Jesuits Druillettes and Dablon passed beyond through Lac St Jean and reached Lake Nicaubau on the watershed between the St Lawrence and Hudson Bay, but they were obliged to turn back because their guides were afraid of meeting the Iroquois.[2] It was toward the west that the most progress appears to have been made, although the years of greatest activity in that quarter were still to come. No one had yet penetrated beyond the westernmost point reached by Jean Nicollet in 1634-35 in the Lake Michigan area, but exploration about Lake Superior had been greatly advanced. Chouart des Groseilliers and his young brother-in-law Radisson arrived there in 1659; in the course of the winter they explored the south shore as far as Chagouamigon near the western end of the lake, and from there crossed to the north shore, returning to Quebec in 1660.[3] The Jesuit Ménard set out that same year with eight Frenchmen and some Ottawa tribesmen, but he perished in 1661 in Wisconsin. Later it was written that, of all the missionaries, it was he who had come "closest to the Sea of China." The dream of reaching Asia by crossing the continent was still alive; the sea of which three sides (the north, east and south) were known to the Lake Superior Indians could be none other than the Asian Sea, or so it was believed.[4]

In this New France with its hazily-defined political structure, where, for instance, the Governor's Council and the *Conseil de la traite* at times seemed to be one and the same, it was the religious institutions that were already the best organized and also the healthiest financially. True, the missionary effort had fallen off greatly in a few short years; in the wake of the disastrous end of the Huron mission, the Iroquois mission had also foundered, and the missionaries had all returned to their bases in the St Lawrence to concentrate henceforth on the Indians in the immediate area. But what the Church had lost in expansion, it had acquired in depth. The Church in New France was no longer solely dependent on an order of missionaries, and, once the Abbé de Queylus was out of the way, higher religious authority was vested entirely in a Vicar Apostolic who had the personal support of the King. The Vicar Apostolic had designated two Grand Vicars, Father Lalemant, Superior of the Jesuits, and the secular priest Charles de Lauson-Charny. The latter presided over the *Officialité*, though this ecclesiastical tribunal was not yet recognized by the State. The clergy was numerous, considering the size of the population; twenty-two priests, of whom fifteen were Jesuits. One ordination had already taken place, that of Henri de Bernières in 1660, and Monseigneur de Laval was soon recruiting churchmen among Canadians. In 1662, he raised Germain Morin to the rank of sub-deacon and conferred the tonsure and minor orders on Louis Jolliet.[5] The Church's auxiliary services were already established; at Quebec, the Jesuits continued to maintain their college, seventeen Ursulines were attending to the education of girls, and sixteen Hospitalières were running the Hôtel Dieu; at Montreal, there were still only four Hospitalières, and their work was in danger of foundering, for their endowment of 20,000 livres from Madame de Bullion was involved in the seizure of La Dauversière's property. Marguerite Bourgeoys had just begun her work of education with the help of three lay companions, who were bound only by a civil contract; the Sisters of the Congregation of Notre Dame, without vows and "with neither veil nor wimple," did not yet constitute a religious community.[6] Each church was administered by a *Fabrique* or council. The only basic structure missing was the parish, but preparations were under way for its creation.

The fragility of this little colony of barely three thousand inhabitants, so primitive politically compared to its religious development, was tragically apparent; in 1660-61 there was a constant feeling that at any moment everyone might pack up and go back to France. With peace reigning at last in Europe, New France should have been strengthened, but the colony continued to live in the state of siege it had known since 1658. No work could be done outside Montreal and Trois Rivières except in sufficient numbers to afford mutual protection. The last of the Hurons were lying low in their miniature fortress near the Château of Quebec. The peace had disintegrated and the Iroquois were masters not only of the routes leading to the interior of the continent but also those leading directly to the St Lawrence. They prowled at will about Montreal, Trois

Rivières and Quebec. They were found on the Saguenay and around Lac
St Jean, and even half way between Lac St Jean and Hudson Bay the
Montagnais were terrified of meeting them. Rumours of a massive invasion
in the spring of 1660 sowed panic everywhere, even in the upper town
of Quebec. But the army of invasion did not appear; it had been diverted
to the Ottawa River, where seventeen Frenchmen and some Indian allies
under the command of Dollard des Ormeaux had gone to ambush some
Iroquois on their way home from their winter hunt. The invaders from
the Richelieu went to the rescue of their brothers, demolished the French
ambushing party at the Battle of the Long Sault and went home with
their furs and prisoners.[7]

The respite was brief, however, lasting only a few months, and then
panic spread anew through the colony. It began in the winter of 1660-61
with a series of evil omens. At Montreal there was an earthquake; at
Trois Rivières "woeful voices" were heard; at Quebec flaming canoes were
seen flying through the air and a girl was haunted relentlessly by demons;
on the Isle of Orleans, an unborn child cried in its mother's belly; in
February 1661 a comet appeared. Barely had these signs been manifested
when the Iroquois "appeared on all sides, like a raging torrent." If in
1660, writes Father Le Jeune, the Iroquois "made us cry loud enough to
be heard in France, now they leave us only tears to weep for our dead."[8]

And the dead were many. In the spring of 1661 the Iroquois captured
thirteen of the French at Montreal, then ten more shortly after, "then
others still, & still others" through the summer. The people of Trois
Rivières looked on helplessly as "sometimes at the very gate of their town,
now men, now children" were carried off. The sénéchal Lauson went to
the Isle of Orleans to drive out a band of Iroquois; his little troop was
massacred and he himself perished with it. The losses of 1661 were estimated at more than seventy Frenchmen. "This year deserves to be
counted among those of calamity & gloom."[9]

And yet the Iroquois who are sowing such terror were almost entirely
the Mohawks, a minor nation which could raise only five hundred men
capable of bearing arms. But, it was written, they "despise the French,
because they have never seen them at war in their country; & the French
have never gone there because they have never tried, until now believing
the pathways to be more impassable than they are." Two regiments would
have been enough to destroy them, but the French settlers were "more accustomed to wielding the hoe than the sword."[10] New France did not have
the military manpower to take the offensive.

The continual siege since 1658 had disrupted all economic activity.
Except on the Côte de Beaupré, farming in the country had been abandoned. In the spring of 1660 there was an "almost total" shortage of
grain, and it became necessary, the following autumn, to prepare a ship-

ment of food from Rouen to save the colony. As for the fur trade, the very lifeblood of the colony, it had come to a complete standstill. Not a single fleet of canoes had been able to come from the Great Lakes in 1659. The following year, because the Battle of the Long Sault had effectively freed the Ottawa River route, Chouart des Groseilliers and Radisson arrived at Montreal with furs worth 200,000 livres. Before this "benediction from Heaven," wrote Marie de l'Incarnation, there was talk of abandoning the country, "in the belief that there was nothing more to be done for the trade."[11] But then the route from the *pays d'en haut* was immediately closed tight again.

Besides being paralysed by the lack of supply, the business of the fur trade was sorely strained by the price of its goods for barter. The middlemen to whom the Communauté des Habitants sold its furs and from whom it bought its trade goods were "small merchants who, having not a sou to their name," were obliged, because of the "credit advanced to them," to pay stiff prices in France for their merchandise. Their resale prices in New France were necessarily stiffer still. Then, on their return to France, these small merchants would sacrifice their beaver to satisfy the demands of their La Rochelle creditors. Owing to the depressed condition of the French market for furs, other merchants in a position to engage in the trade had little taste for doing so. Governor d'Argenson, whose responsibility it was to give effect to the edict of March 7, 1657 stipulating the conditions of the fur trade, judged that, besides forbidding "all *habitans* to trade individually" (from which the cultivation of the land should benefit), it would be necessary to give the Communauté the monopoly of goods for barter and to fix the prices of such goods in advance. He proposed that "a special treaty" be concluded "with a company of merchants who would traffic in this country exclusively of all others." Thus, instead of relying on small, destitute individual merchants, the Communauté would be doing business with a firmly-based company which could buy trade goods at the most advantageous prices, and "the beaver, being all in strong hands" would no longer be "so highly subject to price reductions" in France.[12] This represented a return to the situation existing before 1627. It was only in 1660 that these "strong hands" were brought to the scene, when the Communauté concluded a commercial contract with the Guenet company of Rouen. This contract, signed on February 5 on behalf of the Communauté by René Robineau de Bécancour, guaranteed the Norman company the exclusive right to transport trade goods and food to New France, as well as the monopoly of the trade in beaver. The company undertook in return to pay 60,000 livres per year to the Communauté, which was still responsible for the administrative expenses of the country. The large quantity of furs brought in by des Groseilliers and Radisson in 1660 was indeed profitable to the company, but the following year the trade was once again of little consequence. In November of that second year, moreover, the *Conseil de la traite* broke the contract and designated a new monopolist, Nicolas Juchereau de Saint-Denys, with far less advantageous conditions for the Communauté. This, in short, created a situation much the same as that denounced by d'Argenson. The great fur-trade routes remained blocked in any event.[13]

The Communauté was encountering determined opposition, moreover, as demonstrated by a serious incident in July 1662. The Communauté had decided to establish a warehouse at Montreal, since it alone, in principle, could sell trade goods and purchase the beaver whose export was reserved to Juchereau de Saint-Denys. But the Montrealists raised a vehement outcry against the warehouse, holding tenaciously by their autonomy and invoking the ownership of the island by the Society of Notre Dame. The Jesuit *Journal* goes so far as to use the word "sedition" in reporting this opposition. The merchant Jacques Le Ber was arrested as an accessory to the affair and "his property" was seized. Maisonneuve came to Quebec and prepared to sail for France. Governor Davaugour, all too eager, perhaps, to seize the opportunity of asserting his authority over Montreal, ordered him to give up his planned voyage and return to Montreal to prepare for an inquiry.[14]

This, too, was a period of bitter controversy between the Communauté and the people in general on the one hand and the representative of the Hundred Associates on the other. The business of the Communauté having gone from bad to worse, the Hundred Associates decided that they must hold an inquiry. In 1660 they sent to Quebec from the *Parlement* of Paris an advocate, Jean Peronne Dumesnil, who was vested with the titles of Controller-General, Intendant and Supreme Judge, and who conducted the inquiry with an uncompromising diligence that affronted one and all; soon antagonism to the inquiry was verging on violence. Late in August 1661, Peronne Dumesnil's son was killed during a quarrel. Governor Davaugour, who had just assumed office on presentation by the Hundred Associates, forbade the continuance of the investigation, but Peronne Dumesnil would agree neither to suspend his inquiry nor to temper his severity. In 1662 he was refused access to the Communauté's papers, but he obtained them anyway by forced entry. He continued to do battle with the country's highest authorities until his departure in October 1663. In his report, he accused the Communauté of having misappropriated some three million livres since 1645, and laid the blame upon the Governors, the Bishop, the Jesuits and all those engaged in administration. The inconsistencies of the report were pointed out to Colbert by the royal commissioner Gaudais-Dupont, who went on to explain that, if there were indeed accusations to be brought against the directors of the Communauté, it was for incompetence rather than dishonesty.[15]

This tempest raged for three years, and would alone have been sufficient to perturb the whole colony. But there were other more or less serious quarrels going on at the same time, quarrels within the Church and quarrels between the Church and the State.

Of the internal troubles besetting the Church, some were of little consequence for the outside world. The Hospitalières of Montreal and the Ursulines of Quebec, for example, found themselves at loggerheads with Monseigneur de Laval. Jeanne Mance, a laywoman, had not been able to run the hospital at Montreal alone, but had been offended when the Abbé de Queylus moved to send some Hospitalières from Quebec, and had obtained three Hospitalières from the Institut St Joseph that La Dauversière had founded in 1636.[16] When they arrived in September 1659, Laval ordered them to be attached to the Hôtel Dieu of Quebec, even to submitting to its rules. Jeanne Mance objected to the Bishop's interference in the work of La Dauversière. Finally, in October, Laval authorized the Hospitalières of St Joseph to leave for Montreal, but imposed two harsh conditions on them; they were not to live "in community, in accordance with canonical custom" and they would not be permitted to take in Canadian novices, which prompted Dollier de Casson to write that these nuns were mistaken if, having completed their ocean crossing, they thought they had seen the last of storms; "so great a one did they encounter here, that they could hardly set foot on dry land."[17]

The differences between Laval and the Ursulines of Quebec produced an upheaval no less serious. Laval's first intervention decreed that the mistress of novices should henceforth be elected, which was surprising "in the extreme," wrote Marie de l'Incarnation, adding, "we protested with vigour," but the Bishop "would not hear us." Nor did he stop there; he took it upon himself to modify the rules of the community, cutting out some, adding some, altering others and, complained the Mother Superior, ruining "effectively" the established order. The nuns resisted. "He has given us eight months or a year to think on it, [but] we have already thought on the affair and our decision is already made: we will not accept, unless it be at the extremity of obedience. Nevertheless, so as not to worsen matters, we shall say not a word; for we have to deal with a Prelate who, being a man of very great piety, when once he is persuaded that he is proceeding for the glory of God, will never turn back."[18]

According to Marie de l'Incarnation, Monseigneur de Laval was "most zealous and inflexible." His inflexibility over what he considered to be the glory of God was to make itself felt on the public scene; from 1660 to 1663, his dispute with the Abbé de Queylus and his heavy-handedness in his dealings with the civil authorities shook the little St Lawrence colony more resoundingly than all else .

The Abbé de Queylus, who had been named Grand Vicar by the Archbishop of Rouen but had then been obliged to bow to Laval's authority, repaired to France to argue his cause. In February 1660, however, Laval, in order to head off a schism, obtained *lettres de cachet,* orders issued under the King's personal seal, forbidding de Queylus to return to Canada. With the support of the Society of Notre Dame, the Sulpician secured papal bulls in his favour creating a parish at Ville Marie, which in a sense confirmed the jurisdictional claims of the Archbishop of Rouen. Then, despite the King's order, de Queylus reappeared at Quebec on August 3, 1661, to the surprise and displeasure of the Bishop, who forbade him by letter to leave Quebec and twice requested Governor d'Argenson to bring the weight of his authority to bear. D'Argenson was preparing his own departure and hesitated to intervene. For the third time Laval asked him to enforce the King's order, and at the same time warned de Queylus that he would be suspended *ipso facto* from his sacerdotal functions should he continue his journey. De Queylus slipped away to Montreal anyway, but another *lettre de cachet* and the intervention of the new governor, Davaugour, obliged him to re-embark for France before the year was out. Still worried over the possible outcome of the affair, Laval pursued his adversary as far as Rome itself. He was fearful, he wrote to the Pope, lest de Queylus, "employing new stratagems, & falsely representing our affairs," should obtain new powers. He accused the Sulpicians of Montreal of not showing sufficient devotion "toward the Apostolic See" and of being "moved with the same spirit of disobedience & division" as the Abbé de Queylus. He expressed apprehension, finally, that the intervention of the Archbishop of Rouen in the parish of Ville Marie might raise "altar against altar in our Church of Canada."[19]

In his conflict with the State, it was once again Monseigneur de Laval who had the last word.

On his arrival in 1659, he had found that the Jesuits had little by little acquired a prodigious degree of political power over the twenty-five years of their exclusive ministry, to the benefit of the Church in general. This power had been trimmed briefly during the time of D'Ailleboust, but regained its full force after the arrival of the Vicar Apostolic, the Jesuits' protégé. It was trimmed once again by Governor d'Argenson, but came to the fore stronger than ever in the autumn of 1661 when Governor Davaugour assumed office, for the Jesuit Ragueneau, who had been removed from the public scene in 1656 (in response to the complaints of his own confrères), was placed by Davaugour himself at the head of a "General Council," where he deliberated daily on public affairs with three other notables. He played the same important role on the *Conseil de la traite.* He was, moreover, the one man in whom Laval placed his entire confidence. No other Jesuit in Canada was ever to exert so decisive an influence in the administration of the colony. We need only recall that, from May 1661, Laval, too, had a vote on the Council of Quebec to realize what power the Church wielded in the affairs of New France,[20] a power that crushed at least two governors, d'Argenson and Davaugour.

D'Argenson, whose attitude had hardly ingratiated him with Laval in 1659, complained the following year that the Bishop was encroaching "on the power of others with such ardour that he listens to no one." A number of these disagreements were quarrels over precedence. Today the points at issue may appear quite absurd, but in those days the very structure of a society founded upon recognition of and respect for the established hierarchy was at stake. In 1660, d'Argenson had taken pains to consult the Company of the Hundred Associates on the question of precedence, but by the time he received a reply the Bishop had already had time to make his own arrangements. In November 1660, he decided that the Governor should no longer have the rank of honorary church-warden. The Governor was enraged; he refused to allow himself to be belittled, and "disrespectful" words were uttered with regard to Mon-seigneur de Laval. Then, early in 1661, d'Argenson insisted that his party have precedence over the churchwardens; the Bishop promptly suspended all processions. About the same time, the case of a Huguenot gave rise to "a great turmoil between the powers; a cataclysm was thought to be at hand." Standing firm on the authority of the *Officialité* that he had established, Laval passed judgement on Daniel Vuil as "a relapsed heretic, blasphemer & profaner of the Sacraments." The ecclesiastical tribunal was not yet recognized by the State, however, and an altercation ensued between the Governor and the Bishop, both claiming jurisdiction over the guilty man. In the end Laval had his way. D'Argenson, wearied and disgusted by these interminable fights, disappointed too at not having received the troops he had requested for the defence of the colony, asked to be recalled in 1661, pleading ill health; Laval had in fact already taken steps to have him removed as Governor. Father Ragueneau, who accused d'Argenson of having always been "iniquior" (too unjust) toward the Bishop and the Jesuits, announced his departure as though he were giving tidings of a victory.[21]

The Baron Dubois Davaugour was similarly disposed of in his turn. A high-ranking nobleman known for his brilliant military career, and accustomed to command, Davaugour was, according to Colbert, of "some-what bizarre and intractable character." When he arrived with a hundred soldiers, he soon sized up the colony's situation with his practised soldier's eye. He expressed astonishment that d'Argenson had been able to resist the Iroquois with the ridiculously insufficient forces at his command, and declared that he would go back to France the following year even without being recalled unless he were sent the troops that had been promised.[22] The first months of his administration brought joy to the hearts of Laval and the Jesuits, the latter because Father Ragueneau, as we have seen, was placed at the head of the Council of New France, and Laval because the new governor lent his energetic support to the campaign against alcohol.

The trading of spirits to the Indians had given rise to terrible and continual disorders since the very beginning of the colony, but the multitude of interdictions published since the days of Champlain and Montmagny served only to prove the extent and permanence of the evil. An attempt at supervising the trade in 1657 had not resulted in any improvement. It was the Abbé de Queylus, acting in his capacity as Grand Vicar of the colony, who, on March 31, 1658, had been the first to declare the sale of spirits to the Indians a "mortal sin." Considering this insufficient, Laval decreed excommunication for anyone committing such an act, and on April 18, 1661, he named and excommunicated a man for the first time on these grounds. D'Argenson had been more tolerant, and had only half-heartedly supported the Bishop's interdictions, but Davaugour had no sooner applied the final, secular push in expelling de Queylus upon taking office than he turned, in all his military severity, against the vendors of alcohol. The Huguenot Vuil, caught red-handed selling spirits to the Indians, was "arquebused" in October 1661 on the Governor's order. A man named Laviolette was also shot, and another vendor was whipped. But suddenly everything changed. Father Lalemant attempted to intercede in favour of a woman found guilty of the same crime, and Davaugour decided that, if it were not to be a crime for her, it should not be for anyone. In January 1662, he authorized the sale of liquor for all, which, naturally, caused "a great stir." During the "extraordinary troubles & disorders" which followed, Laval reimposed the penalty of excommunication, having relaxed it briefly. He renewed it in April to include all those responsible for drunkenness among the Indians. The traders, however, scoffed at this, supported as they were "by a secular power which has the stronger hand." The Jesuits were dragged into the quarrel; Father Ragueneau was removed from the Council, and the Jesuit *Journal* notes reprovingly, in April, "This month there has been a change of Council," the Governor "having by his authority set down those who were its members, & installed ten others, 5. to 5. for each four months of the year, the syndics also being set down, & several other new things established."[23]

The little colony, already suffering from administrative instability, religious strife, military and commercial insecurity and shortage of supply, was convulsed and terrorized by these events. Throughout, particularly from 1661 to 1663, appeals were made repeatedly to France. In 1661, Governor Davaugour requested three hundred soldiers for the protection of the country and twelve hundred colonists to assure its establishment, addressing himself to the Prince de Condé, whose father had been Viceroy of New France and who appears to have been playing an important role in France since the death of Mazarin. The Jesuit Ragueneau, who was then still on good terms with the Governor, also wrote to Condé, his former pupil, asking him for a regiment which could be sent to attack the Iroquois by the most direct route, the Hudson River. To make sure that these requests should not fall on deaf ears, Davaugour sent Pierre Boucher, Governor of Trois Rivières, to France. Boucher went to the King and requested help, assuring him that it would be possible "to make in this country a greater and more beautiful kingdom [even] than the Kingdom of France." Father Le Jeune, for his part, declared in his introduction to the *Relation* published early in 1662 that hitherto the Queen Mother had been able to do no more than prevent "the entire ruin of New France"; insisting that the loss of the colony would be prejudicial to the Kingdom, he begged the new King to save "the Fleurs de Lys."[24]

And yet in 1662 there were genuine hopes of an improvement. True, Montreal was still enduring savage attacks in which a number of men perished, including Major Closse, and the Iroquois had begun to carry their incursions into the land of the Mistassins with the intention of reaching Hudson Bay, so that "the source of Beaver should be stanched by the loss of those who transport it to our *habitans*." The Iroquois, however, were diverted from their massive attacks by the wars they were waging on other fronts, in New England against the Abenakis, to the south against the Andastes, to the west against the Sioux, and also on the Great Lakes. They were no longer enjoying their customary success; they were defeated by the Andastes to the south and on Lake Huron by the Saulteurs. They were aware, too, that the French colony was awaiting the arrival of strong reinforcements. Furthermore, as it was later discovered, "sickness, famine & war were greatly depleting their ranks, & led them to fear that they themselves were on the point of desolation." They therefore turned to the French for a reconciliation. The Jesuit Le Moyne, a man of uncommon courage, went to spend the winter of 1661-62 among the Onondagas under the protection of Garakontié; in August 1662 he returned to Montreal, bringing with him eighteen Frenchmen released from captivity. The only real adversaries to be won over now were the Oneidas and the Mohawks, but they were also the most shrewd and devious. In any event, the Iroquois prepared "a distinguished Embassy to come to us with handsome gifts, to invite us to go anew to inhabit their lands."[25] Hopes were raised even higher in the autumn when Pierre Boucher returned. The King had promised a regiment for the following year, and in the meantime New France was to receive a hundred soldiers and two hundred colonists. A royal commissioner, de Monts, arrived with Boucher to look into the situation in the country. On the way, de Monts had stopped at Newfoundland to take possession of Placentia Bay, and had left some thirty colonists and a priest there under the command of Nicolas Gayot, who had been made seigneur of the bay. Upon his arrival in Quebec, de Monts made a rapid examination of the state of affairs and re-embarked on November 3 to report to the King.[26]

But all this was of little consequence, for what New France needed urgently was something close to a complete reconstruction. Bitterly disappointed over the state of his relations with Davaugour, to the point where he was seen, as Marie de l'Incarnation wrote, "to wither where he stood," Monseigneur de Laval did not wait for Boucher's return, but took ship on August 12, 1662, accompanied by the Jesuit Ragueneau; the Governor's secretary hastened to do likewise, in order to defend his superior against these two "powers."[27]

As a result of this succession of appeals issuing from the colony, and particularly the new colonial policy adopted by the young Louis XIV and his minister Colbert, New France was at last to have its reorganization. On his return, Laval was able to announce that he had obtained everything he had asked of the King.[28] The reorganization would be sweeping, and would touch every aspect of the colony's existence.

The Hundred Associates turned over their immense seigneury to the King, having perceived that they were in danger of losing it in any case. The wastefully enormous fiefs granted by the Company were abolished and the seigneurial territory was reunified under the Crown. The Island of Montreal, until then the autonomous fief of the Society of Notre Dame, became the property of the Sulpicians and was integrated into the general administration. Even seigneurial justice ceased to function for a time.[29] The seigneury of the Hundred Associates, once reunited to the King's domain, was raised to the rank of province,[30] and was given a dual government similar to that of certain provinces in France, a governor as the military authority and an intendant as the civil authority. A Sovereign Council was created to serve as court of first instance, legislative council and court of appeal. Quebec officially became a city, with a mayor and aldermen.[31] For the reinforcement of the colony, preparations were made to send a regiment and, to assure its growth, the State launched a well-ordered policy of settlement; to restore the vitality of its trade, steps were taken with a view to creating a powerful commercial organization, the *Compagnie des Indes occidentales* (West Indies Company).

The Church, having played a major role in obtaining this reform, now took advantage of it to strengthen its own framework and consolidate its political power. Laval, having destroyed his second governor, returned triumphant with a new governor of his own choice. Politically, the Vicar Apostolic became the official equal of the Governor, since the two were joint heads of the Sovereign Council, whose members they chose by agreement between them. The King had moreover resolved to request that Rome raise the apostolic vicariate to a bishopric, and the revenues of the Benedictine Abbey of Maubec were granted to the future secular bishop for his maintenance. Monseigneur de Laval founded the Quebec Seminary for the recruitment, training and support of the clergy, made additions to his *Officialité*, and established tithing.[32]

This reform of 1663 did not solve all problems for all time. Though the Bishop agreed to lift his excommunication of those found guilty of trading in alcohol, the alcohol trade remained a cause of friction between Church and State. Rivalry between the "powers," too, was to be as bitter as before, whether between the politically powerful Bishop and the Governor, albeit he was the Bishop's choice, or between the Governor and the Intendant.

Nevertheless, with these sweeping reforms the colony of New France suddenly emerged from the formless and stagnant condition to which it had appeared doomed forever. In 1663 it finally crossed the threshold of the new era that had been planned for it since 1627.

ABBREVIATIONS

A.A.Q.: Archives de l'Archevêché de Québec.
A.N.: Archives nationales de France.
A.S.Q.: Archives du Séminaire de Québec.
B.N.: Bibliothèque nationale de France.
B.R.H.: *Bulletin des recherches historiques.*
C.H.R.: *Canadian Historical Review.*
J.R.: *The Jesuit Relations,* Thwaites edition.
P.A.C.: Public Archives of Canada.
P.A.C.R.: *Annual Report of the Public Archives of Canada.*
R.A.P.Q.: *Rapport de l'Archiviste de la Province de Québec.*
R.H.A.F.: *Revue d'histoire de l'Amérique française.*
T.R.S.C.: *Transactions of the Royal Society of Canada.*

1. Pierre Jeannin, *Les marchands au XVIe siècle* (Paris, 1957), pp. 30, 103.
2. Verrazano's account of his voyage, in *Les Français en Amérique*, ed. Charles-André Julien (Paris, 1946; Vol. I of the 2nd series, *Classiques de la colonisation*, in the collection *Colonies et empires*), pp. 53, 72-74.
3. The text cited by the author is the French version translated from the Italian by René Herval and annotated by him and by Ch.-A. Julien, in *Les Français en Amérique*, pp. 51-76. The Italian text is that of the Cellere manuscript discovered in 1909. It would appear that Verrazano had a number of copies of his account made for friends, but the original addressed to the King of France (and probably written in Latin) has not yet been found.
4. This original route was not followed again until 1562, by Ribault, and then in 1602 by Gosnold, who had acquired a copy of Verrazano's account.
5. *Les Français en Amérique*, pp. 54-55.
6. *Ibid.*, p. 59, Verrazano's Note A.
7. *Ibid.*
8. See Maggiolo's map (1527), which shows the Mare Indicum to the north of Florida, separated from the Atlantic by a narrow isthmus; also the map by Verrazano's brother (1529), which represents the Asian Sea in similar fashion and on which an inscription states that this isthmus is only 6 miles wide.
9. *Les Français en Amérique*, p. 61, Verrazano's Note A.
10. *Ibid.*, pp. 62-63, Verrazano's Note A and editor's notes.
11. *Ibid.* pp. 64-70.
12. *Ibid.*, pp. 70-71.
13. *Ibid.*, p. 75.

14. *Ibid.*, p. 71.
15. *Ibid.*, pp. 65, 69-70.
16. Cited by Ch.-A. Julien in *Les voyages de découverte et les premiers établissements* (Paris, 1948), p. 87, n. 1.
17. *Les Français en Amérique*, p. 73.
18. "Manuscript map, 24 x $71\frac{1}{4}$, composed of two large sheets of vellum, highly coloured, in the Biblioteca Ambrosiana, Milan" (*Sixteenth-century Maps relating to Canada* [Ottawa, 1956], p. 45). See also W. F. Ganong, "Crucial Maps in the Early Cartography and Place-Nomenclature of the Atlantic Coast of Canada" (a series of 9 studies, since republished in one volume by T. E. Layng), III, *T.R.S.C.*, 1931, Sec. II, p. 192; and Bernard G. Hoffman, *Cabot to Cartier* (Toronto, 1961), pp. 122-25.
19. "Large manuscript map of the world, 51 x $102\frac{1}{4}$ inches, in the Biblioteca Vaticana, Rome" (*Sixteenth-Century Maps*, pp. 48-49); see also the Ganong and Hoffman studies cited above.
20. Probably in July, since Verrazano dated his account July 8, and signed it on board the *Dauphine*.
21. On this English voyage of 1527, see *The Precursors of Jacques Cartier, 1497-1534*, ed. H. P. Biggar (Ottawa, 1911), pp. xxix-xxxi, J. Winsor, *Narrative and Critical History of America* (Boston and New York, 1889, 8 vols.), III, 170, 185-86; Ganong, "Crucial Maps, V," *T.R.S.C.*, 1933, Sec. II, pp. 152-53. Hoffman has shown in a recent study that the English ship that went to the West Indies has not yet been identified beyond question, although some historians have taken it to be the *Mary Guildford*. It is therefore still hazardous to

state that John Rut made the voyage from Newfoundland to the West Indies; this voyage may have been made by the other ship. (*Cabot to Cartier*, pp. 117-21.) Nothing remains of this English expedition of 1527 in cartography, except perhaps the Cap de Pratto mentioned by Cartier in 1534.

22. "Jean de Silveira au roi du Portugal," 24 Dec. 1527, in Eugène Guénin, *Ango et ses pilotes* (Paris, 1901), p. 80.

23. *Les Français en Amérique*, p. 76, n. 2.

24. These names appear on a map by Gastaldi about 1550, then on a map by Ruscelli in 1561. The maps are in J. G. Kohl, *A History of the Discovery of Maine*

(Portland, 1869; Vol. I of *Documentary History of the State of Maine*), pp. 226, 233.

25. Map of 1566 by Zaltieri, in M. Trudel, *Atlas historique du Canada français, des des origines à 1867* (Quebec, 1961), map 22.

26. André Thevet, *Cosmographie universelle:* see Ganong, "Crucial Maps, VIII, *T.R.S.C.*, 1936, Sec. II, p. 128; see the Porcacchi map of 1572, in Winsor, *op. cit.*, III, 453.

27. In this period there were already the names Shubenacadie, Tracadie and Passamaquoddy; the resemblance was clearly coincidental, but their existence may explain the ease with which the name Acadie spread over such a large area.

NOTES TO CHAPTER TWO

1. "Extrait de la généalogie de la maison Le Veneur, par le président Hénault," *Nova Francia*, VI (1931), 340-43. President Hénault's work was done in 1723 from the Le Veneur family archives.

2. *Ibid.*, 342.

3. For the period prior to 1532, see documents reproduced in Joüon des Longrais, *Jacques Cartier: Documents nouveaux* (Paris, 1888), pp. 1-17; *A Collection of Documents relating to Jacques Cartier and the Sieur de Roberval*, ed. H. P. Biggar (Ottawa, 1930), pp. 1-35 *passim*.

4. Order from the King, 18 March 1534, in *Coll. of Docs.*, p. 42

5. The names of the ships are not stated in any document. The sailing list has not been found, and the account of the first voyage mentions only Cartier by name; the St Malo pilot is therefore the only member of the expedition whose identity is known to us.

6. Account of Cartier's first voyage, in *Les Français en Amérique*, pp. 79-80. The text cited (pp. 79-112) is that edited by Th. Beauchesne, who has profited from the learned works of Biggar, Ganong, and others. On the various editions of this account and on the authorship of the accounts of the three voyages, see Marcel

Trudel, *Les vaines tentatives*, pp. xvii and 72-73 (n. 25).

7. Order of 19 March 1534, in *Coll. of Docs.*, pp. 43-44.

8. Account cited, pp. 84-85.

9. *Ibid.*, pp. 85-87. For identification of historical with modern place-names, see the commentaries of the editor Beauchesne, those of H. P. Biggar in *The Voyages of Jacques Cartier* (Ottawa, 1924), pp. 1-81, and also the following studies: Ganong, "The Cartography of the Gulf of St. Lawrence, from Cartier to Champlain," *T.R.S.C.*, 1889, Sec. II, pp. 17-58; "Jacques Cartier's First Voyage," *T.R.S.C.*, 1887, Sec. II, pp. 121-36; "Crucial Maps, VI," *T.R.S.C.*, 1934, Sec. II, pp. 149-294; "Crucial Maps, VII," *T.R.S.C.*, 1935, Sec. II, 101-129; H. F. Lewis, "Notes on Some Details of the Explorations by Jacques Cartier in the Gulf of St Lawrence," *T.R.S.C.*, 1934, Sec. II, pp. 117-48.

10. Account cited, pp. 87-88.

11. *Ibid.*, p. 88-91.

12. *Ibid.*, p. 92.

13. *Ibid.* The name Brion has survived to this day; the island was named in honour of Philippe de Chabot, Seigneur de Brion, who became Admiral of France in 1525.

According to Ganong, Cartier may have raised a cross on this island, which was known for a time as Cross Island ("Crucial Maps, VI," *T.R.S.C.*, 1934, Sec. II, p. 185).

14. Account cited, pp. 93-99. Cap d'Espérance was the northern point of Miscou Island; the "conche sainct Martin" is today the harbour of Port Daniel.

15. *Ibid.*, pp. 99-104. The first map to mention the name Gaspé is Levasseur's of 1601. Gaspé Bay was not given a name in 1534, and from 1535 the Gaspé region was called Honguedo.

16. Jacques Rousseau, "Ces gens qu'on dit sauvages," in *Les Cahiers des Dix*, XXIII (1958), 71; W. D. Lighthall, "Hochelagans and Mohawks; A Link in Iroquois History," *T.R.S.C.*, 1899, Sec. II, pp. 199-211.

17. Account cited, pp. 104-112.

18. Commission of 30 Oct. 1534 and Order of the King, 30 March 1535, in *Coll. of Docs.*, pp. 44-45 and 53; *Les Français en Amérique*, p. 119.

19. *Coll. of Docs.*, pp. 45, 53.

20. Account of Cartier's second voyage, in *Les Français en Amérique*, pp. 118-24. "Canada," according to Cartier, meant "town" in the language of the Laurentian Indians. The name at first applied to the small region of Quebec, but it very soon came to have a much broader application. The Iroquois village at Stadacona held its place in the popular traditions of the St Lawrence for many years, for Sagard states that a site on Cape Diamond still bore the name "Fort des Iroquois" in his day.

21. Account cited, pp. 124-35.

22. See A. G. Bailey, "The Significance of the Identity and Disappearance of the Laurentian Iroquois," *T.R.S.C.*, 1933, Sec. II, pp. 97-108.

23. Account cited, pp. 136-44, 148. Beaugrand-Champagne maintained that, in order to reach Hochelaga, Cartier left the St. Lawrence and took to the Rivière des Prairies, on the opposite side of the Island of Montreal ("Le chemin d'Hochelaga," *T.R.S.C.*, 1923, Sec. I, pp. 17-24); Gustave Lanctôt, for his part, has demonstrated that Cartier continued up the St. Lawrence ("L'itinéraire de Cartier à Hochelaga," *T.R.S.C.*, 1930, Sec. I, pp. 115-41). Beaugrand-Champagne's theory has been revived recently by Lucien Campeau s.j. ("Sur les pas de Cartier et de Champlain," in *Cahiers de l'Académie canadienne-française*, 8, pp. 29-33). See also E. Achard, *Le chemin de Jacques Cartier vers la bourgade d'Hochelaga* (Montreal, 1969).

24. Account cited, pp. 144-53.

25. *Ibid.*, p. 154. The fort was where the stream called the Lairet joined the St Charles River from the north; according to Silvio Dumas, who has done some excavation at the site, it was on the west bank of the Lairet. In 1608 there were still "some vestiges, such as a fireplace" and "some great pieces of squared timber, worm-eaten, and some 3 or 4 cannon balls." (H. P. Biggar, ed., *The Works of Samuel de Champlain*, II, 36-37.)

26. Account cited, pp. 154-56, 160-62.

27. *Ibid.*, pp. 170-71.

28. Jean and M.-L. Dufrenoy and Jacques Rousseau, *Les plantes antiscorbutiques*, reprint from the *Revue horticole*, Jan.-Feb. 1954. (3 pp.).

29. Account cited, pp. 168-72.

30. Jacques Rousseau has shown that the *annedda* was the *thuya occidentalis* or white cedar: "L'annedda et l'arbre de vie," *R.H.A.F.* VIII, 2 (Sept. 1954), pp. 171-201; see also *Jacques Cartier et "la grosse maladie"* (Montréal, XIXe congrès international de Physiologie, 1953), which includes a study by Rousseau, "Le mystère de l'Annedda," pp. 105-116 (followed by an English translation); and Dufrenoy and Rousseau, *Les plantes antiscorbutiques*.

31. Account cited, pp. 157-59.

32. *Ibid.*, pp. 173-79.

33. *Ibid.*, pp. 174, 176, 180-83.

NOTES TO CHAPTER THREE

1. Account of Cartier's third voyage (the Hakluyt text) in H. P. Biggar, *The Voyages of Jacques Cartier*, p. 249, and the French version of this text in *Les Français en Amérique pendant la première moitié du XVIe siècle*, p. 187; documents in Biggar, *A Collection of Documents relating to Cartier and Roberval*, pp. 66-67 (gift of the *Hermine*), 75-81.

2. Orders of 14 and 22 Sept. 1538, in *Coll. of Docs.*, pp. 69-70.

3. Commission of 17 Oct. 1540, *ibid.*, pp. 128-31.

4. See Robert de Roquebrune, "Roberval, sa généalogie," *R.H.A.F.*, IX, 2 (Sept. 1955), pp. 157-75.

5. Commission of 15 Jan. 1541, in *Coll. of Docs.*, pp. 178-85.

6. Haro to Charles V, 28 Sept. 1541, *ibid.*, pp. 378-80.

7. Preamble to the project of 1538 (a preamble that was added afterwards), *ibid.*, p. 70.

8. Cartier's commission, 17 Oct. 1540, *ibid.*, pp. 128-29.

9. Roberval's commission, 15 Jan. 1541., *ibid.*, p. 178; orders of 7 and 18 Feb. 1541, *ibid.*, pp. 200, 207-9.

10. Charles V to his ambassador in Portugal, undated letter written in the autumn of 1540, *ibid.*, pp. 108-9.

11. The Spanish ambassador in France to Charles V, 27 Dec. 1540, *ibid.*, pp. 169-71.

12. *Ibid.*, p. 170; Cardinal of Toledo to Charles V, 27 Jan. 1541, *ibid.*, p. 190.

13. Marquis de Aguilar to Charles V, 17 April 1541, *ibid.*, pp. 270-71.

14. The Spanish ambassador in France to Charles V, 3 Nov. 1541, *ibid.*, pp. 403-5; Sarmiento to Los Cobos, 22 Jan. 1542, *ibid.*, pp. 432-33.

15. Statement of Cartier's account, *ibid.*, pp. 480-84; report of a Spanish spy, April 1541, *ibid.*, 278; Cartier's third voyage, in Biggar, *Voyages*, p. 251.

16. Roberval's commission, 15 Jan. 1541, in *Coll. of Docs.*, pp. 181-83.

17. Order to Roberval, 7 Feb. 1541, *ibid.*,

pp. 199-202; decree of the Parlement of Rouen, 9 March 1541, *ibid.*, p. 227.

18. Cartier's third voyage, in Biggar, *Voyages*, pp. 250-51; will dated 19 May 1541, in *Coll. of Docs.*, pp. 292-94; see also *ibid.*, p. 394, n. 1; pp. 480-84.

19. Santiago's report, *ibid.*, pp. 378-80. The observers all gave different totals.

20. *Coll. of Docs.*, pp. 193-94, 225, 394, 442; Biggar, *Voyages*, pp. 253, 256; E. de Cathelineau, "Quel jour Cartier rentra-t-il de son troisième voyage?", *Nova Francia*, V (1930), 97-99; Wallop to Henry VIII, 26 Jan. 1541, in *Coll. of Docs.*, p. 188.

21. Cartier's third voyage, in Biggar, *Voyages*, p. 251.

22. *Ibid.*, 251-52.

23. *Ibid.*, pp. 252-55; *Coll. of Docs.*, pp. 394 and n. 1, 480-84; letter from Nantes to the Portuguese ambassador in France, 12 Nov. 1541, *ibid.*, p. 407.

24. Cartier's third voyage, in Biggar, *Voyages*, pp. 256-59.

25. Where the *annedda* is mentioned in the narrative, we read that it "hath the most excellent vertue of all the trees of the world, whereof I will make mention hereafter" (*ibid.*, p. 254), but the portion of the narrative in which this was to be done (*i.e.*, after the return from Hochelaga) has been lost. This promise of further mention does, however, suggest that the party had had occasion to use the remedy.

26. *Ibid.*, p. 259.

27. Account of Roberval's voyage, 1542-43, in Biggar, *Voyages*, p. 264; evidence given at the Fuenterrabia inquiry, Sept. 1542, in *Coll. of Docs.*, pp. 456-57, 463.

28. *Ibid.*, pp. 451, 457-58.

29. *Ibid.*, p. 457; Roberval's voyage, in Biggar, *Voyages*, p. 264.

30. *Coll. of Docs.*, pp. 304-9; the Chevalier Poyet to the Parlement of Rouen, 10 July 1541, in E. Gosselin, *Nouvelles glanes historiques normandes puisées exclusivement dans les documents inédits* (Rouen, 1873), p. 6; letter from the Spanish ambassador

in France to Charles V, 3 Aug. 1541, in *Coll. of Docs.*, p. 561.

31. Notables mentioned in the documents include Paul d'Aussillon, Seigneur de Sauveterre; Nicolas de Lépinay, Seigneur de Neufville; Robert de Longueval, Sieur de Thenelles; the pilot Jean Fonteneau dit Alfonse; François de Mire, Captains Guinecourt and Macé Jalobert, the Sieurs Noirefontaine du Buisson, Michel Rousseil, Froté, La Brosse, La Salle, Royèze, Levasseur, Talbot and Villeneuve—not forgetting, if they really were of the party, Roberval's niece Marguerite de la Roque, her lover and her nurse.

32. Roberval's voyage in Biggar, *Voyages*, p. 263; Fuenterrabia inquiry, Sept. 1542, in *Coll. of Docs.*, p. 452.

33. Roberval's voyage, in Biggar, *Voyages*, p. 264.

34. *Ibid.*, p. 265.

35. Cathelineau has observed that Cartier must have arrived early in September at the latest, since on Sept. 7 it was noted that Olivier du Breil "died not long ago on the Canada expedition, where he had gone with Jacques Cartier". (Cathelineau, "Quel jour Cartier rentra-t-il de son troisième voyage?" *Nova Francia*, V, 1930, pp. 97-99.)

36. Roberval's voyage, in Biggar, *Voyages*, p. 264; André Thevet, *Les singularitez de la France antarctique* (Paris, 1878; new edition of the 1578 text), p. 430.

37. Roberval's voyage, in Biggar, *Voyages*,

p. 266; see also the extract from the *Cosmographie* of Jean Alfonse in Biggar, *Voyages*, pp. 278-303.

38. Alfonse's *Cosmographie*, *loc. cit.*, pp. 292-93, 296.

39. Roberval's voyage, in Biggar, *op. cit.*, pp. 265-67; Alfonse's *Cosmographie*, *loc. cit.*, p. 299; Roberval's pardon to Paul d'Aussillon, in *Coll. of Docs.*, pp. 445-47.

40. Roberval's voyage, in Biggar, *Voyages*, p. 267.

41. *Ibid.*, p. 268.

42. *Ibid.*; Alfonse's *Cosmographie*, *loc. cit.*, p. 296.

43. Roberval's voyage, in Biggar, *Voyages*, pp. 269-70.

44. Map reproduced in Biggar, *Voyages*, Plate XIV, and in Trudel, *An Atlas of New France* (1968), 20.

45. Roberval's voyage, in Biggar, *Voyages*, pp. 269-70. We do not know whether Alfonse was on this expedition; what he writes about Hochelaga in his *Cosmographie* is rather vague and does not appear to be based on first-hand observation.

46. Roberval's order to Paul d'Aussillon, 11 Sept. 1543, in *Coll. of Docs.*, p. 475.

47. Commission in *Coll. of Docs.*, pp. 471-72. The date of departure is deduced from legal proceedings between Le Breton and Maingard (*Coll. of Docs.*, p. 473n.); if the ship had arrived on or before June 19, the account, which ends on that date, would surely have mentioned it.

48. Roberval's order, 11 Sept. 1543, in *Coll. of Docs.*, p. 475.

NOTES TO CHAPTER FOUR

1. Charles and Paul Bréard, *Documents relatifs à la marine normande et à ses armements aux XVIe et XVIIe siècles* (Rouen, 1889), pp. 51-52, and 53-59 (list of voyages for the years 1574-90).

2. Commissions of March 1577 and 3 Jan. 1578, in Alfred Ramé, *Documents inédits sur le Canada. Deuxième série* (Paris, 1867), pp. 6, 8-10.

3. Charles de La Roncière, *En quête d'un empire colonial. Richelieu* (Paris, 1923; Vol.

IV of *Histoire de la marine française*), pp. 308-9.

4. Marc Lescarbot, *Histoire de la Nouvelle-France*, ed. Edwin Tross (Paris, 1866, 3 vols.), II, 576-77; Biggar, *Works of Champlain*, I, 463-64; Winsor, *Narrative and Critical History of America*, III, 170.

5. Richard Hakluyt, *Discourse concerning Westerne Planting* (Cambridge: Maine Historical Society, 1877; Vol. II of *Documentary History of the State of Maine*), p. 34.

6. *Ibid.*, pp. 26, 84.

7. *Ibid.*, pp. 26, 101.

8. *Ibid.*, pp. 101-3.

9. Ramé, *Documents inédits sur le Canada*, 1865 ed., p. 38.

10. Letters of 29 Aug. 1575, in Ramé, *Documents*, 1865 ed., pp. 32-34; see also 34, n., 36, n.; Longrais, *Jacques Cartier, documents nouveaux*, p. 160.

11. Ramé, *Documents*, 1865 ed., p. 34, n., pp. 38, 40; letters from Noël to Jean Groote, 1587, in Longrais, *op. cit.*, pp. 145-48.

12. Letters from Henry III, 12 Jan. 1588, in Ramé, *Documents*, 1865 ed., pp. 34-44.

13. Merchants' deliberations, 11 March 1588, in Longrais, *op. cit.*, pp. 152-54; "Remonstrances," *ibid.*, pp. 155-56; Council decree, 5 May 1588, *ibid.*, pp. 157-58; letters of revocation, 9 July 1588, in Ramé, *Documents*, 1865 ed., pp. 48-51, and marginal notes, pp. 34-40; see also Ramé, 1867 ed., pp. 10-11.

14. Power of attorney, dated 12 Nov. 1596 and contract of 4 March 1597, in C. and P. Bréard, *op. cit.*, pp. 73-78; E. Gosselin, *Nouvelles glanes historiques normandes*, p.10.

15. J.-C. Taché, *Les Sablons (Ile de Sable)* (Montreal, about 1883), pp. 7-47.

16. Contract of 4 March 1597, in C. and P. Bréard, *op. cit.*, pp. 75-78.

17. Letters patent of 12 Jan. 1598, in Lescarbot, *op. cit.*, II, 398-405; *Edits, ordonnances royaux, déclarations et arrêts du Conseil d'Etat du Roi concernant le Canada* (Quebec, 1854-56, 3 vols.), II, 7-10; Narcisse-Eutrope Dionne, *La Nouvelle-France de Cartier à Champlain, 1540-1603* (Quebec, 1891), App., item H, pp. 354-60.

18. Contracts of 16 March 1598 with Chefdhostel and 18 March 1598 with Girot, in C. and P. Bréard, *op. cit.*, pp. 79-83; Gosselin, *Nouvelles glanes*, pp. 11-14.

19. Joseph Le Ber, "Un document inédit sur l'île de Sable et le marquis de La Roche," *R.H.A.F.* II, 2 (Sept. 1948), p. 203; Gustave Lanctôt, "L'établissement du marquis de La Roche à l'île de Sable," *Canadian Historical Association Annual Report*, 1933, pp. 39-40.

20. C. and P. Bréard, *op. cit.*, pp. 73-78, Lanctôt, *loc. cit.*, pp. 33-36; Le Ber; *loc. cit.*, pp. 199-213.

21. Le Ber, pp. 203-4, 207-8; also contract published as appendix to this article, pp. 211-13.

22. *Works of Champlain*, III, 305-6; C. and P. Bréard, *op. cit.*, pp. 66-69, 73, 75, 78, 91-92; Charles Bréard, *Le vieux Honfleur et ses marins. Biographies et récits maritimes* (Rouen, 1897), pp. 55-57; Gosselin, *Nouvelles glanes*, p. 18. The conditions of the monopoly are taken from a declaration by the merchants of St Malo, in Ramé, *Documents*, 1865 ed., pp. 52-53.

23. Lanctôt, *loc. cit.*, p. 41; Gosselin, *Nouvelles glanes*, p. 17; Le Ber, *loc. cit.*, p. 204.

24. The 400-ton *Don-de-Dieu* (the biggest of the four), commanded by Guillaume Lechevalier, with Henri Couillart in charge of its sailors; the 100-ton *Espérance*, captained by Sébastien Morin; the 120-ton *Bon-Espoir*, commanded by Guillaume Caresme who, in spite of his name, which evokes lenten fasting, was also the "victualler"; the *Saint-Jean*, commanded by Nicolas Tuvache. Documents in C. and P. Bréard, *op. cit.*, pp. 85, 86, and in *Nouveaux documents sur Champlain et son époque*, ed. Le Blant and Baudry (Ottawa, 1967), p. 70.

25. La Roche, "Escrit," quoted by Lanctôt, *loc. cit.*, p. 40; *Works of Champlain*, III, 305-6, 308-9; documents in C. and P. Bréard, *op. cit.*, pp. 93, 96, 97 and n. 1; C. Bréard, *Le vieux Honfleur*, pp. 97-100.

26. *Works of Champlain*, III, 309.

27. C. Bréard, p. 53; C. and P. Bréard, *Documents*, p. 67; Henry Harrisse, *Notes pour servir à l'histoire, à la bibliographie et à la cartographie de la Nouvelle-France et des pays adjacents* (Paris, 1872), pp. 18, 34, 44-45; A.-Léo Leymarie, "Le Canada pendant la jeunesse de Louis XIII," *Nova Francia*, I (1925), 169, n. 2.

28. *Works of Champlain*, I, 96-97; III, 308-10.

29. *Ibid.*, III, 309-10.

30. *Ibid.*, III, 310-11.

31. *Ibid.*, I, 98; III, 311; documents of March, April and Nov. 1602, in C. and

P. Bréard, *op. cit.*, pp. 89-90; Gosselin, *Nouvelles glanes*, p. 19; *Nouveaux documents sur Champlain et son époque*, pp. 48 f., 55-66, 68-74.

32. Letters of 21 and 28 Dec., 1602, in Ramé, *Documents*, 1867 ed., pp. 12-17;

letter from Charles de Montmorency, 3 Jan. 1603, *ibid.*, pp. 19-21.

33. Document of 26 Jan. 1603, *ibid.*, pp. 14-15.

34. C. and P. Bréard, *op. cit*, p. 71.

35. *Works of Champlain*, III, 311.

NOTES TO CHAPTER FIVE

1. Biggar, *Works of Champlain*, I, 127, 141, 158-59, 162.

2. Account of Cartier's second voyage, in *Les Français en Amérique*, pp. 152, 156; Lescarbot, *Histoire de la Nouvelle-France* (ed. Tross), III, 662, 665; R. G. Thwaites, ed., *The Jesuit Relations and Allied Documents* (Cleveland, 1896-1901), XXV, 107; see also A. G. Bailey, "The Significance of the Identity and Disappearance of the Laurentian Iroquois," *T.R.S.C.*, 1933, Sec. II, p. 106, n. 50.

3. Bailey, pp. 97-108.

4. Document of 21 Feb. 1603, *R.H.A.F.*, II, 2 (Sept. 1948), p. 211.

5. Gosselin, *Nouvelles glanes*, p. 20; Régis Roy, "M. de Chaste," *B.R.H.*, 27 (1921), pp. 214-5; H. P. Biggar, *The Early Trading Companies of New France* (Toronto, 1901), p. 46.

6. Letter from the King, 13 March 1603, in Ramé, *Documents inédits sur le Canada*, 1867 ed., pp. 23-25; A.N., série E, vol. 5 A, fol. 248.

7. *Works of Champlain*, III, 313-14; docs. of Feb. and March 1603, in C. and P. Bréard, *Documents relatifs à la marine normande*, pp. 99-101; *Works of Champlain*, I, 100.

8. *Works of Champlain*, III, 315-16.

9. Contract of 27 Dec. 1610, reproduced in *Works of Champlain*, II, 315-17, and in N.-E. Dionne, *Samuel Champlain, Fondateur de Québec et Père de la Nouvelle-France*, I (Quebec, 1891), 399-403. See also *Nouveaux documents sur Champlain*, pp. 10-11.

10. *Works of Champlain*, I, 115-16; see also *Nouveaux documents sur Champlain*, pp. 17-19, 21. His explanations to the Indians of Tadoussac went into print in France before the end of 1603.

11. A.N., Colonies, C^{11}A, I, 114v.

12. *Works of Champlain*, I, 209; *ibid.*, III, 314-15; assignment of the donation of 1601 by a deed of 1625, reproduced by Leymarie, *Nova Francia*, I (1925), 83-85; memorandum published by Hubert Deschamps, ed., *Les voyages de Samuel Champlain, Saintongeais, Père du Canada* (Paris, 1951), p. 354. There appears to be no reason for questioning Champlain's declaration, made toward the end of his career, regarding his voyage to the West Indies. Doubts as to his veracity have been raised, however, by the existence of a work attributed to him but never published by him: *Brief discours des choses plus remarquables que Samuel Champlain de Brouage a reconneues aux Indes occidentales*. In a recent study, L.-A. Vigneras suggests that Champlain may not have made his voyage, or not all of it, with Coloma's armada, as he was supposed to have done; either he had written the *Brief discours* from information gathered in Spain, or perhaps from the papers of his "uncle from Provence," or else he had recounted his voyage at a time when his memory was no longer reliable. (L.-A. Vigneras, "Le voyage de Samuel Champlain aux Indes occidentales," *R.H.A.F.*, XI, 2 (Sept. 1957), pp. 163-200.) To be fair to Champlain, it should be noted that if the work was his, he had not judged it worthy of publication. It should not in any case be classed with his other works. Moreover, the work published under his name, and that not before 1859, was not the original but a copy, whose fidelity may well be questioned. The account of Verrazano's voyage of 1524, too, was long known only through a copy full of errors; it was only after the discovery

of the Cellere manuscript that historians finally gave Verrazano the credit he deserves. Until such time as the original may be found, the *Brief discours* should not be allowed to blot Champlain's record.

13. *Works of Champlain*, I, 96-98.

14. *Ibid.*, 96-106.

15. *Ibid.*, 121-24.

16. *Ibid.*, 125-52.

17. *Ibid.*, 153-65.

18. *Ibid.*, 166-72, 186-88.

19. *Ibid.*, 172, 181-85.

20. *Ibid.*, 170-71.

21. *Ibid.*, 173-80.

NOTES TO CHAPTER SIX

1. Text of vice-admiral's commission, in *Pierre Du Gua, Sieur de Monts: Records*, ed. W. I. Morse (London, 1939), pp. 4-6; letters patent of 8 Nov. 1603, reproduced in Lescarbot, *Histoire de la Nouvelle-France* (ed. Tross), II, 408-14; *Remontrances par le sieur de Mons*, 18 Dec. 1603, in B.N., Dupuy, vol. 318, 107r.-108r.; *Collection de manuscrits relatifs à la Nouvelle-France* (4 vols., Quebec, 1879-88), I, 44 f.

2. *Remontrances*, cited; contract of 10 Feb. 1604, in Gosselin, *Nouvelles glanes historiques normandes*, pp. 24-29; Biggar, *Early Trading Companies*, p. 53. See also *Nouveaux documents sur Champlain*, pp. 80-83, 87 f.

3. Biggar, *Works of Champlain*, I, 234, 239, 276 f., 279, 467 n. 1; III, 322; Lescarbot, *op. cit.*, II, 422; Bréard, *Documents relatifs à la marine normande*, pp. 102, 103.

4. Lescarbot, *op. cit.*, II, 423; *Works of Champlain*, I, 234 and n. 2.

5. Lescarbot, *op. cit.*, II, 423, 425; *Works of Champlain*, I, 234, 237 f., 247.

6. Lescarbot, *op. cit.*, II, 425; *Works of Champlain*, I, 239-252.

7. *Works of Champlain*, I, 254-59; III, 340-43; Lescarbot, *op. cit.*, II, 429.

8. Lescarbot, *op. cit.*, II, 429 f.; *Works of Champlain*, II, 2 f. The date of this concession is given in a petition from Biencourt mentioned in a decree of the Council, 8 Feb. 1624 (A.N., série E, vol. 78 A, 304).

9. Lescarbot, *op. cit.*, II, 430-33; *Works of Champlain*, I, 260-63.

10. *Works of Champlain*, I, 264-68; III, 346 f.

11. *Ibid.*, I, 271 f.; III, 322.

12. Lescarbot, *op. cit.*, II, 436.

13. *Ibid.*, 443 f., 449 f.; *Works of Champlain*, I, 274-78, 301 f., 306.

14. *Works of Champlain*, I, 279 f., 304; Lescarbot, *op. cit.*, II, 445, 448.

15. *Works of Champlain*, I, 278 f.

16. *Ibid.*, I, 280-88, 300; III, 355.

17. *Ibid.*, I, 289-96; III, 352-61.

18. *Ibid.*, I, 297-300; III, 361-63.

19. *Ibid.*, I, 302 f., 306 f.; Lescarbot, *op. cit.*, II, 450 f.

20. *Works of Champlain*, I, 303-5; 322; Lescarbot, *op. cit.*, II, 452, 468; III, 739; *idem*, "Relation dernière," in *J.R.* (Thwaites, *Jesuit Relations*) II, 132.

21. *Works of Champlain*, I, 311; Lescarbot, *Histoire* (ed. Tross), II, 469.

22. *Works of Champlain*, I, 311 f., 363; Lescarbot, *Histoire*, II, 470, 475.

23. *Works of Champlain*, I, 311-55; III, 364-98; Lescarbot, *Histoire*, II, 470-75, 541.

24. *Works of Champlain*, I, 367-69, 371-73; Lescarbot, *Histoire*, II, 478; *idem*, "Relation dernière," in *J.R.*, II, 164.

25. *Works of Champlain*, I, 383; Lescarbot, *Histoire*, II, 520, 567 f.; III, 62, 744; Pierre Biard, s.j., to his Provincial, 31 Jan. 1612, in *J.R.*, II, 22; Biard's relation of 1616, in *J.R.*, III, 204.

26. *Works of Champlain*, I, 369-71, 389 f.; Lescarbot, *Histoire*, II, 479, 526.

27. *Works of Champlain*, I, 322, 374-76; Lescarbot, *Histoire*, II, 479-81; Gabriel Sagard, *Histoire du Canada* (ed. Edwin Tross), p. 9.

28. *Works of Champlain*, I, 377-83; Lescarbot, *Histoire*, II, 481.

29. *Works of Champlain*, I, 383, 385-89; Lescarbot, *Histoire*, II, 520, 567 f.; III, 62, 744.

30. *Works of Champlain*, I, 389 f.; Lescarbot, *Histoire*, II, 526 f.

31. *Works of Champlain*, I, 394-436; III, 399-401, 406 f., 409; Lescarbot, *Histoire*, II, 521-35, 538, 542-51. Regarding the name Port Fortuné, either the choice was ironic, or "fortuné" should be understood in its old sense of "marked by the blows of fortune."

32. *Works of Champlain*, I, 438; Lescarbot, *Histoire*, II, 463, 527, 553; "Les muses de la Nouvelle-France," reproduced in Vol. III of the same edition.

33. *Works of Champlain*, I, 440 f., 446-49; Lescarbot, *Histoire*, II, 465-68, 528 f., 553 f., 556-58, 560; III, 836.

34. *Works of Champlain*, I, 450; Lescarbot, *Histoire*, II, 563.

35. Lescarbot, *Histoire*, II, 563; *Le Mercure françois*, I (Paris, 1619), 296v.

36. Mention of these proceedings is made in a document of 25 June 1633, B.N., Nouvelles acquisitions françaises, vol. 9269, 304 f.; Gosselin, *Nouvelles glanes*, 30 f. See also *Nouveaux documents sur Champlain*, 131.

37. Lescarbot, *Histoire*, II, 565.

38. Decree of 17 July 1607, A.N., série E, vol. 14 A., fol. 71 (copy in P.A.C., MG 3, series 1, vol. 1). See also *Nouveaux documents sur Champlain*, 137 f. The exact date of the revocation is not known, but it must have been in the spring, since at the end of May they heard at Port Royal that the monopoly had been revoked.

39. *Works of Champlain*, I, 459-65; III, 412-16; Lescarbot, *Histoire*, II, 575-77, 579.

NOTES TO CHAPTER SEVEN

1. Biggar, *Works of Champlain*, I, 170 f., 231 f.; IV, 28 f., 31.

2. *Ibid.*, II, 4 f., 8 f., 27; IV, 32, 37; Lescarbot, *Histoire de la Nouvelle-France* (ed. Tross), II, 434 f.

3. *Works of Champlain*, II, 21, 26, 27, 138; III, 213; IV, 118; Bréard, *Documents relatifs à la marine normande*, 110, 112, 113.

4. *Works of Champlain*, IV, 32.

5. *Ibid.*, II, 11-14.

6. *Ibid.*, 16-19.

7. *Ibid.*, 24 f., 32 f., 35 f.; Sagard, *Histoire du Canada* (ed. Tross), I, 272.

8. *Works of Champlain*, II, 25-35; Lescarbot, *Histoire* (ed. Tross), III, 596 f.; *Histoire* (ed. W. L. Grant and H. P. Biggar, 3 vols., Toronto, 1914), III, 303 f.

9. *Works of Champlain*, II, 52, 53, 59-62; Lescarbot, *Histoire* (ed. Tross), IV, 468; "Relation dernière" in *J.R.*, II, 166.

10. Le Jeune, relation of 1630, *J.R.*, XVI, 226-30.

11. *Works of Champlain*, II, 73-83, 89-91, 94-106; IV, 71-80, 89-105; Lescarbot, *Histoire* (ed. Tross), III, 600-602.

12. *Works of Champlain*, II, 108-10; III, 325 f.

13. *Ibid.*, II, 116-19; III, ix (for editor's comment); Bréard, *Documents*, p. 118. Henry Hudson entered Hudson Bay on Aug. 3, 1610; as for Lac St Jean, it was not officially discovered by the Jesuit De Quen until 1647.

14. *Works of Champlain*, II, 118-22, 124-37; IV, 106-17.

15. *Ibid.*, IV, 125.

16. *Ibid.*, II, 138, 142, 171 f.; IV, 118 f.; Lescarbot, *Histoire* (ed. Tross), III, 605.

17. At the end of 1610, when he was about forty, Champlain married a very young Protestant girl, not yet twelve years old, with a good dowry. He received 4,500 livres immediately, but it was understood that the marriage would not be consummated for two years at least. According to some documents made available by the historians Le Blant and Baudry, the first years of this marriage were difficult; Hélène Boullé even left home, and violent family quarrels ensued. See *Nouveaux documents sur Champlain*, pp. 330-35.

18. *Works of Champlain*, II, 157-72, 205, 212, 255; IV, 125, 150, 151, 154.

19. *Ibid.*, II, 171-85, 187-89, 191-98, 200-206, 208-12; IV, 125-40, 141-51.

20. *Ibid.*, II, 215 f.; IV, 34; Le Blant and Delafosse, "Les Rochelais dans la vallée du Saint-Laurent, 1599-1618," *R.H.A.F.*, X, 3 (Dec. 1956), 339 ff.

21. *Works of Champlain*, II, 243 f.; IV, 208 f.; articles accorded to the Comte de Soissons, 27 Sept. 1612, and letters of 8 Oct. 1612, in B.N., Nouv. acq. franç., 9, 269: 39.

22. Commission delivered 15 Oct. 1612 to Champlain by Soissons, in *Works of Champlain*, IV, 209-16; V, 143.

23. For these letters of appointment, see B.N., Nouv. acq. franç., 9,269: 39-42; Gosselin, *Nouvelles glanes historiques*, pp. 32, 34, 38; Biggar, *Early Trading Companies*, pp. 195-96; Ramé, *Documents inédits sur le Canada*, 1867 ed., pp. 36, 37, 38. See also *Nouveaux documents sur Champlain*, pp. 233-41.

24. *Works of Champlain*, II, 245; IV, 217; V, 143.

25. *Ibid.*, II, 252-54; IV, 154.

26. *Ibid.*, II, 255-58; IV, 154-57.

27. *Ibid.*, II, 255, 259, 261-76, 301 f.; IV, 154, 158, 160-75, 200 f.; VI, 242-45 (identification table for the 1632 map).

28. Sagard, *Histoire* (ed. Tross), II, 367; III, 739 f.; Le Jeune's relations of 1633, *J.R.*, VI, 18, and 1636, *J.R.*, IX, 274.

29. *Works of Champlain*, II, 282-94, 296, 304 f.; IV, 181-93, 195.

30. *Ibid.*, III, 37; *Oeuvres de Champlain* (ed. C.-H. Laverdière, Quebec, 1870), IV, 20.

31. *Works of Champlain*, II, 272, 297-303; IV, 196-202; VI, 243 (identification table for 1632 map).

32. *Ibid.*, IV, 220 f., 340 f., 344; edict of Nov. 1613, registered at the Parlement of Rouen on Dec. 14 of that year, in Biggar, *Early Trading Companies*, p. 197; docs. of 14, 15 and 20 Nov. 1613, in B.N., Nouv. acq. franç., 9,269: 183v., 304 f. See also *Nouveaux documents sur Champlain*, pp. 310-21.

NOTES TO CHAPTER EIGHT

1. Documents of Feb. 2 and March 1608, cited in Le Blant, "La famille Boullé," *R.H.A.F.*, XVII, 1 (June 1963), p. 66.

2. See *Monumenta Novae Franciae* (ed. Lucien Campeau), introd. and text of 22 April 1613; also Lescarbot, *Histoire de la Nouvelle-France* (ed. Grant-Biggar), III, 320.

3. Contract in *Factum du procès entre Jean de Biencourt, Sr de Poutrincourt et les Pères Biard et Massé, jésuites* (published 1614, republished 1887 in Paris with introd. and notes by Gabriel Marcel), 11.

4. Lescarbot, *Histoire de la Nouvelle-France* (ed. Tross), III, 608.

5. Biard, relation of 1616, *J.R.*, III, 162-64; Biggar, *Works of Champlain*, IV, 3 f.

6. *Factum*, 18 f.; Lescarbot, *Histoire* (ed. Tross), III, 608 f.; "La conversion des sauvages," in *J.R.*, I, 64-66; "Relation dernière," in *J.R.*, II, 128-32.

7. Lescarbot, in *J.R.*, I, 68; in *J.R.*, II, 164; *Histoire* (ed. Tross), III, 610.

8. According to Adrien Huguet, *Jean de Poutrincourt* (Amiens and Paris, 1932), 306, 308 and n. 2 (citing Rameau, *Une colonie féodale*, 51); but the sole confirmation one finds in the archives goes back only to 1720 (P.A.C., C¹¹D, 10, General Corresp., 1605-1749, 140).

9. Lescarbot, "La conversion des sauvages," *J.R.*, I, 76, 108-12; "Relation dernière," *J.R.*, II, 148; *Histoire* (ed. Tross), III, 610-14.

10. *Factum*, 5 f.; Lescarbot, "Relation dernière," *J.R.*, II, 140, 172.

11. Biard to the General of the Jesuits, 21 Jan. 1611, *J.R.*, I, 130; Biard to the Provincial, 10 June 1611, *J.R.*, I, 140; "Relatio rerum gestarum," *J.R.*, II, 212; Biard, relation of 1616, *J.R.*, III, 166; Lescarbot, *Histoire* (ed. Grant-Biggar), III, 327; *Monumenta* (ed. Campeau), 58 f.

12. Letters from the King, the Queen Mother, Father Coton, and Madame de Guercheville, reproduced in the *Factum*, 5-9.

13. Lescarbot, "Relation dernière," *J.R.*, II, 138; Biard, relation of 1616, *J.R.*, III, 170.

14. Biard to the Provincial, 10 June 1611, *J.R.*, I, 142; Biard to the General of the Jesuits, 21 Jan. 1611, *J.R.*, I, 132-34; *Factum*, 9; Lescarbot, *Histoire* (ed. Grant-Biggar), III, 328; *Works of Champlain*, IV, 5; *Monumenta* (ed. Campeau), introduction.

15. *Monumenta* (ed. Campeau), introd., 203★ to 207★.

16. Test of contract in the *Factum*, 10-13; Lescarbot, *Histoire* (ed. Tross), III, 665-67; *Histoire* (ed. Grant-Biggar), III, 328 f.; *Monumenta* (ed. Campeau), 208★.

17. *Monumenta* (ed. Campeau), 208★ to 210★.

18. Biard, relation of 1616, *J.R.*, III, 176; *Works of Champlain*, IV, 6 f.

19. Biard to the Provincial, 10 June 1611, *J.R.*, I, 156; "Relatio rerum gestarum," *J.R.* II, 218; Biard, relation of 1616, *J.R.*, III, 184.

20. Lescarbot, "Relation dernière," *J.R.*, II, 178, 180; "La conversion des sauvages," *J.R.*, I, 76-78; *Factum*, 20-24; Biard, relation of 1616, *J.R.*, III, 186, 188, 192; Biard to the Provincial, 10 June 1611, *J.R.*, I, 170, 190; "Relatio rerum gestarum," *J.R.*, II, 218.

21. Biard to the Provincial, 10 June 1611, *J.R.*, I, 162; to the General of the Jesuits, Jan. 1612, *J.R.*, II, 90.

22. *J.R.*, II, 86; III, 146; *Factum*, 4; Lescarbot, "Relation dernière," *J.R.*, II, 154.

23. Biard, relation of 1616, *J.R.*, III, 232-34. Although Florida is mentioned, the southern limit of Madame de Guercheville's domain must have been the 40th parallel, since this concession was based on the letters of 1603.

24. *Ibid.*, 234.

25. *Ibid.*, 226, 234, 242; "Relatio rerum gestarum," *J.R.*, II, 232, 234-38; *Factum*, 34, 41 f.; *Works of Champlain*, IV, 11 f.

26. *Factum*, 42-55, 77; Biard to Biencourt and to Capt. L'Abbé, 13 March 1612, *ibid.*, 43-47; Biencourt to his father, 13 March, *ibid.*, 48-50; the same to the same, 14 March, *ibid.*, 50-54; Hébert's account,

13 March, *ibid.*, 54; Poutrincourt to Lescarbot, 15 May 1613, in Lescarbot, *Histoire* (ed. Grant-Biggar), III, 335. On the interdict, see also Campeau, "La grande crise de 1612 à Port-Royal," in *Lettres du Bas-Canada*, XV, 1 (March 1961), 24-26.

27. *Monumenta* (ed. Campeau), introd.; see also Campeau's article cited above, 22 f.

28. Massé to Mme de Guercheville, 10 March 1612, in *Factum*, 59 f. However, this letter was seized by Biencourt and did not reach its destination; it is cited because it represents the opinion of the missionaries.

29. The King to Biencourt, 4 Jan. 1613, in Huguet, *Jean de Poutrincourt*, 398 f.; the General to the Provincial Balthazar, 2 Jan. 1613, in *Monumenta* (ed. Campeau), 269-71.

30. Biard, relation of 1616, *J.R.*, III, 262-72; "Relatio rerum gestarum," *J.R.*, II, 248.

31. Biard, relation of 1616, *J.R.*, III, 62; IV, 8-10; "Relatio rerum gestarum," *J.R.*, II, 250; Capt. Fleury's report, 1614, in *Monumenta* (ed. Campeau), 442 f.

32. Biard to the General of the Jesuits, 26 May 1614, *J.R.*, III, 6; Biard's relation of 1616, *J.R.*, III, 274-76, 278-82; IV, 8-10; "Relatio rerum gestarum," *J.R.*, II, 252, 254; Capt. Fleury's report, in *Monumenta* (ed. Campeau), 443; *Factum*, 70; Lescarbot, *Histoire* (ed. Grant-Biggar), III, 336.

33. "Relatio rerum gestarum," *J.R.*, II, 262-64; Biard, relation de 1616, *J.R.*, IV, 24-28.

34. *J.R.*, II, 266; *J.R.*, IV, 34.

35. Biard to the General of the Jesuits, 26 May 1614, *J.R.*, III, 10-12; Biard, relation of 1616, *J.R.*, IV, 34, 36, 42, 46, 54; Poutrincourt to Lescarbot, 1614, in Lescarbot, *Histoire* (ed. Grant-Biggar), III, 338; complaint of Poutrincourt, 1614, *ibid.*, 339 f.; "Relatio rerum gestarum," *J.R.*, II, 266; Huguet, *op. cit.*, 407, 410 f., 414.

36. Purchas's account in *Forerunners and Competitors of the Pilgrims and Puritans* (ed. C. H. Levermore, New York, 1912), II, 563-66.

37. Biard, relation of 1616, *J.R.*, IV, 50, 54, 56-76; Biard to the General of the Jesuits, 26 May 1614, *J.R.*, III, 4-18; Lescarbot, *Histoire* (ed. Grant-Biggar), III, 341; Poutrincourt to Lescarbot, *ibid.*, 338; Campeau, "La première mission des Jésuites en Nouvelle-France," in *Lettres du Bas-Canada*, XV, 3 (Sept. 1961), 156 f.

38. For the documents (inventoried or reproduced) that relate to the French claims, see Noël Sainsbury, *Calendar of State Papers, Colonial Series, 1574-1660* (Lon-don, 1893); Alexander Brown, *The Genesis of the United States* (Boston and New York, 1897); and above all, the cited *Monumenta* (ed. Campeau).

39. Biard, relation of 1616, *J.R.*, IV, 76-78.

40. Contract of 2 May 1613, summarized in Huguet, *Jean de Poutrincourt*, 397, n. 2; see also *Monumenta* (ed. Campeau), 217*.

41. Poutrincourt to Lescarbot, 1614, in Lescarbot, *Histoire* (ed. Grant-Biggar), III, 343; see docs. of 1613 summarized in Hughet, *op. cit.*, 424, n. 1.

NOTES TO CHAPTER NINE

1. Biggar, *Works of Champlain*, III, 24 f.; IV, 226; Sagard, *Histoire du Canada* (ed. Tross), I, 36.

2. On this question, see Conrad Morin, O.F.M., "La naissance de l'Eglise au Canada," *R.H.A.F.*, I, 2 (Sept. 1947), pp. 243-56.

3. There have been long discussions regarding the name of this first chapel; a recent study demonstrates that it remains unknown: Adrien Pouliot, S.J., *Aux origines de notre dévotion à l'Immaculée-Conception* (La Société historique de Québec, 1956), pp. 2-8.

4. *Works of Champlain*, III, 28-30, 35.

5. *Ibid.*, III, 26, 34-37; IV, 229.

6. *Ibid.*, III, 37 f., 45 f.; IV, 230 f., 237-39.

7. *Ibid.*, III, 49, 53-55, 58, 216; IV, 240, 247.

8. *Ibid.*, III, 56-65, 67, 70, 73, 81, 94; IV, 245, 251-55, 257 f., 260, 267, 277 f.

9. On these speculations, see Morris Bishop, *Champlain* (New York) 1948), pp. 355-59; A. G. Zeller, *The Champlain-Iroquois Battle of 1615* (New York, 1962), pp. 31-37.

10. *Works of Champlain*, III, 66-69, 71-79; IV, 254-65.

11. *Ibid.*, III, 79-81; IV, 265-67.

12. *Ibid.*, III, 39-45, 95, 97, 101-5; IV, 232-37, 278-80, 283-95; VI, 251; Sagard, *Histoire* (ed. Tross), I, 194.

13. For Brûlé's story, related by Champlain, see *Works of Champlain*, III, 213-26 (it is the only source).

14. *Works of Champlain*, III, 169-72; IV, 335-37; Sagard, *Histoire* (ed. Tross), I, 42.

15. On this wintering, see article and doc' of Le Blant and Delafosse, "Les Rochelais dans la vallée du Saint-Laurent," in *R.H.A.F.*, X, 3 (Dec. 1956), 350-53, 358-63.

16. Le Clercq, Chrestien, *Premier établisse-ment de la foy dans la Nouvelle France* (2 vols., Paris, 1691), I, 92-100.

17. *Works of Champlain*, III, 173, 174; IV, 337.

18. Bishop has cast doubt on this voyage of 1617; yet Champlain (whatever Bishop may think of it) writes of this voyage in his 1619 publication; and even if Champlain was in Paris in July 1617 he could have had time to go to Quebec and return to France: in 1613, the voyage from Tadoussac to St Malo had taken only two weeks.

19. Text of the contract reproduced in Le Caron, *Au Roy sur la Nouvelle France*, 14 f. See also *Nouveaux documents sur Champlain*, 361 f.

20. *Works of Champlain*, IV, 342 f.

21. Relation reproduced in Odoric-M. Jouve, O.F.M., *Les Franciscains et le Canada*, I (Quebec, 1915), 58-68. See also *Nouveaux documents sur Champlain*, pp. 349-54.

22. Biard, relation of 1616, *J.R.*, III, 21-282; this relation has been republished by Lucien Campeau, in *Monumenta Novae Franciae*, I, 456-637.

23. Lescarbot, *Histoire* (ed. Grant-Biggar), III, 302.

24. Letter from Biencourt, 1 Sept. 1618,

294   THE BEGINNINGS OF NEW FRANCE

reproduced in *Coll. de manuscrits relatifs à la Nouvelle-France*, I, 57-59.

25. Contrary to the way in which the editor H. P. Biggar presented these documents in *Works of Champlain*, the order of the items relating to this program can only be as follows:
Champlain's petition to the Chamber of Commerce;
articles for submission to the King;
deliberation of the Chamber;
letter to the King and to his Council.

26. Requête de Champlain à la Chambre du Commerce, *Works of Champlain*, II, 339-45.

27. Articles à proposer au roi, *ibid.*, II, 329-39.

28. Délibération de la Chambre du Commerce, *ibid.*, II, 346-51.

29. Lettre au roi et à son Conseil, *ibid.*, II, 326-28.

30. Letter from Louis XIII to the merchant associates, 12 March 1618, *ibid.*, IV, 364 f.

31. Doc. of 20 March 1618, in Sagard, *Histoire* (ed. Tross), I, 28-32; see also Morin's article cited above, *R.H.A.F.*, I, 2 (Sept. 1947), 255 f.; I, 3 (Dec. 1947), 335-41.

32. *Works of Champlain*, III, 182-88, 191-201, 206 f., 211-13; Sagard, *op. cit.*, I, 54-57; Le Clercq, *op. cit.*, I, 122 f., 125 f.

33. *Works of Champlain*, III, 204 f.

34. Sagard, *op. cit.*, I, 62; Le Clercq, *op. cit.*, I, 129 f.

35. *Works of Champlain*, III, 210 f., 229.

36. *Ibid.*, IV, 353-57

37. *Ibid.*, IV, 361-66.

38. *Ibid.*, IV, 366. See also *Nouveaux documents sur Champlain*, 394-96.

39. *Works of Champlain*, V, 5, 7.

40. *Ibid.*, 26, 113; Sagard, *op. cit.*, I, 89, 158.

NOTES TO CHAPTER TEN

1. Montmorency to Champlain, 2 Feb. 1621, in A.N., Colonies, F 3, 3: 106r.; also in Biggar, *Works of Champlain*, V, 14 f.

2. On the de Caëns, see Joseph Le Ber, *Documents inédits*, in *R.H.A.F.*, III, 4 (March 1950): 587-93, and above all, the new and very precise details from Father Archange Godbout on p. 592, n. 8.

3. *Works of Champlain*, V, 15.

4. For the text of the agreement, see B.N., Nouv. acq. franç., 9,269: 186r.-189v.; Fonds français, 8,022: 181r.-186r.; 16,738, doc. 148. At first, in 1620, a period of 11 years was set; the King then extended this by 4 years. It is clear that six families (therefore at least eighteen persons) were to be established in 15 years; the phrase *tous les deux ans* appears in the agreement, but the ambiguity of this text is clarified in several other official documents.

5. *Works of Champlain*, V, 16-18, 22 f.

6. *Ibid.*, V, 25-35.

7. B.N., Nouv. acq. franç., 9,269: 184r.; A.N., V 6, 58: 10; 59: 13; *Works of Champlain*, V, 37 f.

8. *Ibid.*, V, 41-49.

9. Letters of delegation, 18 Aug. 1621, in Sagard, *Histoire* (ed. Tross), I, 80-83; see also B.N., Nouv. acq. franç., 9,269: 47.

10. For the text of the memorandum, see Sagard, *op. cit.*, I, 84-89.

11. On the authorship and the date of this document, as well as on its contents, see Trudel, *Histoire de la Nouvelle-France*, Vol. II: *Le comptoir, 1604-1627*, 283-85, and n. 56.

12. Extraits des Registres du Conseil d'Etat, B.N., Fonds français, 16,738, doc. 143: 10s.

13. Complaint of 18 Jan. 1622, in the cited "Extraits," B.N., Nouv. acq. franç., 9,269: 182r.

14. "Extraits" cited, Nouv. acq. franç., 9,269: 185r.

15. Text of the regulation, *ibid.*, 183r.-186r.; *Nouveaux documents sur Champlain*, pp. 432-43.

16. B.N., Nouv. acq. franç., 9,269: 191r.-v.; 277r.-v.; Fonds français, 16,738, no 132: 3; *Works of Champlain*, V, 61.

17. *Works of Champlain*, V, 113 f.

18. *Ibid.*, 112, 119 f.

19. *Ibid.*, 56 f. The text of these ordinances has not come down to us.

20. "Extraits" cited, B.N., Fonds français, 16,738, doc. 143: 8, 14; P.-G. Roy, *Inventaire des concessions en fief et seigneurie*, I, 1; *Works of Champlain*, V, 133.

21. Camille Rochemonteix, s.j., *Les Jésuites et la Nouvelle-France au XVIIe siècle*, I (Paris, 1895), 137-49; Lucien Campeau, s.j., "Notre-Dame-des-Anges," in *Lettres du Bas-Canada*, VIII, 2 (June 1954), 98.

22. It was not named Notre Dame des Anges, as was later claimed, but St Charles, in honour of a distinguished benefactor, Charles Des Boves, Vicar-General of Pontoise. On this question, see Trudel, *Le comptoir*, p. 321; and Campeau, in the article cited, pp. 77-95.

23. Le Caron to his Provincial, letter of 1624, in Le Clercq, *Premier établissement de la foy*, I, 288. Le Clercq, in 1691, insisted that Father Le Caron had the Jesuits in mind, but this seems improbable. Le Clercq, like Sagard in 1636, was writing in a climate of recrimination and bitterness; after 1632 it had become common for Récollets to say that they had been deprived of their mission by the very ones they had called in.

24. Campeau, article cited, app. I: "Les récollets ont-ils appelé les jésuites?", 95-105.

25. Charles Lalemant, s.j., to Champlain, 28 July 1625, in Sagard, *Histoire du Canada* (ed. Tross), III 789, and in *J.R.*, IV, 170.

26. Sagard, *Histoire*, III, 788; Le Clercq, *op. cit.*, I, 310.

27. On *Auhaitsique* becoming *Ahuntsic* and on the mistaken identification of this Frenchman as a Huron, see Godbout, "Le néophyte Ahuntsic," in *B.R.H.*, 48 (1942), 129-37.

28. The death of Father Viel is discussed in Trudel, *Le comptoir*, pp. 340-42.

29. Charles Lalemant, s.j., to his brother Jérôme, s.j., 1 Aug. 1626, *J.R.*, IV, 226.

30. *Loc. cit.*

31. In the cited letter, p. 218; Charles Lalemant to the General of the Jesuits, August 1626, *J.R.*, IV, 180-82.

32. A.N., V 6, 59: no. 13; see also 61, no. 1.

33. Decree of 7 March 1626, A.N., série E, vol. 86: 66s.; decree of 26 March, *ibid.*, vol. 86: 406; *Works of Champlain*, V, 150-52.

34. On Le Caron's pamphlet, see Trudel, *Le comptoir*, pp. 302-6.

35. Decrees of 7 March and 26 March 1626 (A.N., E, 86: 66s., 406); *Works of Champlain*, V, 150-52.

36. *Works of Champlain*, V, 110, 112.

37. *Ibid.*, 202, 203, 210, 275, 285; Sagard, *Histoire*, IV, 830, 833.

38. Extraits des Registres du Conseil d'Etat, B.N., Fonds français, 16,738, doc. 143: 8, 14.

39. *Pièces et documents relatifs à la tenure seigneuriale* (Quebec, 1852), 53-55, 373; Dionne, *Samuel Champlain*, II (Quebec, 1906), app., 511-13.

40. *Works of Champlain*, V, 235.

41. *Ibid.*, V, 257.

NOTES TO CHAPTER ELEVEN

1. Jacques Rousseau, "L'origine et l'évolution du mot esquimau," in *Cahiers des Dix*, XX (1955), 184, 197 f.

2. Biggar, *Works of Champlain*, V, 168 f.

3. Rousseau, p. 185.

4. *Works of Champlain*, V, 124 f.

5. *Ibid.*, II, 19, 119, 173 f.

6. Sagard, *Histoire du Canada* (ed. Tross), I, 227 f.

7. *Ibid.*, I, 165.

8. *Works of Champlain*, V, 61-65, 69 f., 81 f.

9. Sagard, *Histoire*, II, 519 f.

10. Charles Lalemant, s.j., to his brother Jérôme, s.j., 1 Aug. 1626, *J.R.*, IV, 194.

11. Sagard, *Histoire*, II, 367; III, 739 f., 750.

12. Le Jeune, s.j., relation of 1633, *J.R.*, VI, 18; relation of 1636, *J.R.*, IX, 274.

13. Sagard, *Histoire*, I, 187.

14. *Ibid.*, 227.

15. *Ibid.*, II, 367; Sagard, *Le grand voyage*

au pays des Hurons (ed. George M. Wrong), p. 307; *Works of Champlain*, IV, 281; Brébeuf's relation, 1636, *J.R.*, X, 50; Le Jeune's relation, 1640-41, *J.R.*, XXI, 176, 238.

16. Sagard, *Histoire* (ed. Tross), I, 227; *Le grand voyage* (ed. Wrong), p. 280.

17. *Works of Champlain*, V, 132; Sagard, *Histoire*, II, 287, 327.

18. Sagard, *Histoire*, III, 811.

19. La Roche d'Aillon, letter to a friend, 18 July 1627, in Sagard, *Histoire*, III, 799-809; Sagard, *op. cit.*, III, 810.

20. Le Clercq, *Premier établissement de la foy*, I, 207-11, 219.

21. *Works of Champlain*, V, 73-75, 77-80.

22. *Ibid.*, 117-19, 130-33; Le Clercq, *op. cit.*, I, 260; relation of the Récollet Le Caron, 1624, in Le Clercq, I, 286.

23. *Works of Champlain*, V, 208 f., 214-26, 229-32, 305, 308-12; Sagard, *Histoire*, II, 434-46; Jean E. Murray, "The Early Fur Trade," *C.H.R.*, XIX (1938), 365 ff.

NOTES TO CHAPTER TWELVE

1. Biggar, *Works of Champlain*, VI, 181; Le Jeune, s.j., relation of 1635, *J.R.*, VII, 268.

2. Le Jeune, relation of 1636, *J.R.*, IX, 168.

3. *Works of Champlain*, V, 111; Sagard, *Histoire du Canada* (ed. Tross), I, 107, 174.

4. Sagard, *op. cit.*, I, 178-82; *Works of Champlain*, III, 128.

5. Sagard, *op. cit.*, II, 516 f.; Lescarbot, *Histoire de la Nouvelle-France* (ed. Tross), II, 752.

6. Lescarbot, *op. cit*, III, 780 f.; Sagard, *op. cit.*, III, 698.

7. Sagard, *op. cit.*, I, 202; III, 708; *Works of Champlain*, III, 37 f.; IV, 230 f.

8. Sagard, *op. cit.*, III, 620 f.

9. *Works of Champlain*, II, 283; Lescarbot, *op. cit.*, III, 811; Biard, s.j., relation of 1616, *J.R.*, III, 116; Sagard, *op. cit.*, III, 604.

10. Sagard, *op. cit.*, I, 166.

11. *Ibid.*, I, 267.

12. *Ibid.*, I, 235; *Works of Champlain*, V, 115.

13. Sagard, *op. cit.*, III, 610 f.

14. Le Caron, Récollet, *Au Roy sur la Nouvelle France*, p. 8.

15. *Works of Champlain*, V, 250. Giffard is not identified by name.

16. Le Clercq, *Premier établissement de la foy*, I, 223.

17. Sagard, *op. cit.*, II, 335.

18. Colbert to Talon, 5 April 1667, *R.A.P.Q.*, 1930-31, p. 72.

19. Sagard, *op. cit.*, III, 705, 709; see also the *Dictionnaire, ibid.*, IV (unpaginated); Lescarbot, *Histoire* (ed. Tross), III, 678.

20. Le Jeune, relation of 1633, *J.R.*, V, 110; Biard, relation of 1616, *J.R.*, III, 194, 196, 246; "Relatio rerum gestarum," in *J.R.*, II, 240.

21. *Works of Champlain*, VI, 47.

22. Lescarbot, *op. cit.*, III, 761, 763; Sagard, *op. cit.*, III, 543; Le Jeune, relation of 1636, *J.R.*, IX, 228.

23. Sagard, *op. cit.*, I, 252 f.; Lescarbot, *op. cit.*, III, 707-9.

24. Sagard, *op. cit.*, II, 517; *Works of Champlain*, V, 67.

25. Le Jeune, relation of 1633, *J.R.*, V, 120; relation of 1632, *J.R.*, V, 48-50.

26. *Works of Champlain*, III, 143; Biard, relation of 1616, *J.R.*, III, 132; Lalemant, s.j., to his brother, 1 Aug. 1626, *J.R.*, IV, 202.

27. Biard to the Provincial, 10 June 1611, *J.R.*, I, 166-68; Biard, relation of 1616, *J.R.*, IV, 90-92, 94-96; Sagard, *op. cit.*, I, 112 f.; II, 487-91.

28. Biard, relation of 1616, *J.R.*, III, 104-6.

29. *Works of Champlain*, V, 259.

30. André Vachon, "L'eau-de-vie dans la société indienne," *Canadian Historical Association Annual Report* for 1960, 28 f.

NOTES TO CHAPTER THIRTEEN

1. A.N., V 6, 66: pièce 1. With the help of a legal document of 1628, this refutes the pamphlet of 1644 that accused La Tour of having appropriated some property of Biencourt's.

2. Letters of Charles de La Tour to the king and to Richelieu, July 1627, reproduced in Couillard-Després, *Charles de Saint-Etienne de La Tour* (Arthabaska, 1930), 151 f., 158.

3. A.N., Colonies, E: 107.

4. The Récollet Jamet to Cardinal de Joyeuse, 15 July 1615, reproduced in *Nouvelle-France*, 13 (1914), 439.

5. For this total, see Trudel, *Le comptoir*, p. 428, n. 73.

6. B.N., Fonds français, 16,738, document 143: 8.

7. Lalemant, S.J., to his brother, 1 Aug. 1626, *J.R.*, IV, 216, 226.

8. *Loc. cit.*; B.N., Fonds français, 16,738, doc. 143: 5; decree of 9 July 1622, A.N., E, 87b-88a: 244 v.

9. Memorandum from the Chevalier de Razilly, 26 Nov. 1626, in the *Revue de géographie*, 1886: 374-83.

10. *Le Mercure françois*, XIII, 354-58.

11. Text of the 20 articles of 29 April 1627, in *Edits, ordonnances royaux*, I, 5-11; text of the 31 articles of 7 May following, *ibid.*, I, 12-17.

12. Lauson to Richelieu, 30 June 1627, Archives des Affaires étrangères de France, *Mémoires et documents, France*, vol. 785: 178r.

13. See this list in *Collection de manuscrits relatifs à la Nouvelle-France*, I, 80-85; see also Sulte, *Histoire des Canadiens français*, II, 27-33.

14. Declaration of 6 June 1631, in *Oeuvres de Champlain* (ed. Laverdière), *Pièces justificatives*, XVIII, 16.

15. Gervase Kirke was English, but since his sons were born at Dieppe they were considered to be natives of France; this is why they were regarded as traitors in France, and were burnt in effigy.

16. Biggar, *Works of Champlain*, V, 274-

77; Sagard, *Histoire du Canada* (ed. Tross), IV, 833-35.

17. Letter from Kirke, in *Works of Champlain*, V, 279-82, and in Sagard, *op. cit*, IV, 839-41; Champlain's reply, in *Works of Champlain*, V, 283-85.

18. *Works of Champlain*, V, 287.

19. Sagard, *op. cit.*, IV, 858-65; *Coll. de manuscrits relatifs à la Nouvelle-France*, I, 75, 79.

20. Sagard, *op. cit.*, IV, 858-84.

21. *Works of Champlain*, V, 293-96.

22. Sagard, *op. cit.*, IV, 885; *Works of Champlain*, V, 296-302.

23. *Works of Champlain*, V. 303 f., 313-19, 322-24.

24. *Ibid.*, V, 325 f.; VI, 29-41; 43-49.

25. *Ibid.*, VI, 51 f., 61; Sagard, *op. cit.*, IV, 895 f.

26. Docs. of 8 March and 6 June 1631, in *Oeuvres de Champlain* (ed. Laverdière), *Pièces justificatives* XV, 13; XVIII, 16.

27. Letter of 19 July 1629, in *Works of Champlain*, VI, 53 f.; Champlain's proposals, *ibid.*, 54 f.; see also *ibid.*, 52, 56-59, 128-41, 353 f.; Sagard, *op. cit.*, 898-901. The original text of the treaty of capitulation is in P.A.C., also in *Works of Champlain*, VI, 59 f.; for the date of ratification, see *ibid.*, 60 f.

28. *Works of Champlain*, VI, 61-68; Sagard, *op. cit.*, IV, 904 f.

29. *Works of Champlain*, VI, 70-74.

30. *Ibid.*, VI, 69, 74 f.

31. *Coll. de manuscrits relatifs à la Nouvelle-France*, I, 76, 79; *Works of Champlain*, VI, 97; Captain Daniel's account, *ibid.*, 153-56.

32. Daniel's account, *ibid.*, 153; Sagard, *op. cit.*, IV, 906 f.; *Works of Champlain*, VI, 74-95.

33. Champlain's commission, *ibid.*, VI, 151 f.; the Jesuit Lalemant to his superior, 22 Nov. 1629, *ibid.*, 162-67, and in *J.R.*, IV, 234-45.

34. Daniel's account, in *Works of Champlain*, VI, 153-61; see also VI, 95 f.

35. Docs. of 1629, in *Oeuvres de Champlain* (ed. Laverdière), *Pièces justificatives*, I, 1;

V, 4 f.; *Works of Champlain*, VI, 98-124, 143-150; Sagard, *op. cit.*, 908 f.

36. *Coll. de manuscrits relatifs à la Nouvelle-France*, I, 76, 79.

37. Docs. of 1630, in *Oeuvres de Champlain* (ed. Laverdière), *Pièces justificatives*, VII-XIV, 5-13.

38. *Ibid.*, X, 8 f.

39. *Coll. de manuscrits*, I, 76, 79. The plan for an expedition in 1630 led by Montigny and Daniel was perhaps connected with this; plan reproduced in *Works of Champlain*, VI, 357-60.

40. *Works of Champlain*, VI, 171-81; 198 f.; letters, 1631, in Couillard-Després, *op. cit.*, 191-93.

41. *Works of Champlain*, VI, 181 f., 198-213.

42. Doc. of 1630, in *Oeuvres de Champlain* (ed. Laverdière), *Pièces justificatives*, VII, 5 f.; doc. of 1631, *ibid.*, XVII, 14 f.; another doc. of 1631, *ibid.*, XIX, 17 f.; *Works of Champlain*, VI, 168-71, 182 f., 210 f.

43. Doc. of 1631, in *Oeuvres de Champlain* (ed. Laverdière), *Pièces justificatives*, XIX, 17 f.; *Works of Champlain*, VI, 199 f., 214-17.

44. Text of the treaty of 1632, in *Coll. de manuscrits*, I, 86-97.

45. Commission of 10 May 1632, *ibid.*, I, 110; *Works of Champlain*, VI, 219; Le Jeune, relation of 1632, in *J.R.*, V, 10-42.

NOTES TO CHAPTER FOURTEEN

1. Relation of 1636, in *J.R.* (Thwaites), IX, 132.

2. Relation of 1632, *J.R.*, V, 10, 38.

3. *Ibid.*, 38-40, 44; *Works of Champlain* (Biggar), VI, 183; memorandum of 1637, in Margry, *Découvertes et établissements des Français* (Paris, 1876), I, 14 f.

4. Memorandum of 1637, in Margry, *op. cit.*, I, 3 ff.

5. Relation of 1632, *J.R.*, V, 48; relation of 1633, *ibid.*, 202, 204.

6. Relation of 1633, *J.R.*, V, 238-40, 246-62; VI, 10-18; relation of 1634, VII, 214; relation of 1636, IX, 270-74; X, 76.

7. Relation of 1637, *J.R.*, XII, 186-88.

8. Relation of 1640, *J.R.*, XVIII, 234.

9. *Ibid.*, 230, 232; relation of 1643, *J.R.*, XXIII, 274-78; relation of 1646, XXVIII, 276-78. The dates of departure and return are not given in the documents, but it is known that Nicollet was present at the foundation of Trois Rivières, on July 4, 1634, and he was back at Quebec in August 1635.

10. Le Jeune to the Provincial, 1634, *J.R.*, VI, 76.

11. Relation of 1634, *J.R.*, VII, 212; A.N., Z 1 d, file 103; Sagard, *Histoire du Canada* (ed. Tross), III, 813 f.; *Pièces et documents relatifs à la tenure seigneuriale*, 388; docs. in Cambray, *Robert Giffard*, 22-31, 34-38;

P.-G. Roy, *Inventaire des concessions en fief et seigneurie*, I, 31.

12. Mme Pierre Montagne, *Tourouvre et les Juchereau*, passim.

13. Champlain to Richelieu, 18 Aug. 1634, in *Works of Champlain*, VI, 378; relation of 1635, in *J.R.*, VIII, 18; relation of 1636, in IX, 136.

14. Champlain to Richelieu, *Works of Champlain*, VI, 378.

15. Relation of 1634, *J.R.*, VII, 228; relation of 1635, in VIII, 20.

16. Relation of 1636, *J.R.*, IX, 142.

17. J.-E. Labignette, "Les chevaliers de Malte dans l'Histoire du Canada," *B.R.H.*, 68 (1966), 7-23.

18. Relation of 1636, *J.R.*, IX, 144.

19. On this problem, see P. Deffontaines, *Le rang, type de peuplement rural du Canada français*, Cahier No. 5 of *Cahiers de géographie de l'Université Laval;* Max Derruau, "A l'origine du 'rang' canadien," in *Cahiers de géographie de Québec*, October 1956, pp. 39-47.

20. For a description of the New France of 1641, see M. Trudel, "La Nouvelle-France à l'heure de Ville-Marie," in Cahier No. 8 of the *Cahiers de l'Académie canadienne-française*, pp. 39-48.

21. On the chronology of these events, see M.-C. Daveluy, "Naissance de Ville-

Marie," in Cahier No. 8 of *Cahiers de l'Académie canadienne-française*, pp. 51-57; and above all, by the same author, *La Société de Notre-Dame de Montréal* (Editions Fides, Montreal, 1965), pp. 17-21, 95 f., 103-5, 108-10, 114 f.

22. M.-C. Daveluy, "Naissance de Ville-Marie," in the cited Cahier, 59 f.

23. M.-C. Daveluy, *La Société de Notre-Dame de Montréal*, pp. 119-22, 131-33.

24. Relation of 1641, *J.R.*, XXI, 106; relation of 1642, XXII, 202, 210; Dollier de Casson, *Histoire du Montréal* (Société historique de Montréal, 1868), pp. 31-33.

25. Relation of 1642, *J.R.*, XXII, 210, 212; relation of 1643, XXIV, 262; Dollier de Casson, *op. cit.*, pp. 36-41.

26. *J.R.*, XXIV, 222-28.

27. Relation of 1642, *J.R.*, XXII, 206-8; Dollier de Casson, *op. cit.*, pp. 46-49.

28. Dollier de Casson, *op. cit.*, pp. 54 f.

29. On the land concessions, see E.-Z. Massicotte, "Les premières concessions de terre à Montréal, sous M. de Maisonneuve, 1648-1665," in *T.R.S.C.*, 1914, Sec. I, pp. 215-29.

30. Relation of 1642, *J.R.*, XXII, 34, 246-48.

31. *Ibid.*, 32, 34, 246, 276; relation of 1643, *J.R.*, XXIV, 196, 278; Journal of the Jesuits, *J.R.*, XXVII, 80.

32. Relation of 1672, *J.R.*, LVI, 266; Dollier de Casson, *op. cit.*, pp. 48 f.

NOTES TO CHAPTER FIFTEEN

1. The historian Ganong places this fort at Portland Point, in the present-day port of Saint John (W. F. Ganong, "The Site of Fort La Tour," in *T.R.S.C.*, 1891, Sec. II, p. 74.

2. Agreement of 27 March 1632, in *Collection de manuscrits relatifs à la Nouvelle-France*, I, 85 f.; memorandum of 1700 on Acadia, *ibid.*, II, 354, 364.

3. Letters of 24 Nov. 1632 and 24 Jan. 1633, in Renaudot, *Recueil des gazettes nouvelles*, 37 and 39.

4. Complaint lodged at La Rochelle, 1 Nov. 1632, cited in Couillard-Després, *Charles de Saint-Etienne de La Tour*, pp. 245 f.

5. Letter from the King of England to Sir William Alexander, 4 July 1631, in *P.A.C.R.*, 1912, p. 48; Alexander's order, *ibid.*, pp. 49 f.; Portland to Richelieu, 6 Dec. 1633, *ibid.*, pp. 51 f.

6. A. Godbout, "Le rôle du Saint-Jehan," in *Mémoires de la Société généalogique*, I, 1 (Jan. 1944), 20 f.

7. Memorandum of 1700, in *Coll. de manuscrits*, II, 354; doc. of 1635, in Couillard-Després, *op. cit.*, 250-53; R. Baudry, "Charles d'Aulnay et la Compagnie de la Nouvelle-France," in *R.H.A.F.*, XI, 2 (Sept. 1957), 218-23.

8. R. Le Blant, "La Compagnie de la Nouvelle-France et la restitution de l'Acadie (1627-1636)," in *Revue d'histoire des colonies*, XLII, 146 (1955), 69-93.

9. Memorandum of 1700, in *Coll. de manuscrits*, II, 354, 363; decree of the Council, 1703, cited in Couillard-Després, *op. cit.*, 213; John Hutchinson, *The History of the Colony of Massachusetts Bay* (2nd ed.), pp. 29 f., 46 f.

10. Docs. summarized in Couillard-Després, *op. cit.*, 210-12; Le Blant, "La Compagnie de la Nouvelle-France," 86 f.

11. Le Blant, "Les compagnies du Cap-Breton, 1629-1647," *R.H.A.F.*, XVI, 1 (June 1962), 81-84.

12. Nicolas Denys, *Description geographique et historique des costes de l'Amerique Septentrionale* (published in 1672; republished in French and English by W. F. Ganong, under the title *The Description and Natural History of the Coasts of North America* (Acadia): Toronto, The Champlain Society, 1908), pp. 480-83; Le Blant, "La Compagnie de la Nouvelle-France," in *Revue d'histoire des colonies*, XLII, 146 (1955), 87 f.

13. Denys, *op. cit.*, pp. 476, 479.

14. Letter of 14 April 1633, in Couillard-Després, *op. cit.*, p. 201.

15. Denys, *op. cit.*, p. 474.

16. Razilly to Richelieu, 25 July 1634, cited in Couillard-Després, *op. cit.*, p. 210.

17. Denys, *op. cit.*, p. 483.

18. *Ibid.*, p. 483; Comeau, "Nicolas Denys, pionnier acadien," *R.H.A.F.*, IX, 1 (June 1955), 34.

19. Marcel Delafosse, "La Rochelle et le Canada au XVIIe siècle," *R.H.A.F.*, IV 4 (March 1951), 473.

20. Denys, *op. cit.*, 483.

21, The King to Menou d'Aulnay, 10 Feb. 1638, in *Coll. de manuscrits*, I, 115.

22. Baudry, "Charles d'Aulnay," *R.H.-A.F.*, XI, 2 (Sept. 1957), 226 f.; Couillard-Després, *op. cit.*, pp. 291-98.

23. The King to Menou d'Aulnay, 13 Feb. 1641, in *Coll. de manuscrits*, I, 116 f.; doc. of 24 Feb. 1641, cited by G. Massignon, "La seigneurie de Charles de Menou d'Aulnay," in *R.H.A.F.*, XVI, 4 (March 1963), 475 f.; letter from Père Pacifique de Provins, 24 June 1644, in Couillard-Després, *op. cit.*, pp. 298, 300 f.; doc. of 1 Feb. 1641, cited by Baudry, "Charles d'Aulnay," 220.

24. Decree of 1642, in Couillard-Després, *op. cit.*, p. 302; decree of 6 March 1644, *ibid.*, p. 311; letter from La Tour, 21 Oct. 1644, *ibid.*, p. 300.

25. Baudry, "Charles d'Aulnay," 226-30; Massignon, in the cited article, *R.H.A.F.*, XVI, 4 (March 1963), 473-77; Delafosse, in the cited article, *R.H.A.F.*, IV, 4 (March 1951), 471; Couillard-Després, *op. cit.*, 301-4.

26. John Hutchinson, *The History of the Colony of Massachusetts Bay* (2nd ed.), 128 f.; John Winthrop, *The History of New England from 1630 to 1649* (1853 ed.), II, 51 f., 106.

27. Hutchinson, *op. cit.*, 129-31; Winthrop, *op. cit.*, II, 128-39, 150-63, 464-66.

28. Memorandum from the Capuchins, 20 Oct. 1643, in *Coll. de manuscrits*, I, 117 f.; memorandum from Menou d'Aulnay, in Couillard-Després, *op. cit.*, p. 345.

29. Hutchinson, *op. cit.*, pp. 131-35; Winthrop, *op. cit.*, II, 219-21, 229-32, 236, 241-43, 267 f.; Denys, *op. cit.*, 471 f.; doc.

of 1645, in Couillard-Després, *op. cit.*, pp. 484-89, with commentary, 363-83.

30. Louis XIV to Menou d'Aulnay, 28 Sept. 1645, in *Coll. de manuscrits*, I, 119 f.; the Queen to the same, 27 Sept. 1645, *ibid.*, I, 119; letters patent of February 1647 and confirmation of 13 April 1647, *ibid.*, I, 120-26; *J.R.* (Thwaites), XXVIII, 223; Baudry, "Charles d'Aulnay," *R.H.-A.F.*, XI 2 (Sept. 1957), 231.

31. Baudry, "Charles d'Aulnay," 218-41.

32. *Ibid.*, 232; Le Blant, "Les compagnies du Cap-Breton," *R.H.A.F.*, XVI, 1 (June 1962), 81-94.

33. Denys, *op. cit.*, p. 499; doc. of Oct. 1655, *ibid.*, appendix, 68 f.; Baudry, "Charles d'Aulnay," 232 f.; Delafosse, "La Rochelle et le Canada," *R.H.A.F.*, IV, 4 (March 1951), 474 f.; Massignon, "La seigneurie de Charles de Menou d'Aulnay," *ibid.*, XVI, 4 (March 1963), 479; Le Blant, "La première compagnie de Miscou," *ibid.*, XVII, 3 (Dec. 1963), 363-70.

34. Delafosse, "La Rochelle et le Canada," 473; letters of 25 Feb. 1651, reproduced in Couillard-Després, *op. cit.*, pp. 401-4.

35. Memorandum of 1700, in *Coll. de manuscrits*, II, 356 f.; Massignon, in the cited article, *R.H.A.F.*, XVI, 4 (March 1963), 474, 480.

36. Doc. of Oct. 1655, in Denys, *op. cit.*, appendix, p. 69; *J.R.*, XXXVI, 142-44.

37. Docs. of 1652 and 1653, in *Coll. de manuscrits*, I, 132, 140; memorandum of 1700, *ibid.*, II, 357.

38. Text of the contract, in Couillard-Després, *op. cit.*, pp. 408-12.

39. Memorandum of 1700, in *Coll. de manuscrits*, II, 358; Denys, *op. cit.*, 466; appendix, 69.

40. Concession of 1653, in Denys, *op. cit.*, appendix, 57-60; governor's letters patent, *ibid.*, appendix, 61-67; Baudry, "Quelques documents nouveaux sur Nicolas Denys," *R.H.A.F.*, IX, 1 (June 1955), 24 f.

41. Doc. of 1654, in *Coll. de manuscrits*, I, 144; Denys, *op. cit.*, p. 466.

42. Text of the treaty of capitulation, 1654, in *Coll. de manuscrits*, I, 145-49; letter

from the Capuchin Ignace, 1656, in *P.A.C.R.*, 1904, app. H, 9; memorandum of 1700, in *Coll. de manuscrits*, II, 374.

43. Text in Couillard-Després, *op. cit.*, pp. 166-168; see also *ibid.*, p. 451.

44. Doc. in *Coll. de manuscrits*, I, 151-55; Denys, *op. cit.*, p. 467; Couillard-Després *op. cit.*, p. 441.

45. Godbout, "Le rôle du Saint-Jehan," in *Mémoires de la société généalogique*, I, 1 (Jan. 1944), 19-30; Baudry, "Charles d'Aulnay," *R.H.A.F.*, XI, 2 (Sept. 1957), 234.

46. Debien, "Engagés pour le Canada au XVIIe siècle, vus de La Rochelle," *R.H.A.F.*, VI, 2 (Sept. 1952), 177-233; 3 (Dec. 1952), 374-407; Massignon, in the cited article, *R.H.A.F.*, XVI, 4 (March 1963), 476f.; Baudry, "Charles d'Aulnay," 234 f.

47. Baudry, *loc. cit.*

48. Doc. cited in Couillard-Després, *op. cit.*, p. 222.

49. Denys, *op. cit,*, 479; *J.R.* V, 200, 291; VIII, 156-67; XXXII, 34, 52-54; Winthrop, *History of New England* (1859 ed.), II, 128; doc. in Couillard-Després, *op. cit.*, pp. 484-89; Baudry, 'Charles d'Aulnay," 236.

50. Memorandum of 20 Oct. 1643, in *Coll. de manuscrits*, I, 117 f.; letter from the Capuchin Ignace, 1656, *P.A.C.R.*, 1904, app. H, 7 f.

51. Letter from the Capuchin Ignace, 6 Aug. 1653, in *Coll. de manuscrits*, I, 136-40; letter from the same, 1656, in *P.A.C.R.*, 1904, app. H, 3-11; letters from Père Pacifique de Provins to the Secretary of the Propaganda, 12 Dec. 1641 and 9 March 1644, in Couillard-Després, *op. cit.*, pp. 284 f.

52. Letter from the Capuchin Ignace, 1656, in *P.A.C.R.*, 1904, app. H, 7; *J.R.*, XXIV, 310; XLIII, 22.

NOTES TO CHAPTER SIXTEEN

1. Journal of 1645, in *J.R.* (Thwaites), XXVII, 76.

2. Relation of 1643, *J.R.*, XXIII, 268; relation of 1644, XXV, 108, 112; *Articles accordez entre les directeurs et associez en la Compagnie de la Nouvelle France; et les deputez des habitants dudit pays*, issued in print 1645, in A.S.Q., *Polygraphie*, 4: 3.

3. Request to the governor, 20 Oct. 1646, A.S.Q., *Faribault*, 2: 158. In an order of 1653, the judge Pierre Boucher excluded from trade "certain individuals who are not habitants" and who nevertheless were engaged in fur-trading; he forbade "all persons who are not habitants to do any trading of goods." (Ordinance of 26 July 1653, in *B.R.H.*, XXXII, 1926: 188.)

4. Journal of 1645, *J.R.*, XXVII, 76, 98; journal of 1646, XXVIII, 156, 234.

5. Letter from Jérôme Lalemant, s.j., 31 March 1644, in *J.R.*.., XXVII, 62; journal of 1645, XXVII, 76, 78, 84; relation of 1645, XXVII, 136, 250-68; 278-302; journal of 1646, XXVIII, 168-

70, 230, 234; relation of 1646, XXVIII, 266, 290-302; XXIX, 246.

6. Journal of 1647, *J.R.*, XXX, 172; relation of 1647, XXX, 220; relation of 1648, XXXII, 178.

7. Prohibition of 6 Sept. 1645, A.S.Q., *Faribault*, 1: 42; journal of 1645, *J.R.*, XXVII, 102.

8. Journal of 1646, *J.R.*, XXVIII, 154-56.

9. Journal of 1645, *J.R.*, XXVII, 88-90, 98.

10. Journal of 1647, *J.R.*, XXX, 186; orders of Montmagny, 16 May and 21 Sept. 1646, A.S.Q., *Faribault*, 1: 46, 58.

11. Journal of 1646, *J.R.*, XXVIII, 238.

12. *Ibid.*; journal of 1647, *J.R.*, XXX, 186, 190.

13. Text of the regulation of 1647, *P.A.C.R.*, xxv-xxvii.

14. Text in Cambray, *Robert Giffard*, pp. 152-56.

15. Journal of 1649, *J.R.*, XXXIV, 62.

16. This Article 17 gave to Frenchmen born in Canada and to Christian Indians the freedom to "come and live in France

whenever they wish, and there to acquire, will and inherit property and to accept gifts and legacies," but it appears that there was no similar provision for them in Canada itself.

17. Election of Jacques Hertel and of Charles Sevestre, A.S.Q., *Faribault*, 1: 71, 78.

18. "Ordres pour le voyage de France, 1650," and "Pouvoirs donnés au sieur Bourdon" by Father Lalemant, in *R.H.A.F.*, V, 1 (June 1951), 118-21.

19. Relation of 1635, *J.R.*, VIII, 60.

20. Relation of 1636, *J.R.*, XXVIII, 274.

21. Relation of 1649, *J.R.*, XXXIV, 122, 136: relation of 1652, XXXVIII, 66; relation of 1660, XLV, 204; order of 9 July 1644, in *Ordonnances, commissions*, I, 5; Montmagny's order 9 July 1645, A.S.Q., *Faribault*, 1: 40a.

22. Relation of 1647, *J.R.*, XXX, 220, 230-48; relation de 1648, XXXII, 126, 178-82, 188.

23. Journal of 1648, *J.R.*, XXXII, 102.

24. Relation of what occurred in Huronia, 1648, XXXIII, 70-72, 116, 120, 122, 124, 128-34.

25. *Ibid.*, 80, 88; letter from Father Ragueneau to the General, 1 March 1649, XXXIII, 252-54; journal of 1649, XXXIV, 52; Lalemant to the Provincial, 8 Sept. 1649, XXXIV, 82.

26. Relation of 1649, *J.R.*, XXXIV, 122-32, 196, 202-210, 222; Ragueneau to the General, 13 March 1650, XXXV, 24, 26; relation of Huronia, 1650, XXXV, 78-84; Lalemant to the Provincial, 9 Sept. 1649, XXXIV, 82.

27. Journal of 1649, *J.R.*, XXXIV, 50, 56, 58; relation of 1649, *ibid.*, 228-34; relation of 1650, XXXV, 200; Lalemant to the Provincial, 9 Sept. 1649, XXXIV, 82.

28. Ragueneau to the General, 13 March 1650, *J.R.*, XXXV, 20; relation of 1650, *ibid.*, 106-60, 182-88; relation of 1657, *J.R.*, XLIII, 262-64.

29. Ragueneau to the General, *J.R.*, XXXV, 22; letter from Mère Marie de S. Bonaventure, 29 Sept. 1650, *J.R.*, XXXVI, 58; relation of 1650, XXXV, 74-76, 186-204, 206, 214; relation of 1651,

XXXVI, 178, 180, 202; journal of 1651, *ibid.*, 116.

30. Journal of Father Buteux, *J.R.*, XXXVII, 42; letter from Father Buteux, 4 Nov. 1651, *ibid.*, 68; relation of 1651, *ibid.*, 66.

31. Marie de l'Incarnation to her son, 17 May 1650, in *Ecrits spirituels et historiques* (ed. Dom A. Jamet; 4 vols., Paris, (1929-39), IV, 279; the same to the same, 30 Aug. 1650, *ibid.*, IV, 295 f.; agreements of 14 Oct. 1650, A.S.Q., *Faribault*, 1: 86.

32. "Narré du voyage," in *J.R.*, XXXVI, 104-6.

33. Relation of 1647, *ibid.*, 182-206.

34. *Collection de manuscrits relatifs à la Nouvelle-France*, I, 127-29; see also *Documents Relative to the Colonial History of the State of New-York* (ed. Brodhead-O'Callaghan; Albany, 1855), IX, 5.

35. "Narré du voyage," in *J.R.*, XXXVI, 82-106.

36. Letter from the Council of Quebec, 20 June 1651, in *Coll. de manuscrits*, I, 127-29; journal of 1651, *J.R.*, XXXVI, 128, 146.

37. Relation of 1652, *J.R.*, XXXVIII, 62.

38. Extract from the account-books of the Council of Quebec, 15 Nov. 1651, in *R.H.A.F.*, V, 1 (June 1951), 121-23; journal of 1650, *J.R.*, XXXV, 40; M. Delafosse, "La Rochelle et le Canada au XVIIe siècle," *R.H.A.F.*, IV, 4 (March 1951), 476-78.

39. Relation of 1653, *J.R.*, XL, 210.

40. Ordinances of 1653, *R.A.P.Q.*, 1924-25, 378 f.

41. Relation of 1652, *J.R.*, XXXVII, 134-44; XXXVIII, 48, 56-58; journal of 1652, XXXVII, 112-14; journal of 1653, XXXVIII, 192; relation of 1653, XL, 96-110.

42. Relation of 1653, *J.R.*, XL, 162, 168.

43. *Ibid.*, 156; journal of 1653, XXXVIII, 180, 198; relation of 1654, XLI, 46, 80.

44. Relation of 1653, *J.R.*, XL, 220; relation of 1654, XLI, 36, 84-86, 90-129, 132.

45. Relation of 1653, *J.R.*, XL, 218.

46. *Ibid.*, 214.

47. *Ibid.*; order of 28 April 1654, *R.A.P.Q.*, 1924-25, 383 f.

48. Relation of 1653, *J.R.*, XL, 78-82; relation of 1654, XLI, 42, 76.

49. "Copy of two Letters," *J.R.*, XVI, 210-12; Le Jeune to Mère S. Bonaventure, 10 March 1656, *ibid.*, 236-38.

50. Relation of 1656, *J.R.*, XLII, 30, 218.

51. Concession, 12 April 1656, *J.R.*, XLI, 244-46; relation of 1656, XLII, 36, 52, 56; XLIII, 134-85; journal of Father Dablon, 1655-1656, XLII, 60-215.

52. Relation of 1654, *J.R.*, XLI, 200-202; relation of 1657, XLIII, 128.

53. Relation of 1656, *J.R.*, XLII, 32, 228-38; journal of 1656, XLII, 252-58; relation of 1657, XLIII, 114-16, 198-206; XLIV, 76; journal of 1657, XLIII, 48, 52-54, 60.

54. Relation of 1658, *J.R.*, XLIV, 152, 310-14; letter from Ragueneau, 21 Aug. 1658, *ibid.*, 152-62; relation of 1660, XLV, 208-10.

55. Preamble to the decree of 7 March 1657, in *P.A.C.R.*, 1943, XXV.

56. Decree of 7 March 1657, *P.A.C.R.*, 1943, XXV-XXVII.

57. Letters from Argenson, 5 Sept. 1658, in *B.R.H.*, 27 (1921), 300, 302, 306, 308, 333.

58. Letters cited, *ibid.*, 301.

NOTES TO CHAPTER SEVENTEEN

1. Relation of 1633, *J.R.* (Thwaites), V, 190.

2. *Ibid.*, 136, 138, 180, 188, 216; relation of 1634, *J.R.*, VII, 226; Le Jeune to the Provincial, 1634, VI, 82.

3. Relation of 1636, *J.R.*, IX, 282-98; relation of 1637, XII, 40-46.

4. Relation of 1636, *J.R.*, IX, 104; relation of 1637, XII, 46-52, 90, 108-112; relation of 1638, XIV, 232-56.

5. Relation of 1640, *J.R.*, XIX, 62-66; relation of 1642-43, XXIV, 102.

6. Relation of 1635, *J.R.*, VII, 264; relation of 1636, VIII, 226; IX, 148.

7. Letters of foundation reproduced in Rochemonteix, *Les Jésuites et la Nouvelle-France au XVIIe siècle*, appendix II of vol. I, 454, f.; see also I, 205-207.

8. Declaration of 1663, in *J.R.*, XLVII, 258; *Papier terrier de la Compagnie des Indes occidentales*, 58, 63.

9. Relation of 1636, *J.R.*, IX, 106, 300; journal of 1648, XXXII, 80-82, 106; journal of 1649, XXXIV, 62.

10. Letters of foundation, in Rochemonteix, *op. cit.*, app. II of vol. I, 454; see also doc. and commentary, *ibid.*, I, 209, f.; relation of 1650-51, *J.R.*, XXXVI, 174; Declaration of 1663, *J.R.*, XLVII, 258.

11. Relation of 1642-43, *J.R.*, XXIV, 102.

12. Relation of 1634, *J.R.*, VI, 144, 148; relation of 1638, XIV, 204.

13. *Ibid.*, 204-6; relation of 1639, *J.R.*, XVI, 74; *Inventaire des concessions en fief et seigneurie*, I, 295.

14. Journal of 1646, *J.R.*, XXVIII, 238, 246; journal of 1649, XXXIV, 62; Declaration of 1663, XLVII, 262.

15. Journal of 1646, *J.R.*, XXVIII, 184; Mère de l'Incarnation à la Supérieure des Ursulines de Tours, 13 Sept. 1640, in *Écrits* (ed. Jamet), III, 207.

16. Relation of 1656-57, *J.R.*, XLIII, 220-222; journal of 1657, *ibid.*, 48; Declaration of 1663, XLVII, 262.

17. Relation of 1636, *J.R.*, VIII, 234; letter from Mme d'Aiguillon, in the relation of 1639, XVI, 24; *Annales de l'Hôtel-Dieu de Québec* (ed. Jamet), 10 f.; *Inventaire des concessions*, I, 155.

18. *Inventaire*, I, 142, 147-49; V, 139-41; *Papier terrier*, 121-23.

19. Relation of 1639, *J.R.*, XVI, 10; Marie de l'Incarnation, 20 March 1635, in *Écrits* (ed. Jamet), III, 46; Poncet to Marie de l'Incarnation, autumn 1638, *ibid.*, III, 109; Marie de l'Incarnation to Mme de La Peltrie, Nov. 1638, *ibid.*, III, 111-13.

20. Hospitalières: Mère Saint-Ignace (Marie Guenet), Superior, aged about 29 years; Mère Saint-Bernard (Anne Le Cointre), 28 years; Mère Saint-Bonaventure-de-Jésus (Marie Forestier), 22 years. Ursulines: Mère de l'Incarnation (Marie

Guyart), Superior, 40 years; Mère Saint-Joseph (Marie de La Troche), 23 years; Mère Sainte-Croix (Cécile Richer), 39 years.

21. Relation of 1639, *J.R.*, XVII, 20-22; *Annales de l'Hôtel-Dieu* (ed. Jamet), 19-21; letter from Mère Sainte-Croix, 2 Sept. 1639, in *Ecrits* (ed. Jamet), III, 151 f., 154.

22. *Annales*, 21, 26 f., 28 f., 30, 33, 49, 87 f., 98.

23. Letter from Marie de l'Incarnation, 3 Sept. 1640, in *Ecrits* (ed. Jamet), III, 179; from the same, 16 Sept. 1641, *ibid.*, III, 248; from the same, 26 Aug. 1644, *ibid.*, III, 370 ff.; letter from Mère Sainte-Croix, 2 Sept. 1639, *ibid.*, III, 155 f.

24. Letter from Marie de l'Incarnation, 29 Sept. 1642, *ibid.*, III, 299 f., 306.

25. Letter from the same, 1 Sept. 1651, *ibid.*, IV, 308-313; from the same, 13 Sept. 1651, *ibid.*, IV, 329.

26. Doc. *ibid.*, III, 115; IV, 59-63; letter from Marie de l'Incarnation to her son, 30 Aug. 1644, *ibid.*, III, 393; letter from the same, 1656, in *Lettres de la R. M. Marie de l'Incarnation* (2 vols., Paris, 1876; ed. Abbé Richaudeau), II, 93-104; from the same, 15 Oct. 1657, *ibid.*, II, 121.

27. Marie de l'Incarnation to her son, 2 Oct. 1655, *ibid.*, II, 82; 1652, *ibid.*, II, 7; 15 Oct. 1657, *ibid.*, II, 120; 24 Aug. 1658, *ibid.*, II, 126; 24 Sept. 1654, *ibid.*, II, 68; 1659, *ibid.*, II, 140; *Annales*, in *Ecrits* (ed. Jamet), IV, 131 n.

28. Letter from Marie de l'Incarnation, 16 Sept. 1641, in *Ecrits* (ed. Jamet), III, 248; *ibid.*, 212-14; letter to her son, 24 Sept. 1654, in *Lettres* (ed. Richaudeau), II, 67; *Les Ursulines de Québec*, I, 142.

29. Relation of 1639, *J.R.*, XVI, 238; XVII, 58; relation of 1640, XIX, 134; relation of 1645-46, XXIX, 256; relation of 1649-50, XXXVI, 48.

30. Relation of 1640, *J.R.*, XIX, 136; relation of 1645-46, XXIX, 256-58; letter from Father Ragueneau, 13 March 1650, in Rochemonteix, *op. cit.*, II, 108, n. 1.

31. Doc. on the *donnés*, in *J.R.*, XXI, 292-307; letter from Father Chaumonot, 24 May 1640, *J.R.*, XVIII, 10; study in Rochemonteix, *op. cit.*, I, 388-94.

32. Relation of 1642, *J.R.*, XXII, 270; letter from Father Garnier, 1643, XXIII, 236; letter from Father Brébeuf, 23 Sept. 1643, XXIII, 246; relation of 1642-43, XXIII, 266, 268; relation of 1644-45, XXVIII, 38; letter from Father Lalemant, 31 March 1644, XVII, 67; letter from Father Ragueneau, 13 March 1650, XXXV, 18.

33. Relation of 1639, *J.R.*, XVI, 58, 250.

34. Relation of 1637, *J.R.*, XIV, 40-42, 66.

35. Relation of 1635, *J.R.*, VIII, 100, 132, 154; relation of 1636, VIII, 246; X, 10; relation of 1637, XIII, 39; XIV, 106; relation of 1638, XV, 38; letter of Father Du Peron, 1639, XV, 188; relation of 1639, XVI, 58; relation of 1640, XIX, 76-78, 122, 232; relation of 1640-41, XXI, 134; relation of 1642, XXIII, 22; relation of 1642-43, XXIII, 266; relation of 1645-46, XXIX, 260; relation of 1647-48, XXXIII, 68; relation of 1649-50, XXXV, 74. The statistics given in these Relations are as follows:

1634-35: 22 baptisms (as many as in the St Lawrence)

1635-36: 86 (115 in the St Lawrence)

1636-37: 250

1637-38: more than 100 (150 in the St Lawrence)

1638-39: 300 (out of 450 in all of New France)

1639-40: more than 1,000 (the year of the great epidemic)

1640-41: 100

1641-42: 120

1642-43: 100

1643-44: more than the preceding year

1645-46: 164

1646-47: more than 500

36. Relation of 1642, *J.R.*, XXII, 34-36, 268-70; relation of 1643-44, XXVI, 180; relation of 1644-45, XXVIII, 44; letter from Father Ragueneau, 1 March 1649, XXXIII, 258; relation of 1648-49, XXXIV, 146; relation of 1649-50, XXXV, 106 ff., 146 ff.; journal of 1650, XXXV, 52-56.

37. Relation of 1653-54, *J.R.*, XLI, 90-129; "Copy of two Letters," XLI, 224-228; relation of 1655-56, XLII, 60-215; re-

lation of 1656-57, XLIII, 134-85, 282; XLIV, 34 52-78; relation of 1657-58, XLIV, 154, 172.

38. Relation of 1636, *J.R.*, IX, 208.

39. Father de Quen to the General, Oct. 1656, in Rochemonteix, *op. cit.*, II, 184 n.; Father Poncet to the same, 1655, *ibid.*, II, 198 n.

40. Dollier de Casson, *Histoire du Montréal*, 114 f.

41. Conrad Morin, O.F.M., "Les tentatives du secrétaire François Ingoli, pour l'érection d'un évêché au Canada, 1631-1641," in the report of the *Société canadienne d'histoire de l'Eglise catholique*, for 1944-45, I, 69-82.

42. Résumé of the proceedings of the Assemblées du Clergé de France, in Daveluy, *La Société de Notre-Dame de Montréal*, pp. 57-59; Marie de l'Incarnation to her son, 11 Oct. 1646, in *Ecrits* (ed. Jamet), IV, 109-11.

43. The Hundred Associates to the General of the Jesuits, June 1651, in *J.R.*, XXXVI, 68-73; Rochemonteix, *op. cit.*, II, 197-201.

44. App. XI, in Rochemonteix, *op. cit.*, II, 479 ff.; also *ibid.*, II, 239 ff., 278-81.

45. App. X, *ibid.*, II, 477 f.; app. XI, *ibid.*, 479 f.; journal of 1653, *J.R.*, XXXVIII,

184; Father de Quen to the General, 3 Sept. 1658, in Rochemonteix, *op. cit.*, II, 216, n. 1.

46. Journal of 1657, in *J.R.*, XLIII, 58, 62-64; doc. in Rochemonteix, *op. cit.*, II, 222; decree of Governor d'Ailleboust, A.S.Q., *Séminaire*, 6: 5.

47. Journal of 1658, *J.R.*, XLIV, 104; letters from d'Argenson, in *B.R.H.* 27 (1921), 307 f., 330, 337; Father de Quen to the General, 3 Sept. 1658, and Father Vimont to the same, 6 Sept. 1658, in Rochemonteix, *op. cit.*, II, 228, n. 3.

48. Father Pijart to the General, 26 Aug. 1658, *ibid.*, II, 231, n.l.; Father de Quen to the same, 3 Sept. 1658, *ibid.*, II, 233, n. 4; same to the same, 6 Sept. 1658, *ibid.*, II, 234, n. 4; Father Ragueneau to the same, 20 Aug. 1658, *ibid.*, II, 235.

49. Letters from Rome, 1657 and 1658, app. XI, *ibid.*, II, 479-500; app. XII, *ibid.*, II, 502-10; letter of 1664, app. XII, *ibid.*, II, 511; Marie de l'Incarnation to her son, 1659, in *Lettres* (ed. Richaudeau), II, 140; Abbé Faillon, *Histoire de la colonie française en Canada*, II, 333.

50. Journal of 1659, *J.R.*, XLV, 110-112, 116; letter from the King, in Faillon, *op. cit.*, II, 341; Rochemonteix, *op. cit.*, II, 198-200; Faillon, *op. cit.*, II, 346 ff.

NOTES TO CHAPTER EIGHTEEN

*On population and the distribution of seigneurial land and land *en censive* (conceded to censitaires), supporting documentation for this entire chapter will be found in my two volumes, *La population du Canada en 1663* and *Le terrier du Saint-Laurent en 1663*.

1. 12,827,149¾ arpents in 68 fiefs; 469,193½ arpents in 33 sub-fiefs; 1,698 arpents in 3 sub-sub-fiefs.

2. In the *Report of the Canadian Historical Association* for 1969, pp. 26-36, I published a study on this subject entitled "Sur la formation d'une oligarchie terrienne dans le Saint-Laurent." The figures contained in this study were tentative only; certain of them are corrected herein.

3. Rue Sault-au-Matelot, Rue Saint-Pierre or d'Argenson, Rue Neuve, Rue Notre-Dame, Rue Sous-le-fort, a street leading to the Cul-de-Sac, Rue de la fontaine Champlain.

4. Rue Notre-Dame and Rue Saint-Pierre intersect Rue Saint-Jean and Rue Saint-Louis, which become Saint-Michel and Saint-Joseph in their extensions toward the St Lawrence.

5. This rise of land was levelled in the nineteenth century. Its site is largely covered by the present Place Viger.

6. At Quebec, one mill per 219 people; at Trois-Rivières, one per 231; at Montreal one per 298.

7. Of the 7, one was born at sea, 3 in the

British Isles (England, Scotland and Ireland), one in Switzerland and two in Belgium.

8. In order of numerical importance in immigrant origin, Normandy, Aunis, Perche, Poitou, Paris, Maine, Saintonge, Anjou, Ile-de-France, Orléanais, Brittany, Champagne, Angoumois and Picardy.

9. Omitted are 16 women of marriageable age whose civil status, married or single, is unknown.

10. Of 183 bourgeois for whom we have full information, 42, or 23% could not sign their names; 4 were merchants and 38 were master tradesmen.

NOTES TO CONCLUSION

1. Marie de l'Incarnation to her son, 12 Oct. 1655, in *Lettres* (ed. Richaudeau), II, 86; *Inventaire des concessions en fief et seigneurie*, I, 176 f.; *Papier terrier de la Compagnie des Indes occidentales*, 112, 180, 241 f., 347 f.

2. Relation of 1660-61, *J.R.*, XLVI, 250-92.

3. Relation of 1659-60, *J.R.*, XLV, 234-38.

4. *Ibid.*, 220-24; relation of 1662-63, *J.R.*, XLVIII, 116-42; Lalemant to the General, 18 Aug. 1663, XLVII, 248.

5. A.A.Q., registre A, 27 f.; "Relatio missionis canadensis anno 1660," in *Mandements*, I, 24-26.

6. "Déclaration des terres," Oct. 1663, in *J.R.*, XLVII, 258; "Relatio" cited, in *Mandements*, I, 27; *Histoire de la Congrégation de Notre-Dame*, I, 54-70.

7. Journal of 1661, *J.R.*, XLVI, 172-74; relation of 1660-61, *ibid.*, 286-92; *Annales de l'Hôtel-Dieu de Québec* (ed. Jamet), 113-15; Marie de l'Incarnation to her son, 25 June 1660, in *Lettres* (ed. Richardeau), II, 150; "Dollard des Ormeaux," by André Vachon, *Dictionnaire biographique du Canada*, I, 274-83.

8. Relation of 1660-61, *J.R.*, XLVI, 202-4; Marie de l'Incarnation to her son, Sept. 1661, in *Lettres*, II, 207-9.

9. Relation of 1660-61, *J.R.*, XLVI, 206-20.

10. Relation of 1659-60, *J.R.*, XLV, 200, 206, 212-14.

11. Journal of 1660, *ibid.*, 148, 160; decree of the Conseil d'Etat, 1 Sept. 1660, in *P.A.C.R.*, 1899, supplement, p. 50; Marie de l'Incarnation, 17 and 23 Sept. 1660, in *Lettres*, II, 167, 174.

12. Letters of Governor d'Argenson, 1658' in *B.R.H.*, 27 (1921), 298-303, 306 f., 332.

13. Journal of 1660, *J.R.*, XLV, 156; relation of 1661-62, XLVII, 152; "Extrait des registres du Conseil privé," 20 Feb. 1660, in *Nouvelle-France, Documents historiques* (1893 ed.), I, 4; report by Peronne Dumesnil, published in *B.R.H.*, 21 (1915), 173, 198; "Robinau de Bécancour," by Jean-Guy Pelletier, in *Dic. biog. du Can.*, I, 588 f.

14. Journal of 1662, *J.R.*, XLVII, 288.

15. Reports by Peronne Dumesnil and Gaudais-Dupont, in *B.R.H.*, 21 (1915), 169-73, 193-200, 225-31; journal of 1661, *J.R.*, XLVI, 182; doc. in Cambray, *Robert Giffard*, 196-201; "Peronne Dumesnil" by Marie Baboyant, and "Gaudais-Dupont" by André Vachon, in *Dic. biog. du Can.*, I, 334 f., 550 f.

16. These first Hospitalières were Judith Moreau de Brésoles, Superior; Catherine Macé, Marie Maillet and Marie Morin.

17. *Annales de l'Hôtel-Dieu de Québec* (ed. Jamet), 106 f.; Marie de l'Incarnation to her son, 17 Sept. 1660, in *Lettres*, II, 170; Dollier de Casson, *Histoire du Montréal*, 126 f., 140; Faillon, *Histoire de la colonie française*, II, 357-60; Daveluy, *Jeanne Mance*, 106-9, 194 f.

18. Marie de l'Incarnation, 13 Oct. 1660 and 13 Sept. 1661, in *Lettres*, II, 182; 193.

19. Lettres de cachet, 1660, A.A.Q., registre A, 179; Laval to d'Argenson, Aug. 1661, *ibid.*, 140 f.; Laval to Queylus, Aug. 1661, *ibid.*, 140, 142; Laval to the Pope, 22 Oct. 1661, in A.A.Q., *Copies de lettres*, I, 27; Faillon, *op. cit.*, II, 472-94.

20. Journal of 1661, *J.R.*, XLVI, 186;

letter from d'Argenson, 4 July 1660, in Faillon, *op. cit.*, II, 468 f.; d'Avaugour to Condé, in *J.R.*, XLVI, 148-53; report by Peronne Dumesnil, *B.R.H.*, 21 (1915), 173-98.

21. Letter from Laval, 20 Oct. 1659, *R.A.P.Q.*, 1939-40, 191; letter from d'Argenson, 7 Sept. 1660, in Faillon, *op. cit.*, II, 469; journal of 1660, *J.R.*, XLV, 146, 164; doc. of 1661, A.S.Q., *Polygraphie*, 2: 33; journal of 1661, *J.R.*, XLVI, 162-66; *Mandements*, I, 29 f.; Ragueneau to the General, 15 Sept. 1661, in Rochemonteix, *op. cit.*, II, 307, n. 2; Marie de l'Incarnation to her son, Oct. 1661, in *Lettres*, II, 214 f.; doc. in Faillon, *op. cit.*, II, 496; instructions to Talon, 27 March 1665, in *R.A.P.Q.*, 1930-31, p.5.

22. D'Avaugour to Condé, 13 Oct. 1661, in *J.R.*, XLVI, 150; Marie de l'Incarnation to her son, Oct. 1661, in *Lettres*, II, 215; Colbert to Tracy, in Rochemonteix, *op. cit.*, II, 312 f.

23. Relation of 1633, *J.R.*, V, 320; *Ordonnances, commissions*, I, 5; A.S.Q., *Faribault*, I, 70; journal of 1657, *J.R.*, XLIII, 76; journal of 1658, XLIV, 92; journal of 1660, XLV, 150; journal of 1661, XLVI, 170-72, 186; journal of 1662, XLVII, 274, 278; orders of 24 Feb. and 30 April 1662,

in *Mandements*, I, 42 f., 43 f.; Marie de l'Incarnation to her son, 10 Aug. 1662, in *Lettres*, II, 221.

24. "To the King," in the relation of 1660-61, *J.R.*, XLVI, 196-98; journal of 1661, *ibid.*, 186; Ragueneau to Condé, 12 Oct. 1661, *ibid.*, 146-49; d'Avaugour to Condé, 13 Oct. 1661, *ibid.*, 148-53; Marie de l'Incarnation to her son, 6 Nov. 1662, in *Lettres*, II, 225.

25. Relation of 1661-62, *J.R.*, XLVII, 138-53; 174-219; relation of 1662-63, XLVIII, 74-80; relation of 1663-64, *ibid.*, 248.

26. Journal of 1662, *J.R.*, XLVII, 292; Marie de l'Incarnation to her son, 6 Nov. 1662, in *Lettres*, II, 223-25.

27. Letter of 10 Aug. 1662, *ibid.*, II, 222; journal of 1662, *J.R.*, XLVII, 284.

28. Laval to the cardinals, 24 Oct. 1663, A.A.Q., *Copies de lettres*, I, 19.

29. Dollier de Casson, *Histoire du Montréal*, 173 f.

30. Marie de l'Incarnation to her son, 1663, in *Lettres*, II, 267.

31. *Edits, ordonnances royaux*, II, 6.

32. Mésy to Lalemant, 1664, *P.A.C.R.*, 1899, supplement, p. 51; A.A.Q., register A, 28, 38 f.; *Mandements*, I, 44-47.

SELECT BIBLIOGRAPHY

The era preceding 1663 has been called "pre-history," and not without justification considering the paucity of source material available to the historian.

The first period, 1524 to 1603, which is dealt with in my volume entitled *Les vaines tentatives*, is the most poorly documented of all. There is just enough to piece together the bare essentials of the first explorations of New France: a report by Verrazano; an account of Cartier's voyage of 1534, which is only a copy of the lost original; an account of Cartier's voyage of 1535-36, published in 1545 but of unknown authorship and based on an original that has never been found; an account of the voyages of 1541-43, preserved only through an English text by Richard Hakluyt which is incomplete, breaking off just before revealing what the reader feels must be the key to the story; on the Brazilian and Florida ventures, just enough documentation to provide a sequence of the principal events. There is no coherent series of archives on the activities of the French in North America during the sixteenth century, even for the important voyages undertaken in the name of the king, let alone those other voyages undertaken by fishermen or merchants on their own initiative. Consequently, we must make do with fragments gathered one by one from here and there, and published with the care of a collector mounting his specimens. Among such collections we should note two edited by H. P. Biggar, *The Precursors of Jacques Cartier, 1497-1534* (Ottawa, 1911) and *A Collection of Documents Relating to Jacques Cartier and the Sieur de Roberval* (Ottawa, 1930), and one by Joüon des Longrais, *Jacques Cartier. Documents nouveaux* (Paris, 1888), as well as some documents brought to light by Alfred Ramé, and others by Robert Le Blant. Documentary fragments of a cartographic nature are to be found in several important works: Henry Harrisse, *The Discovery of North America* (London and Paris, 1892) and *Notes pour servir à l'histoire, à la bibliographie et à la cartographie de la Nouvelle-France* (Paris, 1872); W. F. Ganong, *Crucial Maps in the Early Cartography and Place-Nomenclature of the Atlantic Coast of Canada*, originally published in the *Transactions of the Royal Society of Canada* and republished by Theodore E. Layng in one volume with annotations (Toronto, 1964); and mention should be made of a study by Bernard G. Hoffman, *Cabot to Cartier: Sources for a Historical Ethnography of Northeastern North America, 1487-1550* (Toronto, 1961).

Generally speaking, then, we know only certain major events of this period, while others of possibly great importance are hardly more than suspected (for example, in the St Lawrence region, voyages made between 1543 and 1603; rivalries, sometimes deadly, between French merchants; the attempt at settlement on Sable Island; and the great ethnological revolution among the Amerindians of the St Lawrence). If complete documentation ever came to light, the history of the period might have to be rewritten in a quite different way. As it is, any historiographer attempting to record the knowledge acquired and transmitted by historians would find he had material better suited to archaeology than to history—lively polemic over details, arising from a faulty reading of some inscription on an old map, or hypotheses having absolutely no historical foundation. Since events of this period are known only in outline, without the circumstances in which they occurred, historians of our sixteenth century all have the same things to say; only personal style distinguishes one writer from another, and not always even that. Neverthe-less, there are some who deserve special mention for the very copiousness of their works: Justin Winsor and his colleagues, authors of *Narrative and Critical History of America* (8 vols., Boston, 1889), which represented the sum of historical, biblio-graphical and cartographic knowledge at that time and is still worth consulting; N.-E. Dionne, whose *Nouvelle-France de Cartier à Champlain, 1540-1603* (Quebec, 1891) is still useful; John Bartlet Brebner, whose *Explorers of North America, 1492-1806* (1955 edition) is an excellent aid; and S. E. Morison, who in *The Euro-pean Discovery of North America: The Northern Voyages, A.D. 500-1600* (New York, 1971) brings under review all the exploration accomplished by the end of the sixteenth century.*

For the second period, 1604-1627, which is dealt with in my volume entitled *Le comptoir*, the documentation is more plentiful but still fragmentary and scattered, leaving us once again with less than a complete historical picture. The published sources are impressive at first sight. The writings of Lescarbot, Champlain, the Jesuits (particularly on Acadia) and the Récollets (the most important being Sagard) are rich in information, but do they effectively portray a quarter-century? Among those who kept records of events, only Champlain was present throughout the period, and it is recognized that he tended to record only his own part in them; for his writings, we have used H. P. Biggar's six-volume edition, *The Works of Samuel de Champlain* (Toronto, The Champlain Society, 1927-35). The Jesuit Biard was in Acadia only from 1611 to 1613, and yet he was the most prolific of the Jesuits in New France during this period. His writings are included in an in-valuable collection edited by R. G. Thwaites, *The Jesuit Relations and Allied Docu-ments* (73 vols., Cleveland, 1896-1901), and in a more recent work by Lucien Campeau, S.J., *La première mission d'Acadie, 1602-1616* (Quebec, 1967), this being the first volume of *Monumenta Novae Franciae*, a compilation of Jesuit documents of which Volume II covering the years 1617-34 will appear shortly. Marc Lescarbot, author of *Histoire de la Nouvelle-France* (published in Paris in 1866) was in Acadia for only a year, 1606-7. Similarly, a year was all that the the Récollet Gabriel Sagard spent in Canada, though he wrote two important works, *Le grand voyage au pays des Hurons*, first published in France in 1632 and republished by George M. Wrong with an English translation (Toronto, The Champlain Society, 1939), and *Histoire du Canada et voyages que les Frères Mineurs Recollects y ont faicts pour la conversion des Infidelles*, first published in Paris in 1636 and republished in four volumes by Edwin Tross (Paris, 1866). The observations of Biard, Lescarbot and Sagard, moreover, were conditioned by hotly disputed circumstances. And many documents have been lost. For example, it is known that the Jesuits wrote a great number of letters from 1625 to 1627. but only four have been found. The Récollets, considering their long stay in the St Lawrence, have left a very meagre list of archives: the notebook of remonstrances of 1621, two pamphlets, fragments of memoranda, a single formal account, the memorandum of 1637, and four letters; it is fortunate that we have Sagard's *Long Journey* and his *Histoire du Canada*.

Administrative archives originating in New France during this period are very rare indeed. For Acadia, we look in vain for civil registers or deeds of land con-cession. For Canada, all we have is a few pages of civil registers reconstituted from memory in 1640 and manifestly incomplete. The texts of the ordinances published by Champlain on 12 September 1621 have not been found, nor the records of evi-dence in the disputes at Tadoussac involving the de Caëns, nor the record of the general assembly of 1621, nor the letters written by Champlain to the king in 1620 and on the occasion of the Le Baillif affair in 1622. Even administrative archives produced in France are in no case coherent. Normally there should have been complete series of documents, pertaining to the de Caëns, for example, but in fact

*For a detailed bibliography of the period 1524-1603, see my volume *Les vaines tentatives* (Montreal, 1963), pp. xi-xxii and 6.

we find no more than fragmentary series containing little more than summaries of documents or allusions to documents no longer to be found. Archives that we have used in France are as follows: at the Ministère des Affaires étrangères, Fonds France and Fonds Amérique; at the Archives nationales, the Colonies series, C¹¹A, E, and F³; series E, Conseils du Roi, Conseil des Finances; the series V⁴ and V⁶, and Z¹D; at the Bibliothèque nationale, Fonds français, Nouvelles acquisitions françaises, vol. 203 of the Collection Clairambault and vol. 318 of the Collection Dupuy. At the Public Archives of Canada a number of documents in MG 3 and MG 6 were used, most of them copies from archives in France. Two recent publications throw new light on some events of the period: Robert Le Blant and René Baudry, *Nouveaux documents sur Champlain et son époque*, Vol. I (Ottawa, 1967) for the years up to 1622, and the first volume of Lucien Campeau's *Monumenta Novae Franciae*, mentioned above.

However, one cannot hope to gain new insight into a period from documents of this kind alone; an attempt was therefore made to supplement the information obtained from them with some further study of geographic knowledge in these years 1604-1627. We are far from short of material for the study of exploration, thanks to Champlain's writings and an abundance of cartography (which is no more difficult to interpret in this period than later, since map-making improved very little during the remainder of the seventeenth century). We have also noted an important sociological phenomenon in the mutual influence of the European and Amerindian cultures; the Europeans in the New World would never be quite the same again; and for the Amerindians there began a rapid change in ways of life and thought.

On the central personage of the period, we note two important biographies: Morris Bishop's *Champlain: The Life of Fortitude* (New York, 1949) and a very recent work by Samuel Eliot Morison, *Samuel de Champlain: Father of New France* (Toronto, 1972).*

For the period of the Hundred Associates, 1627-1663, the documentation is much more plentiful; however, while it is sufficient for a historian's purposes in some respects, in others it is only partial, or even totally lacking. Though these were the years of the Hundred Associates' régime, none of the Company's administrative archives are to be found; they were probably destroyed in fires during the Parisian insurrection of 1871. All the minutes of meetings have disappeared, other than a few excerpts needed for royal or private administrative purposes, and not a single one of the Company's account books is known to exist. Missing also, though lost in quite recent times, are Governor Montmagny's letters. Usually, the material a historian can expect to find most easily is official correspondence, but for these early years of New France there is hardly any.

For the most important manuscript sources, archives in France were consulted: at the Archives des Affaires étrangères, Fonds Angleterre, in Correspondance politique, 1625-1783, and in Mémoires et Documents, 1592-1805, Fonds Amérique, 1592-1785, Fonds France, 1611-1763, and Fonds Rome; at the Archives de la Charente-Inférieure, Etudes Menon, Sacré and others; at the Archives de la Marine, series A¹, B², B³ and B⁴; at the Archives nationales, Fonds Colonies for the series C¹¹ A, C and D, F²A, F³, E, F, V⁶, X, Y and Z; at the Bibliothèque nationale, the 500 de Colbert, Collection Clairambault, Fonds français, and Nouvelles acquisitions; at the Ministère de la Guerre, vols. 42, 56 and 71 of the Archives historiques, 1626-1759.

The Public Archives of Canada, in the MG section, has copies, photostats or microfilms of documents representing a considerable part of the collections mentioned above. Also assembled are copies or microfilms of documents in the public and private archives of Quebec, particularly in Manuscript Group No. 8, which

*For the period 1604-1627, the reader will find a much more detailed bibliography in my book *Le comptoir* (Montreal, 1966; Vol. II of *Histoire de la Nouvelle-France*), pp. xxiii-xlix.

comprises documents relating to the early years of Quebec, Trois Rivières and Montreal, and to the seigneuries, as well as parish archives and registers. At the Public Archives we used, in addition to these, the series C.O. 1, Colonial Papers, General Series, 1597-1697 (vols. 5, 6, 9, 12, 13) and the Faillon and Saint-Sulpice collections.

Private archives for the period before 1663 are rather meagre. At Quebec, in the Archives of the Province of Quebec, we note some administrative papers; in the Archives of the Archbishopric: Documents du Vatican, Registre A, Copies de lettres, vol. I, Registre des confirmations, vol. I; at the Seminary of Quebec, the following collections: Faribault (containing a great many administrative papers), Séminaire, Lettres, Registre A, and Polygraphie (in which one finds documents relating to the Fabrique of Notre Dame, the Ursulines and the Hospitalières); in the Notre Dame parish archives, the civil register (of which records prior to 1640 were reconstituted from memory); at the Hôtel Dieu, besides the Annales, are found the series Chroniques (which records admissions and dowries) and Obédiences, and the invaluable Terrier des anciens titres (register of old land titles); at the Ursuline convent, the Annales, the Livre des entrées (most useful with its lists of pupils), the Registre des antrées, Vêtures et Professions, the Constitutions, the letters of Marie de l'Incarnation, and a number of accounting documents. At Trois Rivières there are the archives of the Bishopric with the oldest civil register in the country, and the Seminary archives with some miscellaneous documents. In Montreal there are archives at the Seminary of St Sulpice, which have been reproduced in part for the Public Archives of Canada, and also at the Hôtel Dieu, where one may find the Annales and much other documentation, little of which remains unpublished. The old archives of the Congregation of Notre Dame were lost in a fire in the late nineteenth century; unhappily there remain only such documents as could be found in other archives of the country, and those saved from oblivion by publication before the event. Finally, there are notarial records in the judicial archives of Quebec, Trois Rivières and Montreal; for the period of the Hundred Associates, we are fortunate to have a complete set on microfilm.

Considering the fragmentary nature of the documentation, the number of printed sources may appear considerable, but these publications vary a great deal in quality.

The published collections of administrative documents do not amount to much: Collection de manuscrits contenant lettres, mémoires et autres documents historiques relatifs à la Nouvelle-France (4 vols.; Quebec, 1883), and Nouvelle-France. Documents historiques (Quebec, 1893), of which only the first volume has appeared; some important documents for the period of the Hundred Associates are reproduced in Edits, ordonnances royaux, déclarations et arrêts de Conseil d'Etat du Roi concernant le Canada (3 vols.; Quebec, 1854-56), in Ordonnances, commissions, etc., etc., des gouverneurs et intendants (2 vols.; ed. P.-G. Roy, Beauceville, 1924), and in Mandemants des évêques de Québec, Vol. I (Quebec, 1877). For the study of external relations, E. B. O'Callaghan's Documents Relative to the Colonial History of the State of New-York (15 vols.; Albany, 1853-1887) is still very useful.

There are important published sources for other documents belonging to this period of the seventeenth century, but apart from Champlain's works and Lescarbot's Histoire, mentioned above, all are concerned with religious history. Of the seventy-three volumes of The Jesuit Relations (Thwaites edition), forty-three are taken up by the Relations for the years 1627-1663, to which the editor has added the Journal and various letters. When Lucien Campeau, s.j., has completed the publication of his Monumenta, historians will have at their disposal even more documentation. There are also Marie de l'Incarnation's Ecrits spirituels et historiques, published in four volumes by Dom A. Jamet (1929-1939), her Lettres in the two-volume Richaudeau edition of 1876, and the Correspondance published by Dom Oury (Solesmes, 1971), as well as the Annales de l'Hôtel-Dieu de Québec, 1636-1716, published by Jamet in 1939.

A number of inventories published by the Archivist of the Province of Quebec have been a constant source of assistance: Inventaire des concessions en fief et *seigneurie, fois et hommages et aveux et dénombrements* (6 vols.; Beauceville, 1927-29); *Papier terrier de la Compagnie des Indes occidentales, 1667-1668* (Beauceville, 1931); *Inventaire d'une collection de pièces judiciaires, notariales, etc., etc.* (2 vols.; Beauceville, 1917); *Inventaire des greffes de notaires* (21 vols.; Quebec, 1942-64); *Inventaire des testaments, donations et inventaires du régime français* (3 vols.; Quebec, 1941); and various other inventories published in the *Rapport de l'archiviste de la Province de Québec*.

Finally, as with the two previous periods, leaving aside numerous studies on restricted subjects and regions, we mention some general studies of recent date that deal with the period of the Hundred Associates: Gustave Lanctôt, *Histoire du Canada*, Vol. I, *Des origines au régime royal*, published in Montreal in 1962 and in an English translation (Toronto, 1963); Marcel Trudel, *Le terrier du Saint-Laurent en 1663* (Ottawa, 1972), *La population du Canada en 1663* (Montreal, 1972), and *La seigneurie des Cent-Associés* (Montreal 1973), the third volume of *Histoire de la Nouvelle-France*. Four other studies, though of wider range, may be found useful for the bearing they have upon this period in the early history of New France: W. J. Eccles, *The Canadian Frontier, 1534-1760* (New York, 1969) and *France in America* (New York, 1972); George T. Hunt, *The Wars of the Iroquois* (Madison, Wis., 1960 ed.); Andrew Hill Clark. *Acadia: The Geography of Early Nova Scotia* (Madison, Wis., 1968).

INDEX

THE CANADIAN CENTENARY SERIES

A History of Canada in Eighteen Volumes

The Canadian Centenary Series is a comprehensive history of the peoples and lands which form the Dominion of Canada.

Although the series is designed as a unified whole so that no part of the story is left untold, each volume is complete in itself. Written for the general reader as well as for the scholar, each of the eighteen volumes of *The Canadian Centenary Series* is the work of a leading Canadian historian who is an authority on the period covered in his volume. Their combined efforts have made a new and significant contribution to the understanding of the history of Canada and of Canada today.

W. L. Morton, Vanier Professor of History, Trent University, is the Executive Editor of *The Canadian Centenary Series*. A graduate of the Universities of Manitoba and Oxford, he is the author of *The Kingdom of Canada; Manitoba: A History; The Progressive Party in Canada; The Critical Years: The Union of British North America, 1857-1873;* and other writings. He has also edited *The Journal of Alexander Begg and Other Documents Relevant to the Red River Resistance.* Holder of the honorary degrees of LL.D. and D.LITT., he has been awarded the Tyrrell Medal of the Royal Society of Canada and the Governor General's Award for Non-Fiction.

D. G. Creighton, former Chairman of the Department of History, University of Toronto, is the Advisory Editor of *The Canadian Centenary Series*. A graduate of the Universities of Toronto and Oxford, he is the author of *John A. Macdonald: The Young Politician; John A. Macdonald: The Old Chieftain; Dominion of the North; The Empire of the St. Lawrence* and many other works. Holder of numerous honorary degrees, LL.D. and D.LITT., he has twice won the Governor General's Award for Non-Fiction. He has also been awarded the Tyrrell Medal of the Royal Society of Canada, the University of Alberta National Award in Letters, the University of British Columbia Medal for Popular Biography, and the Molson Prize of the Canada Council.